A Culture of Sufism

SUNY series in Medieval Middle East History
Jere Bacharach, editor

A Culture of Sufism

Naqshbandīs in the Ottoman World, 1450–1700

~

Dina Le Gall

State University of New York Press

Published by
State University of New York Press, Albany

Printed in the United States of America

For information, contact State University of New York Press, Albany, NY
www.sunypress.edu

Production by Diane Ganeles
Marketing by Susan M. Petrie

Library of Congress Cataloging-in-Publication Data

Le Gall, Dina.
A culture of Sufism : Naqshbandīs in the Ottoman world, 1450–1700 / Dina Le Gall
p. cm. — (SUNY series in medieval Middle East history)
Includes bibliographical references (p.) and index.
ISBN 978-0-7914-6245-4 (alk. paper)—978-1-4384-4872-5 (pb alk. paper)
1. Naqshabandīyah—Turkey—History 2. Naqshabandiyah—Middle East—History. 3. Sufism—Turkey—History. 4. Sufism—Middle East—History. 6. Islam—Middle East—History. I. Title II. Series.

BP189.7.N35L44 2004
297.4'8—dc22

2003069325

10 9 8 7 6 5 4 3 2 1

To my mother and in memory of my father

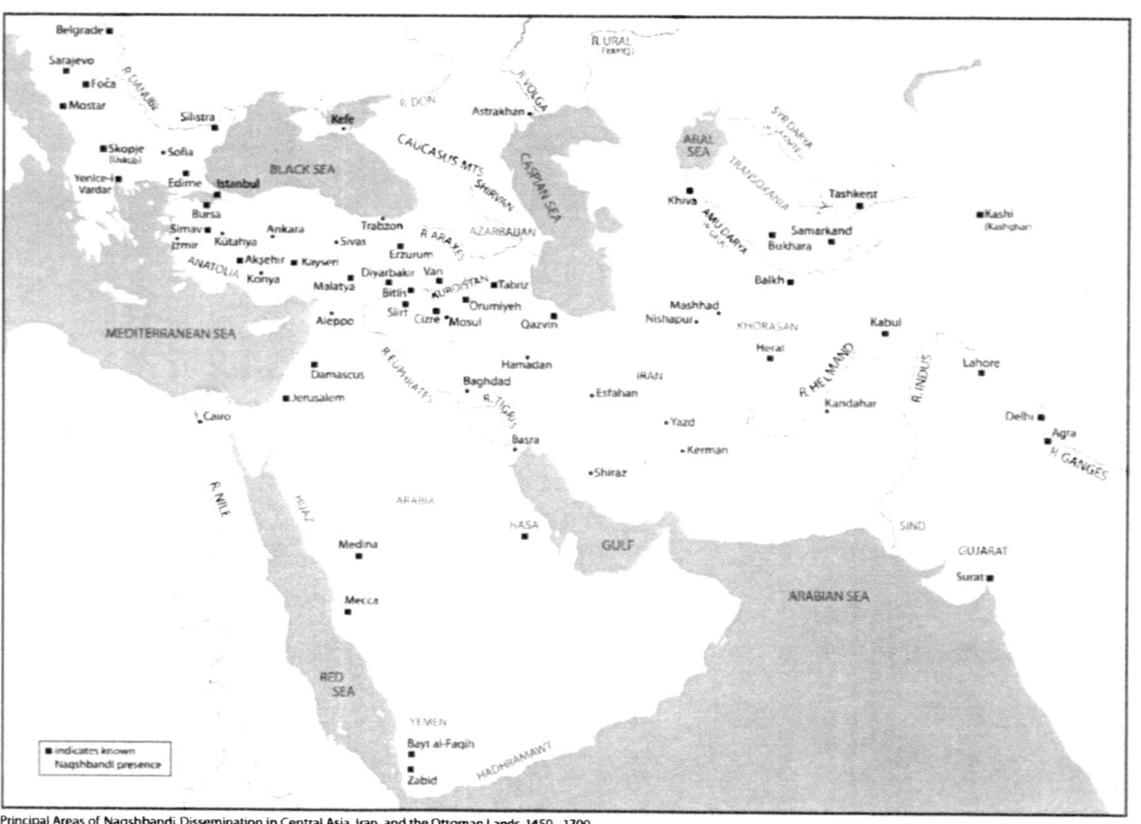

Principal Areas of Naqshbandi Dissemination in Central Asia, Iran, and the Ottoman Lands, 1450–1700

Contents

Acknowledgments

Over the long journey of researching and writing this book I incurred a great many debts, intellectual and other. To Bernard Lewis, who supervised the dissertation as which the book began, I am indebted for sharing with me his wisdom and his vast knowledge of Islamic history and for his unfailing trust and encouragement. Michael Cook offered insights, discussed with me many difficult questions, and read and commented on the manuscript at various stages. Many others read, contributed references, asked or answered questions, criticized, and shared ideas, thereby saving me from a host of errors and helping steer my thinking into new and productive directions. While apologizing to those whom I have overlooked—there are bound to be some—I would like to thank especially the following: Yeşim Arat, Butrus Abu-Manneh, Jere Bacharach, Jean-Louis Bacqué-Grammont, Beth Baron, Devin DeWeese, Yohanan Friedmann, Marc Gaborieau, Jo Ann Gross, Şükrü Hanioğlu, Jane Hathaway, Frederick de Jong, Cemal Kafadar, the late Nehemia Levtzion, Hossein Modaressi, Jürgen Paul, Leslie Peirce, Steve Reinert, Barbara von Schlegell, Emmanuel Sivan, John Voll, Gabriel Warburg, Michael Winter, and Yael and Evyatar Zerubavel. The late Martin Dickson answered many questions with his signature erudition and enthusiasm. I have learned much from Hamid Algar, if indirectly. My husband and colleague, Michel Le Gall, read and discussed with me numerous versions of this book since its inception at Princeton University, when we were both graduate students. While I owe a great debt of gratitude to all these individuals, I am of course responsible for errors and misconceptions that remain.

Much of the research for this book was based on source materials obtained from the rich manuscript collections of the Süleymaniye, Istanbul University, and Topkapı Palace Libraries in Istanbul, the Dār al-Kutub and Al-Azhar Mosque Libraries in Cairo, the Staatsbibliothek in Berlin, the

Bibliothèque Nationale in Paris, the India Office and British Libraries in London, and Firestone Library of Princeton University (which provided also most of the printed works that I consulted). I am grateful to the staffs of all these institutions for their patience, kindness, and professional help in gaining access to invaluable materials, sometimes under less than ideal circumstances.

At different stages of this project, I received financial assistance from a number of institutions and foundations, including Princeton University's Graduate School and Department and Program of Near Eastern Studies, the American Association of University Women, the Institute of Turkish Studies, the Harold W. Dodd Foundation, the Provost of Macalester College, St. Paul, and the Faculty of Arts and Sciences of Rutgers, the State University of New Jersey. I would like to express my thanks to all of them for their generosity.

Thanks are also due to Sue Conn for her help in producing the map, Wyatt Benner for his copyediting, and to Michael Rinella, Diane Ganeles, and Susan M. Petrie of State University of New York Press for their expert guidance throughout the publication process.

Finally, I wish to thank Michel, Maya, and Daphna for many and varied sacrifices made lovingly over the years, Joan and Louis Le Gall for their moral support, and my mother and late father for nurturing my interest in history and for teaching me, by example, how to combine critical thinking with empathy.

Note on Transliteration

The perennial problem of transliteration in Islamic studies is compounded in this book by a very broad geographic scope (from Central Asia to Iran, Arabia, Anatolia, and the Balkans), along with the central role that long-distance travel and the routine crossing of and bridging over linguistic boundaries played in the story told here. No system of transliteration can capture the diversity that all this entails while being both consistent and grammatically and aesthetically pleasing. Indeed, in more than a few instances compromises have been made on all these counts.

My first aim in transliterating technical terms and personal names from Arabic, Persian, and Ottoman Turkish has been to achieve as much consistency as possible and to reflect the universal Islamic character of phenomena central to this study. With this in mind I have tried to Arabize as much as possible, rendering in Arabic form and vocalization most Islamic terms and group names irrespective of the context of their appearance. For example, I have written *sharīʿa* rather than *şerīʿat* and Naqshbandiyya rather than Nakşbendiye even when the context is Ottoman and Turkish-speaking (though for a Sufi lodge, I have used *zāwiya* in a generic way and mostly *tekke* in Turkish-speaking Ottoman contexts). Similarly, individuals who came to Anatolia and the Balkans from Central Asia or Iran retain the Perso-Arabic forms of their names irrespective of the new lives and careers that they built in new contexts (thus Aḥmad Bukhārī, wherever his career took him).

In the case of more specific Ottoman terms and group names, as well as titles of and quotations from sources in Ottoman Turkish and names of individuals who were born and spent their entire careers in Turkish-speaking environments in Anatolia and the Balkans, I have used Ottoman-Turkish forms (avoiding modern Turkish altogether, again with a view to emphasizing the universal Islamic nature of the phenomena discussed here). In such instances I have followed the transliteration tables of the *International Journal of Middle East Studies* (with diacritical marks throughout but long vowels indicated only in words of Arabic and Persian origin). What results are forms such as *şeyhülislām, tekke, ʿilmiye, ḳāżī ʿasker, ġāzī,* Bektaşiye, Ḳızılbaş, or Şaʿbān Efendi (with some exceptions: for example Ḳāḍīzādelis with ḍ, because this form has become common). In transliterating from Persian, I have departed from Arabic much more minimally. The main change has been substituting v for w, as in Ṣafavids.

To reduce clutter somewhat, I have written a few frequently used or well-recognized words (tariqa, madrasa, shaykh, Sufi, sultan, vezir) without italics and diacritical marks. Likewise, geographic names that appear in general atlases are written in the forms found there, with transliteration added on first appearance when this seems warranted.

Introduction

Unlike Western fascination with the mystical insights and poetry of great Sufi masters, which has a long history, scholarship on tariqa Sufism is relatively young. As long as paradigms of an inevitable trajectory of tradition-to-modernity and of postclassical "cultural decline" reigned in the historiography of Muslim societies, there was little interest in the tariqas, either in the sense of systems of mystical guidance or in that of Sufi brotherhoods.[1] For many Western as well as Muslim observers, they were simply an aspect of a disappearing traditional order. Not a few, among them Western scholars, Soviet observers of Central Asian Islam, and Muslim reformers of different hues, viewed them as part of the decline and one of the very causes of the "corruption" of Muslim societies. Then there was the *littérature de surveillance* genre originating with colonial officials and scholars. Their main concern was with nineteenth-century tariqas, especially in North Africa, and with that in mind they created and disseminated an image of the tariqas as networks of religious fanaticism and anti-European military and political activism.

The appearance of Spencer Trimingham's *The Sufi Orders in Islam* in 1971 may be seen as heralding a new beginning. His was not only a comprehensive study that set out to explore doctrinal, devotional, organizational, and social aspects of the tariqas; in addition, it would soon become the standard work around and against which scholars were constructing new research agendas and arguments.[2] Among other things, Trimingham was one of the first to identify a new, "reformist" style of tariqa Sufism in the eighteenth and nineteenth centuries—what in time came to be the subject of considerable scholarly debate under the rubric of "neo-Sufism."[3] Still, in fundamental ways Trimingham's own thinking continued to be embedded in the old paradigms. He, too, imagined the tariqas as a manifestation of a disappearing traditional order. Moreover, he believed that inherent in the very institutionalization that they represented was a "narrowing" of the Sufi quest that in time led to Sufism's descent into "legalism," "conformity," and "decay."[4]

It took somewhat longer for what we may more properly call a "new" interest in the study of tariqa Sufism to develop—this time as both a symptom and catalyst of a broader emerging critique of the old historiographic paradigms. Writing in the past two to three decades, scholars belonging to this generation have adopted a variety of approaches and organizing principles. Some have centered their investigation on an individual Sufi master,[5] while others have focused on a mode of exercising spiritual authority,[6] a particular Sufi lodge or center,[7] a certain geographic region of the Islamic world,[8] or an individual tariqa.[9] As a group, however, all these scholars are bound together by an approach that views the tariqas as historical phenomena and by their interest in social and cultural aspects of tariqa Sufism along with the doctrinal and political ones. They have abandoned and in some cases explicitly criticized the old notion of the tariqas as an aspect of decline, and have instead sought to gain a new understanding of their ubiquity and of the various roles that they played in all postmedieval or post-Mongol Muslim societies, including their role as instruments of Islamization, social integration, or cultural transmission, among other things.

It is to this ongoing collective effort of newly studying post-Mongol tariqa Sufism that the present investigation into the early dissemination of the Naqshbandiyya in the Ottoman world belongs. What I have tried to produce here is more than an account of Naqshbandī doctrine or practice, and more than a map of the Naqshbandī dissemination in the Ottoman world. Much of my exploration is geared toward understanding how various historical realities, themselves dynamic and changing, affected the proliferation of this tariqa and the manner in which its practitioners experienced their Sufi affiliation and constructed for themselves a place in society. Among the many issues brought to bear on the picture are geopolitics, patterns of communications and travel, devotional practice, teaching styles, intellectual tastes, patronage, spatial arrangements, writing and linguistic adaptability, ways of connecting with a sacred past and with the invisible world of the "friends of God," and modes of constructing, deploying, and bequeathing spiritual authority. These concerns have also shaped my choice of sources (most in Arabic or Ottoman-Turkish, some in Persian): rather than great classics or foundational texts of the Sufi or Naqshbandī tradition, I have relied on an array of more modest and sometimes more mundane sources, ranging from devotional manuals to spiritual genealogies, treatises, biographical and hagiographical literature, chronicles, travel accounts, city histories and geographies, surveys of Sufi lodges, and records of charitable endowments. Many of these sources remain in manuscript form.

At the center of the inquiry stands a much-neglected historical phase of a tariqa that has otherwise drawn considerable scholarly attention, among other things due to its rich literary production, distinctive devotional regimen, and reputation for political engagement. Interest in this tariqa has also stemmed from the broad scope of its geographic expansion, along with its very endurance: from Tīmūrid Transoxania, where it emerged between the thirteenth and fifteenth centuries, it spread within another century or so to India, western China, Iran, Anatolia, Arabia, and the Balkans, and somewhat later to the Caucasus and all the way to Indonesia. It continues to be active today, especially in Turkey, Central Asia, Afghanistan, the Indian subcontinent, and also among Muslim communities in the West. Over the past three decades different devotees, aspects, and historical phases of this tariqa have been explored by a good number of scholars, among them Hamid Algar, Butrus Abu-Manneh, Bakhtiyar Babad anov, Martin van Bruinessen, Arthur Buehler, Devin DeWeese, Joseph Fletcher, Jo-Ann Gross, İrfan Gündüz, J. G. J. ter Haar, Fritz Meier, Jürgen Paul, and Florian Schwartz. Important substantive and interpretive lacunae nevertheless remain.

One phase that remains almost entirely ignored is that of the early Ottoman Naqshbandiyya (ca. 1450–1700). Interest in the Naqshbandiyya has been everywhere uneven. Much of it has focused on two branches that became active in the eighteenth and nineteenth centuries: the Indian-born Mujaddidiyya, so called after the epithet *mujaddid-i alf-i thānī* ("the Renewer of the Second Millennium") of its eponym Aḥmad Sirhindī, and the Arab-Ottoman Khālidiyya, itself a Mujaddidī offshoot.[10] In the Ottoman context, where during the nineteenth century Naqshbandīs (of the Khālidī branch) were quite visible and influential, the still prevalent common wisdom has it that the tariqa had been brought over only about a century earlier by Mujaddidīs coming from India, and then underwent a dramatic revitalization at the hands of their Khālidī successors. Despite a presence in Istanbul, Anatolia, Arabia, and the Balkans that might span generations, pre-Mujaddidī Naqshbandīs have thus been nearly ignored.[11]

As a result, we have only limited understanding of how the first Naqshbandī dissemination into the Ottoman lands, beginning in the fifteenth century, was integral to the historical moment during which this tariqa was carried out of Transoxania, or of how the Naqshbandī proliferation was affected by the great geopolitical upheaval that was the Ṣafavid takeover of Iran. We remain even less well informed about the ways in which the Naqshbandī consolidation in different parts of the empire intersected with various Ottoman realities, from prevailing intellectual tastes among the Ottoman urban elite, to the state's efforts to limit the amassing of independent power and to rein in "heretics," to singular but momentous historical developments such as the emergence of Istanbul as an imperial Muslim capital, the incorporation of the Arab provinces into the empire, or the struggle of the Ottoman state against the Shīʿī Ṣafavids of Iran. Myriad other aspects of the workings of the tariqa in Ottoman society remain obscure—for example, how Naqshbandīs distinguished themselves from other Sufis, attracted a following, built a public identity, created spiritual lines, mobilized patronage, made use of space, or became involved in the life of various communities; how followers of the tariqa conceived of their attachment to it; and in what environments Naqshbandīs made a particular mark or were able to establish lasting structures. Before anything else, it is these issues that the present book seeks to explore, both in order to gain a better understanding of Naqshbandī history and of the workings of premodern tariqas, and as a window into Ottoman society and culture and into aspects of the less well known "middle Ottoman centuries."

From a historiographic point of view, the mention of the "middle Ottoman centuries" (commonly taken to begin around the end of Süleymān's reign) should point to the importance of studying a tariqa such as this—and tariqas in general—if only because this provides a counterpoint to the common practice of privileging state structures along with phenomena that fall neatly under them.[12] The Naqshbandī vitality of our period clearly transcended political borders and was little dependent on dynastic politics. As the careers of a number of seventeenth-century shaykhs well demonstrate, from a Naqshbandī perspective there was little relevance to the divide between the Ottoman "golden age" and "middle centuries" (and, for that matter, to the related implication of post-Süleymānic stagnation or decline). The irrelevance of the divide is underscored even more dramatically, of course, by the vigorous Mujaddidī expansion of the eighteenth century.

The central historiographic problems that the present book seeks to address relate, however, to another instance of privileging—that of the Mujaddidiyya and Khālidiyya. On the face of it, privileging these two latter-day Naqshbandī branches may seem to result simply from the lineal and literary predominance that they established as a corollary of their dramatic expansion throughout and beyond the regions in which the tariqa had been active before. As growing numbers of Naqshbandīs came to trace themselves through the new lineages, and especially as Sirhindī's influential *Maktūbāt* and other Mujaddidī and Khālidī writings began to circulate in print and took over as the tariqa's defining literature, older lineages of direct Central Asian origin were gradually marginalized. In time, the two latter-day lineages eclipsed and almost erased the memory of earlier historical phases—except the very early history of the tariqa in Transoxania, from the time of the eponym Bahā' al-Dīn Naqshband (d.791/1389) and his immediate spiritual ancestors to that of 'Ubaydullāh Aḥrār (d. 895/1490), two generations after him. This amnesia of sorts affected Naqshbandīs themselves, while at the same time shaping the direction of scholarship, which came to focus almost exclusively on later phases in the tariqa's history.

But the scholarly privileging of the Mujaddidiyya and Khālidiyya has been more than simply the result of lineal or literary predominance. I propose that it is related to, and symptomatic of, a whole pattern of biases in Sufi, Ottoman, and Islamic historiography, and that together these biases have obscured not only our understanding of the Naqshbandiyya, but also that of organized Sufism and of the relationship between Sufism and Islamic orthodoxy. To begin with, Sufi, Ottoman, and more generally Islamic historiography have all at one time or another tolerated and suffered from the habit of reading back better-known or more compelling nineteenth-century realities and images into what were taken to be similar phenomena from the past in lieu of exploring the latter in their own right and within their proper historical contexts. Second, a number of specific nineteenth-century modes of thinking have encouraged a view of the tariqas as overly organized and politicized, and of Sufism itself as inherently antithetical to Islamic orthodoxy. I am referring here, on the one hand, to colonial and *littérature de surveillance* images of the tariqas as grand organizational networks for political activism,[13] and, on the other, to late nineteenth-century modernist and Salafī thinking, with their branding as backward and obscurantist a host of practices and beliefs—from visiting tombs and seeking the intercession of saints to mystical and esoteric approaches to Qur'ān interpretation.[14]

Third, more recently, arguments advanced by the proponents of the "neo-Sufi" thesis have reinforced some of these modes of thinking, however inadvertently. Beginning with Fazlur Rahman over four decades ago, a series of scholars have posited the emergence, in the eighteenth and nineteenth centuries, of a new style of reformist, outward-looking, activist, neoorthodox, and presumably demysticized Sufism. Among other things, new or "reformed" tariqas (with the Mujaddidiyya and Khālidiyya sometimes given pride of place) are said to have moved away from informal and loose forms of Sufi affiliation, become stripped of their metaphysical and ecstatic character, relinquished the quest for a direct mystical union with God, and disavowed the teachings of the thirteenth-century mystic Muḥyī al-Dīn Ibn al-'Arabī. Instead, it is argued, they came to insist on tighter and more exclusive Sufi affiliation, developed a new focus on the Prophet and a renewed interest in the study of Prophetic traditions, and placed at the center of their vision strict adherence to the Holy Law (*sharī'a*) and the Prophet's practice (*sunna*), commitment to the socio-moral reconstruction of Islamic society, and political and military activism in defense of Islamic rule and the *sharī'a*-based order.[15] Granted, those who have identified this kind of Sufism have characterized it specifically as a new phenomenon that emerged under changing circumstances in the eighteenth and nineteenth centuries. But the schema that they created has had its own dynamics; for example, it suggests certain connections and configurations (such as that orthodoxy equals devotional sobriety, political engagement, and disavowal of metaphysical and mystical speculation) as though they were inherent or inevitable.

These various habits and modes of thinking warrant our scrutiny for more than one reason. From a strict Naqshbandī perspective, they have been at play in producing and reinforcing a view of the Naqshbandiyya that is exceedingly reliant on the Mujaddidiyya and Khālidiyya and that casts this tariqa as a perpetual instrument of political activism in defense of the *sharī'a*-based order. In broader terms, they have been similarly at play in producing and reinforcing a series of related paradigms. One portrays the tariqas as huge, centralized organizations geared to political and military activism in defense of Islam. Another postulates a sharp divide between popular Sufism, on the one hand, and orthodox tariqas, on the other, with the latter presumably the bearers of a rigorous orthodoxy that is antithetical to a host of Sufi devotional practices and even to mystical speculation itself. A third (which is perhaps a variant of the second paradigm) views Islamic orthodoxy as uncompromisingly anti-Sufi, in a manner resembling the stance of today's "neo-Wahhābī" movements.

Some of these (and related) paradigms have recently drawn criticism or come under investigation. Especially influential, though only indirectly related to the study of Sufism, have been recent studies of Islamic legal discourse, which are transforming our understanding of the meaning of "orthodoxy" in Islamic contexts by illuminating the subtle but continuous dynamism that went into the articulation of the law over the generations. Closer to home,

Ahmet Karamustafa has challenged in *God's Unruly Friends* the paradigm of separating between two strands of Islam, one high, normative, or official, the other low, antinomian, or popular. In particular, he has demonstrated the dubiousness of subsuming what he calls "dervish renunciatory piety" of the Islamic later middle period under the rubric of a presumably unchanging "popular" or "unorthodox" religiosity.[16] Barbara von Schlegell has called into question the polarized model of law versus mysticism through an analysis of the seventeenth-century Damascene scholar and Sufi 'Abd al-Ghanī al-Nābulusī and his defense of music, saintly intercession, tomb visitation, and adherence to mystical speculation of the Ibn al-'Arabī school.[17]

Inasmuch as it can help expose and transcend some of the nineteenth-century modes of thinking mentioned above, a careful investigation of the early Ottoman Naqshbandiyya fits into this same broad project, especially as it relates to the study of organized Sufism, early-modern tariqas, and the relationship between Sufism and Islamic orthodoxy. One would want to explore, in this regard, a number of intriguing dynamics and configurations that the Naqshbandiyya of our period exhibited. In what follows I set out to examine, for example, how pre-Mujaddidī Ottoman Naqshbandīs combined a self-image and public image of rigorous *sharī'a*-abidance with a commitment to mystical excellence and with a claim to mystical superiority, sometimes of an extravagant nature. I explore their understanding of orthodoxy: to what extent they conceived of it in terms of personal observance or devotional practice, or constructed it as a public stance of pushing for a stricter implementation of the *sharī'a* in society. I investigate the manner and the extent to which the Naqshbandī proliferation was dependent on tight organization or on political activism or instrumentality. And I ask how at a time of heightened Ottoman-Ṣafavid conflict in the early and middle years of the sixteenth century Naqshbandīs were able to combine a recent memory of Ṣafavid persecution in Iran and a distinctly Sunnī spiritual genealogy (traced via the first caliph, Abū Bakr) with open veneration of the *imāms* (the descendants of the Prophet and the supreme leaders of the Muslim community according to Shī'ī doctrine) and with an attitude that was seemingly less than combative toward the Ṣafavid regime in Iran and its Ḳızılbaş followers inside Anatolia.

The book consists of two parts, one organized along geographic regions and the second proceeding thematically. Chapter 1 explores how spiritual deputies or successors (*khalīfas*) of 'Ubaydullāh Aḥrār, along with Central

Asian pilgrims to the Hijaz and somewhat later refugees from Ṣafavid Iran, disseminated the Naqshbandiyya westward to Arabia and the Ottoman lands. Special attention is given to the unique role of Aḥrār in training and sending off *khalīfa*s and to the notion that his was a conscious "missionary" endeavor, one that he did not spell out, but that was implicit in the conduct of some of his immediate *khalīfa*s and later spiritual descendants. A second theme of this chapter revolves around the impact of the Ṣafavid rise to power in Iran on the Naqshbandī dissemination, such as the persecution of Naqshbandīs inside Iran and the constraints imposed on travel between Central Asia and the Ottoman lands. (The more general politicizing and embittering of formerly benign Sunnī-Shī'ī relations is addressed in later chapters).

Chapter 2 focuses on Naqshbandīs in the Ottoman capital. Among other things, it examines how immigrant shaykhs and their local spiritual descendants developed a reputation as the teachers of a rigorously *sharī'a*-abiding tariqa and the purveyors of both mystical insights and a broader Persian literary culture; how they had Sufi lodges (*tekke*s) built for their disciples; how they attracted a following, some but not all of it hailing from the capital's learned and governing elite; and how they established enduring spiritual lines as a means of sustaining the presence of the tariqa in the city for over two centuries.

Chapter 3 moves to Anatolia and the Balkans, where despite the work of a series of shaykhs trained in Istanbul or Transoxania the presence of the tariqa was more ephemeral. The inquiry begins with the Balkans then focuses on some parts of Anatolia (in the broad geographic sense). In Anatolian Kurdistan, in particular, a lasting Naqshbandī presence developed, much of it under the aegis of a spiritual line that reconfigured common practices, among other things introducing a hereditary and communal style of leadership and a less-than-sober devotional regimen. It was under special war-related circumstances in this frontier area that for a time during the early seventeenth century the Ottoman authorities were led to grant a Sufi shaykh and his family more latitude than they usually cared to allow. This was the context for the unusual career of Shaykh Maḥmūd Urmavī, a Naqshbandī who built himself up as a powerful charismatic figure, drew a massive community-wide following, and engaged openly in politics.

Chapter 4, devoted to the Arab lands, begins by exploring a number of factors that perhaps constrained the dissemination of the tariqa into these quarters. Issues of geography and travel figure here, along with cultural tastes and the apparent uncongeniality of a devotional regimen based on the silent method of *dhikr* ("recollection of God") for followers of the Shāfi'ī legal rite.

The discussion then shifts to the Holy Cities of the Hijaz, set apart, as they were, by their role as the hub of the annual pilgrimage (*ḥajj*) and as the locus of large "foreign" Muslim communities. Two enduring pre-Mujaddidī lines of Indian origin developed in this environment, though only after the turn of the seventeenth century.

Following a thematic organization, part 2 of the book begins, in chapter 5, with a discussion of the Naqshbandī construction of orthodoxy. Since devotional sobriety appears to have been very much at the core here, the first task is to examine how the devotional regimen of the tariqa was constructed and how it was made into the emblem of rigorous adherence to the *sharī'a* (or to what Naqshbandīs might call *al-'amal bi'l-'azīma*, "acting with strictness"). A second task is to consider how a second Naqshbandī commitment that was no less central—the commitment to mystical excellence, and indeed superiority—was reconciled and interwoven with the emphasis on *sharī'a*-abidance. This involves an examination of a series of emphases and pursuits that were all at the heart of the Naqshbandī conception of mystical excellence: a view of shaykhs as the ultimate *murshid*s (intimate guides along a path of spiritual transformation), the technique of *rābiṭa* (fixing the picture of the shaykh in the imagination as a vehicle for the flow of divine energy), a deep-seated belief in the ability of practitioners to communicate with the "friends of God," and Naqshbandīs' devotion to the dissemination of the mystical teachings of Muḥyī al-Dīn Ibn al-'Arabī. A third task centers on the Naqshbandī Bakrī *silsila* (chain of initiatic descent that connects Sufis to the Prophet via consecutive individual links): did the concept of spiritual descent via the Prophet's companion and first caliph, Abū Bakr (rather than via his cousin and son-in-law, 'Alī b. Abī Ṭālib, as in many other tariqas), function essentially as a spiritual marker, and how? Or was it transformed—especially once Shī'ī-Sunnī relations had been politicized and embittered by the advent of the Ṣafavids to power in Iran—into a political emblem of staunch Sunnī identity or even hostility to all things Shī'ī?

Chapter 6 addresses the issue of the Naqshbandiyya's assumed propensity for political activism in defense of the *sharī'a*-based order. It questions especially the thesis of this tariqa's instrumental role in the critical sixteenth-century Ottoman battle against the Ṣafavids and Ḳızılbaş. Did Ottoman Naqshbandīs play a significant role in this battle? Did they exhibit a particular hostility toward the Ṣafavids, and in what ways? Were they particularly well equipped to restrain or co-opt the Ḳızılbaş of Anatolia? What evidence do we have for the ways in which the Ottoman governing elite rewarded Naqshbandīs for such roles? Or is the notion of the Naqshbandī instrumentality in the anti-Ḳızılbaş campaign perhaps informed by much later historical realities and images?

Chapter 7 approaches the early Ottoman Naqshbandiyya as a network and an instrument of cultural transmission and integration. Rejecting common notions of tariqas as tight-knit organizations and of Sufi dissemination as necessarily a political or missionary endeavor, special attention is paid here to a series of little-explored organizational and especially cultural modes and preferences that Naqshbandīs exhibited, either in continuation of older Sufi or Islamic habits or in new ways. These include a propensity for long-distance travel, commitment to writing and copying, linguistic adaptability, attachment to "vertical" traditions going back in time, and the ability of shaykhs to operate and disseminate the tariqa from specialized and endowed institutions as well as from more generic spaces such as public and neighborhood mosques. A number of distinctive Naqshbandī practices and pursuits are also examined here—for example, the bequeathing of spiritual authority to nonrelatives, an apparent knack for the dissemination of Persian literary culture, and the privileging of shaykhs as *murshid*s and of the intimate shaykh-disciple relationship (*ṣuḥba*), even to the extent of ritualizing this bond through the practice of *rābiṭa*. In some ways, this focus on modes of cultural transmission and integration serves as a fitting conclusion to the whole study.

Part I

Dissemination

1

From Transoxania to the Ottoman Lands

The first wave of Naqshbandī transmission to Arabia and the Ottoman lands took place during the second half of the fifteenth century, less than a century after the death of the eponym, Muḥammad Bahā' al-Dīn Naqshband, and just as Naqshbandīs were beginning to establish their predominance among Sufis in Transoxania and Khorasan. The most important early carriers of the tariqa westward were immediate successors and, in time, more remote spiritual descendants in the line of 'Ubaydullāh Aḥrār, though along with these came descendants of other spiritual lines, various pilgrims on their way to the Hijaz, and, somewhat later, displaced Naqshbandīs from Ṣafavid Iran. The intensity of this first wave of expansion later subsided, but individual Naqshbandīs—again, most typically ensuing from Aḥrār's line—continued for generations to travel westward from Transoxania and to refurbish the ranks of the Ottoman Naqshbandiyya, even during times when the hostility of Iran's Shī'ī Ṣafavid rulers compelled them to take circuitous ways. It was only from the seventeenth century on that India, with its own Naqshbandī communities of Aḥrārian descent, became a second origin of westward Naqshbandī expansion, first to Arabia and then, under the aegis of the Mujaddidī branch and with newly enhanced intensity, to other destinations, including the Ottoman capital.

As a prelude to examining the establishment of the tariqa in the Ottoman realm and its relationship with and functioning within the Ottoman state and Ottoman society, the present chapter asks questions about the actual process of dissemination from Transoxania: Who were the individual agents of transmission? What motives and expectations drove them? What routes and logistical infrastructure did they use? How were they affected by political upheavals and changes in communications, especially those connected to the Ṣafavid takeover of Iran at the beginning of the sixteenth century? How was the Naqshbandī dissemination organized (or was it)? And what does this tell us about Sufi expansion as a "missionary" endeavor?

THE BIRTH OF A TARIQA: FROM KHWĀJAGĀN TO NAQSHBANDIYYA

The concept of the illustrious eponym who founds a tariqa, in the double sense of mystical way and Sufi brotherhood, is powerful, yet in several ways problematic.[1] Sufis might celebrate a tariqa founder—that is, an individual from whom a specific mystical way is believed to have derived its distinctive features—while at the same time viewing their respective mystical ways as traditions extending via the *silsilas* all the way back to the Prophet Muḥammad. Moreover, historically tariqas did not emerge ex nihilo but rather developed their distinctive features over time. Nor did their eponymous founders think of themselves as founder of a tariqa—usually they came to be cast in that way by later generations. Sometimes a kind of "retrospective teleology" is provided. The process is detectible in the account of the Naqshbandiyya's emergence out of the earlier Central Asian Sufi current known as the Ṭarīqat-i Khwājagān (the "Way of the Masters"), as it is given in later sources, especially the early sixteenth-century *Rashaḥāt-i 'ayn al-ḥayāt* of Fakhr al-Dīn 'Alī Kāshifī. As Jürgen Paul and Devin DeWeese have shown, the *Rashaḥāt* and related literature made Bahā' al-Dīn Naqshband the teleological "goal of all previous developments" by forgetting or suppressing the importance of collateral lines—that is, those lines of the Khwajāgānī tradition in thirteenth- and fourteenth-century Transoxania that did not lead to Bahā' al-Dīn.[2] It is only with these caveats in mind that we can fruitfully look at the emergence of the Naqshbandiyya out of the Ṭarīqat-i Khwājagān, or consider Bahā' al-Dīn its founder.

In the eyes of the later Naqshbandī tradition as it is expressed in the *Rashaḥāt*, the emergence of the tariqa went as follows: Bahā' al-Dīn was the disciple of Amīr Kulāl, himself a spiritual descendant in the fifth generation of 'Abd al-Khāliq Ghujduvānī, from whom Naqshbandīs begin to designate their *silsila* "Khwājaganī."[3] Like the preceding four *silsila* links that separated him from Ghujduvānī, Amīr Kulāl practiced and taught a vocal method of *dhikr*, thus deviating from the mystical way of Ghujduvānī, with its silent method of recollection acquired from the quintessential mystical guide of Qur'ānic origin, Khiḍr. It was Bahā' al-Dīn who, guided by the "spiritual presence" (*rūḥāniyya*) of Ghujduvānī, reverted to the silent *dhikr*, thereby resurrecting Ghujduvānī's legacy and at the same time establishing a distinct mystical way, to become the Naqshbandiyya, out of the Khwājagānī tradition as it had been practiced by his immediate *silsila* predecessors.[4] This Naqshbandī view informs Hamid Algar's conclusion that the separation of Bahā' al-Dīn from Amīr Kulāl and his disciples whenever they practiced vocal *dhikr* "may be thought of as marking the final crystallization of the Naqshbandīya, with silent *dhikr* . . . established as normative for the order."[5] The later Naqshbandī view is not sufficient, however, to determine when and how the notion of a new way derived from Bahā' al-Dīn arose in the eyes of practitioners. Scholars of the history of the tariqa in Central Asia are increasingly choosing to express the murkiness of the transition by using the construct Khwājagān-Naqshbandiyya until quite late[6] (though for the Ottoman Naqshbandiyya I myself find the hyphenated construct unwarranted, despite the continued appearance of "Khwājagān" occasionally).

On the basis of an array of fourteenth- and fifteenth-century sources originating in various Khwājagānī and Naqshbandī spiritual lines, Jürgen Paul has described the Ṭarīqat-i Khwājagān as a current of mystical teachings (rather than a Sufi brotherhood), to which subscribed a cluster of loosely constructed local groups in Transoxania during the thirteenth through the fifteenth centuries, some urban, some rural. Khwājagānī followers did not share a fixed set of common practices. What brought them together was their claim to being the spiritual followers of Ghujduvānī (who died around the turn of the thirteenth century), their common understanding of the "good Muslim life," and their sense that—at a time of religious upheaval and restructuring following the Mongol conquest—they were being inundated by things that they viewed as un-Islamic.

Based in Qaṣr-i 'Ārifān outside of Bukhara, Bahā' al-Dīn was the leader of one of these local groups. It was during his lifetime that growing competition over followers emerged, making the issue of silent versus vocal *dhikr* into an important marker of identity. Bahā' al-Dīn and his followers adopted the silent method as their own and condemned practitioners of vocal recollection. Several other groups and spiritual lines (as well as different types of *dhikr*) continued to exist at this time, and even during the following generation, when the immediate spiritual successors of Bahā' al-Dīn began to construct around him the image of primacy that would find its full expression in the *Rashaḥāt*. By the time of the *Rashaḥāt*, moreover, the Khwājagān-Naqshbandiyya had undergone several changes in doctrine and devotional practice (at least some of them projected back onto Bahā' al-Dīn). Furthermore, under the leadership of 'Ubaydullāh Aḥrār, they became a more structured and hierarchical organization that was centered around Aḥrār's complex in Samarkand. In addition, there developed an interregional or international network extending far outside the Bukharan oasis, and indeed outside Transoxania.[7]

From the perspective of the development of the Khwājagān-Naqshbandiyya vis-à-vis that of other Central Asian Sufi groups among which they eventually came to predominate—and on the basis of Naqshbandī and other, especially Yasavī, sources—DeWeese has drawn a picture that is somewhat different in several respects. He argues that in Central Asia throughout the fourteenth and much of the fifteenth century, the concept of a genealogical Sufi chain or *silsila* did not command the significance that it would come to have later on as the quintessential principle around which tariqas were to be organized. Sufis of this period might identify themselves in reference to other principles (for example, a distinctive spiritual technique); it was only during the late Tīmūrid period that groups defined by their *silsila* became truly important. As for Naqshbandīs specifically, the story of Bahā' al-Dīn's initiation by the "spiritual presence" of the long-deceased Ghujduvānī, which appeared first in a very early hagiography, the *Anīs al-ṭālibīn*, may itself indicate that in the eyes of Bahā' al-Dīn and his immediate successors the notion of an unbroken *silsila* was not yet central. Even through much of the fifteenth century, Naqshbandīs appear to have viewed the *silsila* with some ambivalence. Kāshifī's *Rashaḥāt*, completed in 909/1503–4, functioned at one level as the very instrument of propagandizing the notion of *silsila*-centered Sufism in these quarters.

In DeWeese's analysis the rise of the Khwājagān-Naqshbandiyya between the thirteenth and fifteenth centuries was fueled primarily by competition over followers with other Sufis; this competition came to an end only when the Naqshbandiyya had become established as the predominant tariqa in Central Asia in the sixteenth century. The principal competitors of the Khwājagān-Naqshbandīs were the Yasavīs, whose practice of hereditary succession and communal leadership allowed them to play an important role in the Islamization, albeit nominal, of whole communities. It was in this context that the Khwājagān-Naqshbandīs came to position themselves as the advocates of Muslim observance, and specifically as the challengers to Sufis whom they portrayed as too willing to extend to groups that were insufficiently attentive to Muslim observance the formal symbols of affiliation—robes, Sufi lodges, written licenses to transmit a tariqa, and so on.[8]

While some aspects of the process through which the Naqshbandiyya emerged out of the Ṭarīqat-i Khwājagān remain contested or unresolved, several points can be made with a degree of confidence about the period following Bahā' al-Dīn. First, the generation of Bahā' al-Dīn's immediate successors—'Alā' al-Dīn 'Aṭṭār, Muḥammad Pārsā, and Ya'qūb Charkhī—was already critical for the promotion and the dissemination of the new way, if not necessarily under the designation Naqshbandiyya.[9] Second, within another generation the tariqa became extremely well established in both Transoxania and Khorasan. In Herat in Khorasan, a Khwājagānī-Naqshbandī community and spiritual line first developed around 'Aṭṭār's *khalīfa* Sa'd al-Dīn Kāshgharī (d. 860/1456). Before long Herat became the capital of the late Tīmūrid sultan Ḥusayn Bāyqarā (d. 911/1506) and, by extension, the foremost cultural center of the eastern Islamic world. In this city Naqshbandīs were intimately involved with the *'ulamā'* (scholars of the religious and legal sciences) and with circles associated with the court, and the tariqa came to dominate the spiritual life of the elite. Particularly important in securing for Naqshbandīs these intellectual and social gains was the great poet and scholar 'Abd al-Raḥmān Jāmī. Jāmī was not much of a "transmitting shaykh" in the sense of one who devotes himself to the training of disciples and *khalīfas*; instead, his contribution to the consolidation of the tariqa in Herat derived from his influential writings and his great personal prestige. Among others, he brought along as a friend of the tariqa (and perhaps an initiated Naqshbandī disciple) 'Alī Shīr Navā'ī, the wealthy landowner, author and poet, patron of the arts, friend and adviser of Ḥusayn Bāyqarā, and probably the most influential figure in the cultural life of Bāyqarā's court and capital. Navā'ī's association with the tariqa was in turn a catalyst as much as it was a consequence of the Khwājagān-Naqshbandiyya's success in Herat.[10]

In Samarkand, at the same time, the Naqshbandiyya was gaining predominance, especially thanks to Shaykh 'Ubaydullāh Aḥrār, who combined influence in the Tīmūrid court of Sultan Abū Sa'īd (and later of his son Aḥmad) with prestige among the city's *'ulamā'*, accumulation of vast landed property, and the construction of a "system of patronage" in support of the area's urban and settled rural population.[11] Aḥrār's political and economic ventures in Samarkand of the late Tīmūrids will concern us again in chapter 6. Here we shall focus on his role in disseminating the tariqa (henceforth referred to simply as Naqshbandiyya) from Transoxania, especially to Anatolia, Arabia, and the Balkans.

AGENTS OF TRANSMISSION

Individual Naqshbandīs were traveling west from Transoxania and Khorasan from the very early days of the tariqa. Bahā' al-Dīn Naqshband is said to have gone on the pilgrimage twice. So did his *khalīfa* Muḥammad Pārsā, who died in Medina in 822/1420, and, a generation after him, the founder of the Herat Naqshbandiyya, Sa'd al-Dīn Kāshgharī.[12] In Anatolia, it has been suggested that the first Naqshbandīs arrived at the turn of the fifteenth century with the army of Tīmūr; this would explain how Muḥammad Pārsā's encyclopedic work, the *Faṣl al-khiṭāb*, was brought over, to be translated into Ottoman Turkish during the reign of Murād II. One of these early carriers of the tariqa is known to us in some detail. A *khalīfa* of Bahā' al-Dīn by the name Rukn al-Dīn Bukhārī, he settled in Amasya, where a *tekke* was built for him in 807/1405–6.[13]

Other carriers of the tariqa arrived in Anatolia and the Balkans during the reign of Meḥmed II. Isḥaq Bukhārī-i Hindī had the sultan build for him in the Aḳsarāy neighborhood of the capital the *tekke* known in time as Hindīler.[14] In Bursa, an immigrant by the name Aḥmad Ilāhī distinguished himself as a mosque preacher and the author of a trilingual treatise on *sulūk* (the "traveling" along the mystical path by means of a devotional discipline); then a local follower, the finance director (*defterdār*) Dervīş Efendi, established for him a mosque and *khānqāh* complex in the Yuğurtlu Baba neighborhood.[15] In Sarajevo, according to chronograms on tombs in the *tekke*-mausoleum of Ǧāzīler, two Naqshbandīs, Şemsī Dede and 'Aynī Dede, arrived with the Ottoman army of conquest in 866/1461–62; apparently they died in battle shortly afterwards.[16]

But it is only later in the fifteenth century, especially in connection with a series of *khalīfa*s of 'Ubaydullāh Aḥrār, that one can speak of a whole wave of Naqshbandī transmission to Anatolia, Arabia, and the Balkans (along with central and western Iran). The most important carriers of the tariqa westward at this time were 'Abdullāh Ilāhī and Aḥmad Bukhārī, respectively a *khalīfa* and a disciple of Aḥrār. They first settled and established a Naqshbandī circle in Ilāhī's native town of Simav in western Anatolia, then moved to the capital after the death of Meḥmed II in 886/1481, and there established the prosperous and lasting Naqshbandī line that remained the center of the Istanbul Naqshbandiyya until the coming of Naqshbandī-Mujaddidīs from India around the turn of the eighteenth century.[17] Another *khalīfa* of Aḥrār, Bābā Ḥaydar Samarqandī, lived for a time in Mecca, then settled in Eyüp outside the walls of Istanbul, where Sultan Süleymān built for him a mosque that came to carry his name.[18] Bābā Ni'matullāh b. Maḥmūd from Nakhichevan in the Caucasus may also have been a disciple of Aḥrār in Samarkand, though he owed his authorization to impart Naqshbandī guidance to another spiritual line (for this, see below). He ended up settling in

Akşehir in central Anatolia, where he distinguished himself as a scholar and the author of several works on the mystical teachings of Muḥyī al-Dīn Ibn al-ʻArabī.[19] ʻAbdullāh Ilāhī and some of his disciples disseminated the tariqa also in parts of the Balkans. Ilāhī spent the end of his life writing and training disciples in Yenice-i Vardar (in modern Greece) at the invitation of a provincial governor, Evrenoszāde Aḥmed Beğ.[20] His *khalīfa* Bedreddīn Baba (or at least this is how Bedreddīn is described by a later source) settled and became a shaykh in Edirne.[21]

Two of Aḥrār's *khalīfas* settled in Mecca and Damascus, at the time still under Mamlūk rule. Ismāʻīl Shirvānī, originally from the Caucasus, lived and taught in Mecca for four decades, having as one of his disciples a great grandson of Aḥrār, Khwāja Muḥammad Qāsim. According to Ṭaşköprüzāde, he visited Anatolia during the reign of Bāyezīd II, though we are told nothing of his activities or impact there.[22] Another *khalīfa* originally from Central Asia, Mawlānāzāda Utrārī, traveled to Mecca with Aḥrār's license to teach (*ijāza*), and then settled in Damascus, where ʻAbd al-Raḥmān Jāmī visited him after the pilgrimage of 878/1473.[23] Muḥammad Badakhshī, a disciple who may have accompanied Utrārī from Samarkand, also settled in Damascus; we are told that Sultan Selīm I paid him two visits in that city shortly after the Ottoman conquest of 922/1517.[24] Three other *khalīfas* of Aḥrār were responsible for introducing the Naqshbandiyya to central and western Iran in the last decades before the Ṣafavid conquest: Sirāj al-Dīn ʻAbd al-Wahhāb and Muḥammad Amīn Bulgharī to Tabriz,[25] and ʻAlī Kurdī to Qazvin. ʻAlī Kurdī, a scion of a family of descendants of the Prophet (*sayyids*), who had come to seek Aḥrār's guidance from Amadiyah (ʻAmādiyya) in Kurdistan, enjoyed in Qazvin a remarkable career, at least for a time. He attracted a distinguished following from among the city's most prominent *ʻulamā'*, *sayyid* and saintly families, including Abū Saʻīd Qazvīnī, who was a grandson of the Sufi shaykh Bāyazīd Khalkhāl, and Mīrak Khālidī, who was a judge (*qāḍī*) and a descendant of the early Muslim commander Khālid b. al-Walīd. A number of *khalīfas* continued to train disciples in the city after Kurdī had been chased away and eventually killed by the Ṣafavids in 925/1519.[26]

All these individuals and their travels are significant in illuminating Aḥrār's role in the Naqshbandī dissemination westward as well as the nature of the enterprise in which he was engaged. Later I shall argue that the early Ottoman Naqshbandiyya teaches us that it is not necessarily useful to try to understand the universal appeal and geographic expansiveness of a tariqa such as this (certainly in the period at hand) in terms of a missionary organization, or a centralized or hierarchical endeavor, or a political enterprise of battling to protect the *sharī'a*-based order, be it at the service of the state or against it. Yet if pre-Mujaddidī or pre-Khālidī Naqshbandīs engaged in anything close to missionary organizing, this would have been represented by the comings and goings apparently orchestrated by Aḥrār, and especially by the large number of his *khalīfas* who traveled west at this time, settling in different locales and taking up writing, teaching, and the training of disciples.

Several aspects of Aḥrār's personality reinforce the impression that he was consciously engaged in what we may call a grand missionary effort. First, he was not only a Sufi shaykh, and one who cultivated disciples and *khalīfas* with a vigor that aroused fear and resentment among the competition,[27] but was in addition a man of keen political and organizational instincts, who presided over substantial economic ventures as well as a network of political contacts and patronage.[28] Second, and more directly significant from our perspective here, as a transmitting shaykh Aḥrār trained as *khalīfas* mostly nonrelatives, a fair number of whom had come to seek him out from afar and then were sent off to engage in teaching the tariqa in faraway places. Granted, the practice of authorizing nonrelatives as *khalīfas* was by that time a Naqshbandī tradition of sorts.[29] But the training and dispatching of disciples who had come from afar was an innovation—one that Aḥrār used effectively as a tool for widespread dissemination.

Here are some examples. 'Abdullāh Ilāhī, who had come to train with Aḥrār from Simav in Anatolia via Istanbul, later returned as his *khalīfa*. 'Alī Kurdī had also come from afar, in time returning not to his native Amadiyah in Kurdistan, but to Qazvin in Iran. Ismā'īl Shirvānī had come to seek Aḥrār from Shirvan in the Caucasus, then traveled as his *khalīfa* to Mecca. Mawlānāzāda Utrārī, originally from Central Asia, traveled with Aḥrār's *ijāza* to the Hijaz, then Damascus; when 'Abd al-Raḥmān Jāmī visited him in 878/1473, he found him still corresponding with his spiritual master. All these careers illustrate Aḥrār's practice of dispatching *khalīfas* to engage in disseminating the tariqa in faraway places and how this practice was reinforced by his training of nonrelatives, and especially of disciples who had come originally from afar. Such individuals naturally made better candidates for missions of this sort than sons, relatives, or other locals, whether because of their own connections and expectations, or those of the shaykh. It is noteworthy, too, that several of the individuals described here did not return as *khalīfas* to their places of birth, but rather proceeded to new locations, in what seems to have been part of a plan orchestrated by Aḥrār.

One could speculate, of course, that rather than being the product of one man's missionary vision, the wave of Naqshbandī *khalīfas* traveling west from Samarkand at this time was the product of changing geopolitical circumstances. Istanbul, in particular, had the pull of an emerging new Muslim imperial capital, with its potential for lavish official patronage. But the circumstances under which ʿAbdullāh Ilāhī moved to the capital—it was rather reluctantly, after several years in his native Simav—suggest that before the beginning of the sixteenth century Istanbul was still less than an obvious magnet for Naqshbandī immigrants.[30] ʿAbd al-Raḥmān Jāmī chose to avoid it altogether: when he received an invitation from Meḥmed II while traveling through Damascus in 878/1473, he hastened instead (perhaps out of political calculations) to Aleppo, Diyarbakır, and the Aqquyunlu capital of Tabriz.[31] Even as late as 955/1548, Abū Saʿīd b. Ṣunʿullāh Kūzakunānī, a refugee from Ṣafavid persecution who settled first in Aleppo, exhibited little interest in the Ottoman capital, planning instead to travel all the way to India, where he hoped to take advantage of some old connections.[32] The travel of *khalīfa*s of Aḥrār to Arabia also does not seem to have hinged on grand geopolitical changes, coming as it did some time before the Ottoman conquest of the Arab lands, and before the Ṣafavid rise to power in Iran at the turn of the sixteenth century.

A comparison with the contemporary Naqshbandī circle of Saʿd al-Dīn Kāshgharī in Herat also underscores Aḥrār's unique practice of sending *khalīfa*s far off. The Kāshgharī line assumed a more local character, with scores of individuals living and teaching in and around Herat until the dislocations wrought by the Ṣafavid conquest of Khorasan in 916/1510.[33] Granted, this line too was carried west, where, in time, it proliferated and enjoyed considerable success. ʿAlāʾ al-Dīn Maktabdār, a disciple originally from the Khorasanī countryside, not only spawned an enduring line of spiritual progeny in Central Asia, but also trained one Ṣunʿullāh Kūzakunānī (the father of Abū Saʿīd), who returned as his *khalīfa* to his own birthplace of Tabriz.[34] It was a *khalīfa* of Kūzakunānī who authorized the afore-mentioned Bābā Niʿmatullāh, later a resident of Akşehir famous for his expertise in the teachings of Ibn al-ʿArabī. Other spiritual descendants in time fled Ṣafavid rule in the Tabriz area to Anatolia, where the line stemming from Kūzakunānī was spectacularly successful around Diyarbakır, then prospered for centuries in Bursa.[35] Still, as geographically widespread Kāshgharī's line became through the spiritual progeny of Maktabdār and Kūzakunānī, it did not evince the intensity of dispatching *khalīfa*s to far away destinations that was a hallmark of the spiritual line of Aḥrār from its very beginning.

One may add here that not only during the generation of Aḥrār's immediate *khalīfa*s but for two centuries and more—as Naqshbandī visitors, pilgrims, and immigrants from Transoxania continued to come to the Ottoman lands, if less frequently—several of the more distinguished of these travelers were spiritual descendants of Aḥrār, especially via the line of Makhdūm-i A'ẓam Aḥmad Kāsānī (d. 949/1542–43).[36] The most important of these was Aḥmad Ṣādiq Ṭāshkandī (d. 994/1586), a much-respected Naqshbandī shaykh already in Transoxania. He arrived in the Ottoman capital in the late sixteenth century and there built a prosperous new career and established what became a much-enduring line of Naqshbandī shaykhs and *tekke* incumbents. Aḥmad Ṣādiq also set out to spread the tariqa to Arabia, where in the words of his disciple and biographer it had become "extinct" by his time.[37] Another immigrant from Transoxania and spiritual descendant of the line of Aḥmad Kāsānī, the poet Ḥaydar Rasā, settled in the Bülbül Dere neighborhood of Üsküdar, where he established one of those Bukharan Naqshbandī *tekkes* known as Buhara or Özbek; he died in 1112/1700–1701 and was replaced as shaykh of the *tekke* by Muḥammad Niyāz, also a Bukharan and spiritual descendant of Aḥmad Kāsānī.[38] Two other spiritual descendants of the same line made their impact especially in Mecca and Damascus. Muḥammad Ḥusayn al-Khwāfī (d. 1087/1676–77) married into a Meccan *sayyid* family and attracted a coterie of local disciples. Abū Sa'īd al-Balkhī (d. 1091/1681) lived for a time in Mecca and in Eyüp outside the walls of Istanbul, where he is said to have attracted many disciples. More than anything else, however, he made his mark by initiating one individual—the prolific Damascene scholar and author 'Abd al-Ghanī al-Nābulusī.[39]

Even if the above does suggest that 'Ubaydullāh Aḥrār engaged in a deliberate endeavor of "missionary organizing," it may be futile to expect to find in our sources any explicit expression of a great design of spreading the tariqa from Transoxania to all these distant places. First, in the eyes of travelers themselves goals such as pilgrimage, study, and propagating the tariqa were often intertwined. One could have been sent off or embarked on a long trip with a view to propagating a new Sufi creed and devotional regimen, while at the same time seeking to perform the pilgrimage, or meet distinguished scholars, or resolve issues related to personal circumstances or to competition over a master's succession. Such seems to have been the case of Aḥmad Ṣādiq Ṭāshkandī's travel to Istanbul after the death of his spiritual master in Transoxania, or of Ḥaydar Rasā's immigration after the "misfortune" that we are told had befallen him in his native Bukhara. Second, our sources (be they devotional manuals, chronicles, or biographical or hagiographical literature) are more apt to discuss actions than intent, and are thus not well suited to illuminate matters such as a missionary vision.

There was however a fitting discursive format—the account of a Sufi's dream—that Naqshbandī practitioners of our period could use to express such sentiments, and we do have one striking example of this in the treatise-cum-hagiography that Muṣṭafā al-Ṣādiqī, a disciple of Aḥmad Ṣādiq Ṭāshkandī, wrote under the title *Al-Manhaj al-muwaṣṣil ilā al-ṭarīq al-abhaj*. In his work, Ṣādiqī tells us that his master had already become the foremost Naqshbandī shaykh of his circle in Transoxania, but then he decided to leave this illustrious career behind and travel all the way to Istanbul, having been commanded in a dream "to spread the perfume of this radiant tariqa in the . . . hearts of the people of Rūm, the Arabs, and the Persians and to sow the aromatic seeds of its rules of conduct (*ādāb*) in the . . . bosoms of the inhabitants (*m.k.a.n*, probably a copyist's error for *s.k.a.n*) of Yemen, India, and Daylam".[40]

This statement, albeit retrospective (and rhetorical in its formulation and metaphors, as might be expected in this genre) is the only explicit expression that we have of the grand sense of missionary endeavor that apparently informed Aḥrār's practice of sending off *khalīfas*—granted, not from the master himself, but from spiritual descendents who may have inherited this sentiment from him.[41]

IN THE SHADOW OF ṢAFAVID PERSECUTION

From the perspective of a tariqa that had just recently begun its dissemination out of Transoxania in several directions, the Ṣafavid takeover of Iran at the turn of the sixteenth century was a development of potentially major—and detrimental—repercussions. As we have seen, there had been an old Naqshbandī center going back to Sa'd al-Dīn Kāshgharī in Herat, to which *khalīfas* of both Kāshgharī and Aḥrār later added new circles in Qazvin and Tabriz. Under more hospitable circumstances a Naqshbandī presence probably would have emerged in other parts of Iran, and in turn this could have established at least a modicum of geographic continuity between the original home of the tariqa in Transoxania and the new centers now developing in India to the south and in Anatolia, Arabia, and the Balkans to the west. But the fashioning of Iran into a Shī'ī state, as the Ṣafavids set out to do, created a fundamentally different environment for Naqshbandīs throughout this vast country and in neighboring areas. Intermittent military operations between the Ṣafavids and their Sunnī neighbors in Transoxania and the Ottoman Empire, breakdowns of public order, and some attempts to impose blockades on travel via Iran hindered the ability of immigrants, pilgrims, and visitors from Transoxania to travel freely, sometimes compelling them to travel at risk to their safety or to seek lengthy and arduous routes circumventing Iran. Inside the Ṣafavid realm, the conversion of a largely Sunnī population to Shī'ism called for the suppression of a tariqa that in the eyes of the new rulers was not simply an expanding rival Sufi brotherhood but also one that they saw as having a potentially uncompromising Sunnī bent to it by dint of its Bakrī *silsila*.

Beside these transformations in communications and in Iran's domestic political climate, the Ṣafavid rise to power might affect Naqshbandīs in other ways. Given the military and political battles that soon ensued between the Ṣafavids and their Sunnī Ottoman neighbors, and more generally the grand changes that were occurring in Sunnī-Shī'ī relations (and in the political meaning of Shī'ism itself), what was at stake was the very spiritual and political identity of a tariqa that had just begun its westward diffusion from Transoxania, and whose Bakrī spiritual genealogy had already stamped it as distinctly Sunnī. One would want to know whether the new political climate affecting not only Iran but the Ottoman realm as well led Naqshbandīs to become more consciously Sunnī than before. Did they transform a notion of Bakrī descent that they had originally understood as a spiritual marker into a notion of more open political significance, or even an emblem of hostility to Shī'īs? Was the distinct form of silent *dhikr* associated with this tariqa perhaps reinforced, if not created, by Naqshbandīs in Iran who were compelled to resort to a kind of Ṣafavid-engendered Sunnī *taqiyya* (the dissimulation of religious practice under duress that is more typically associated with Shī'ī minorities)?[42] Did Ottoman Naqshbandīs rally to the help of the Ottoman state in its political battles against the Ṣafavids and their Ḳızılbaş adherents inside Anatolia, and with what consequences? While these are all highly significant questions, the present and following sections address only those that relate to communications and to Iran's domestic politics, while leaving issues that are better discussed in the context of the Naqshbandiyya's establishment within the Ottoman state and Ottoman society to be taken up in chapters 5 and 6.

According to Said Arjomand, the Ṣafavid campaign against Sufis and Sunnīs in Iran began immediately under Shāh Ismā'īl I (r. 907/1501 to 930/1524), with the Naqshbandiyya "the first order to be ferociously suppressed." By the end of this shāh's reign the tariqa is said to have become "effectively extirpated in central and western Iran," apparently an extrapolation from Algar's statement that "soon [after its establishment in these regions] all trace of the Naqshbandiyya was extirpated from Western and Central Iran by the Ṣafavids, for whom the slaughter of Sunni scholars and shaykhs was an essential part of establishing Shi'i supremacy".[43]

The picture that emerges from sixteenth-century Naqshbandī sources is somewhat more complex. The Ṣafavids may well have sought to extirpate the tariqa, as well as other manifestations of Sunnism, but this was not easily achieved in central Iran, and certainly not in border areas such as Khorasan or Azerbaijan. In time, the Naqshbandī presence did disappear throughout the country. However, this was the product of a protracted process that lasted some fifty years in Herat and Qazvin and over a century in Tabriz and its environs. It involved instances of outright repression, of flight or emigration to Sunnī territories beyond the border, and of shaykhs who simply withdrew from teaching or proselytizing. Nor was emigration out of Iran always a response to direct and outright repression by the regime: it might be induced by the inauspicious atmosphere that the establishment of a Shī'ī state entailed, or by the actual or anticipated loss of patrons, or simply by the growing difficulty of living among Shī'ī neighbors who became increasingly arrogant as Ṣafavid rule was becoming more entrenched.

In Herat the persecution of Naqshbandīs began shortly after the conquest of 916/1510, when the Ṣafavids had the tomb of 'Abd al-Raḥmān Jāmī burnt, leading his only surviving son to leave the city and resettle in the town of Owbeh (Awbah), some one hundred miles to the east.[44] Six other of the ten Naqshbandī shaykhs who according to the *Silsilanāma-yi khwājagān-i Naqshband* of Qazvīnī lived in Herat at the time of the conquest left at unknown dates for Bukhara, Kandahar, Gujarat, and Damascus. Another two apparently managed to stay behind in the city for several decades.[45] Still another, the author of the *Rashaḥāt*, Fakhr al-Dīn 'Alī Kāshifī, continued to live in Herat for over twenty years. Then he, like Jāmī's son before him, moved east to Owbeh, apparently seeking in the Khorasanī hinterland a refuge from the inauspicious atmosphere, if not the outright repression, that prevailed in the city itself.[46]

Naqshbandīs were not alone in seeking refuge outside of the city and further afield. As Maria Subtelny has shown, the "unfavorable climate" that the Ṣafavid conquest initially engendered for "cultural and intellectual life" led various "cultured elements" to leave Herat for western Iran, India, and Transoxania. In 918/1512 the new Ṣafavid authorities allowed a caravan of some five hundred such immigrants to leave for Transoxania, where Sunnī Uzbek rulers had replaced the Tīmūrids a few years earlier.[47] At the same time, Sunnism was hardly stamped out in this province, in which Ṣafavid control remained fragile for some time. The century after the initial Ṣafavid arrival in Khorasan saw a number of Uzbek invasions from Transoxania. On several occasions, Uzbek governors were established in various parts of Khorasan, while Herat itself came under siege or was taken over by Uzbek forces for several short periods, and once for over ten years.[48] Martin Dickson has shown that, at least for the first quarter-century of Ṣafavid rule in this area, Sunnīs or crypto-Sunnīs managed to survive, developing a peaceful coexistence of sorts with Shīʿī neighbors and reemerging "publicly and vengefully" every time Herat changed hands between Ṣafavids and Uzbeks.[49]

From Qazvin, we have firsthand testimony for the suppression of the Naqshbandiyya in the *Silsilanāma-yi khwājagān-i Naqshband* of Muḥammad Qazvīnī. Here Ṣafavid persecution began in 925/1519, when the carrier of the tariqa to Qazvin, *sayyid* ʿAlī Kurdī, was expelled to Tabriz, and there killed;[50] still, it took another half century for the tariqa to disappear completely. A number of *sayyid* ʿAlī's *khalīfa*s who hailed from some of the city's most prominent scholarly and saintly families remained unharmed after his expulsion and continued to live and train disciples in Qazvin for several decades.[51] Qazvīnī's father, Ḥusayn, himself a Naqshbandī shaykh of the line of Aḥrār who had come to Qazvin independently of *sayyid* ʿAlī, was one of those who stayed during all this time.[52] It seems that what eventually led to the disappearance of the tariqa from Qazvin was the establishment of the city as the new Ṣafavid capital around the middle of the sixteenth century.[53] The new Qazvin must have been a less comfortable place for Sunnīs to continue living and practicing, and before long there was apparently a new wave of persecution. It was during this period that Qazvīnī's father was forced to flee to Damascus, where a few years later his son completed his *Silsilanāma*.[54]

In Tabriz the situation was somewhat different. Here the suppression of the Naqshbandiyya was not complete until the beginning of the seventeenth century, if only because Ṣafavid rule over Azerbaijan and the Muslim khanates of Transcaucasia did not become firmly established until then. During the preceding century the area had changed hands several times. First the Ṣafavids wrested it from Aqquyunlu rule in the summer of 906–7/1501. Then the Ottomans occupied Tabriz shortly in 920/1514, 941/1534, and 955/1548, before recognizing Ṣafavid rule over Tabriz, Nakhichevan, and Yerevan in the Peace of Amasya in 962/1555. Through a more determined military effort begun in 986/1578, the Ottomans established themselves more permanently in much of Azerbaijan and Transcaucasia, but then the Ṣafavids led by Shāh ʿAbbās reversed these territorial gains in 1010–20/1600–1610, with the new border stabilized along a line running close to that of today.[55]

The Tabriz Naqshbandīs were closely affected by this succession of military and political vicissitudes. Ṣun'ullāh Kūzakunānī, who had introduced the tariqa into this area, fled to Kurdish-ruled Bitlis in Anatolia shortly after the first Ṣafavid conquest, though later he returned, homesick (*ḥubb al-waṭan*, "love of homeland," is the term used by his biographer), and apparently his life was spared by order of Shāh Ismā'īl.[56] One of his *khalīfa*s, Darvīsh Akhī Khusrawshāhī, and a *khalīfa* of the latter, Ilyās Bādāmyārī, may have been spared Ṣafavid persecution altogether; they both died in their native villages near Tabriz.[57] Other spiritual descendants of this line sought refuge in Ottoman territory: 'Alījān Bādāmyārī in the village of Akhtarīn near Aleppo, and Aḥmad Efendi, known as Mūmjī Pāshā, in Çiçeḳli near the Black Sea town of Giresun.[58]

One can gain a sense of how some Naqshbandīs may have survived in the face of Ṣafavid persecution from the story of Kūzakunānī's son, Abū Sa'īd. He was born in Tabriz shortly before the Ṣafavid takeover and grew up there during the reign of Shāh Ismā'īl, then was led to seek refuge in Anatolia under Shāh Ṭahmāsp. Impressed by the success of a scholar from Qazvin who had fled to Anatolia in the disguise of a pilgrim to the Hijaz, Abū Sa'īd, accompanied by an aged paternal uncle, tried a similar tactic; but the two were caught and imprisoned by the shāh's agents, and had their property confiscated. It was only after some time in prison that, in 953/1546, Abū Sa'īd was able to flee to Ardabil, where two years later he joined the Ottoman army on its return to Anatolia after a brief occupation of Tabriz. For some time he lived in Aleppo supported by a small sultanic allowance; then he moved to Istanbul, where he was to enjoy some popularity and the patronage of a number of high-ranking Ottoman officials.[59]

Some speculation is necessary if one is to unravel the circumstances of two later escapes from the Tabriz area. Of Muḥammad Bādāmyārī, a spiritual descendant of Ṣun'ullāh Kūzakunānī via Darvīsh Akhī Khusrawshāhī and Ilyās Bādāmyārī, we are told that Ṣafavid tyranny caused him to flee with a retinue of dependents and disciples to Orumiyeh (Urūmiyya), west of the lake of that name. In his new place of residence he established himself as a shaykh of wide appeal, attracting a following among both the common folk and the elite and authorizing two sons as *khalīfa*s.[60] Bādāmyārī may have escaped on the occasion of the Ottoman withdrawal from Tabriz in 955/1548, or perhaps he continued to live near Tabriz for some years (though not after 978/1570, the year from which dates Qazvīnī's account). When he relocated to Orumiyeh, it was still under the control of the Ṣafavids (or their vassals), as it would be until the early 990s/1580s. Perhaps the difference was that here the pressure on Sunnīs was less severe than in Tabriz, just as in Khorasan it was less severe in the town of Owbeh than in the capital, Herat. Or it may be that what allowed Muḥammad Bādāmyārī to continue to engage in Sufi teaching and training unharmed was a family ancestry that, according to Qazvīnī, won him respect among local Shī'īs. One thing that information about Bādāmyārī and his disciples demonstrates rather clearly is that this particular Naqshbandī circle did not resort to practicing a silent form of the *dhikr* as a form of *taqiyya*, a dissimulation of religious practice under duress. As we see in chapter 3, practitioners of this spiritual line adopted from secondary Kubravī and Nurbakhshī affiliations of Bādāmyārī's spiritual master a dramatic vocal *dhikr* that they practiced along with the Naqshbandī silent one and that continued to be a hallmark of this spiritual line for centuries.

One of Bādāmyārī's sons, Shaykh Maḥmūd, who grew up in Orumiyeh, moved in time to Ottoman Diyarbakır, where he launched a spectacular career and won much fame under the sobriquet Rūmiye Şeyhī, "the shaykh from Orumiyeh."[61] About the circumstances of this move again very little is said in the sources, though we know that it must have taken place before 1020/1611, when the shaykh had a son, Ismā'īl, born in Diyarbakır.[62] It would seem that like the move of a Naqshbandī from Yerevan who, we are told, escaped to Bursa when his hometown fell into the hands of the "wicked *ṭā'ifa*,"[63] that of Shaykh Maḥmūd, too, was caused by the reestablishment of Ṣafavid rule in Azerbaijan and parts of the Caucasus as a result of Shāh 'Abbās's military onslaught of the 1010–20/1600–1610. Thus, this move was part of a larger historical moment. It was at this time that the Naqshbandiyya disappeared for good from the Tabriz area and more generally from the Ṣafavid realm, ending a presence that had begun vigorously in the Herat of Ḥusayn Bāyqarā and earlier, then dwindled gradually toward extinction after the Ṣafavid takeover of Iran at the beginning of the sixteenth century.[64]

ṢAFAVID POWER AND CHANGING PATTERNS OF COMMUNICATIONS

The Ṣafavid rise to power was not only an event of momentous sectarian significance. Along with the incorporation of the Arab lands into the Ottoman Empire and with the growing European presence and power in the Indian Ocean, it was one of several monumental changes that from about the turn of the sixteenth century were transforming geopolitics and communications throughout the area from Central Asia to India, Arabia, and Anatolia.[65]

From a Naqshbandī perspective, Ṣafavid rule spelt not only repression of Naqshbandīs within the country, but also the endangering and obstruction of communications between Central Asia and the Ottoman lands via Iran and thus the travel of the Transoxanian pilgrims, visitors, or immigrants who were the natural agents for refurbishing the newly emerging Naqshbandī presence in Anatolia, Arabia, and the Balkans. Granted, the vastness of Iran and the survival of Sunnīs or crypto-Sunnīs everywhere would have made the imposition of a blockade on individual travel impossible even had the Ṣafavids pursued such a policy.[66] Moreover, economic considerations sometimes compelled them to be more concerned with ensuring—and actively encouraging—the continued flow of trade.[67] Still, travel was often obstructed and sometimes cut off, whether through the imposition of sanctions or in consequence of military hostilities and the breakdown of public order that attended them.[68] Naturally, the ups and downs of travel hinged to a considerable extent (as did the fortunes of Sunnīs inside Iran) on the ever-changing balance of power and military and diplomatic relations between the Ṣafavids and their Sunnī neighbors to the east and west.[69]

Some travelers were compelled to seek an alternative to traditional routes via Iran in a northern route traversing the steppes north of the Caspian and Black Sea. Leading from Khiva in Khwārazm on the Amu Darya (Oxus River) to the eastern and northern shores of the Caspian, then Astrakhan, the regions under the control of the Noghay princes and the Crimean khāns in the Lower Volga and Don, Kefe in the Crimea, and across to the southern shore of the Black Sea, this route was highly hazardous: long, physically and logistically arduous, and exposed to attacks by tribal populations. Still, at times it became the best or only available route.[70] We know of travelers on this route especially from several years in the mid-sixteenth century, when Ottoman authorities took a series of measures to facilitate travel in order to keep open communications with their Uzbek allies in Transoxania.[71]

The years 958/1551 and 959/1552 saw several diplomatic parties traveling on the northern route in both directions. Especially for a returning party traveling east in the spring of 959/1552, there are documents showing how the Ottoman authorities in Istanbul sought to secure the safety and provisioning of the travelers by enlisting the cooperation of Ottoman provincial governors on the first leg of the trip, and of local Noghay princes farther along.[72] Another famous mission of this time (whose precise circumstances remain less than clear) involved a detachment of three hundred Janissaries equipped with cannons who traveled from Istanbul to Samarkand at the request of Khān 'Abd al-Laṭīf; they arrived safely (apparently after the khān's death), but on their return trip four years later disappeared somewhere north of the Caspian, in the vicinity of Astrakhan.[73] The most famous traveler on the northern route was the Ottoman mariner Sīdī 'Alī Re'īs. He arrived in Samarkand by land after a naval mission that had taken him to India, and from Samarkand set out to return home in 962/1555 with an entourage of some fifty companions. The group made it to the mouth of the Ural (Yayiq) River north of the Caspian, and there was stopped and forced to return to Khwārazm because of the recent Russian conquest of Astrakhan. However, by then the Ottoman-Ṣafavid Peace of Amasya, signed earlier that year, had created new opportunities: rather than risking another trip along the now doubly imperiled northern route, Sīdī 'Alī Re'īs and his companions set out again on one of the traditional Iranian routes via Mashhad, Rayy, Qazvin, and Baghdad, and arrived in Istanbul in 964/1557.[74]

Some of those traveling on the northern route were civilians, especially Transoxanian pilgrims to the Hijaz, as we see in a pilgrimage caravan returning to Samarkand, also in 959/1552.[75] From about the same time dates the trip of the eminent Transoxanian Naqshbandī and Kubravī shaykh 'Abd al-Laṭīf Makhdūm-i Jāmī, who was returning home after several years in the Ottoman capital. We are told that 'Abd al-Laṭīf chose to travel via the dangerous northern steppes rather than risk travel through Iran. He did make it to Khwārazm, where he died in 963/1556, though some of his less-fortunate companions are said to have found their death somewhere along the way at the hands of "infidel Circassians."[76]

As we see in the story of 'Alī Re'īs, the Peace of Amasya (962/1555) combined with the Russian conquest of Astrakhan in 964/1556 (and three years later, the failed Ottoman attempt to reconquer that city) to create a new configuration: travel via Iran, and even via the new Ṣafavid capital of Qazvin, became more attractive for some time, while travel on the northern route was made even more complicated than it had been before. For some years after 996/1588, the Ottomans were able to keep the northern route open, albeit with difficulties, having regained control of the western shores of the Caspian. Then the campaigns of Shāh 'Abbās and ensuing Ottoman-Ṣafavid wars during the first decades of the seventeenth century again imperiled travel both through Iran and on the northern route. It was only after the Treaty of Zohab (1049/1639), which ushered in a long period of Ottoman-Ṣafavid peace, that travel overland via Iran became once again feasible and attractive.[77]

Despite the challenges to travel through Iran, it is clear from casual references to the travel of Naqshbandī pilgrims, visitors, and immigrants from Transoxania that communications were never severed completely: Naqshbandī travelers made the trip from Central Asia to the Ottoman lands in virtually every decade of the two centuries and more of Ṣafavid rule, though often this was via circuitous routes or at a high cost. In fact, it may be that the obstacles to travel via Iran and the emergence of the alternative route via the northern steppes coalesced with the Ottoman conquest of the Arab lands during the second decade of the sixteenth century and the ensuing establishment of an imperial pilgrimage route from Istanbul, with the result that traditional pilgrimage routes from Transoxania via Iran were being replaced for good with more northerly ones going to Anatolia. Itineraries of Naqshbandī pilgrims from Transoxania during the fifteenth century show them traveling along several Iranian routes: a northern one via Herat, Nishapur, Qazvin, Tabriz, Diyarbakır, Aleppo, and Damascus; a central route following the same itinerary to Qazvin and thence to Hamadan and Baghdad; and a southern one going from Herat to Kerman or Yazd, and from there onward via Shiraz.[78] After the Ṣafavid rise to power in Iran and the Ottoman conquest of the Arab lands, and especially once the annual pilgrimage caravan from Istanbul became a highly organized state affair, more Central Asian pilgrims were choosing northern itineraries that took them all the way to Istanbul, where they would join the imperial Ottoman caravan for the last leg of their travel to the Hijaz via Damascus.

Evidence for this new pattern of pilgrimage (most of it from a later period) survives in some of those Naqshbandī *tekke*s and places of accommodation for Transoxanian pilgrims that especially Bukharan founders took to establishing in various places along the pilgrimage route, or routes, from Central Asia. Bursa had one such *tekke* from sometime in the sixteenth century. Greater Istanbul had two from the late seventeenth century and another two from the eighteenth.[79] A legend originating in one of these latter institutions, the *tekke* of Sulṭāntepe in Üsküdar, invokes explicitly this mode of pilgrimage by relating how the *tekke* was built (in this case by Sultan Muṣṭafā III in 1171/1757) in the place where pilgrims from Transoxania traveling through Istanbul used to set up their tents annually. As different versions of the legend have it, the travel of these pilgrims through Istanbul was predicated either upon the custom of visiting on the way the tomb of Eyüp Sulṭān (the Prophet's companion Abū Ayyūb al-Anṣārī), or upon the need to obtain permission from the Ottoman authorities to perform the pilgrimage.[80]

CONCLUSION

The Mujaddidī dissemination of the eighteenth century was clearly not the beginning of the Naqshbandiyya's widespread geographic expansion. The process began with dissemination throughout Transoxania and Khorasan in the fifteenth century. Later in that century the tariqa was being carried far and wide—to Kashghar, India, and, most important from our perspective, to Anatolia, Iran, Arabia, and the Balkans. It would be two more centuries before the main channel of Naqshbandī expansion west from Transoxania was superseded by the vigorous transmission from India associated with the Mujaddidiyya, and later the Khālidiyya.

Much of the Naqshbandī dissemination of the period examined here was connected to 'Ubaydullāh Aḥrār, who brought to the tariqa unprecedented political and organizational sensibilities and skill, and whose mode of operation came closest to "missionary organizing" of anything exhibited by pre-Mujaddidī or pre-Khālidī Naqshbandīs. Granted, explicit expressions of missionary sentiments are not something that our sources are likely to furnish; and, indeed, apart from one retrospective statement of this kind we are left to reconstruct Aḥrār's missionary vision and plan from circumstantial evidence. Especially pertinent in this regard turns out to be his practice of training nonrelatives who had come to seek him out from afar, then sending them off as *khalīfa*s to their places of birth or to altogether new destinations. It is primarily through the activities of a series of these *khalīfas* that Naqshbandī circles emerged during Aḥrār's lifetime and in the following century in various places throughout Iran, Anatolia, Arabia, and the Balkans.

The takeover of Iran by the Shī'ī Ṣafavids at the beginning of the sixteenth century was naturally detrimental for a Sunnī tariqa that had just begun its expansion west from Transoxania and Khorasan. In this chapter we have seen how the establishment of Ṣafavid rule led to the gradual dwindling and disappearance of the tariqa throughout Iran, though not with the speed or the ferocity suggested by some scholars. Military hostilities and attempts at imposed blockades also obstructed—though never blocked completely—the westward travel of Transoxanian Naqshbandīs, and these obstacles to travel, along with the suppression of Naqshbandīs inside Iran, turned this vast country into a void that separated the Naqshbandī centers of Transoxania and to a lesser extent India from those of Anatolia, Arabia, and the Balkans.

The question of how the Ṣafavid rise to power might influence the Naqshbandī spiritual and political identity through the grand transformation that it effected in Sunnī-Shīʿī relations and in the political meaning of Shīʿism itself is best addressed within the following discussion of the Ottoman Naqshbandiyya. In chapter 5, I shall argue that even the heightened sectarian tensions of this time did not lead Ottoman Naqshbandīs to reconfigure immediately a Bakrī *silsila* that had been originally a spiritual marker into an emblem of political identity or of hostility to Shīʿīs. Chapter 6 treats some of the political repercussions of the rise of the Ṣafavids within Ottoman society and considers the ways in which Naqshbandīs were affected by and became involved in the ensuing battles, especially those surrounding the Ḳızılbaş adherents of the Ṣafavids inside Anatolia.

2

Istanbul

ESTABLISHING A PRESENCE

It was during the reign of Sultan Bāyezīd II at the end of the fifteenth and beginning of the sixteenth century that a Naqshbandī presence was established solidly in Istanbul for the first time. Some Naqshbandīs had arrived in the newly conquered capital already under Meḥmed II, who developed an interest in these carriers of the tariqa from Transoxania, perhaps because of the reputation that they and their teachers had gained as experts in the mystical teachings of Muḥyī al-Dīn Ibn al-'Arabī.[1] From the *Rashaḥāt-i 'ayn al-ḥayāt* we learn that in 877/1473 the sultan extended an invitation, albeit unsuccessfully, to 'Abd al-Raḥmān Jāmī, who was traveling through Syria on his return from the pilgrimage.[2] Another Naqshbandī, probably the immigrant from Bukhara Aḥmad Ilāhī, who settled in Edermit and later in Bursa, was commissioned to write a commentary on the *Miftāḥ al-ghayb* of Ibn al-'Arabī's closest disciple and exponent, Ṣadreddīn Ḳonevī.[3] The sultan also had a *tekke* established in the Aḳsarāy neighborhood of the capital for a Naqshbandī immigrant by the name Isḥaq Bukhārī-i Hindī, assigning to it income from the pious endowment (*waqf*) of the recently completed imperial mosque complex of Fātiḥ. One of the residents of the *tekke* (which in time came to be known as Hindīler) was an officer of the Palace Service, the *silāḥdār ağa.*[4] Yet Bukhārī-i Hindī apparently did not produce a *khalīfa* who could succeed him as *tekke* incumbent (*pōstnishīn*) or continue to initiate disciples and thus perpetuate his spiritual line. The work of establishing a more solid Naqshbandī presence in the capital fell to 'Abdullāh Ilāhī and Aḥmad Bukhārī, newly arrived from Transoxania via Anatolia at the beginning of Sultan Bāyezīd's reign.

About the move of these two carriers of the tariqa to the capital there has been some confusion. The introduction to the *Risāle-i molla Ilāhī* (at least in some of the copies that have survived), suggests that they arrived under Sultan Meḥmed, since the *Risāle* is said to be the transcript of a sermon that Ilāhī delivered at the Aya Sofya Mosque in 874/1469, with the sultan in attendance.[5] However, our main informant on Ilāhī's career, the eminent Bursan writer Maḥmūd Lāmi'ī Çelebi, who was Ilāhī's spiritual descendant, is unambiguous in dating his move to the capital to the aftermath of Sultan Meḥmed's death. Perhaps it was one of the copiers of the *Risāle* who started the myth of the public delivery of this so-called sermon in the presence of the Sultan. Mustafa Kara believes that the attribution of the *Risāle* to Ilāhī is altogether mistaken. Like the commentary on the *Miftāḥ al-ghayb*, this too was a work of Aḥmad Ilāhī of Bursa that was attributed erroneously to the more famous Istanbul shaykh of the same name.[6]

According to the account of Lāmi'ī Çelebi in his Turkish translation-adaptation of Jāmī's *Nafaḥāt al-uns* (with an appendix featuring the biographies of some thirty Anatolian shaykhs), Ilāhī had been to the newly conquered capital as a young student before embarking on the trip that took him to Samarkand, where 'Ubaydullāh Aḥrār initiated him into the tariqa.[7] Returning as Aḥrār's *khalīfa*, probably in the late 870s/early 1470s, he settled in his native Simav in western Anatolia, where soon an impressive circle of disciples and followers emerged around him.[8] Aḥmad Bukhārī, a scion of an important Bukharan *sayyid* family and a disciple of Aḥrār who became Ilāhī's trainee, accompanied his new spiritual master to Simav, there serving as the group's prayer leader (*imām*) and the shaykh's obedient right-hand man, who routinely performed many of the menial tasks involved in the maintenance of the household-*tekke*. From Simav the reputation of Ilāhī spread to Istanbul. Gifts and invitations began arriving from the powerful of the capital, including from the onetime chief military judge (*ḳāżī 'asker*) Mağnısalı Çelebi.[9] Yet the shaykh was little impressed with this attention, and preferred to stay in Simav. At one point, he allowed Bukhārī to travel to the capital and scout the situation, but again decided to stay behind, having received a message encoded in a line of Persian verse in which his disciple advised: "The man whose mind is at peace is he who seizes the skirt of the Beloved and holds to a corner."[10]

In the end it was the political upheavals following Sultan Meḥmed's death in 886/1481 that led Ilāhī to the capital. Though sparing in detail, Lāmi'ī Çelebi is unambiguous about the time, stating that it was the events of the interregnum (*feterāt*) that caused the move.[11] Even clearer is the statement of Ṭaşköprüzāde, according to which the shaykh was compelled to move to the capital because of disturbances that broke out in the area of Simav in the wake of the sultan's death.[12] Be that as it may, it was during the reign of Sultan Bāyezīd that Ilāhī and Bukhārī established the foundations of an enduring Naqshbandī presence in the capital (Bukhārī continuing in this role after Ilāhī's move to Yenice-i Vardar, and until his own death in 922/1516). Together the two gained for the tariqa a solid footing in an imperial capital that was growing in size and population, and where other Sufis—especially the Khalwatīs, but also Mevlevīs and Bayramīs—were settling and having their first *tekkes* set up at about the same time.

Lāmi'ī Çelebi's account captures a certain duality that characterized Ilāhī throughout his career. By temperament he was indifferent to the company and patronage of casual followers from among the rich and powerful, and preferred to devote himself to writing and to the training of a small coterie of disciples whose every thought he could monitor during daily sessions, and whom he was able to lead to a state of "presence with God" (*ḥużūr*, Ar. *ḥuḍūr*). In addition to Bukhārī, these intimate trainees included the *'ālim* from Kürre-i Nuḥās on the Black Sea shore, Uzun Muṣliḥüddīn; another budding *'ālim* later known as Lüṭfullāh Üskübī; and especially 'Ābid Çelebi, a judge and descendant of Jalāl al-Dīn Rūmī who gave up his career to become Ilāhī's disciple. Üskübī later moved with Ilāhī to Yenice-i Vardar, then carried the tariqa west to Skopje (Üsküb). 'Ābid Çelebi remained in the capital. He built a mosque with quarters for residents near his home in the Fātiḥ district, and there served as shaykh until his death a few years after Ilāhī's.[13]

Perhaps because he preferred the guiding of a few intimate disciples to the commotion of a large and distinguished following, when he moved to the capital Ilāhī chose as his quarters the "dilapidated and derelict" rooms of the madrasa attached to the Zeyrek Mosque in Fātiḥ, where he had been a student in his youth, over the presumably well-endowed and more fitting *tekke* offered by the once *ḳāżī'asker* Mağnısalı Çelebi. Indeed, before long he sought to flee the excessive attention that the capital's elite showered on him—and the distraction that this posed to his serious disciples. Accepting the invitation of an admirer, the district governor (*sancaḳ beğī*) Evrenoszāde Aḥmed Beğ, he moved to the quieter setting of Yenice-i Vardar (in Modern Greece), where he died shortly after, in 896/1491.[14] Despite this reluctance, Ilāhī nevertheless created around himself and the tariqa an aura that attracted precisely the large and eminent (and presumably more casual) following toward which he was so ambivalent. State officials, high-ranking *'ulamā'*, the capital's rich, and other grandees (*mevālī-i 'aṣr, a'yān, ekābir, erbāb-i devlet, aṣḥāb-i kasrat*) are said to have gathered around him at Zeyrek.[15] Such followers would have been drawn to him not only because of his reputation as a powerful mystical guide, who had trained with 'Ubaydullāh Aḥrār in Samarkand, and had communed with the spirit of Bahā' al-Dīn Naqshband at his tomb in Bukhara. They would have been attracted, too, by his expertise in the mystical teachings of Ibn al-'Arabī and his personal acquaintance with 'Abd al-Raḥmān Jāmī, that icon of the cultural splendor of Ḥusayn Bāyqarā's Herat and of a literary Persian culture that the intellectual elite of the new imperial capital much coveted.[16]

Along with training his more intimate disciples and catering—albeit reluctantly—to the larger following at Zeyrek, Ilāhī was a prolific writer. Typical is the *Meslek eṭ-ṭālibīn*, in which he touches on distinct Naqshbandī matters within broader and more generic discussions about the relationship between tariqa and *sharī'a*, the conduct of shaykhs and disciples, ascetic exercises, Sufi morals, and the Sufi's struggle against the desires of the uncontrolled soul. Among other things, the *Meslek* emphasizes rigorous adherence to the Prophet's *sunna* along with a Malāmatī-inspired rejection of ostentatious behavior, including ostentatious piety.[17] Ilāhī hails the silent *dhikr* as the most perfect form of recollection; but rather than the mechanics of the Naqshbandī *dhikr*, he is more interested in continuous *dhikr* as a weapon in the general Sufi battle against inattentiveness.[18] The *Meslek* is also revealing in its language. Ilāhī, who wrote in the three major Islamic languages of his time—Arabic, Persian, and Ottoman Turkish—makes it clear in the introduction that his choice of Turkish here was deliberate: this was to allow him to introduce a legacy of mystical thought that was available only in Arabic and Persian to followers who did not know these languages.[19]

Becoming Ilāhī's principal successor in the capital when the latter had moved to Yenice-i Vardar, Aḥmad Bukhārī approached the dissemination of the tariqa in a somewhat different manner. He was little educated in the exoteric Islamic sciences and not a prolific writer, though he wrote a treatise on the Naqshbandī way and a collection of glosses on Rūmī's *Masnavī*.[20] He too, like Ilāhī, was a transmitter of mystical insights derived from Ibn al-'Arabī and Rūmī. But he seems even more interested than his master had been in teaching the Naqshbandiyya as a distinct mystical and devotional way. Lāmi'ī Çelebi describes his sessions of Sufi training (*irshād*), which were anchored in the tariqa's central devotional and pedagogical methods: "His way was that of strictness in the performance of religious duties, relinquishing desire, continuous silent recollection, intimate companionship [between shaykh and disciple], withdrawal from people, eating and talking exiguously, performing night vigils and day-time fasting, guarding oneself against religious innovation, following the Prophet's practice, and concentrating one's being upon God while holding aloof from the concerns of this world."[21]

Bukhārī clearly emerges as more comfortable than his master with the hustle and bustle of Istanbul and with lobbying for the attention and patronage of the city's governing and learning elite (apparently he was capitalizing on the respect that he enjoyed thanks to his illustrious Khwājagānī and *sayyid* descent, as manifested in his common epithet Emīr). There must be an element of hyperbole in Lāmiʿī Çelebi's statement that most of the shaykh's followers were former judges, madrasa professors, or men who were otherwise associated with the high echelons of the Ottoman religious/learned hierarchy, the *ʿilmiye*.[22] Among his disciples, benefactors, and *khalīfas* we recognize individuals who clearly hailed from more modest backgrounds.[23] Still, Lāmiʿī's account makes it clear that like his master—and, indeed, without the latter's ambivalence—Bukhārī built around himself a distinguished circle of followers.

Along with catering to this following and training a number of prominent *khalīfas*, Bukhārī embraced the establishment of material foundations for his spiritual line. Within a little more than two decades, he had three Naqshbandī *tekkes* established in the capital. The first one, soon to emerge as the most eminent Naqshbandī institution of the capital, was located near the Fātiḥ mosque complex. It had several rooms for residents, along with a mosque that was reportedly built through the generosity of Sultan Bāyezīd. Here Bukhārī himself served as shaykh until his death in 922/1516, when he was succeeded by his *khalīfa* and son-in-law Maḥmūd Çelebi. A second *tekke*, also combining a mosque with residential quarters, was built in the neighborhood of Ayvānsarāy (or Balāṭ), up the Golden Horn, to accommodate the growing number of disciples. However, because this institution did not have a proper *waqf* supporting it, it slipped away from Naqshbandī control after Bukhārī's death; it was only in the mid-seventeenth century that one Muṣliḥüddīn Muṣṭafā, a shaykh who had married a female descendant of Bukhārī's, reendowed and reinstated the premises as a Naqshbandī *tekke*. The third Emīr-i Bukhārī Tekke was located outside the city walls in Edirne Ḳapı, and had as its first shaykh Bukhārī's son-in-law Maḥmūd Çelebi. It consisted at first of a mosque and residential quarters that Bukhārī built and his successor enlarged; later Sultan Süleymān had a congregational mosque added to the complex.[24]

From the perspective of 922/1516, the year of Bukhārī's death, the sixty years or so since the Naqshbandiyya had first appeared in Istanbul, and especially the thirty-five years since Ilāhī's arrival at Zeyrek, were ones in which the tariqa had become solidly established in the Ottoman capital. It had gained a reputation as a distinct mystical and devotional way whose shaykhs emphasized rigorous *sharī'a*-abidance while offering superior mystical progress as well as a link with a coveted mystical and cultural legacy from Iran and Transoxania. It had attracted distinguished followers, including many *'ulamā'*, as well as material favor, some of it from high-ranking officials and even sultans. In addition, several sites where the Naqshbandī way was taught and its devotional regimen conducted had been established or procured, though a number of them did not continue as Naqshbandī institutions beyond one generation: the Emīr-i Bukhārī Tekke in Ayvānsarāy passed after its founder's death to non-Naqshbandī heirs; the Hindīler Tekke probably lost its Naqshbandī connection for a while; the mosque of 'Ābid Çelebī apparently continued as a public mosque, though one offering accommodation to Naqshbandī and Mevlevī dervishes; and even at Zeyrek, where an important Naqshbandī circle had come together around 'Abdullāh Ilāhī, Ilāhī's replacement as *pōstnishīn* was a Khalwatī shaykh, Bālī Efendi (who later made his principal impact in Sofia, Bulgaria).[25]

Indeed, by 922/1516 the Khalwatiyya had probably become the capital's most prominent tariqa and the Ottoman sultans' favorite. After Sultan Bāyezīd had come to the throne in 886/1481, having defeated his brother Cem, he invited from his earlier seat of Amasya (where he had been governor during his father's sultanate) a spiritual guide and perhaps political collaborator, the Khalwatī shaykh Meḥmed Cemāleddīn Aḳsarāyı (known as Çelebi Efendi). The shaykh was installed in a large and lavishly endowed mosque complex that the future grand vezir Koca Muṣṭafā Paşa established in a converted Byzantine church between Aḳsarāy and the fortress of Yediḳuḷe. The mosque was to become both the center of the district named after the founder and the citadel of the Istanbul Khalwatiyya for many years.[26]

In the analysis of Nathalie Clayer, Bāyezīd II was the first of a long series of sultans who sought spiritual counsel from Khalwatī shaykhs and favored this tariqa for its critical collaboration in the Ottoman campaign of "Sunnitization" and of eliminating heterodoxy.[27] Others have suggested that the Khalwatiyya suffered a temporary stagnation under Selīm I, or that this sultan was for a time suspicious of the Khalwatīs before he became reconciled to the influence that they wielded from their center in Koca Muṣṭafā Paşa.[28] Either way, by 922/1516, the Naqshbandiyya may be said to have been well established in the Ottoman capital, but it was clearly not the most important, most favored, or most quickly proliferating tariqa. This must be taken into account as we go beyond 922/1516, and examine how the Istanbul Naqshbandiyya fared beyond the generation of the "founders," what kind of tariqa it became, how it was distinguished from its counterparts, who was attracted to it, and what elements allowed it to expand, prosper, or at least endure, as it certainly did all the way to the Mujaddidī efflorescence of the eighteenth century.

SPIRITUAL LINES AND CONTINUITY

Before moving on to discuss followers, patronage, and the role of *tekkes*, the present section seeks to draw attention to a phenomenon that can be easily overlooked—namely, the very endurance of the spiritual line that began with Ilāhī and Bukhārī.

After Bukhārī's death the line (or, more accurately, "tree") that issued from him evolved primarily around two circles.[29] One began with his *khalīfa* and son-in-law Maḥmūd Çelebi (d. 938/1531–32). He was the first incumbent of the Emīr-i Bukhārī Tekke in Edirne Ḳapı, then moved after his master's death to the one in Fātiḥ but retained strong ties to his original *tekke*, which was sometimes called after him. Shortly before his death, he made over in *waqf* to this institution a considerable sum of money and several pieces of real estate that facilitated a major enlargement and renovation of the premises.[30]

We know of spiritual descendants of Maḥmūd Çelebi spanning about a century and a half. One of his *khalīfas*, Mişmelzāde Meḥmed Efendi, settled and initiated a number of Naqshbandī disciples in the *tekke* adjacent to the Molla Fenārī Mosque in the citadel of Bursa.[31] The shaykh's prized *khalīfa* and son-in-law, 'Abdüllaṭīf, and a *khalīfa* of the latter, Meḥmed Cemālzāde, were the incumbents of the Emīr-i Bukhārī Tekke in Fātiḥ for some five decades before this post was taken over by other spiritual descendants of Bukhārī. 'Abdüllaṭīf, whom Nev'īzāde 'Aṭā'ī describes as the "head of the Khwājagānī *silsila*" (*serḥalḳe-i silsilet-i hōcagān*) in the Fātiḥ *tekke*, is notable for his connections within the *'ilmiye*, his ability to mobilize material support for the *tekke*, and his training of a number of disciples and *khalīfas*, including Meḥmed Cemālzāde, the onetime Khalwatī shaykh, and Muṣṭafā Sürūrī, for whom the vezir Ḳāsım Paşa had built a madrasa in Galata across the Golden Horn from Istanbul.[32] In the Edirne Ḳapı *tekke* the line issuing from Maḥmūd Çelebi was even more lasting, though less distinguished. Beginning with Ḥaccı Halīfe Menteşevī, four and perhaps eight of his spiritual descendants were the incumbents of this *tekke* before this position passed in 1086/1675 to spiritual descendants of another Naqshbandī line.[33]

A second circle that ensued from Aḥmad Bukhārī and whose mark was to be felt in the capital for some time began with Bukhārī's younger *khalīfa*, Ḥekīm Çelebi (d. 974/1567). After his master's death, the young Ḥekīm Çelebi spent some time as a "pious resident" (*mujāwir*) in the Holy Cities of the Hijaz, then lived off a modest allowance in Istanbul and Bursa. During that time he was introduced to the then chief equerry (*mīrāhūr-i evvel*) of the palace and future grand vezir, Rüstem Paşa, perhaps by the poet from Filibe Baba Maḥmūd Riżā'ī, who was simultaneously a disciple of the shaykh and the private tutor of the *mīrāhūr*.[34] Some ten years later the association with Rüstem led to the establishment in Fīl Dāmī, between Bāyezīd and Aḳsarāy, of a *tekke* supported by a sultanic *waqf*, to which Ḥekīm Çelebi was assigned as shaykh. It was around this *tekke* that he began to develop his own circle and initiatic line—though always as "the *khalīfa* of Emīr-i Bukhārī."[35]

In time the Fīl Dāmī *tekke* and the spiritual line spawned by Ḥekīm Çelebi evolved into important agents of Naqshbandī dissemination. Disciples associated with this circle appear several times in our sources in connection with the production and use of devotional Naqshbandī literature. Moreover, in the two centuries after the shaykh's death, spiritual descendants of his came to officiate in all the *tekke*s ensuing from the line of Aḥmad Bukhārī. The Fīl Dāmī *tekke* itself had as shaykhs seven of his spiritual descendants (Muṣṭafā Naḳşbendzāde, Ya'ḳūb Ilāhīzāde, Aḥmed Tirevī, Ibrāhīm Efendi, 'Osmān Bosnevī, Mu'abbir Ḥasan, and Muṣṭafā Efendi Esīrī Damadı);[36] one of these, Tirevī, was a well-connected *'ālim* and the preceptor of several *khalīfas*,[37] and two others, Bosnevī and Esīrī Damadı, were famous preachers in some of the capital's major imperial mosques.[38] Two other of Ḥekīm Çelebi's spiritual descendants, Meḥmed Ḳavaḳlızāde and Şa'bān Efendi, were the incumbents of the Emīr-i Bukhārī Tekke in Fātiḥ for ten years or so beginning in 993/1585.[39] Another two—the triple Naqshbandī-Khalwatī-Mevlevī *khalīfa* Ḥasan Feyżī Simkeşzāde, and his son, the historian-biographer Meḥmed Şeyhī—were the incumbents of the Edirne Ḳapı *tekke* for some six decades, from 1086/1675 to 1145/1732.[40] When the Emīr-i Bukhārī Tekke in Ayvānsarāy, which had slipped out of Naqshbandī control upon the founder's death, was reinstituted in the mid-seventeenth century, it too had as shaykhs some of Ḥekīm Çelebi's spiritual descendants (via Aḥmed Tirevī). Yūsuf Efendi and 'Osmān Efendi were *pōstnishīn*s from 1079/1668 to 1137/1725; an earlier *pōstnishīn* may have been Ya'ḳūb Ḳayṣeriyeli, another of Tirevī's *khalīfa*s and an imperial mosque preacher of some renown.[41]

All this represents unusual lineal continuity. We know of many other Naqshbandī shaykhs who came to the capital from Transoxania and elsewhere over the years and who commanded respect and drew a following, not least among the city's elite; yet from most of these other carriers of the tariqa no lines of much permanence evolved. We may recall that Isḥaq Bukhārī-i Hindī had an endowed *tekke* built for him by Sultan Meḥmed II; still, he did not spawn a spiritual line. Nor did a known spiritual line issue from Bābā Ḥaydar Samarqandī, the *khalīfa* of 'Ubaydullāh Aḥrār, who came via Mecca to Eyüp, where in time Sultan Süleymān had a mosque built for him.[42] The same may be said about several others. A second Aḥmad Bukhārī, who settled in the Unḳapanı neighborhood of the capital, where large crowds regularly came to seek his famous *baraka* (grace or charisma), also did not generate a spiritual line.[43] Nor did a line issue from Muḥammad b. Kamāl al-Dīn Farkandī, a visitor via Mecca following the pilgrimage of 980/1573, who was adopted by the capital's elite thanks to his learning and his kinship with the eminent *şeyhülislām* (chief jurisconsult of the empire) Ebüssu'ūd Efendi.[44]

Clearly, the development of enduring lines was not simply a matter of *tekkes*, and certainly not of formal and properly endowed *tekkes*, as is clear from a comparison between Isḥaq Bukhārī-i Hindī, who did not train any *khalīfa* in his *tekke* endowed by the sultan, and 'Abdullāh Ilāhī, who trained several in the "dilapidated" premises of the Zeyrek madrasa. Evidently, too, lineal continuity required more than individual shaykhs who attracted followers, initiated disciples, taught devotional practice and mystical insights, exuded *baraka*, or conducted sessions of silent *dhikr*. For lines of any permanence to evolve, shaykhs also needed to have a commitment to the continuous training of *khalīfas*. The spiritual progeny of Ilāhī and Bukhārī seem to have had a distinct commitment to such training, and especially to the training of *khalīfas* who were not family members. Perhaps this was a practice that Ilāhī and Bukhārī inherited from 'Ubaydullāh Aḥrār and then bequeathed to their spiritual descendants (though they apparently did not appropriate from Aḥrār the attendant procedure of dispatching *khalīfas* to faraway destinations).

Two other aspects of the way in which shaykhs of this line went about bequeathing their spiritual authority and securing lineal continuity may be noted here. First, they were prepared to train and authorize as *khalīfas* individuals who had affiliations with other tariqas—for example, Meḥmed Cemālzāde, Şa'bān Efendi, and Simkeşzāde—and they were apparently able to make these individuals' Naqshbandī identity paramount. Second, as energetic, or respected, or lavishly supported as they might be, they saw themselves and were seen by others as the *khalīfas* of their spiritual preceptors and as the last links in a *silsila* inherited from them: none of them tried to launch the kind of autonomous or breakaway lines that were common in the contemporary Khalwatiyya.[45] It should be noted, however, that the Naqshbandī literature itself was silent on many of these points (though not on spiritual succession or multiple affiliations, as we shall see later). No distinction was made, for example, between shaykhs who initiate disciples and those who train *khalīfas*—both types were subsumed under the generic term *murshid*. It is only in circumstantial evidence that we can detect the special importance that the spiritual progeny of Ilāhī and Bukhārī assigned to the training of *khalīfas* (and of nonrelatives, for that matter).

Finally, an additional perspective on the issue of *khalīfas* and continuity may be had from the fortunes of the only lasting pre-Mujaddidī Naqshbandī line beside that of Ilāhī and Bukhārī to have developed in the Ottoman capital. It originated with Aḥmad Ṣādiq Ṭāshkandī, the scion of a venerable *sayyid* family from Bukhara and a spiritual descendant of Aḥrār via Makhdūm-i Aʿẓam Aḥmad Kāsānī. Aḥmad Ṣādiq's career and *silsila* are known to us in unusual detail from the *Al-Manhaj al-muwaṣṣil ilā al-ṭarīq al-abhaj*, authored by his disciple Muṣṭafā al-Ṣādiqī. According to this account, after having trained with Kāsānī and his *khalīfa* Muḥammad Islām Jūybārī, he went on to become the foremost Naqshbandī shaykh of Transoxania, so much so that Kāsānī's son, Khwāja Isḥāq, instructed his own *khalīfas* to seek renewed initiation from him. Then, shortly after Jūybārī's death in 971/1563, Aḥmad Ṣādiq left this brilliant career to go to Istanbul, having been commanded in a dream to "spread the perfume" of the tariqa far and wide.[46]

In his new residence the shaykh embarked on a new career, attracting a large and prominent discipleship. One of his followers was the *şeyhülislām*, Ebüssuʿūd Efendi, and Sultan Murād III himself is said to have had an audience with him and "pledged to him his faithful *irāda* [discipleship?] and perfect genuine love." When the shaykh died in the devastating Istanbul plague of 994/1586, much came to a standstill: the historian Selānīkī relates that the capital's high officialdom, along with many shaykhs and *ʿulamāʾ*, attended his funeral services held at the Fātiḥ Mosque and that at the sultan's orders the work of the Imperial Council was suspended for three days.[47] As we see in another chapter, the shaykh also had an abiding interest in the Arab lands. A few years before his death he traveled on one of his several pilgrimages to Mecca with a large retinue, making this a grand occasion for spreading the tariqa along the way.[48]

What makes Aḥmad Ṣādiq pertinent to the issue of lines and continuity is the long line of Istanbul Naqshbandī shaykhs that ensued from him and that was rather different from that of Ilāhī and Bukhārī. It passed from Aḥmad Ṣādiq to his son and *khalīfa*, Ḍiyā' al-Dīn Aḥmad, who had probably accompanied him from Transoxania and who became the incumbent of the original Emīr-i Bukhārī Tekke in Fātiḥ after the death of Ṣa'bān Efendi in 1002/1593. It may be that Aḥmad Ṣādiq himself was the first of this line to become the *tekke*'s incumbent, although this is suggested only by a much later source, perhaps one that viewed him as more fitting than his son to have brought this old and venerable Naqshbandī institution under the leadership of shaykhs newly arrived from Transoxania. Be that as it may, from Ḍiyā' al-Dīn Aḥmad the position of shaykh went to a cousin and new immigrant from Transoxania, Faḍlallāh Efendi, and after him to a series of descendants of the same line and family, who remained the incumbents of the *tekke* for close to two centuries.[49]

While certainly long lasting, this was an altogether different affair from the line of Ilāhī and Bukhārī and, as we see below, from the practice of nonhereditary "spiritual" succession that had become distinctive of Naqshbandīs in many locales.[50] Rather than nonhereditary spiritual descendants, the successors of Aḥmad Ṣādiq were all *khalīfa*s-cum-biological progeny, whether sons, brothers, or nephews. Theirs was a Naqshbandī line as well as a family patrimony centered on a single *tekke* (though not quite akin to the phenomenon of hereditary families of shaykhs and shrine caretakers that are known to us from other environments and from other, often more localized, tariqas).

TEKKES AND INSTITUTIONAL ARRANGEMENTS

By way of introduction, a note about the use of *tekke* and *zāwiya* in this study is in order. It has been suggested that in Mamlūk Syria and Egypt, *ribāṭ*, *khānqāh*, and *zāwiya* were distinct institutions, the first housing both Sufis and the poor (of both sexes), the second generally a large royal or princely foundation housing hundreds of Sufis but not assigned to a specific shaykh or tariqa, and only the third reserved specifically for a Sufi shaykh and his disciples.[51] In the Ottoman environment, too, we are told that the term *zāwiya*, as opposed to *tekke*, could be employed to refer specifically to small urban institutions or to dervish hospices on the road or in mountain passes.[52] However, sources used in the present study do not bear out such neat distinctions. Except in a few cases (for example one description of the Emīr-i Bukhārī Tekke in Fātiḥ that makes the *zāwiya*, with its cells for residents, a component of the whole *tekke* complex), the term *tekke* tends to appear in our sources interchangeably with *zāwiya* and *khānqāh*, and sometimes *dargāh*.[53] Contemporaries seem to have seen no clear difference between such institutions, so that terminology is not likely to reveal much about the configuration of individual ones. To avoid constant shifting between terms, I use *tekke* in sections of the book that deal with Anatolia and the Balkans, and *zāwiya*, in a more generic sense, elsewhere.

Naqshbandī shaykhs of the capital taught mysticism, trained disciples, and conducted the tariqa's devotional rites under a variety of institutional and spatial arrangements, and not necessarily from endowed or specialized institutions. There was clearly no extensive network of specialized *tekke*s of the kind that the Mujaddidiyya and especially Khālidiyya of the capital would have much later (in 1256/1840, there would be fifty-three Naqshbandī *tekke*s in the capital, all but four of them active).[54] Some shaykhs operated from private residences or from private mosques that they established, and in some cases endowed, near their residences. Muṣṭafā Sürūrī (d.969/1562) had a successful teaching career, having his own madrasa built by the vezir Ḳāsım Paşa in the neighborhood of that name across the Golden Horn. But personal and political doubts caused him to vacillate between madrasa teaching and the tariqa; in addition to his madrasa he built near his residence in the same neighborhood a small mosque where he taught students and, after a fall from grace toward the end of his life, catered to the stevedores and boatmen of the nearby imperial dockyards.[55] ʻAbdullāh Ilāhī's *khalīfa* ʻĀbid Çelebi also taught the tariqa from a private mosque that he established near his house in the Fātiḥ district. However, this mosque had rooms for Naqshbandī and Mevlevī dervishes, as well as a *waqf* that the shaykh founded and to which his followers added several others during the few decades after his death in 903/1497–98.[56] A second Aḥmad Bukhārī (d. 994/1586), who settled in Unḳapanı on the Golden Horn, became especially renowned for receiving the many seekers of his *baraka* in his private residence; after his death the site became a place of visitation (*ziyāra*), where Sultan Murād III had a tomb built.[57] Even Aḥmad Ṣādiq Ṭāshkandī may fall into this category: although a few years after his death his immediate descendants became the incumbents of the old Emīr-i Bukhārī Tekke in Fātiḥ, the bulk of our evidence suggests that Aḥmad Ṣādiq himself was not based in the *tekke*.[58]

Of course, every tariqa had its share of shaykhs who operated out of homes or private (or public) mosques, if simply because they could not command the kind of material patronage that would make available more specialized premises. In this regard it may be instructive to compare the contemporary Naqshbandiyya and Khalwatiyya. We have noted that as of the reign of Bāyezīd II the latter became the favorite of almost every sultan and the recipient of extensive material patronage, much of it in the form of lavish *tekkes*, such as the one in the Koca Muṣṭafā Paşa complex. The Naqshbandiyya was certainly not as lavishly supported. But whether they were or were not able to command sufficient material support (as we shall see, there were ways to mobilize patronage from outside the governing elite), some Naqshbandī shaykhs may also have not been that eager to acquire *tekkes*. For one thing, the Naqshbandī devotional regimen and pedagogy—highly sober, independent of paraphernalia, emphasizing one-on-one relations between shaykhs and intimate trainees, and calling upon disciples to pursue the mystical path while immersed in society—allowed shaykhs to conduct the tariqa's rites and train disciples without access to institutionalized and endowed *tekkes*. In addition, shaykhs may have continued to harbor the ambivalence toward *tekkes* that some of their early spiritual ancestors in Transoxania had expressed.[59]

'Abdullāh Ilāhī himself may be of relevance here. As we have seen, for some time he was reluctant to move from his home-*tekke* in Simav to the capital, and having moved he chose as his base the "dilapidated" premises of the madrasa attached to the Zeyrek Mosque, where he had been a student in his youth, instead of a presumably endowed *tekke* offered by the onetime *ḳāżī'asker* Mağnısalı Çelebi. Moreover, when he eventually fled the excessive attention that he was getting at Zeyrek to the quieter setting of Yenice-i Vardar, Ilāhī apparently did not attempt to secure a successor at Zeyrek: while his principal *khalīfa*, Aḥmad Bukhārī, who had a rather different approach to *tekkes*, proceeded to have a number of them established elsewhere, Ilāhī's replacement at Zeyrek, Bālī Efendi, was a Khalwatī shaykh. Careers such as that of Ilāhī and Aḥmad Ṣādiq Ṭāshkandī (and a few others) are a reminder that while specialized *tekkes* were undoubtedly important sites for the dissemination of the tariqa, the personal influence that a shaykh could wield through training disciples, conducting the tariqa's ritual, writing, and interacting with casual followers was not predicated upon the size or level of institutionalization of his *tekke*, and could exist outside the context of a specialized *tekke* altogether. Nor is the number or size of the tariqa's specialized *tekkes* an accurate indication of its influence in the capital at any given time.

Given the possibility of a lingering Naqshbandī ambivalence toward *tekkes*, along with the ability of shaykhs of this tariqa to conduct devotional rites without paraphernalia, we might expect more of them to have been based in public mosques, especially those in which they might officiate as preachers or prayer leaders. Some did—notably the famous imperial mosque preachers Ya'ḳūb Ḳayṣeriyeli, Muṣṭafā Esīrī Damadı, and 'Osmān Bosnevī (the latter doubling as a preacher and *tekke* incumbent)[60] and others (Mu'abbir Ḥasan, 'Umar Bākī, Muṣliḥüddīn Efendi) who were preachers in less prominent mosques.[61] But Naqshbandī shaykhs propagating the tariqa out of mosques, madrasas, and other public institutions were not particularly common in the capital. As we shall see, in Bursa this was a more prevalent, or at least more visible, configuration. The majority of the capital's better-known Naqshbandī shaykhs operated out of specialized institutions that came into being when a patron or a series of patrons (and in some cases the shaykh or his relatives) made the premises available and provided for maintenance and for living expenses for functionaries and residents through *waqf*. Such were the Emīr-ī Bukhārī Tekkes in Fātiḥ, Edirne Ḳapı, and (in time) Ayvānsarāy, the Hindīler Tekke, which Sultan Meḥmed II established in the Aḳsarāy neighborhood for Isḥaq Bukhārī-i Hindī, the Ḥekīm Çelebi Tekke in Fīl Dāmī, with its sultanic *waqf* incorporated into that of the Süleymāniye Mosque, and the two Bukharan *tekke*s of the Sulṭānaḥmed and Bülbül Dere neighborhoods, the latter in Üsküdar.

*Tekke*s' sources of funding varied considerably. The Hindīler Tekke in Ayvānsarāy and apparently the Ḥekīm Çelebi Tekke in Fīl Dāmī came into being through acts of sultanic beneficence, and their *waqf*s were part of the great sultanic *waqf*s supporting the Sulṭān Meḥmed and Süleymāniye Mosques.[62] The Bukharan *tekke*s of Sulṭānaḥmed and Bülbül Dere (known as Buhara or Özbek/Özbekler) belonged to a distinct category of institutions that appear in several locations besides the capital. These were *tekke*s that Bukharan benefactors established in various places along the pilgrimage route to Mecca to provide accommodations for pilgrims from Transoxania. Their shaykhs had to be Bukharans or married Bukharan women, and the *tekke*s usually had a Naqshbandī affiliation or Naqshbandī ties.[63] Another distinct mode of patronage associated with a number of Naqshbandī *tekke*s emerges from the *İstanbul Vakıflan Tahrîr Defteri*, edited by Barkan and Ayverdi. This register gives a neighborhood-by-neighborhood account of all the nonsultanic *waqf*s that existed in Istanbul *intra muros* in the mid-sixteenth century, each *waqf* with the name of the founder and information about assets, expected income, beneficiaries, administrators, and allocations for specific expenses. As it turns out, the *waqf*s supporting a number of Naqshbandī instituitions—the Emīr-i Bukhārī Tekkes in Fātiḥ and Edirne Ḳapı and the 'Ābid Çelebi Mosque—were actually packages, each consisting of a series of small *waqf*s that were established over several decades by the founding shaykh and his followers. Their assets were typically cash or modest pieces of rentable urban real estate.

The Edirne Ḳapı *tekke*, for example, had some thirty *waqfs* created for it during the thirty-odd years before the register was made. The largest ones were founded by the *tekke*'s first shaykh, Maḥmūd Çelebi, and his wife, Fāṭima Hātūn (the daughter of Aḥmad Bukhārī); they consisted of rentable urban property as well as sums of money amounting to about fifty thousand *aḳçe* each. Maḥmūd Çelebi also endowed some of the *tekke*'s premises, including residential buildings and a kitchen. All the other *waqfs* supporting this institution were far more modest in scale, consisting of either a few pieces of real estate or a sum of money totaling as much as a few thousand *aḳçes*. The founders appear to have been rank-and-file disciples—scribes, small religious functionaries, a private tutor, bureaucrats, craftsmen, and their wives or freed slaves. Only about half of them were *'askerīs* (members of the Ottoman non-taxpaying military-administrative elite), and then somewhat marginally, that is, by dint of descent from the family of a shaykh, a scribal or low *'ilmiye* position, or some religious education. There was not a single prominent *'ālim* or state official among them.[64] Much the same can be said of the benefactors and the *waqfs* supporting the Emīr-i Bukhārī Tekke in Fātiḥ, except that this institution had one *waqf* founder of note in Pirinçci Sinān Ağa, the (retired) official responsible for the rice supply to the palace of Meḥmed II.[65] The 'Ābid Çelebi Mosque was the beneficiary of considerably fewer *waqfs*, but out of the same mold in terms of sources of income, founders, and manner of establishment.[66]

What these *waqf* packages demonstrate is that there was another, albeit less lucrative, way for *tekkes* to be established and supported other than through the patronage of the wealthiest and most powerful benefactors from the Ottoman governing elite. All three institutions mentioned here may have been given gifts by the high and mighty: the Emīr-i Bukhārī Tekkes in Fātiḥ and Edirne Ḳapı are said to have had their respective mosques built by two sultans, Bāyezīd II and Süleymān.[67] But they were all founded and secured a continuous existence in a cumulative effort that was launched by shaykhs and their disciples—individuals who were not necessarily part of the governing elite and clearly did not belong to its upper echelons. The process began with the founding shaykh endowing property in order to secure its use for his disciples after his death. Additional *waqfs* were gradually added by his followers, and assigned to pay for maintenance, equipment, foodstuffs, and allowances for functionaries and residents. All the *waqfs* concerned were small or medium in size, and unlike those that prominent *'askerīs* typically established in favor of the large religious-educational complexes of the capital, they had their assets in cash or urban real estate—not in *waqf* villages spread over the countryside.[68] Finally, while the phenomenon of "cumulative *waqfs*" certainly had its analogues in *tekkes* of other tariqas, the register of 953/1546 mentions it exclusively in a Naqshbandī connection; of several thousand *waqfs* appearing in the register, it is only those assigned to the Emīr-i Bukhārī Tekkes in Fātiḥ and Edirne Ḳapı that are lumped together under the specific designation *evḳāf ül-mürīdīn ve'l-muḥibbīn* (roughly "disciples' *waqfs*"), which is meant to indicate this kind of cumulative mode.

Where these *waqf* packages differed much less dramatically from a sultanic *waqf* such as that supporting the Ḥekīm Çelebi Tekke was in the size of their expected income. From records appearing in the *Süleymaniye Vakfiyesi*, edited by Kürkçüoğlu, we learn that the *waqf* of the Ḥekīm Çelebi Tekke included specific allocations of some 30,000 *aḳçe* annually, suggesting that its expected total annual income may have been larger, but not tremendously so.[69] By comparison, the anticipated annual income from the *waqfs* supporting the Emīr-i Bukhārī Tekkes in Fātiḥ and Edirne Ḳapı amounted to about 22,000 and 23,000 *aḳçe* respectively. The *waqfs* supporting the 'Ābid Çelebi Mosque were considerably more modest, but they too were expected to yield over 10,000 *aḳçe* annually. In comparison with the great *waqfs* of Istanbul—foundations yielding hundreds of thousands of *aḳçes* annually, albeit typically supporting several institutions in and outside of the capital—an annual income of 10,000 or 20,000 and even more than 30,000 *aḳçe* was undoubtedly small.[70] To make another comparison, at this time 20,000 *aḳçe* (a little over 60 *aḳçe* per day) would have been the salary of a professor of middle rank or a small-town judge.[71] As contemporary *tekkes* go annual incomes of this order were nevertheless respectable, though not grand. Most of the seventy or so *tekkes* mentioned in the Istanbul *waqf* register of 953/1546 were assigned much lower incomes, typically amounting to a few hundred *aḳçes* annually in addition to the use of the premises. Five *tekkes* were secured incomes roughly similar to those of the four Naqshbandī institutions discussed here.[72] Four *tekke* or mosque complexes were assigned higher incomes amounting to between 50,000 and 150,000 *aḳçes* annually.[73] And seven others were to be the beneficiaries of large or very large *waqfs*, yet ones that supported more than a single institution.[74] In all, the four Naqshbandī institutions for which we have records were the beneficiaries of medium-size *waqfs*. The incomes they could expect were nowhere near those of the sultanic or vezirial foundations supporting the great mosque complexes of the capital, and they were inferior, too, in comparison with those of the most financially privileged *tekkes*, both metropolitan and provincial. They nevertheless exceeded the incomes assigned to numerous other *tekkes*, which were typically supported by a single piece of real estate or a sum of money of equivalent value.

In terms of physical configuration, too, the four Naqshbandī institutions discussed here were small or medium sized. From the section of the 953/1546 register devoted to the Edirne Ḳapı *tekke*, we learn that some thirty years after its establishment this institution comprised a mosque (later to be replaced by a congregational mosque), an assembly room for the performance of the tariqa's rites, three rooms for resident disciples, four adjoining buildings for the founder's descendants and the mosque's prayer leader and muezzin, kitchen and dining facilities, a cemetery, and two gardens (with amenities such as mats and blankets, prayer rugs, oil lamps, bathing jugs, dining tables, cooking and eating utensils, and storage crates, as well as several volumes of the Qur'ān and a few other books).[75] The 'Ābid Çelebi Mosque had, according to its original *waqf* from 900/1494, five rooms for dervishes.[76] The Emir-i Bukhārī Tekke in Fātiḥ was apparently larger: the account ascribing to it sixteen rooms for disciples comes from the eighteenth century,[77] but already one of the original sixteenth-century *waqfs* supporting it envisaged ten Qur'ān readers, including the mosque's prayer leader and muezzin and several resident disciples.[78] This too was only a medium-sized *tekke*, however. It was nowhere in the league of *tekkes* such as Hüdā'ī or Koca Muṣṭafā Paşa, or of some of capital's Mevlevī institutions, with their rooms for thirty or forty residents, or even more.

Some light is shed on the indispensability of a proper *waqf* for a *tekke*'s lasting existence—and more generally on the ways in which *tekkes* came into being—by the fortunes of another Emīr-i Bukhārī Tekke, that located in Ayvānsarāy up the Golden Horn. We learn from the *Ḥadīḳat ül-cevāmi'* of Ayvānsarāyı that because this site was the private property (*mulk*) of the first shaykh, Aḥmad Bukhārī, and because it was not supported by a proper *waqf*, when the shaykh died the property was claimed by legal heirs (*verese*). Apparently these individuals were not associated with the tariqa—which is not surprising, given the proclivity of Naqshbandī shaykhs for spiritual over hereditary family succession—and as a result the site slipped out of Naqshbandī control and ceased to exist as a Naqshbandī *tekke* for over a century. It was only in the mid-seventeenth century that the property reverted to Naqshbandī use, having come into the hands of a female descendant of Bukhārī who married a Naqshbandī shaykh. A *tekke* was reinstituted, with the said shaykh, Muṣliḥüddīn Muṣṭafā, as its incumbent. To secure its future existence, Muṣliḥüddīn established, in turn, a *waqf* that presumably gave over the premises for the use of future shaykhs. According to the *Ḥadīḳa* (written about another century later), a series of ten shaykhs followed, all of them Naqshbandīs.[79]

However, even a *waqf* (be it sultanic, "cumulative," or other) was not sufficient to make an institution "Naqshbandī," or in other words to earmark a *tekke* for the use of a certain tariqa. What founders usually stipulated in the endowment deeds was that a *tekke*'s premises were to provide housing for resident disciples and sometimes for the founder and his progeny, and that income accruing from certain assets would cover daily expenses (for food, lighting, and such) and pay for certain functions and functionaries—the mosque's prayer leader and muezzin, *waqf* administrators, readers of chapters of the Qur'ān, reciters of litanies in the founder's honor, and providers of services such as cooking, cleaning, and gardening (all apparently resident disciples). The identity of a *tekke*'s shaykh, and certainly matters of succession, were not necessarily settled by *waqf* founders, at least not in institutions of the kind discussed here, where the office of the shaykh (*mashyakha*) was not a family patrimony. In fact, *waqf* records available to us often refer to the shaykh of a *tekke* only in his capacity as the prayer leader (*imām*) of the mosque; it is "to the *imām* of the mosque" (sometimes doubling as the *waqf* administrator) that a fixed allowance was commonly assigned.

A founder of an institution such as a madrasa or *tekke* could, of course, earmark it for a certain individual—as was the case with Isḥaq Bukhārī-i Hindī or Ḥekīm Çelebi—and in other cases the incumbent himself would have been the founder, as was 'Ābid Çelebi. But these matters were not necessarily determined through *waqf* documents, which also did not designate the manner of succession, and certainly did not assign *tekke*s to "the Naqshbandī tariqa" or their *mashyakha*s to "shaykhs of the tariqa."[80] Securing a *tekke* for the continuous use of a tariqa—at least during periods when these issues were not decided by the state—depended on shaykhs themselves, whose prerogatives apparently included the appointing of successors.[81] This underscores once again the importance of shaykhs' commitment to the training and authorization of *khalīfa*s. If they were to last as institutions associated with a certain tariqa, *tekke*s needed not only ongoing patronage through *waqf*, but also shaykhs who were committed to training *khalīfa*s and securing them as future incumbents. When this did not happen, a *waqf* would not be of much use, as is evident from the Hindīler Tekke of Aḳsarāy, which enjoyed only a short-lived career as a Naqshbandī institution despite its sultanic *waqf*.

~

Naqshbandī *tekke*s of the capital and the circles of disciples (sing. *ṭā'ifa*, *ḥalqa*, *jam'iyya*, Tur. *ṭā'ife*, *ḥalḳe*, *cem'iyet*) that congregated around them generally operated independently of each other and did not constitute an institutionally bound or hierarchical network. Followers sought out and became attached to individual spiritual masters; they are not known to have frequented multiple shaykhs or *tekke*s and certainly were not subject to a graded system of "membership" that was valid across the capital's Naqshbandiyya, let alone "across the tariqa." Shaykhs, too, were not transferred among various Naqshbandī institutions in accordance with higher considerations, as was the practice of contemporary Mevlevīs and perhaps Khalwatīs, though they might train in one *tekke* and then become the incumbents in another, especially when such institutions were associated with the same spiritual line.[82]

One unusual case in which a shaykh tried to subject one Naqshbandī *tekke* to another emerges from the 953/1546 register of Istanbul *waqf*s, and specifically from a *waqf* that in 937/1531 Aḥmad Bukhārī's *khalīfa* Maḥmūd Çelebi, who was then the shaykh of the Emīr-i Bukhārī Tekke in Fātiḥ, established for the Emīr-i Bukhārī Tekke in Edirne Ḳapı, where he had been shaykh before. One stipulation of the founder was as follows:

> The shaykh of the *zāviye* of Hazret-i Emīr Buhārī . . . adjacent to the mosque of Sultan Mehmed Hān [inside the city walls] will be the supervisor (*nāẓir*) [of the endowment of the Edirne Ḳapı *tekke*]. Every month, the individual officiating as the endowment's administrator (*mütevelli*) will hand over to [him] the said income, which he will then allocate for the [necessary] expenses. Once a year, on the first day of the year, the shaykh of the old *zāviye* [in Fātiḥ], in his capacity as *nāẓir*, along with the muezzin of the [Fātiḥ] *zāviye* and the rest of its resident community, will convene in one place with the *imām* of the [Edirne Ḳapı] mosque, its *mü'ezzin* and the rest of its resident community to review the functioning of the endowment. The account books (*defter*s) of the administrator and collector will be inspected separately, and if anything is found to be inconsistent with the conditions laid down by the founder, they will be held liable and will be dismissed and replaced by others.[83]

We cannot tell for sure what led Maḥmūd Çelebi to try to subject the Edirne Ḳapı *tekke* to that of Fātiḥ in the disposal and supervision of its *waqf* income. Was he trying, shortly before his death, to make the primacy of the original Emīr-i Bukhārī Tekke in Fātiḥ an institutional matter rather than simply one of seniority or prestige? Was this part of an attempt to establish himself as a kind of "supershaykh" at a time when his own *khalīfa* was the incumbent of the Edirne Ḳapı *tekke*, and his fellow *khalīfa*, Ḥekīm Çelebi, had already become the incumbent of his own *tekke* in Fīl Dāmī? Whatever the shaykh's motives, it would be unwise to project from this case to the wider realities of the tariqa or of the capital's Naqshbandiyya. Here were two *tekke*s that were bound to each other in unusual ways: they had been built just a generation earlier to accommodate the disciples of one individual, Aḥmad Bukhārī; moreover, before he moved to the Fātiḥ *tekke*, Maḥmūd Çelebi had been the first shaykh of the one in Edirne Ḳapı. In cases where no such ties existed, this kind of attempt to create institutional interdependence between *tekke*s would have been much less plausible.

Another characteristic of the whole network of Istanbul *tekke*s (if "network" is at all apt) may be noted. Most Naqshbandī institutions of the capital during the period discussed here were located either in the area between Fātiḥ, Unḳapanı, and Aḳsarāy, or up the Golden Horn—from Ayvānsarāy and Edirne Ḳapı to Eyüp outside the city walls. Two were located in Ḳāsım Paşa across the Golden Horn and in Bülbül Dere in Üsküdar, both outside Istanbul proper. Until the establishment of the Özbek Tekke of Sulṭānaḥmed at the end of the seventeenth century, there was not a single Naqshbandī *tekke* in Istanbul *intra muros* outside the areas of Fātiḥ-Unḳapanı-Aḳsarāy and Ayvānsarāy-Edirne Ḳapı. Together all these neighborhoods constituted only part of the overall inhabited area of the capital during this period, and not the most densely populated part at that.[84] Other tariqas, for example the Khalwatiyya and Mevleviye, had major *tekke*s located elsewhere in the city, the first in Samaṭya and the second in Yeni Ḳapı, Ḳāsım Paşa, Galata, and Beşiktaş.[85] Perhaps what contributed to this Naqshbandī concentration was the religious attractiveness that the presence of the Fātiḥ Mosque and the tomb of the Prophet's companion Abū Ayyūb al-Anṣārī imparted to the districts of Fātiḥ and Eyüp. Interestingly, the two areas of Fātiḥ-Unḳapanı-Aḳsarāy and Ayvānsarāy-Edirne Ḳapı-Eyüp were to remain major Naqshbandī centers after the introduction of the Mujaddidiyya into Istanbul in the eighteenth century: despite the expansion and building activity of the Mujaddidī and Khālidī phases, which carried the tariqa, among other directions, all the way up the Bosphorus, in 1840 over 40 percent of Naqshbandī *tekke*s of the capital were still located in the two areas delineated above.[86] These neighborhoods cannot be said to have developed, however, into anything resembling a "Naqshbandī space" in the sense of a continuous area of strong Naqshbandī influence, if not predominance. Perhaps one of the factors that militated against the emergence of a distinct sphere of influence of this kind was precisely that absence of institutional ties among different *tekkes* that has been noted above.

PENETRATING SOCIETY

If the Naqshbandiyya was "the order of the ulama," as has been suggested, in the Ottoman capital of our period it was both more and less than that.[87] Numerous men of religion were indeed attracted to this tariqa. This is not only suggested by hagiographers such as Lāmi'ī Çelebi or Muṣṭafā b. Hayreddīn, with their hyperbolic assertions that most of Aḥmad Bukhārī's disciples came from the upper echelons of the *'ilmiye* or that Şa'bān Efendi, a century later, had as his "heart and soul" disciples "most [of the capital's] glorious *'ülemā* and illustrious shaykhs."[88] The same connection is reflected in the profusion of Naqshbandī disciples and shaykhs among the minor religious functionaries (mosque preachers and prayer leaders, personal tutors, calligraphers, copiers of *fatwās*) that fill the *mashā'ikh* chapters in the biographical dictionaries. It emerges, too, from an examination of twenty high-ranking *'ulamā'* of the reigns of Süleymān through Murād IV for whom Nev'īzāde 'Aṭā'ī gives specific tariqa affiliations: twelve of them were Naqshbandīs, with Zaynīs constituting a distant second.[89]

The Naqshbandī-*'ulamā'* connection was neither exclusive nor as elitist as the remarks of the hagiographers imply: of the several patterns that it assumed, only one involved members of the *'ilmiye* proper, those scholars who graduated from the prestigious educational institutions and then went on to pursue careers in madrasa teaching and the law.[90] Such were, for example, the biographer Ṭaşköprüzāde, the *ḳāżī 'askers* Ḳızıl 'Abdurraḥmān Amasyalı, Mağnısalı Çelebi, and Sālim Efendi, and the *qāḍī* of Istanbul Kurd Ḳāsım 'Alī, all Naqshbandī followers.[91] Individuals of this type tended to be casual followers of the tariqa, though some of them are said explicitly to have been initiated or to have taken the *ṣuḥba* of a shaykh. Others married into a shaykh's family or became the benefactors of a shaykh and his *tekke*, as was Ḳızıl 'Abdurraḥmān, who built for the Emīr-i Bukhārī Tekke in Fātiḥ an endowed Qur'ān school, in the garden of which he is buried.[92]

Most men of religion who became associated with the tariqa were much less senior. Usually they were individuals who had received a madrasa education and perhaps gained positions as mosque preachers or prayer leaders, but had not embarked on a full-fledged *'ilmiye* career as professors or judges. ʿAbdullāh Ilāhī, Maḥmūd Çelebi, Ḥekīm Çelebi, Şaʿbān Efendi, and many other of the tariqa's most distinguished shaykhs fall into this category. Such individuals were, of course, not unique to the Naqshbandī constituency: they can be found throughout the ranks of many other tariqas.[93]

There was perhaps another, middle category consisting of individuals who turned to the tariqa after having abandoned more successful *ʿilmiye* careers. We know in some detail of several such *ʿulamā'*-turned-Naqshbandīs, usually low- or middle-ranking professors or judges who became disenchanted with the learned establishment. A case in point is that of Muṣṭafā Sürūrī. Conflicting personal loyalties and predilections, along with *ʿilmiye* infighting, led him to give up a teaching position in the madrasa that the vezir Ḳāsım Paşa had built for him in Galata across the Golden Horn from Istanbul and become instead the *khalīfa* of shaykh ʿAbdüllaṭīf of the Emīr-i Bukhārī Tekke in Fātiḥ. In time, Sürūrī returned to his madrasa, now combining madrasa teaching with reading the *Masnavī* in a nearby mosque and giving Sufi training in another private mosque that he had built near his house. Later he left a second time to become the tutor of one of Sultan Süleymān's sons, Prince Muṣṭafā. But in his last years, after the downfall and execution of the prince, he was again at his mosque, teaching students and patronized by the boatmen and stevedores of the nearby imperial dockyards.[94]

While not one of these patterns of men of religion becoming associated with the tariqa was uniquely Naqshbandī, together the many instances of such individuals (of varying ranks) who became Naqshbandī disciples amounted to a phenomenon that several contemporary observers found noteworthy. Writing in the mid-sixteenth century, the biographer Laṭīfī was particularly explicit about this issue, attributing the special attraction that the Naqshbandiyya held for men of religion to the fact that it was judged most in keeping with rigorous observance of Islam's Holy Law:

> Of all the ways of the shaykhs, this way [in particular] is considered by *şerīʿat*-minded *ʿülemā'* to be in conformity with the Prophet's practice and the Holy Law. It is for this reason that most men of religion . . . who choose withdrawal [and take up the devotional life] opt for this way.[95]

If the Naqshbandī promise of fidelity to the *sharīʿa* was so critical in the ranks of the *ʿulamā'*, among the capital's governing and intellectual elite and the Ottoman dynasty and court a no less powerful promise must have been that of superior mystical teaching and training, along with the Naqshbandī association with a Perso-Islamic literary culture that this milieu equated with intellectual sophistication and panache and that was much coveted.[96] We have seen the interest that Meḥmed II took in Naqshbandī immigrants from Bukhara who had gained a reputation as experts in the mystical teachings of Ibn al-ʿArabī, having a *tekke* built for one and commissioning another to write a commentary on the *Miftāḥ al-ghayb* of Ṣadreddīn Ḳonevī. Other individuals from the capital's political and intellectual elite must have been drawn to the reputations of shaykhs who wrote Persian verse, taught or commented on Persian language and literature, composed *muʿammā* (that genre of wordplay that had been a favorite at the court of Sultan Ḥusayn Bāyqarā in Herat), or conducted public reading sessions of Rūmī's *Masnavī*. Interestingly, such pursuits were not limited to immigrants from Bukhara or to individuals such as ʿAbdullāh Ilāhī, who had a personal acquaintance with the Herat of Ḥusayn Bāyqarā or with luminaries of the stature of ʿAbd al-Raḥmān Jāmī. Many Anatolians by birth, among them Maḥmūd Çelebi, Ḥekīm Çelebī, Muṣṭafā Sürūrī, Meḥmed Ḳavaḳlızāde, Molla Münşī Aḳḥiṣārı, and Ḥasan Feyżī Simkeşzāde, also engaged in similar activities.[97] Of all these pursuits, reading the *Masnavī* was perhaps the most important means of recruiting prominent followers. The historian Ṭaşköprüzāde came to know his Naqshbandī preceptor, Maḥmūd Çelebi, by reading the *Masnavī* with him.[98] The same is said of the grand vezir Rüstem Paşa, who as a young palace official read the *Masnavī* with Ḥekīm Çelebi, later becoming his "lifelong disciple" and building (or having Sultan Süleymān build) his *tekke* in Fīl Dāmī in the Aḳsarāy neighborhood.[99]

The attraction was spiritual and intellectual, not necessarily political. Along with Ḥekīm Çelebi and his lifelong spiritual mentoring of Rüstem Paşa, there were other Naqshbandī shaykhs who established similar relationships with high-ranking Ottoman officials, members of the Ottoman court, and even sultans. Here suffice it to mention Aḥmad Ṣādiq Ṭāshkandī, who became a spiritual mentor of Sultan Murād III, or Şaʿbān Efendi, who had the same sultan seek his spiritual intervention and visit him in the Emīr-i Bukhārī Tekke in Fātiḥ more than once.[100] However, Murād had apparently more influential Sufi confidants in two Khalwatī shaykhs: Ḥasan Ḥüsāmeddīn ʿUşşāḳī and the popular Şuccāʿ.[101] Moreover, we recall Clayer's thesis, according to which Khalwatī shaykhs had become the political favorites of the Ottoman sultans from the days of Bāyezīd II in consequence of their championing of the Ottoman campaign against "heterodoxy" and the help that especially a number of Khalwatī branches (the Sünbüliye, Cemāliye, and Şemsiye-Sīvāsiye) extended to a series of Ottoman sultans in this regard.[102] Naqshbandīs did not come to provide such political services or to enjoy such political patronage.

As we will see in chapter 6, they too have been portrayed as agents of the antiheterodox, and especially anti-Ḳızılbaş, Ottoman campaign of the time; but this proposition appears to be a projection back from nineteenth-century images more than a reflection of sixteenth-century realities.

It is much more difficult to learn about the involvement of Naqshbandī shaykhs with the wider urban population, since the contemporary biographers, hagiographers, and chroniclers who produced the pertinent sources were less interested in this constituency and less inclined, as a matter of literary convention, to write about it. It is unlikely that the reputation of this tariqa for rigorous adherence to the *sharī'a* and its emphatically sober devotional regimen made it less attractive among the more popular urban milieus (as we will see in the discussion of the Ḳāḍīzādelis in chapter 6, individuals of this background might well become militantly involved in campaigns of enforcing the *sharī'a* on others, too). One thing that can be established with some confidence, however, is that Naqshbandī shaykhs of the capital eschewed communal leadership and campaigns of mass recruitment. They did not employ the techniques of recruiting whole communities that are known from other tariqas (and from the Naqshbandiyya of Kurdistan)[103] and they certainly did not count among their ranks anybody resembling the Aleppan Ikhlāṣ al-Khalwatī, with his one hundred thousand disciples, or his *khalīfa* Muḥammad Ghazzī, who is said to have initiated "the majority of the people of Damascus" in mass ceremonies held during two visits to that city.[104] Naqshbandī shaykhs, too, made deliberate efforts to reach the wider public, but these were typically of a more subtle nature, such as writing in (or translating into) Ottoman Turkish in order to reach less-learned or less-aristocratic followers who did not know Persian. 'Abdullāh Ilāhī was explicit about this goal in the introductions to the *Meslek eṭ-ṭālibīn* and the *Ervāḥ ül-müştāḳīn*, as was Muṣṭafā b. Hayreddīn in his translation of Qazvīnī's *Silsilanāma*.[105]

Some Naqshbandī shaykhs were better placed than others to make inroads among the larger urban population by serving as preachers in some of the capital's two hundred or so congregational mosques, and especially its series of imperial mosques (those large complexes that had been endowed over the centuries by members of the Ottoman dynasty). Because attendance at the communal Friday service was expected of the whole community, the position of preacher, and especially of imperial mosque preacher, provided holders direct and prestigious access to the public (though also considerable government scrutiny in what became, from sometime in the sixteenth century, government-appointed positions).[106] Among Naqshbandīs, a series of spiritual descendants of Ḥekīm Çelebi via Aḥmed Tirevī—'Osmān Bosnevī, Ya'ḳūb Ḳayṣeriyeli, Ḥasan Feyżī Simkeşzāde, and 'Umar Bākī—especially distinguished themselves as mosque preachers, the first two serving in some of the capital's premier imperial mosques.[107] Bosnevī will be discussed at length in chapter 6 in connection with his active involvement, as preacher in the Süleymāniye Mosque, with the puritanical Ḳāḍīzādeli movement. His fellow *khalīfa* Ḳayṣeriyeli, who served in the Sultan Selīm and Bāyezīd Mosques, may have been of a more learned temperament: his sermons are said to have been written down and to have gained him much fame.

Those who might be among Bosnevī's or Ḳayṣeriyeli's listeners, that is, the common Istanbulites—artisans, shopkeepers, food vendors, small bureaucrats—whom the Naqshbandī shaykhs might attract as followers, remain largely unknown. From the biographical dictionaries, which are led by literary conventions to focus on men of religion, shaykhs, and high-ranking officials, we only learn the names of a few such disciples, among them the weaver Ḥāk Muṣliḥüddīn Menteşevī, the dealer in printed goods Aḥmed Başmacı, and the son of a junior military administrator, Mu'abbir Ḥasan.[108] One exceptional source that provides less-biased information—and depicts a more occupationally and socially diverse picture of the Naqshbandī discipleship—is the Istanbul *waqf* register of 953/1546, discussed in the preceding section. The register introduces some sixty founders of *waqfs* that were earmarked entirely or partially to the support of Naqshbandī *tekkes*. The founders are identified by name and honorific and sometimes by position or occupation, followed by an enumeration of the endowed assets, their value, the annual income that they were expected to yield, and prescribed allocations.

By far the largest number of Naqshbandī benefactors that appear in the register can be placed in the ranks of the bureaucracy or the religious establishment. Some are identified by position or occupation—a scribe, a mosque prayer leader, or a private tutor of a prince. Some appear with titles such as *hōca*, *çelebi*, *efendi*, or *mevlānā*. Some were the progeny or freed slaves of *'ulamā'*, *sayyids*, or shaykhs. A few others were craftsmen or master craftsmen (among them a stonemason and a carpenter), though interestingly not one is identified as a merchant. It is impossible to gauge with any certainty to which echelon of their respective careers or occupations *waqf* founders belonged, but several indications suggest that most of them did not come from the upper ranks. Only one founder, Pirinçci Sinān, was a known state official (the officer in charge of the rice supply to the palace of Meḥmed II), and his *waqf* was to benefit primarily the mosque carrying his own name, with only the paid administrator designated as a Naqshbandī follower.[109] One other Naqshbandī benefactor mentioned in the register was identified as a *paşa*, and another three as the progeny of *paşas*.[110] Only one of the founders bearing the titles *hōca*, *çelebi*, *mevlānā*, or *efendi*, a Mevlānā Muḥyiddīn, is identified by his position (as the tutor of one of the Ottoman princes); presumably, none of his colleagues carrying these titles held a position worth mentioning.[111] The typical size of *waqfs* that these founders set up also suggests that most of them did not come from the upper echelons of society. Most of the *waqfs* appearing in the register were, by the size of their assets or their expected annual income, small or even trivial.[112] Somewhat larger ones were likely to have been founded by the shaykh of the recipient *tekke* or a family member.[113]

WAQF-MAKING AND THE WOMEN OF THE TARIQA

The Istanbul *waqf* register of 953/1546 not only helps to complement and modify the picture of a primarily aristocratic or learned discipleship that the biographical literature suggests; it also provides information about seventeen female *waqf* founders in support of some of the capital's Naqshbandī *tekkes*.[114] This information is valuable, because most other sources available to us keep silent about the "women of the tariqa."

There was nothing that would ban women from becoming Naqshbandī disciples. We know, for example, of the mother of Muḥammad Rūjī, a literate woman of a religious bent who was initiated by Sa'd al-Dīn Kāshgharī in fifteenth-century Herat.[115] Nineteenth-century Indian Mujaddidī sources admonished shaykhs to refrain from touching the hand of, or from communing with, a female adept without the presence of a guardian.[116] However, there were ways to get around such dangers. Cemal Kafadar has shown how an eighteenth-century Khalwatī woman communicated with her shaykh via letters in which she recorded her dreams.[117] Interestingly, one of the few female disciples mentioned in our sources also appears in a similar connection: identified only as *pīrzen* ("an old woman"), she used to frequent 'Abdullāh Ilāhī at the Zeyrek madrasa and had him interpret her dreams, one of which he resolved through clues in the *Futūḥāt al-makkiyya* of Ibn al-'Arabī.[118] Naqshbandī shaykhs might also find the technique of *rābiṭa* (fixing the shaykh's picture in the imagination as a vehicle for the flow of divine energy) particularly useful with female adepts, because once learned and internalized this technique could ideally be practiced without physical contact or even proximity. Female disciples might similarly benefit from the Naqshbandī emphasis on an individual and continuous mode of the *dhikr*, one that did not require any paraphernalia and that could be practiced outside a *tekke*—in fact, anywhere. Altogether we may surmise, then, that despite the general silence of our sources, some other women apart from Ilāhī's *pirzen* became adepts, practiced the tariqa's ritual, or "took the *ṣuḥba*" of a Naqshbandī shaykh, either similarly seeking to have dreams interpreted or in other ways.[119]

Women could also be touched by the tariqa through its involvement in disciples' life-cycle events. Naqshbandīs did not encourage celibacy. Some disciples were surely initiated as unmarried young men, and it may be that some young men who came from afar to seek a shaykh's training, having left behind extended families and social networks, found in the tariqa that "social outlet for unmarried young males" that Hans Joachim Kissling highlighted some half a century ago.[120] But most Naqshbandī shaykhs and disciples had families, as is suggested not only by the principle of "solitude within society" (*khalvat dar anjuman*), but also by biographers who thought it important to identify specifically a number of shaykhs and disciples who remained unmarried or childless.[121] Celebrations associated with families' life-cycle events—births, circumcisions, marriages, deaths—would constitute natural occasions for the tariqa or a shaykh to be involved; moreover, much of this could easily take place in the privacy of disciples' homes or in sex-segregated gatherings. That we hear nothing of such occasions except for the casual reference to a shaykh's daughter who was given in marriage to his prized *khalīfa* is perhaps a matter of convention of not discussing women and family because of considerations of privacy and decorum.[122]

Granted, given their insistence on rigorous *sharī'a*-abidance, Naqshbandīs would have had to enforce the sexual segregation of disciples (as is emphasized by the Indian Mujaddidī sources mentioned above).[123] In turn, this would have rendered it difficult—perhaps nearly impossible—for female disciples to participate in communal devotional practice in *tekke*s or mosques alongside the men, and would have left women much-constrained in terms of their ability to express their Naqshbandī affiliation *publicly*. A woman might mark her affiliation with the tariqa by adopting a new style of conduct or dress: of the wife of 'Abdullāh Ilāhī's *khalīfa* 'Ābid Çelebi, we hear that she was a scion of an important *'askerī* family and that she supported her husband's decision to give up his *'ilmiye* career and become a Naqshbandī disciple. We are not told that she was initiated herself, but rather that she substituted a new "religious garb" (*al-thiyāb al-dīniyya*) for her former "fineries" (*thiyāb al-zīna*).[124]

Apart from affecting a new behavior or adopting a new style of dress, a woman could mark publicly her affiliation with the tariqa by becoming the benefactor of a Naqshbandī institution—and here the Istanbul *waqf* register of 953/1546 provides some help. From the register we learn about several women who were actively involved with the ṭariqa as benefactors of Naqshbandī *tekkes*, and who specified in detail through *waqf* documents how the income from their endowed property was to be disbursed (whether, and how much of it, on *tekke* functionaries, Qur'ān readers, foodstuffs, lighting, repairs, and *waqf* administrators). Two of these women, Ziyāde Hātūn (most probably the wife of Aḥmad Bukhārī) and Fāṭima Hātūn (his daughter and wife of his *khalīfa* Maḥmūd Çelebi), established the largest of all the *waqfs* in support of the capital's Naqshbandī *tekkes* except for those founded by their husbands (and shaykhs of the *tekkes*). Ziyāde Hātūn's cash *waqf* in support of the Emīr-i Bukhārī Tekke in Fātiḥ consisted of 46,000 *akçes*; that of Fāṭima Hātūn in support of the Edirne Ḳapı *tekke* was made up of 45,000 *akçes* in cash along with real estate in the vicinity of the Sultan Meḥmed Mosque (a residential building, a barn, and three shops). The wife of 'Ābid Çelebi, identified here as Sittişāh Hātūn, also established a *waqf* in support of her husband's mosque, this one based in the income from several shops. Other female founders (among them a daughter of a *paşa* and two daughters and two freed slaves of shaykhs) are less clearly identified in the register, except one who was the freed slave (*'atīqa*) of Aḥmad Bukhārī. Their *waqfs* were smaller, but still good-sized; most of them were based on small urban real estate or cash of several hundred to several thousand *akçes*.[125] The point here is not that women could own substantial property or become significant participants in *waqf*-making, or that husbands and wives might divide *waqfs* between them in an attempt to protect family wealth from confiscation—this much the scholarship of the past thirty years has made abundantly clear, especially for Ottoman and Mamlūk women.[126] What is important from our perspective is that such patronage was one obvious way in which women could mark *publicly* their Sufi affiliation, especially in tariqas where rigorous fidelity to the *sharī'a* and to its provisions of sexual decorum would have prevented these women from participating in nonsegregated communal rituals.

3

Anatolia and the Balkans

Before the arrival of the Mujaddidīs and Khālidīs in the eighteenth and nineteenth centuries, the Naqshbandiyya was not one of the great tariqas of Anatolia and the Balkans. In several parts of the Balkans (Sarajevo, Mostar, Edirne, Yenice-i Vardar), Naqshbandīs established a substantial presence, sustained through the work of various shaykhs and *tekke*s and the patronage of local officials. In Anatolia in the broad geographic sense (outside Istanbul), their presence was generally sporadic, with two principal exceptions: Bursa, where it was extensive and enduring, and Anatolian Kurdistan, where for a time it was even spectacular.

There were the occasional Naqshbandī shaykhs and circles in various Anatolian towns. Bābā Ni'matullāh b. Maḥmūd Nakhchivānī (d. 902/1496–7), originally from the Caucasus, settled in Akşehir, where he distinguished himself as the author of a commentary on the *Fuṣūṣ al-ḥikam* of Ibn al-'Arabī, a treatise on *waḥdat al-wujūd*, and a (still extant) Qur'ānic exegesis.[1] Two trainees in the Istanbul line of Ilāhī and Bukāhrī, Şa'bān Efendi and Maḥmūd Efendi, known as Ḥāccı Oğlupazarı Şeyhī (d. 1085/1674–5), spent time respectively in Mudurnu, midway between Istanbul and Ankara, and in Bilecik near the Black Sea, the first as a Naqshbandī *khalīfa* and the second as a mosque functionary and madrasa professor.[2] In the village of Çiçekli near Giresun, Aḥmad Efendi Mūmjī Pāshā of the Tabriz line of Ṣun'ullāh Kūzakunānī found refuge from Ṣafavid repression.[3] In Kayseri, Evliyā Çelebi found the tombs of two recently deceased Naqshbandī shaykhs, Seyfullāh Efendi and 'Abdulṣamad.[4] In Amasya, there was an early and enduring Naqshbandī presence. Built and endowed in 807/1404–5 for a *khalīfa* of Bahā' al-Dīn Naqshband by the name of Rukn al-Dīn Bukhārī, the Maḥmūd Çelebi Tekke was probably the first Naqshbandī *tekke* in Anatolia (though it soon passed into the hands of Khalwatī shaykhs). Another early institution, the Yā Vadūd Tekke built in 857/1453 for a *khalīfa* of Sa'd al-Dīn Kāshgharī, continued to function into the nineteenth century, apparently under Naqshbandī shaykhs.[5] Still, with the exception of the last *tekke*, all these represented sporadic instances rather than an overt and continuous Naqshbandī presence. It was in the Balkans that a more continuous presence of the tariqa developed, and in Bursa and Kurdistan that it became, respectively, extensive and spectacular.

CAPITAL AND PROVINCE, TOWN AND COUNTRYSIDE

In trying to account for this pattern of diffusion, we may begin by noting that few Naqshbandīs took part in the kind of early Sufi expansion that Ömer Lutfî Barkan charted in his "Osmanlı İmparatorluğunda bir İskân ve Kolonizasyon Metodu." Barkan described dervishes, especially of heterodox inclinations, who, since the fourteenth century, had been immigrating to newly conquered territories, participating in military campaigns, settling in areas deserted by Christians and in strategic points near passes or on caravan roads, cultivating land, creating the nuclei around which developed future villages, and thus spreading Islamic culture.[6] That Naqshbandīs featured little in such activities could have been a matter of temperament and orientation, but time too must have played a role here: early Naqshbandī immigrants arrived in Anatolia and the Balkans a bit too late to take part in this brand of Sufism; only Şemsī Dede and 'Aynī Dede, who are said to have reached Bosnia with the army of Meḥmed II in 867/1463, and perhaps a few later Naqshbandīs in the Balkans, could be considered part of the tail end of this early phase.

Once they had established a presence in Istanbul as of the late fifteenth and early sixteenth centuries, Naqshbandīs could have turned their *tekke*s there into the fountainhead from which shaykhs would disseminate the tariqa to the towns of Anatolia and the Balkans (and, in time, the Arab lands). But little of this, too, transpired, especially in comparison with the energetic Khalwatī expansion of this time. It may be that the opportunities available in the capital made further expansion less attractive. Or perhaps the Istanbul Naqshbandiyya simply did not give rise to someone with the acute sense of mission and energy that 'Ubaydullāh Aḥrār had shown and that would be necessary for this kind of diffusion to be set in motion. The first to exhibit such Aḥrārian inclinations would be Shaykh Khālid, the nineteenth-century eponym of the Khālidiyya (originally from Kurdistan). He dispatched a large number of *khalīfas* to carefully chosen destinations and thus helped create for the first time in the tariqa's history an extensive Naqshbandī presence throughout Anatolia, and, to a lesser extent, in the Balkans and the Arab lands.[7]

Other dynamics that may have shaped the Naqshbandī dissemination in this time period are suggested by a comparison with the contemporary Khalwatiyya. For one thing, the Khalwatīs commanded more extensive material support, especially from the Ottoman governing elite. Istanbul Naqshbandī shaykhs, too, attracted official and elite patronage that gave them some access to the Ottoman court and governing circles or led to the establishment and endowment of a number of *tekkes* in the capital. But this patronage was considerably smaller than that accorded to Khalwatīs, and perhaps not one that could help generate and sustain expansion from the capital into the provinces.

Or, to continue the Khalwatī comparison, it may be that the matter was at heart one of devotional identity and organizational preferences—to put it differently, that given their style of devotional sobriety and *sharī'a*-abidance and their modes of initiating disciples and attracting followers, Naqshbandīs were neither particularly prone nor well equipped to operate in rural areas, to function as agents of conversion among non-Muslim populations, or to play a role in taming the various heterodox elements that were ubiquitous throughout much of Anatolia and the Balkans at this time.[8] Khalwatīs, especially of the more "orthodox" branches, are said to have become highly active in the Balkans at this time, especially as collaborators in a grand Ottoman project of disciplining or co-opting non-Muslim and heterodox populations (what Nathalie Clayer has termed "Sunnitization").[9] Perhaps what drove them was not simply "adamant orthodoxy," but specifically the orthodoxy of those who were now eager to become politically useful and acceptable by erasing the memory of their own less-orthodox beginnings a century or so earlier. The devotional sobriety and *sharī'a*-abidance that Naqshbandīs placed at the center of their identity were rather different and turned out to be attractive especially in urban milieus, and less suitable for making inroads among heterodox and rural populations.[10] As I argue in chapter 6, notions of the Naqshbandiyya as an agent of the state's battle to co-opt the heterodox appear to be projections back from much later paradigms more than a reflection of fifteenth- or sixteenth-century realities.[11]

Naqshbandīs were also not well equipped to provide the kind of support system for the central government that Suraiya Faroqhi has charted in her study of the Bektaşīs of Anatolia, a support system under which *tekke*s set up in rural areas might function as respected mediators between peasant and nomadic populations.[12] Naqshbandīs were clearly not set up to work among nomadic populations and, except in Kurdistan, we do not meet them cultivating a following among peasants, either. Among pre-Mujaddidī Naqshbandīs there was no one of the mold of the Khalwatī shaykh Faḍlallāh (d. 1039/1629), a Bosnian settled in Damascus who was "fond of associating with peasants," or that of the Sa'dī shaykh from Aleppo Abū'l-Wafā' (d. 1010/1601–2), who had peasants commonly attend his sessions of *dhikr*.[13] In Kurdistan, the only area throughout Anatolia and the Balkans where pre-Mujaddidī Naqshbandīs became for a time spectacularly widespread among both urban and rural populations, shaykhs reconfigured common Naqshbandī devotional and organizational modes. For example, they introduced a practice of hereditary and communal leadership and combined Naqshbandī with less-sober Kubravī and Nūrbakhshī devotional practices. Granted, Kurdistan was also sui generis in several other ways. We shall see below how the spectacular Naqshbandī dissemination in this area was a product not only of recast orthodoxy or modes of succession and dissemination, but also of particular geographic circumstances, ethnic and sectarian configurations, and the unusual war—with a Shī'ī Muslim neighbor—that dominated the political and social climate of this area during much of the period in question.

As a caveat it should be noted—especially given the role that Naqshbandīs in Transoxania had played among the settled rural population—that even if they were poorly equipped for operating among peasants or especially among heterodox populations, Naqshbandīs could still have a presence in the numerous towns that dotted Anatolia and the Balkans. And probably they did, in more places than those currently known to us.[14] We should remember, in this regard, that our knowledge about the presence of the tariqa in all these regions is still partial and tentative inasmuch as it originates mostly in narrative sources that were written in the capital and from a metropolitan perspective. It has not been possible, as part of the present study, to consider more than the occasional provincial and urban histories, geographies, or biographical literature, let alone the documentary material (such as endowment deeds and administrative decrees) for all or even parts of Anatolia and the Balkans. As important as it is, a more systematic examination of these materials is feasible only in the context of individual regional or city histories, or of a collaborative project of mapping the presence of multiple tariqas in all these areas.[15]

THE BALKANS

In several areas of the Balkans—Thrace, Macedonia, Bulgaria, Kosovo, Bosnia—there was a Naqshbandī presence long before the coming of the first Mujaddidīs from India in the eighteenth century. In a number of places, it was ʿAbdullāh Ilāhī and his disciples who introduced the tariqa. Ilāhī settled in Yenice-i Vardar after an illustrious but somewhat dissatisfying career in Istanbul. Evrenoszāde Aḥmed Beğ, the provincial governor at whose invitation he moved, built for him a mosque, where he was able to devote himself to the training of a small coterie of disciples and to writing (at least two of his known works belong to this period). In 896/1491, Ilāhī died and was buried in the mosque, which soon became a popular place of visitation and part of a complex containing also a madrasa and a *tekke*.[16] When Evliyā Çelebi visited Yenice-i Vardar some two centuries later, he found the memory and impact of Ilāhī still strong. Not only did the tomb, inside the mosque complex, continue to draw pilgrims, but, as Evliyā put it, the whole town was colored by the "spiritual presence" (*rūḥaniyet*, Ar. *rūḥāniyya*) of Ilāhī. Many of the inhabitants were *ehl-i ṭarīḳ* (Sufis, or perhaps Naqshbandīs), and local women were "all Rābiʿa al-ʿAdawiyya" (in reference to the eighth-century female Basran mystic): pious, virtuous, and reluctant to venture into the public space.[17]

Bedreddīn Baba, a *khalīfa* of Ilāhī (or at least this is how he is identified by a later source) was probably the first to carry the Naqshbandī tradition to Edirne in Thrace.[18] Another *khalīfa*, the *ʿālim* and poet Lüṭfullāh Üskübī, moved west to Skopje (Üsküb), there becoming a preacher in the Yaḥyā Paşa Mosque and converting many of the "infidel shepherds" of the nearby mountains.[19] Perhaps it was this individual who attracted to the tariqa a fellow *ʿālim* and poet from nearby Prizren, Sūzī Çelebi (d. 928/1522), who left in Prizren an endowed mosque and school complex and who is known primarily for having "taken the company" of the famous *ğāzī* Mīhāloğlu ʿAlī Beğ and for the *Ǧazavātnāme-i ʿAlī Mīhāloğlu* in fifteen thousand verses that he subsequently wrote.[20]

From Evliyā Çelebi's account of Edirne we learn that there was also direct Naqshbandī travel from Central Asia to this area over the years. Among the fourteen *tekke*s that Evliyā mentions in his description of the city, two were apparently Naqshbandī institutions of Central Asian provenance, perhaps of the kind seen also in Istanbul, Bursa, Jerusalem, and Cizre in Kurdistan (where Central Asian pilgrims on their way to the Hijaz were afforded accommodation). The first *tekke*, named after one Abū Isḥāq

Kārūnī, housed dervishes subscribing to the Khwājagānī-Naqshbandī *silsila*; the second, adjacent to the city's Great Mosque and named after one Ṭāshkand Bābā, was said to be specifically "a *tekke* of Uzbeks."[21] Another immigrant from Central Asia, known only as Muḥammad Bukhārī (or Buharalı) came via Istanbul and settled in Silistra, not far from the mouth of the Danube, in 990/1582. From Nev'īzāde 'Aṭā'ī, who served as *qāḍī* in Silistra a quarter century after his death, we learn that he left an impression especially as an ascetic and worker of miracles, one of which involved a premonition of the revolt of Michael of Wallachia in 1003/1594.[22]

From the western Balkans, we know especially of a number of Naqshbandī *tekke*s in several parts of modern Yugoslavia thanks to scholarship that has began to tap Ottoman archival sources from this area. In Sarajevo, the first Naqshbandīs—Şemsī Dede and 'Aynī Dede—are remembered as having come with the Ottoman army of conquest in 867/1463, and then died in battle. Their burial place, the Ǧāzīler Tekke, endured and became part of the fabric of local society, as is evident from court documents from 973/1565, and specifically a petition in which residents of the surrounding neighborhood asked the *qāḍī* to appoint to the *tekke* an acting shaykh to replace the incumbent who was leaving on the pilgrimage to Mecca.[23] Around the turn of the sixteenth century or before, a governor of Bosnia by the name Iskender Paşa added to the Ǧāzīler Tekke a second and more lavishly supported Naqshbandī institution that was named after him. This *tekke* was part of a large mosque complex that included also a soup kitchen (*'imāret*), a guesthouse (*müsāfirhāne*), a caravansaray, waterworks, and a bridge; its *waqf* was based in income from shops, watermills, and sizable landholdings (50 *ciftliks*).[24] By the late seventeenth century, there were Naqshbandī *tekke*s also in Mostar, Foča, and Belgrade. In Mostar, sometime before 1021/1612, one Ḳoşḳī Meḥmed Paşa built and endowed an eleven-room mosque and *tekke* complex called after him, whose *mashyakha* he assigned to his brother Maḥmūd Baba and after him to Sufischolars versed in Qur'ānic exegesis, *ḥadīth*, and theology. A second *tekke* was built and endowed before mid-century by one Ibrāhīm Ağa Şarıca, whose name it assumed.[25] In Foča, Evliyā Çelebi singled out the Bāyezīd Baba Tekke, known to be a Naqshbandī institution, which he described as overlooking the market and having attached gardens and vinyard, a kitchen, and several private apartments.[26] In Belgrade, according to a court document from 1091/1680, a *khalīfa* of the Naqshbandī shaykh 'Alī Samarqandī built a *tekke* whose *mashyakha* was assigned to a fellow *khalīfa*, Meḥmed b. Şeyh 'Īsā, and after him to his biological progeny. The founder also established a modest *waqf,* one substantial enough, however, to provide for the *tekke*'s maintenance along with charity to the poor.[27]

Writing especially about Bosnia and Herzegovina, D emal Ćehajić has suggested that in this region

> the Naqshbandiyya, as an orthodox *ṣūfī* association, established close . . . connections with the Ottoman government [and became] a base of Ottoman ideology and Ottoman policy. . . . The Ottoman administration made use of Naqshbandis in the struggle against heterodox dervishes. As a reward . . . distinguished headmen of the Naqshbandiyya were granted estates and . . . financial support or subvention from the governors . . . thus [becoming] included in the structure of the Ottoman feudal system.[28]

But this is far-fetched as a conclusion from the available evidence—be it the living memory of Şemsī and 'Aynī Dede as fallen *ğāzī*s in the army of conquest, or the patronage that several Ottoman officials, especially the governor of Bosnia, Iskender Paşa, extended to Naqshbandīs. More than this evidence, Ćehajić's assessment seems to be informed by a common (and sometimes unsubstantiated) view—that the orthodox Sufi tariqas functioned as agents of the Ottoman struggle against heterodoxy.[29]

Rather than understanding the Naqshbandī dissemination in the Balkans primarily as a product of collaboration in the Ottoman expansion and antiheterodox campaign, it seems sounder to view it as the result of several interconnected dynamics: the influence of a powerful shaykh such as 'Abdullāh Ilāhī, patterns of travel and pilgrimage from Transoxania, Ottoman military expansion, various strands of official and local patronage, and some of those practices (such as participation in campaigns or "converting infidels") that Barkan has identified especially among earlier dervishes in the Balkans. Be that as it may, while in the Balkans the pre-Mujaddidī Naqshbandiyya was not on a par with some other tariqas,[30] nor with the later Mujaddidiyya and Khālidiyya, clearly pre-Mujaddidī Naqshbandīs did establish here a substantial and continuous presence. In some places the tariqa also became well integrated into local society, be it through the reputation for asceticism of Muḥammad Bukhārī in Silistra, or the enduring spirituality of 'Abdullāh Ilāhī in Yenice-i Vardar, or the series of Naqshbandī *tekkes* in the western Balkans that attracted local and official patronage, offered space for conducting the tariqa's ritual, housed resident disciples, or fed or extended charity to the local poor.

KURDISTAN

In Anatolian Kurdistan, especially in the areas between Diyarbakır and Lakes Van and Orumiyeh (Urūmiyya), Naqshbandīs of our period enjoyed a much more extensive presence than anywhere else in Anatolia west of Istanbul and Bursa, at times even a spectacular one. In some places they would maintain a continuous presence into the nineteenth century, when this region became even more closely associated with the tariqa in connection with the expansion of the Khālidiyya.

There is no obvious explanation for the early Naqshbandī dissemination in Kurdistan. It may be, as Martin van Bruinessen has noted, that "the Kurds had for centuries shown an inclination towards mysticism, often of the less orthodox varieties, and were to continue doing so."[31] But in itself this cannot account for the widespread appeal of the consciously orthodox and devotionally sober Naqshbandiyya, however Naqshbandīs in this region might reconfigure this orientation.[32] As Shāfi'īs, too, Kurds were perhaps less likely than Ḥanafī Muslims (as were most Naqshbandīs in Central Asia, India, and western Anatolia) to be attracted to a tariqa whose devotional regimen was so inextricably bound with the silent *dhikr*. As we learn from the seventeenth-century Medinese Naqshbandī shaykh Ibrāhīm al-Kūrānī, who was originally a Kurd from Shahrazūr, Shāfi'īs considered the vocal *dhikr* a "key to the religion" and a more excellent method than the silent one.[33]

Patterns of communications also did not favor the dissemination of the Naqshbandiyya to Kurdistan, at least not after the late fifteenth century. First, following the move of the Aqquyunlu capital from Diyarbakır to Tabriz in 873/1468, the crucial commercial route on which silk used to travel from the Caspian shore to Diyarbakır and then Aleppo began its diversion to Bursa (now going via Erzurum, considerably north of Diyarbakır).[34] Then the travel of Central Asian pilgrims on the traditional Herat-Nishapur-Qazvin-Tabriz-Diyarbakır route was obstructed by the Ṣafavid takeover of Iran at the turn of the sixteenth century and the military operations, political battles, and breakdown of public order to which it gave rise. As we have seen in chapter 1, some pilgrims found an alternative in the "northern route" via Astrakhan and the lower Volga and Don to Istanbul, whence they would continue their travel on the imperial pilgrimage route via Damascus that the Ottomans had established after their conquest of the Arab lands. All these changes meant that from the early sixteenth century at least Central Asian Naqshbandīs (as opposed to Naqshbandī refugees from Iran) were unlikely to arrive in Kurdistan in any significant numbers (though some did, as we shall see below). Despite all this, during the sixteenth and especially the seventeenth century, Anatolian Kurdistan was the one area in Anatolia apart from Istanbul and Bursa where the Naqshbandiyya prospered and became widely disseminated.[35]

We have little positive evidence for the presence of Central Asian Naqshbandīs in Kurdistan either before or after these grand changes in communications. 'Alī Kurdī, a native of Amadiyah (midway between Mosul and Lake Van) who traveled to Transoxania and there trained with 'Ubaydullāh Aḥrār, returned as Aḥrār's *khalīfa* not to his native Amadiyah but rather to Qazvin in Iran.[36] It may be, however, that he had become interested in Aḥrār in the first place by having heard about him from Central Asian Naqshbandī travelers to Kurdistan. Perhaps such travelers had established a presence by then in the town of Cizre, up the Tigris and northwest of Amadiyah, where in the seventeenth century Evliyā Çelebi visited a Naqshbandī-Khwājagānī shrine and *tekke* of Indians (or perhaps Afghans) and Central Asians (*Hindī ve Özbekī ve Çaghatāyī ve Qomuq qavmı*).[37]

Cizre comes up in another possible Naqshbandī connection—namely, as the place where one 'Alī, the great grandfather of the Naqshbandī and Qādirī shaykh Ismā'īl Faḳīrullāh (d. 1147/1735), had been raised and educated before he moved to the village of Tillū near Şiirt (Şi'ird), there establishing an enduring family line of shaykhs and scholars. Our information about Shaykh Ismā'īl and his ancestor 'Alī comes from the *Ma'rifetnāme* of Ibrāhīm Ḥaḳḳı Erżurūmī, Ismā'īl's *khalīfa* and son-in-law. We are told that Shaykh Isma'īl was the head of a substantial mosque complex in Tillū, a wielder of some local political influence, a "perfect spiritual guide" (*murşid-i kāmil*) in the Naqshbandī and Qādirī tariqas, and a man versed in Islamic learning, whose library contained several hundred volumes including works of Shāfi'ī jurisprudence. His reputation was widespread, as is demonstrated by the letters and vows that he received not only from local Kurdish chiefs but also from Muslim dignitaries in Mecca and India and from members of the Ottoman court and central administration. As for 'Alī, according to the *Ma'rifetnāme* he was an Arab by speech and descent and a prominent *'ālim* from Cizre who moved to Tillū at the turn of the sixteenth century (or perhaps this was later, unless he was a more removed ancestor of Shaykh Ismā'īl than a great-grandfather). In Tillū 'Alī became the teacher, preacher, and prayer leader of the village's only congregational mosque, in which capacities he was succeeded by several descendants. Perhaps 'Alī moved to Tillū in order to embark on a new career as a Sufi shaykh, having been initiated in Cizre by one of those Central Asian Naqshbandīs whose *tekke* Evliyā Çelebi was to report in the mid-seventeenth century. This much, however, the *Ma'rifetnāme* does not make explicit.[38]

Evliyā Celebi's *Seyāḥatnāme* is our most comprehensive source for the dissemination of the Naqshbandiyya in Kurdistan in the seventeenth century, and by extrapolation earlier. Along with the Central Asian *tekke* that he encountered in Cizre, Evliyā described a number of Naqshbandī institutions and shaykhs throughout Kurdistan, some that probably owed their Naqshbandī connections to travelers from Central Asia, and others that were clearly associated with refugees from Ṣafavid Iran or their descendants. Bitlis, southwest of Lake Van, was said to have had twenty Naqshbandī, Bektaşī, and Gulshanī *tekke*s, the majority of which Evliyā believed to have been Naqshbandī, since the local population consisted primarily of Shāfi'īs (it is unclear whether by this he meant Kurds, or rather Sunnī, as opposed to Ḳızılbaş).[39] In Nāmervān, a fortress closer to Erzurum, he encountered a population of several hundred households that he described as devout Sunnīs (*dīndār* and *ehl-i sünnet*) and subscribing to the Naqshbandī tariqa.[40]

In Akhlāṭ, north of Lake Van, the traveler met a Sufi by the name Ḥasan Dede who had "achieved perfection in the *ṭarīḳ-i hōcagān*." Because no refugee connection is mentioned, it may be that Ḥasan had acquired his Naqshbandī connection from Central Asian travelers.[41] Or he may have been connected to the Akhlāṭ *tekke* mentioned by Muḥammad al-Ṭabbākh, whose incumbents combined Naqshbandī and Nūrbakhshī affiliations and presided over a centralized system of shaykhs active in places as faraway from Akhlāṭ as Aleppo.[42] As we will see below, a combination of Naqshbandī and Nurbakhshī affiliations characterized also the most important Naqshbandī line of Kurdistan—that of the Urmavī shaykhs—and there it derived from a spiritual ancestor who had been active in Azerbaijan before the Urmavīs moved to Anatolia as refugees from Ṣafavid persecution. It may be that the Akhlāṭ shaykhs, too, had their Naqshbandī origins in Azerbaijan (and perhaps in the Urmavī line itself), rather than in Naqshbandīs who had come to Kurdistan as travelers or pilgrims directly from Transoxania.

We know of Naqshbandī refugees from Iran coming to Kurdistan from immediately after the Ṣafavid conquest. Ṣun'ullāh Kūzakunānī, a spiritual descendant of the line of Sa'd al-Dīn Kāshgharī in Herat and the founder of the Tabriz Naqshbandiyya, fled to Kurdish-ruled Bitlis shortly after Tabriz became the Ṣafavid capital in 907/1501, though he did not stay for long and perhaps did not make an impact in Bitlis, unless some of the town's Naqshbandīs that Evliyā met much later owed their spiritual origin to him.[43] Another refugee who did become involved in propagating the tariqa in

Kurdistan was one Maḥmūd Efendi from Shirvan, of whose activities we learn from an informant originally from Sivas in Central Anatolia who later became associated with the Naqshbandī circle of Ḥekīm Çelebi in Istanbul. In a note that this informant, Ibrāhīm Sīvāsī, appended to a copy of a treatise in the use of this Istanbul circle, the *Risāle-i şerīfe-i mağrūbe fī uṣūl-i ṭā'ife-i 'aliye-i Naḳşbendiye*, he writes about two Naqshbandī groups (*ṭā'ifes*), one from the town of Gaziantep ('Aynṭāb) and the other from the area between Gaziantep and Mar'aş with followers all the way north to Elbistan, in the direction of Sivas. Members of both groups refused to accept pensions from patrons and insisted upon living by means of regular occupations. The first of the two groups had been initiated by the aforementioned Maḥmūd Efendi, who had come from Shirvan sometime in the 940s/1530s and was in time buried back in his hometown, where his tomb became a common pilgrimage site for his numerous followers. Sīvāsī makes it a point to emphasize that the members of this group were "good people," a curious remark that he may have deemed necessary because of their contacts with Shirvan (at the time of writing again under Ṣafavid rule), or simply because they lived in a distant region of the empire with which his fellow Naqshbandīs in Istanbul had little familiarity. He hints at no unusual practices of this group that might warrant this remark.[44]

The Urmavīs, who became the predominant Naqshbandī line of seventeenth-century Kurdistan, also had their origins in a refugee from Ṣafavid rule. This was one Ḳoçbaba or Ḳocağa, whom we have met in chapter 1 as Muḥammad Bādāmyārī. He fled the Tabriz area to Orumiyeh sometime before 978/1570; and there he built a *tekke* and appointed two sons as *khalīfas*. In time, one of his sons, Maḥmūd, fled further west to Diyarbakır, where, in the two decades or so before he was put to death in 1048/1639, he established himself as the foremost Naqshbandī shaykh of Kurdistan, with huge followings deep into Ṣafavid-ruled territory in Azerbaijan and the Caucasus. All the Ottoman chroniclers of the seventeenth century covered in some detail the career of Shaykh Maḥmūd;[45] but none was aware of his spiritual descent, which emerges from an obscure (and apparently never-used) devotional manual in the Süleymaniye Library collection, the *Şerā'iṭ ve-naṣā'iḥ-i meşā'ih*.[46] By reading the *Şerā'iṭ* (whose anonymous author was a disciple of Shaykh Maḥmūd) in combination with the *Silsilanāma* of the refugee from Iran Muḥammad Qazvīnī, we learn that Ḳocağa was another name of Muḥammad Bādāmyārī, a spiritual descendant of the line of Sa'd al-Dīn Kāshgharī and 'Abd al-Raḥmān Jāmī in Herat. It was Kāshghārī's *khalīfa* 'Alā' al-Dīn Maktabdār who authorized in Herat a disciple from the Tabriz area, Ṣun'ullāh Kūzakunānī, who then carried the tariqa back to his native village near Tabriz, and there authorized one Darvīsh Akhī Khusrawshāhī. From the latter the line passed to Ilyās Bādāmyārī from the adjacent village of Bādāmyār, and from him to a fellow native of the village, Muḥammad, known as Ḳocağa.[47]

Several characteristics that became in time the hallmark of the Urmavīs go back to Ḳocağa. First, drawing on his family's *sayyid* descent and experimenting with a new style of Sufi leadership, he began to transform the line into which he had been initiated from one built on nonhereditary "spiritual" succession and the training of individual disciples and *khalīfas* (as was common among Naqshbandīs at this time) into a hereditary family line exercising leadership over whole communities. To perpetuate his authority in his family, he trained as *khalīfas* two sons: 'Alī, to whom he bequeathed his *tekke*, and Aḥmed, who trained his more famous brother Maḥmūd, with whom he moved to Diyarbakır.[48] Shortly after his move to Orumiyeh, Ḳocağa also developed a reputation as the "leader of low and high" (*qā'id-i khavāṣṣ va-'avāmm*), clearly a reference to more than the training of an intimate coterie of disciples and *khalīfas*.[49] Indeed, several accounts of the career of Ḳocağa's son Maḥmūd suggest that the unusually large following that in time this shaykh was able to gather around himself was rooted in communal loyalty to the family. As the historian Peçevī put it, "most of Kurdistan" was devoted to Shaykh Maḥmūd, his father, or his brother; in this line saintly authority was bequeathed "from father to son."[50]

A second innovation of Ḳocağa concerns devotional practice—and here again the *Şerā'iṭ* provides important clues. We know from several later sources that the Urmavī shaykhs practiced a vocal *dhikr*, one that set them apart devotionally from other Naqshbandīs, with their common practice of silent recollection. The historian Na'īmā relates that disciples commonly gathered to recite this *dhikr* in the congregational mosque adjacent to Shaykh Maḥmūd's *tekke* in Diyarbakır.[51] When in 1065/1655 Evliyā Çelebi visited the *tekke*, whose shaykh was then Maḥmūd's son Ismā'īl, he witnessed a dramatic vocal *dhikr* that induced in practitioners a state of intoxication and bewilderment (*mest va ḥayrān vālih ve sergerdān*).[52] Later spiritual descendants of the Urmavī line who relocated to Bursa practiced both silent and vocal *dhikr* and recited daily Kubravī litanies; one of them wrote a sequel to the *Awrād-i fatḥiyya* of 'Alī Hamadānī and a treatise discussing Nūrbakhshī devotional practice.[53] From the *Şerā'iṭ*, which charts a daily regimen of Naqshbandī, Kubravī, and Nūrbakhshī litanies performed in this line,[54] we learn that the origin of all these practices was Ilyās Bādāmyārī, who received them before he was initiated into the Naqshbandiyya from two sources: his Nūrbakhshī father 'Īsā and a Kubravī by the name 'Abd al-Ḥayy Gilānī. Ilyās then bequeathed these practices to his Naqshbandī *khalīfa* Muḥammad Bādāmyārī, alias Ḳocağa. Most revealing of all, Ilyās bequeathed to Ḳocağa a Kubravī "saw *dhikr*" (*zikr-i arra*) "in which a sawing sound is produced in the practitioner's throat while reciting the formula *ḥayy ḳayyūm*."[55] It was probably this originally Kubravī *dhikr* that Evliyā Çelebi later encountered in the Naqshbandī Urmavī *tekke* in Diyarbakır.

The mix of devotional practices that Ḳocağa introduced into the Urmavī line was clearly attractive to several generations of shaykhs and their followers, perhaps because of the inclination of Kurds toward "heterodox mysticism," as Bruinessen has noted. Interestingly, while they clung to the unusual mix, adherents of this line nevertheless identified themselves and were identified by others simply as Naqshbandīs (or Khwājagānīs). Unlike a contemporary Medinese spiritual line that was defined by its multiple tariqa affiliations, shaykhs of the Urmavī line did not develop a tradition of conferring multiple *silsila*s or tariqa affiliations on disciples.[56]

Finally, another measure of Ḳocağa that served to define the Urmavī line was his relocation from Bādāmyār to Orumiyeh—fleeing "Qizilbāsh (Tur. Ḳızılbaş) tyranny," as Qazvīnī put it. The move put him within what was by then at least a half-century-old tradition of Naqshbandī shaykhs seeking refuge from Shī'ī Ṣafavid rule in neighboring Sunnī territories, such as Shībānid Transoxania, Mughal India, or the Ottoman Empire. In addition, when he reestablished himself in Orumiyeh, Ḳocağa became both a communal Sufi leader and a "promoter of the Prophet's *sunna*." Perhaps the Urmavīs were beginning to define themselves in defiance of the Shī'ī Ṣafavids whose oppression drove Ḳocağa (and later his son Maḥmūd) to flee west. Their *silsila*, too, departed from other Naqshbandī *silsila*s of the time by putting particular emphasis on Abū Bakr and even assuming, in one of its versions, what the sequel to the *Şerā'iṭ* called *nisbet-i kulliye-i bekriye*, that is an exclusive Bakrī affiliation devoid of any reference to 'Alī.[57] This too must have proven appealing to the Kurdish (and Azerī) Sunnī-Shāfi'ī followers of the Urmavīs at a time when war with the Shī'ī Ṣafavid rulers of Iran dominated political and social conditions throughout this area.

A CHARISMATIC SHAYKH AND HIS DEMISE

In time Ḳocağa's third son, Maḥmūd, known to the Ottoman chroniclers as Rūmiye Şeyhī, "the shaykh from Orumiyeh," also sought refuge in Ottoman territory; he moved to Diyarbakır and there had a *tekke* and congregational mosque built and became a Sufi leader of spectacular influence. The sources do not indicate when this move occurred, or even what brought it about.[58] As Bruinessen has noted, an ambitious young shaykh could have been attracted by Diyarbakır's importance as a major military, commercial, and administrative center that was well connected by road to many parts of Anatolia, Syria, Kurdistan, and Azerbaijan.[59] Still, circumstances suggest that the move from Orumiyeh came at the time of the reestablishment of Ṣafavid control in the years 1010–20/1600–1610 (the shaykh had a son born in Diyarbakır in 1020/1611); Shaykh Maḥmūd thus not only relocated to an important and well-connected Ottoman center, but also found refuge in a city that was bound to be much more hospitable than his birthplace for a Naqshbandī shaykh who made a point of emphasizing his Sunnī Bakrī *silsila* and whose father had been a refugee from Ṣafavid rule and a "promoter of the Prophet's *sunna*."

All the principal Ottoman chroniclers of the seventeenth century were fascinated by the story of Shaykh Maḥmūd, his huge following, his style of leadership and political maneuvering, and finally his execution at the sultan's orders in 1048/1639 (which was rumored to have been caused by his dabbling in alchemy in collaboration with a daughter of the Druze rebel Fakhr al-Dīn of the Ma'n family).[60] We are told that the "entire population" of Diyarbakır and its vicinity were firm believers in the shaykh, and that his epithet 'Azīz (the "beloved" or "saintly") was invoked everywhere in the popular oath formula "by the head of 'Azīz." Beyond the city, his following extended to the whole of Kurdistan and farther away, from Erzurum, Mosul, and Urfa to Van and even to "distant areas" of Iran, perhaps Yerevan and Tabriz. Everywhere there were devotees of the family and "loving servants" of the shaykh who came in droves to see him in the Diyarbakır *tekke* or regularly showered on it votive offerings, alms, and other gifts of money and possessions. Followers came from the "common people" (*'avāmm*) as well as men of distinction, wealth, and power, among them Ottoman officials and prominent merchants from Tabriz and Yerevan. From another perspective, they included both "Kurds and *a'cām*," the latter perhaps a reference to Sunnīs in Ṣafavid-ruled Azerbaijan.[61] According to a common rumor, the shaykh had over forty thousand followers (*mürīdīn* and *muḥibbīn*) or, in the more dramatic formulation of critics of his excessive influence, "forty thousand naked, fairy-sounding servants and disciples weeping with divine love."[62]

Several factors combined to generate this unusual popularity. At one level it was the product of the shaykh's powerful charisma, which complemented the tradition of communal family leadership that his father had already established at the family's first base in Orumiyeh. Beyond that, there were important historical circumstances at work. A century-old intermittent war during which this area had changed hands several times between Ottoman and Ṣafavid rulers, and had served as the launching pad for Ottoman campaigns, ended in the years 1010–20/1600–1610 in a Ṣafavid victory and the establishment of the Ottoman-Ṣafavid border close to its line of demarcation of today.[63] The years of the shaykh's prominence in Diyarbakır, in the aftermath of this victory, were dominated by costly (and for a long time abortive) Ottoman efforts to recapture Tabriz and Yerevan, and then Baghdad, which had fallen to the Ṣafavids in 1032/1623. These circumstances buttressed the shaykh's popularity among a local population that was burdened by war and its effects, be it constant insecurity, frequent deployment of large Ottoman armies, disruption of agriculture, requisitioning of foodstuffs, or the imposition of various irregular taxes.[64] The *tekke* in Diyarbakır, with its lavish offerings from wealthy patrons, was the place where a stream of visitors from the entire region were routinely fed or bestowed with the shaykh's "benevolence" (*ni'met*).[65] More importantly, the shaykh was perceived as someone who could intervene on behalf of the local people, petition the Ottoman authorities, or represent to them war-related grievances and pleas. In addition, whether the Urmavī family itself was of Azerī or Kurdish descent—their origins in Bādāmyār near Tabriz might suggest the first—what mattered under the circumstances was religious rather than ethnic or linguistic identity. The fact that the Urmavīs were adamant Sunnīs, along with their history of seeking refuge from Ṣafavid "tyranny" in Ottoman territory, could not but inspire devotion in both the Sunnī Kurds and Azerīs who apparently made up the bulk of Shaykh Maḥmūd's following.

It is against this backdrop that the shaykh's political involvement is best understood. Drawing on personal charisma along with the tradition of family communal leadership, and operating in a frontier region that was faraway from the center of the empire yet critical enough as a launching pad for military campaigns against the Ṣafavids, he succeeded in establishing himself as a local dignitary of sorts, capable of playing a double role. For the local people he was someone who could act as protector or lobbyist with the Ottoman authorities, while for the latter he was serviceable because of his perceived ability to encourage—or discourage—local support or at least quiescence during an ongoing war. The shaykh behaved and comported himself both as a Sufi master and as a local dignitary. In the fashion of Sufi shaykhs everywhere, he inspired stories of dreams and predictions, for example one dream in which he foresaw Sultan Murād's conquest of Baghdad, and another in which he envisioned his own demise and execution.[66] At the same time he took care to be "dressed like a merchant."[67] Several times he also joined other local notables (*a'yān*) in organizing lavish receptions for the imperial entourage when it was passing by Diyarbakır en route to campaigns, or in showering on the sultan presents, from crates of Diyarbakır melons to Arabian horses.[68]

Sometimes the shaykh made his appearance on such occasions at the head of his own entourage—once reportedly coming to welcome the sultan outside the city of Diyarbakır accompanied by "3000 cloaked dervishes."[69] In the Yerevan campaign of 1045/1635 he accompanied the imperial army and, according to one account, was involved in the negotiations and correspondence leading to the city's surrender, even receiving a local envoy in his tent.[70] On another occasion he angered the sultan when disciples of his gave vent to their demoralization and their sense of being abandoned by their rulers by storming into the imperial encampment and raising the old refrain *al-mulk 'aḳīm* (Ar. *'aqīm*), "dominion [or seeking it] leads to the severance of ties."[71] Yet another story—somewhat reminiscent of accounts about 'Ubaydullāh Aḥrār's call for the abolition of the Mongol *damgha* tax in late Tīmūrid Samarkand—has the shaykh meeting with the sultan's entourage in Aleppo on the eve of the Baghdad campaign and there successfully petitioning for a reduction of the *'avāriż* taxes recently imposed on Diyarbakır households.[72]

Shaykh Maḥmūd's execution at the behest of Murād IV following the Ottoman capture of Baghdad in 1048/1638 was the subject of much speculation among contemporaries as well as among the string of later Ottoman chroniclers who covered this incident. As mentioned, according to one story that circulated in several variants the shaykh's demise resulted from his dabbling in alchemy in collaboration with the daughter of the executed Druze chieftain Fakhr al-Dīn, who had found refuge in his household after her father's death. During one of his meetings with the sultan's entourage when the latter was passing through Diyarbakır, the shaykh is said to have handed over to the sultan a bar of yellowish metal produced by the woman, and received a considerable sum of money for further experiments. When later the sultan found out that the money had been squandered with no gold produced, he ordered that the woman and her accomplice be put to death.[73]

Whatever the precise nature of Shaykh Maḥmūd's collaboration with the daughter of Fakhr al-Dīn, the decision of the Ottoman authorities to put him to death after the victory in Baghdad is easily accounted for by the very political balancing act in which he had been engaged—along with the changing political and military situation of the time. It appears that what had made him suspect all along was his wide influence and his dabbling not in alchemy, but in politics. Various enemies and critics had spread rumors that he was planning to use his vast influence to mount a Mahdist revolt and seize political power, as earlier Sufi leaders had done or attempted to do in places as faraway as Morocco and Iran, and just shortly before in the region of Eskişehir in Anatolia.[74] Until the victory in Baghdad the Ottoman authorities had had good reason to overlook the potential threat inherent in the shaykh's mode of action. But once Baghdad had been taken and the border question with Iran had been settled for some time, his help—real or potential—in eliciting local support became much less valuable than before. Tolerating the activities of a charismatic leader with a large and devoted following in a volatile frontier area now seemed ill-advised, and getting rid of the shaykh had become a political necessity.[75]

Shaykh Maḥmūd's death and his style of action shed light on the degree of maneuvering that was available to Ottoman Naqshbandī shaykhs of this time. In some ways his political style and goals are reminiscent of those of Aḥrār in Samarkand; but he never came close to the latter either in building for himself an economic power base, or in the scope of his political influence—which was exercised in a decidedly provincial context. Moreover, the shaykh's unusual political involvement and style were clearly shaped and made possible by unusual circumstances. His numerous devotees were attracted to him by the services (again, real or perceived) that he was able to offer against the ravages of war as much as by religious promise or devotional style. The Ottoman authorities, too, were led by the exigencies of war in a distant region of the empire to allow a shaykh who they hoped would inspire local quiescence to engage in what under other circumstances would have been much less tolerable. It was apparently these circumstances, along with personal charisma, the family's tradition of communal leadership, and perhaps the peculiar mix that already Ḳocağa had introduced into Urmavī devotional practice that produced this unusual instance of a Naqshbandī shaykh who was both hugely popular and politically influential.

From Shaykh Maḥmūd and his brother ensued a spiritual and family line of some continuity both in Kurdistan and later in Bursa. The Diyarbakır *tekke* was still known as "the *tekke* of Şeyh Rūmī" when Evliyā Çelebi visited it several decades after the shaykh's death. The new incumbent was Maḥmūd's son Ismāʿīl Çelebi (d. 1080/1669–70), whom the father had appointed as his successor when he had been told in a dream that his death was near. Ismā'īl continued to command a devoted following and was sought out by high officials. He was succeeded as shaykh by his son Aḥmed Çelebi, whose principal reputation was as a composer and musician, and then by Ḳara Muṣṭafā, a *sayyid* and apparently a brother.[76] In the Orumiyeh *tekke*, which apparently continued to operate under Ṣafavid rule, the *mashyakha* moved from Ḳocağa to his son 'Alī, then to a grandson and great-grandson, Ṣiddīḳ and Ebvābī 'Ācizī, all *sayyids*.[77] In Van, a *khalīfa* of Shaykh Maḥmūd, Vanlı Ḳara 'Abdullāh, became the incumbent of what Evliyā Çelebi later called "the Hōcagān-i Rūmiye Tekke."[78] Two other *khalīfas* of Shaykh Maḥmūd, Ḳaramān and Ḥaccı Meḥmed, apparently took the Urmavī line to Erzurum.[79] Two others fled farther west after his execution, taking his spiritual line to Bursa, where it exhibited remarkable endurance and survived into the twentieth century.

BURSA

The first Naqshbandīs arrived in Bursa during the reign of Meḥmed II, roughly when their counterparts were coming to the Ottoman capital (and still before the arrival in Istanbul of 'Abdullāh Ilāhī and Aḥmad Bukhārī). We are somewhat unclear about the circumstances under which a Bukharan by the name Aḥmad Ilāhī was drawn to the tariqa and about his spiritual genealogy; he is said to have been associated with Malāmatī and Khalwatī shaykhs before an "old spiritual master" initiated him into the Naqshbandiyya. Before long, he made a reputation for himself as a mosque preacher and the author of a trilingual Arabic-Persian-Turkish treatise on *sulūk*, the disciplined progress along the mystical path. Then a follower, the finance director (*defterdār*) Dervīş Efendi, established for him the complex of congregational mosque, *tekke*, and cells for residents that came to be known as Yuğurtlu Baba (apparently after the founder of the original mosque and neighborhood). In support of the complex, Dervīş Efendi founded a *waqf*, whose income and administration he assigned to the shaykh's progeny.

A long line of biological descendants known as the Ilāhīzādeler and associated with the *tekke* ensued. From Ilāhī the *mashyakha* passed to his son and *khalīfa* Meḥmed (d. 900/1495).[80] Later it passed to another biological descendant, Ya'ḳūb Ilāhīzāde (d. 990/1582 or shortly afterward), by then already a veteran of the Naqshbandī Ḥekīm Çelebī Tekke in Istanbul, where he had been shaykh for a number of years beginning in 979/1571–72.[81] A long series of other biological descendants were interred in the family's burial ground in Yuğurtlu Baba; after Ya'ḳūb Ilāhīzāde, his family members no longer served as shaykhs, however, choosing instead various *'ilmiye* careers.[82] In time both the spiritual line that began with Aḥmad Ilāhī and the functioning of the *tekke* came to an end; we do not know when precisely this happened, except that by the early eighteenth century the complex was in ruins, with nothing remaining but the graveyard.[83]

Not long after the incumbency of Ya'ḳūb Ilāhīzāde in Yuğurtlu Baba we hear of another Bursan Naqshbandī *tekke*, this one short-lived, in the neighborhood of Incirlice. The founder was one Ḥasan Efendi, a native Bursan and spiritual trainee of Shaykh Isḥāq Efendi of Samarkand. Ḥasan was also a preacher in Bursa's Great Mosque, where he used to conduct public sessions of *dhikr* until an assembly of *'ulamā'* had him barred from these activities as a result of a scandal ensuing from his endorsement of triple *ṭalāq* divorce. Not long afterward, the *tekke* itself ceased to function, when in 1016/1607–8 Ḥasan was killed by a group of Celāli "brigands" (*eşḳiyā'*).[84]

From sometime during the sixteenth century Bursa was also the site of one, and later another, of those Bukharan Naqshbandī *tekkes* (called Buhara or Özbek/Özbekiye) that Bukharan founders built for the accommodation of Central Asian pilgrims on their way to the Hijaz. Bursa's first Bukharan *tekke* was located in a large and well-attended building in the Pınarbaşı neighborhood of the citadel, adjacent to the 'Izzeddīn Beğ Mosque, where the shaykhs used to conduct public recitations of the Naqshbandī *khatm-i khwājagān* litany. The *tekke* must have existed at least from the mid-sixteenth century, as we learn from the tombstone of one Süleymān Efendi, a shaykh who died and was buried there in 978/1570–71. It is, however, only from the eighteenth century that we know the identity of some of the incumbents by name and spiritual affiliation. By that time, although the stipulation that shaykhs had to be Bukharan still held, several of them were Mujaddidīs, a spiritual affiliation that they must have acquired while traveling on the pilgrimage, perhaps in Mecca.[85]

A similar institution known as the Buhara Ḳalenderhāne or the Ğar-ı 'Āşıḳān Tekke came into being sometime in the seventeenth century. A Naqshbandī practitioner by the name Uzbek 'Abd al-Raḥmān Bābā, who had come to Bursa via Diyarbakır, died and was buried in the *tekke* in 1157/1744–45. Earlier there had been at least two other shaykhs, whom tombstones in the attached graveyard identify simply as 'Abd al-Ṣamad and Bahā' al-Dīn.[86]

In Bursa it seems that a particularly large number of Naqshbandī shaykhs operated not from specialized *tekkes* but instead from public or neighborhood mosques where they officiated as mosque preachers or prayer leaders. Meḥmed Efendi Mişmelzāde (d. 931/1524–25), a spiritual descendant of Aḥmad Bukhārī and Maḥmūd Çelebi in Istanbul, was the preacher of the Molla Fenarī Mosque and the shaykh of the attached *tekke*. We know of at least one disciple of his, an immigrant from Amasya by the name ʻAṭā'ullāh Efendi (d. ca. 980/1572–73), who was drawn to him through his public preaching at Molla Fenarī, and who later became himself the prayer leader of the Naʻlabandoğlu neighborhood mosque.[87] Aḥmed Başmacı (d. 1008/1599–1600), a native Bursan and also a spiritual trainee in the line of Aḥmad Bukhārī in Istanbul, became the prayer leader of the Naḳḳāş ʻAlī Mosque in the citadel.[88] Another Bursan disciple of the same Istanbul line, one ʻAlī Efendi (d. 1040/1630–31), became upon his return the preacher and prayer leader of the ʻAlā'eddīn Beğ Mosque and Tekke, also in the city's citadel.[89]

Among shaykhs trained in other than the Istanbul line of Aḥmad Bukhārī, we may mention Muṣliḥüddīn Halīfe (d. ca. 1001/1591–92), an immigrant from Karasu on the Black Sea shore, who became the prayer leader of the Sultan Murād Mosque, and there distinguished himself particularly as an expert on the *Fuṣūṣ al-ḥikam* of Ibn al-ʻArabī.[90] Ḥāccı Meḥmed Ḥalabī (d. 1010/1601) and Meḥmed Misḳalı (d. 1017/1608), both followers of a Damascus-born shaykh known by the *nisba* Shāmī, also became mosque functionaries, the first in Bursa's ʻAbdī Çelebi Mosque and the second in Mudanya on the Sea of Marmara.[91] So did a later immigrant from Bukhara known as Pīr Muḥammd Uzbek (d. 1077/1666–67); he became the shaykh of the school (*muʻallimhāne*) adjacent to the Ḳavaḳlı Mosque in the citadel, where he is known to have conducted regular sessions of the Naqshbandī *dhikr*.[92]

Along with shaykhs based in *tekke*s or public and neighborhood mosques, Bursa had a Naqshbandī luminary of another breed in Maḥmūd Lāmiʻī Çelebi (d. 938/1531–32), the famous poet and *khalīfa* of Aḥmad Bukhārī. Lāmiʻī hailed from a prominent local family. His father was a finance director under Bāyezīd II and his grandfather, Naḳḳāş ʻAlī, was the founder of the mosque called after him in the city's citadel and one of those Bursa residents who had been taken with the returning army of Tīmūr to Samarkand, whence he brought back the art of painting-carving (*naqsh*). Despite his authorization by Bukhārī, Lāmiʻī Çelebi did not become a "transmitting shaykh" who trains disciples and produces *khalīfa*s, nor one who conducts the Naqshbandī ritual. His importance—both for the tariqa and more generally—lay instead in his being a prolific poet and writer. As a transmitter into Ottoman Turkish of a series of themes and stories from Persian literature, some of which he adapted from later versions in Chaghatay, he epitomized those Ottoman Naqshbandī authors and litterateurs who were responsible for the tariqa's association with a Persian literary culture for which there was much demand among Ottoman intellectual circles. He took special interest in two fellow Naqshbandīs and authors from late Tīmūrid Herat, 'Abd al-Raḥmān Jāmī and 'Alī Shīr Navā'ī, some of whose works he either translated or used as a model. In terms of disseminating the tariqa, especially Lāmi'ī's translation of Jāmī's *Nafaḥāt al-uns* was important. This work not only made available in Ottoman Turkish an account of the Naqshbandī *silsila* from the early Khwājagān to Sa'd al-Dīn Kāshgharī and 'Ubaydullāh Aḥrār; through a sequel featuring the biographies of a number of Anatolian shaykhs, it also helped promote an awareness of the continuity between Aḥrār and his Anatolian spiritual descendants.[93] Finally, more than simply a translator of Jāmī, Lāmi'ī may be thought of as a Naqshbandī shaykh-poet-author in the very tradition of which Jāmī was the earliest and perhaps foremost model.

One circle and line of Bursan Naqshbandīs worthy of a separate discussion ensued from a group of spiritual descendants of the Urmavī line of Kurdistan who immigrated west after the death of their spiritual master, Shaykh Maḥmūd, in Diyarbakır. One *khalīfa* of Shaykh Maḥmūd, Ibrāhīm Efendi (d. 1065/1654–55), settled in Bursa and there instituted regular sessions of *dhikr*.[94] Another *khalīfa* and nephew of the shaykh, Açıḳbaş Maḥmūd, known also by the pseudonym Resmī (d. 1077/1666), traveled first to Egypt, then came to Istanbul and finally to Bursa; there he made the Dāya Hātūn Mosque in the neighborhood of that name the principal meeting place of his circle, though he also held regular sessions of *dhikr* in several other locations, including the city's Great Mosque. Açıḳbaş Maḥmūd seems to have inherited some of his uncle's charisma, political bent, and manner of Sufi *irshād*. Like the latter, he is reported to have initiated thousands of disciples, and it was probably because of this practice that at some point he was summoned to the capital, where according to one story the grand vezir, Köprülü Meḥmed Paşa, and the *şeyhülislām*, Esīrīzāde Meḥmed Efendi, almost had him put to death.[95] Another story told of the shaykh also reminds us of the conduct of his famous uncle: when Sultan Meḥmed IV was passing near Bursa in 1069/1658–59, Maḥmūd slaughtered a horse received from the Celālī Ḥasan Paşa the year before, and ceremoniously presented it to the royal entourage, declaring that it was "fitting for a horse taken from the enemy to be slaughtered for none other than the sultan."[96]

Açıķbaş Maḥmūd and a series of his successors at Dāye Hātūn preserved several Kubravī and Nūrbakhshī practices that the Urmavīs of Kurdistan inherited as a result of an early spiritual affiliation of one of their ancestors. Either Açıķbaş Maḥmūd himself or his nephew and successor, Ahī Maḥmūd b. Ķāsım (d. 1090/1679), wrote a piece on the Nūrbakhshī *silsila* and a commentary and sequel to the *Awrād-i fatḥiyya* of 'Alī Hamadānī.[97] Another successor, 'Abdullāh Efendi (d. 1159/1746), was a reader of the *Awrād* and a practitioner of Kubravī rites.[98] Two shaykhs by the name Meḥmed (d. 1176/1762 and 1192/1778, respectively) engaged in a series of practices that had been the hallmark of the Urmavīs of Kurdistan: along with the Naqshbandī *khatm-i khwājagān* recital, they read the *Awrād*, practiced certain Kubravī rites, and conducted sessions of both silent and vocal *dhikr*.[99]

Like their spiritual ancestors in Kurdistan, Bursa's Urmavīs adopted also a hereditary mode of succession. When one shaykh of the Dāye Hātūn Tekke, Muṣṭafā Efendi (d.1110/1699), died without leaving biological progeny, the office went temporarily to a Mujaddidī shaykh by the name 'Abdülkerīm Müfīd, but then it reverted to a *khalīfa* of the former incumbent, and then to a long series of this shaykh's biological-cum-spiritual descendants.[100] Although by this time, already well into the eighteenth century, Mujaddidī newcomers were replacing and eclipsing the earlier shaykhs of direct Transoxanian origin in many places, this was not to be the case in the circle centered around Dāye Hātūn. In this *tekke*—in time dubbed the "old" Naqshbandī *tekke* to distinguish it from another one known as the "new"—shaykhs came routinely from the same family, and this all the way from the mid-seventeenth century down to the twentieth.[101]

Altogether in Bursa there was a continuous Naqshbandī presence—one involving a series of separate circles with their respective shaykhs, institutions, and spiritual affiliations—for close to five centuries, from the time of Aḥmad Ilāhī and the Yuğurtlu Baba Tekke during the reign of Meḥmed II down to the twentieth century. Despite the geographic proximity, this was not, in terms of lineal origins, an extension of the Naqshbandiyya of the capital. Some of Bursa's Naqshbandīs were trained in Istanbul, especially in the line of Ilāhī and Bukhārī. Others were immigrants from Bukhara, or Transoxanian pilgrims sojourning in one of Bursa's Bukharan *tekke*s, or local trainees of various Bukharan or Anatolian shaykhs. At least in one case, the diversity of origin of the city's Naqshbandīs led also to a diversity of organizational modes and devotional practice: Naqshbandīs of the Urmavī line brought with them from Kurdistan a hereditary mode of succession along with the mixed Naqshbandī and

Kubravī devotional regimen that had characterized their spiritual ancestors back east. One of these immigrants, Açıḳbaş Maḥmūd, perhaps tried to replicate in Bursa also the political maneuvering and communal leadership style of his famous Urmavī ancestor, though here the Ottoman authorities were even less inclined than in faraway Kurdistan to allow such behavior.

In Bursa we have a good example of how specialized *tekke*s were less than critical for the diffusion of the tariqa. Apart from the two *tekke*s that Bukharan founders built for Central Asian pilgrims on their way to the Hijaz, over the years the city had few specialized Naqshbandī *tekke*s, and even fewer ones that lasted more than one or two generations. Most Naqshbandī shaykhs operated from neighborhood or other public mosques of which they were the appointed preachers or prayer leaders. This must be taken into account when one is presented with numerical data about *tekke*s. In his *Seyāḥatnāme*, Evliyā Çelebi mentioned three (unnamed) Naqshbandī *tekke*s in comparison with seventeen Khalwatī institutions, nine Qādirī ones, and one each affiliated with the Zaynī, Gulshanī, Sa'dī, Rifā'ī, Badawī, Celvetī, Bektaşī, and Mevlevī tariqas (the last one particularly large and lavishly adorned).[102] The substantial divergence between the number of Naqshbandī and Khalwatī *tekke*s fits with the picture that we have seen in Istanbul and the Balkans.[103] But we must keep in mind that in Bursa the number of Naqshbandī *tekke*s would have been a particularly poor indicator of the tariqa's influence, because so many of its shaykhs operated there from generic institutions rather than specialized ones.

4

Arabia

CONSTRAINTS ON EARLY TRANSMISSION

Individual Naqshbandīs traveled as pilgrims to the Holy Cities of the Hijaz, the Ḥaramayn, from the very early days of the tariqa in Transoxania, and as was common with all pilgrims undertaking the long and arduous journey from distant lands, they might spend time somewhere on the route, and especially sojourn in the Ḥaramayn as "pious residents" (*mujāwirūn*).[1] Bahā' al-Dīn Naqshband himself is said to have gone on the pilgrimage twice, and his *khalīfa* Muḥammad Pārsā died in Medina in 822/1420.[2] A series of Naqshbandī pilgrims and pious residents from the fifteenth century includes Sa'd al-Dīn Kāshgharī, 'Abd al-Raḥmān Jāmī, 'Alā' al-Dīn Ābīzī, known as Maktabdār, and Muḥammad Rūjī.[3] The last two apparently intrigued some of their Meccan acquaintances with their distinctive *dhikr* and daily routine. But generally these early pilgrims treated their sojourns as occasions for studying from local scholars, not as opportunities for initiating disciples or disseminating the tariqa.

Of a different kind were a number of individuals who settled in Mecca and Damascus toward the end of the fifteenth century, at a time when *khalīfas* of 'Ubaydullāh Aḥrār were traveling west also to other destinations, especially in Iran and Anatolia. Ismā'īl Shirvānī, a *khalīfa* of Aḥrār who traveled to the Hijaz after his master's death in 895/1490, remained in Mecca for the next four decades, teaching *ḥadīth* and Qur'ānic exegesis and training Sufi disciples.[4] Two other *khalīfas* of Aḥrār—Bābā Ḥaydar Samarqandī and Mawlānāzāda Utrārī—spent some time in the Hijaz, then proceeded elsewhere, the first settling in Istanbul and the second in Damascus.[5] 'Alā' al-Dīn Kirmānī, a *khalīfa* of Sa'd al-Dīn Kāshgharī in Herat, left for the Hijaz sometime before the Ṣafavid takeover of Khorasan in 916/1510 and spent in

Mecca the rest of his life.[6] In their new places of residence, these individuals initiated some disciples, thus becoming part of the wave of westward transmission from Transoxania that characterized these years. But little of the impact that they made was upon the local society; instead, they seem to have directed their energy mostly toward other visitors who had come to the Hijaz as pilgrims or *mujāwirūn*. Ismā'īl Ṭālishī, 'Abd al-Ghafūr Sāwijī, and Muḥammad Badakhshī—respectively, disciples of Shirvānī, Kirmānī, and Utrārī—had come from Iran and Transoxania.[7] Another disciple of Shirvānī, Zakariyā al-Bihārī, who made Mecca his home for some six decades, was originally from India. Of all these individuals, Bihārī is the only one who taught several local scholars of note; as a Sufi master, too, he had in Ghaḍanfar al-Nahrawālī (also an immigrant) one disciple whose spiritual descendants in Arabia spanned several generations.[8]

Once a Naqshbandī presence was established in the Ottoman capital at the end of the fifteenth century, and especially after the Ottoman takeover of the Hijaz in 923/1517, when a relatively safe and much-traveled imperial route was made available to pilgrims and other civilian traffic, we hear of numerous Naqshbandīs traveling on the pilgrimage from Istanbul. Some made the pilgrimage multiple times, and others stayed as pious residents in the Ḥaramayn or along the way. Among them were distinguished propagators of the tariqa in the Ottoman capital such as Aḥmad Bukhārī, Ḥekīm Çelebi, 'Abdüllaṭīf, and Muṣṭafā Sürūrī.[9] Yet we hear of almost no pilgrim from Istanbul training *khalīfas*, initiating disciples, or propagating the tariqa along the way. Even Aḥmad Bukhārī, who spent more than a year as a *mujāwir* in Mecca and Jerusalem (before the Ottoman conquest), apparently did not put his talent and propensity for transmission to use in these places, at least not openly.

The only explicit evidence for this "failure" comes from the *Al-Manhaj al-muwaṣṣil ilā al-ṭarīq al-abhaj*, the little-known Arabic treatise that one Muṣṭafā al-Ṣādiqī wrote at the instruction of his spiritual master, Aḥmad Ṣādiq Ṭāshkandī, with whom he went on the pilgrimage from Istanbul in 991/1583.[10] Aḥmad Ṣādiq was in several ways an exception to the pattern charted here. Originally a *khalīfa* of Makhdūm-i A'ẓam Aḥmad Kāsānī in Dahbīd, near Samarkand, according to his disciple and biographer he established himself as a prominent shaykh when he was still in Transoxania. He then left to embark on a second career in Istanbul, having been commanded in a dream "to spread the perfume of this radiant tariqa" to the Arabs, Persians, and the people of Rūm, Yemen, India, and Daylam.[11] Among other things, the shaykh sought to make inroads among Arabic speakers through the work, expounding the Naqshbandī *silsila* and devotional practice, that he instructed his disciple to write. Preceding by at least two decades a similar work by Tāj al-Dīn al-'Uthmānī, this was probably the first Naqshbandī manual written in Arabic and intended for Arabic speakers.

In addition, Aḥmad Ṣādiq approached his pilgrimage of 991/1583 as a grand occasion for personally teaching and spreading the tariqa along the way.[12] He set out from Istanbul with a large retinue of disciples, going by sea via Egypt and returning via Jerusalem and Damascus. During his sojourn in Jerusalem, he initiated the future madrasa professor and Ḥanafī *muftī* of the city, 'Abd al-Ghaffār al-Qudsī.[13] In Damascus we hear of the shaykh presiding over a lavish ceremony in memory of the Prophet's birthday (the *mawlid al-nabī*) at the Umayyad Mosque; with many local men of religion and shaykhs in attendance, he distributed sweets and drinks to the audience and bestowed garments (*malābis*) on his disciples. There were other stops in several towns along the way—presumably in the Hijaz or on the return journey via Syria—during which the shaykh made contacts with local people.

Instructive is Ṣādiqī's description of his master's exploits along the pilgrimage route as part of a campaign of "regenerating" and "reinstituting" a tariqa that had become "extinct" in these quarters (*wa-laqad kāna indarasat hadhihi al-ṭarīqa fa-aḥyāhā wa-indamasat arkān al-sulūk fīhā fa-abdāhā*).[14] As a description of the impact of Aḥmad Ṣādiq's activities (though perhaps not of his vision), this is clearly an exaggeration. Apart from 'Abd al-Ghaffār al-Qudsī, we know of no disciple of note that he initiated, and no local Naqshbandī circle or line that he established. But the reference to a tariqa that had become extinct by this time—even if also part hyperbole—supports our impression that neither Central Asian pilgrims, nor Naqshbandīs who traveled to the Hijaz from Istanbul, had done much to establish the tariqa in the Holy Cities or in other places along the way by this time. A century after the first arrival of Aḥrār's *khalīfas* from Transoxania, Aḥmad Ṣādiq found no Naqshbandī presence to speak of either in the Ḥaramayn or along the pilgrimage way, for example in Jerusalem or Damascus.

It took somewhat longer before a more substantial and enduring Naqshbandī presence developed for the first time in Arabic-speaking environments, primarily in the Ḥaramayn. Increasingly, and even before the dramatic expansion of the Mujaddidiyya from India, this was the work of Indian carriers of the tariqa. As of the turn of the seventeenth century, it was they who established Naqshbandī spiritual lines of note (to be discussed in the following two sections) in both Mecca and Medina.[15] Mention should be made as well of two Transoxanian Naqshbandī travelers who made inroads among Arabic speakers during that time. The first, Muḥammad

Ḥusayn al-Khwāfī (d. 1087/1676–77), a spiritual descendant of 'Ubaydullāh Aḥrār via the line of Makhdūm-i A'ẓam Aḥmad Kāsānī, settled in Mecca, where he married into a local *sayyid* family and initiated some prominent disciples. Among them were the Shāfi'ī *'ālim* and *imām* of Mecca's Great Mosque, 'Alī b. 'Abd al-Qādir al-Ṭabarī (d. 1070/1659–60), and Ḥasan Ibn al-'Ujaymī (d. 1113/1702), the scholar and author of the *Khabāyā al-zawāyā*. Khwāfī himself wrote or translated a number of works, notably a Naqshbandī treatise entitled the *al-Ṭarīqa al-muḥammadiyya*, and he developed a reputation especially for reciting with his disciples the Naqshbandī *khatm-i khwājagān* litany.[16]

A second spiritual descendant of the same line, Abū Sa'īd al-Balkhī (d.1092/1681), made a mark especially in Damascus, where he initiated the eminent scholar and author 'Abd al-Ghanī al-Nābulusī (d.1143/1731). In turn, Nābulusī became a prominent transmitter of the Naqshbandī tradition, although he was not much of an initiating shaykh (nor, according to a recent biographer, a typical disciple who receives training in a systematic discipline from a living spiritual master). One medium of his Naqshbandī influence was a popular and much-copied commentary that he wrote, at Abū Sa'īd's instruction, on a Naqshbandī treatise-manual by the Meccan Tāj al-Dīn al-'Uthmānī. More generally, his influence reminds us of that of 'Abd al-Raḥmān Jāmī in fifteenth-century Herat. Like that of the famous Heratī poet, Nābulusī's importance as a Naqshbandī lay not in training disciples or conducting the ritual, but in the allure and stature that he conferred on the tariqa through his reputation as a Sufi, scholar, and author.[17]

Why did the tariqa take so much longer to establish any substantial or enduring presence in the Arab lands than it did in Istanbul or even in Anatolia and the Balkans? And why did it not develop much of a presence anywhere in this area outside the Ḥaramayn until after the expansion of the Mujaddidiyya in the late seventeenth and early eighteenth centuries?[18] On these important questions I can offer only informed conjectures. Clearly the matter cannot be reduced to one of physical communications. Through the institution of the pilgrimage and the practice of "pious residence," Naqshbandīs from different quarters—Central Asia, Istanbul, and in time India—were traveling to the Hijaz and spending time in the Ḥaramayn in every generation. The process in which, during the seventeenth century, a series of Naqshbandīs from India carved for the tariqa a more substantial presence in the Hijaz was connected precisely to that tradition of pilgrimage.

For Istanbul and Ottoman Naqshbandīs, the establishment of the well-organized imperial pilgrimage route via Damascus following the Ottoman takeover of the Hijaz in 923/1517 made traveling on the pilgrimage relatively safe and routine. Central Asian Naqshbandīs faced many more hurdles, of course. We have seen in chapter 1 how the rise of the Ṣafavids to power at the beginning of the sixteenth century affected the pilgrimage from Central Asia, as politics and war often blocked traditional pilgrimage routes via Iran. We have seen, too, how a northern route via the steppes north of the Caspian Sea became an alternative of sorts, with Central Asian pilgrims traveling this route to Anatolia, then continuing their trip on the imperial pilgrimage route via Damascus. Other pilgrims from Central Asia continued to travel via various Iranian routes (especially during periods of relative quiet), and still others came via India and then by sea. All in all, Central Asian pilgrims never stopped coming to the Hijaz during the two centuries or so of Ṣafavid rule.

Not only travel from Central Asia but that from India, too, could involve considerable challenge once the Ṣafavids took control of Iran and the Portuguese established their hegemony in the Indian Ocean at the turn of the sixteenth century. Naim Farooqi has studied the Ṣafavid and particularly Portuguese harassment of Indian pilgrims traveling by land and sea. He has charted the ineffective attempts of Indian Muslim rulers, and a number of Ottoman sultans, to dislodge the Portuguese from India, to limit their power at sea, or, alternatively, to cooperate with them in the interest of securing the safety of sea travel. And he has shown that after the Portuguese power had begun to wane later in the seventeenth century, European pirates came to pose an even greater challenge to the pilgrimage, having found in merchant and pilgrim ships returning from the Hijaz one of their most lucrative targets.[19] Still, these obstacles—admittedly not in the same league as the difficulties attending travel by land from Central Asia—did not prevent the dissemination of the tariqa from India to Arabia either in Mujaddidī or pre-Mujaddidī times.[20]

Nor is there much evidence to support the idea that the introduction of the Naqshbandiyya to the Arab lands at this time was impaired by the presence of powerful local tariqas. Of all these places, it was rather in Egypt that numerous local tariqas were well established.[21] Yet this did not prevent the introduction of another "foreign" import, the Khalwatiyya, which Turks from Tabriz and Diyarbakır first brought to Egypt at the beginning of the sixteenth century, a few decades after the emergence of this tariqa in the region between Azerbaijan and Shirvan. Indeed, in Egypt the Khalwatiyya (whose early carriers emphasized piety, asceticism, and charisma more than Islamic learning or orthodoxy) quickly attracted a diverse following. It became entrenched not only within the Mamlūk elite and, after the Ottoman conquest of 923/1517, within the new provincial administration and among the Janissaries and cavalrymen of the Ottoman army, but also—though at first to a lesser degree—among Arabic speakers. Before long, the newly arrived tariqa became self-perpetuating, and it would last in Egypt continuously until modern times.[22] Michael Winter has described the introduction, at this very time, of another Sufi import, in Syria, where admittedly local tariqas were not as well-established at the turn of the sixteenth century. This was a branch of the Shādhiliyya that Shaykh 'Alī Ibn Maymūn had brought from North Africa. Unlike the Egyptian Khalwatiyya, however, this Shādhilī branch remained rather ephemeral; it failed to develop a sustained presence beyond the first generation of local initiates.[23]

Language, too, is unlikely to have posed a major obstacle to Naqshbandī transmission in the Arab lands. As Aḥmad Ṣādiq Ṭāshkandī understood, as a measure of propagating the tariqa in this environment one would have to provide prospective disciples with Arabic materials expounding its devotional regimen, history, and *silsila.* But making such materials available should not have been difficult. The carriers of the tariqa from Transoxania to Istanbul had exhibited an impressive linguistic adaptability and commitment to the translation of early Naqshbandī works from Persian into Turkish. What had been done for Turkish could have been done for Arabic, in which most potential transmitters would have had some proficieny to begin with.[24]

Can limited transmission to Arabia be attributed to the fact that Naqshbandīs in Istanbul were simply not that bent on disseminating the tariqa? These Naqshbandīs appear often oblivious to the Arab lands both as an arena for potential expansion and as the venue where, before long, an independent Naqshbandī tradition of Indian origin would emerge. Nor did they demonstrate an interest in the Naqshbandī community that since the end of the sixteenth century was burgeoning in India itself. The one continuous attachment that they nurtured was to the tariqa's origin in Transoxania, whence newly arrived shaykhs often replenished their ranks. One might think that Istanbul Naqshbandīs were not particularly bent on expansion to far-off destinations, but, as we saw in chapter 3, there were *khalīfa*s who went forth from the capital to introduce the tariqa to several places in Anatolia and the Balkans. By contrast, we hear of almost no Istanbul-based shaykhs propagating the tariqa in the Hijaz and the Arab lands. To this there was one exception—that of Aḥmad Ṣādiq Ṭāshkandī.

It may be that Istanbul Naqshbandīs, and perhaps potential carriers of the tariqa from Transoxania—all Ḥanafīs—did not expect to make significant inroads among Arabic speakers not because of linguistic difficulties, but rather because most Arabic speakers (at least in the East, the Mashriq, as opposed to North Africa) were Shāfi'īs by legal rite (*madhhab*), and thus less likely to find the Naqshbandī devotional regimen congenial. Not that being Shāfi'ī precluded one from becoming Naqshbandī: in some places the opposite was true. As we will see below, disciples of the line of Ibrāhīm al-Kūrānī in seventeenth-century Arabia were predominantly Shāfi'īs, as were the numerous followers of the Urmavīs of Kurdistan (granted, both lines in which the Naqshbandiyya was taught in conjunction with other tariqas). In the nineteenth century, the Khālidiyya, whose eponym was himself Shāfi'ī, attracted large Shāfi'ī followings, for example in the eponym's native Kurdistan, and later in Indonesia.[25] Still, it cannot be accidental that the main strongholds of the Naqshbandiyya throughout its history—Central Asia, India, and Anatolia—were all areas where the Ḥanafī legal school predominated, and it may be that one factor contributing to this pattern was the attitude of adherents of different legal rites to devotional matters. Shāfi'īs, we learn from Ibrāhīm al-Kurānī, would have been less than naturally inclined to follow a devotional regimen that had a silent form of the *dhikr* at its center, since they not only considered the vocal recollection entirely acceptable, but also valued it as the "original method," a method superior (*afḍal*) to that of silent *dhikr*, and a "key to the religion of Islam."[26]

It is easy to see how this predilection might make Arabic-speaking Shāfi'īs less likely to be attracted to the Naqshbandiyya—and make would-be disseminators of the tariqa less likely to pursue these Shāfi'īs as a potential audience. Moreover, precisely because of the Naqshbandiyya's strong Ḥanafī connections, after the Ottoman conquest of the Arab lands in the early sixteenth century some Arabic-speaking Shāfi'īs may have come to view this tariqa as one "of the Ottoman center," and thus less than attractive culturally and politically.

Two other cultural predilections might similarly have affected the attractiveness of the tariqa in Arabic-speaking environments. In Istanbul and elsewhere in Anatolia and the Balkans Naqshbandīs acquired a reputation as the defenders and disseminators of the mystical teachings of Ibn al-'Arabī and as the carriers and perpetuators of a much-coveted Perso-Islamic literary culture. A lifelong relationship with a shaykh might start, for example, when a would-be disciple attended his public readings of Rūmī's *Masnavī*. By contrast, in Arabic-speaking environments it appears that neither enthusiasm for Ibn al-'Arabī and certainly not the Naqshbandī expertise in Persian literary culture had the same effect. Here the mystical teachings of Ibn al-ʿArabī did not become as influential as in the Persian- and Turkish- (and later Urdu-) speaking world.[27] Even more clearly, Arabic-speaking scholars, intellectuals, and litterateurs were less eager to partake in that Perso-Islamic literary culture that for Ottoman intellectuals was a mark of sought-after elegance and sophistication. Perhaps they entertained a cultural or intellectual pride that made such borrowing unwarranted. Be that as it may, as McChesney has put it, it was "only the Arabophone areas of North Africa and the Fertile Crescent" that were apparently able to "resist" the lure (or the "imperialism") of a Persian literary culture that was otherwise "virtually co-extensive with Islamdom."[28]

In the two following sections, devoted to two spiritual lines that a series of Naqshbandīs from India established in Mecca and Medina during the seventeenth century, we shall pay attention to these issues of *madhhab* and devotional practice, the teaching of Ibn al-ʿArabī, and the lure (or lack thereof) of Persian literary culture—and to the ways in which they might be implicated in the Naqshbandiyya's attractiveness and dissemination among Arabic speakers.

AN INDIAN TRANSPLANT AND HIS ARABIAN DISCIPLES

Even if the Arab lands were viewed as less than fertile ground for Naqshbandī dissemination, the Ḥaramayn, as the destination of the pilgrimage, always retained a special allure. Two decades after Aḥmad Ṣādiq Ṭāshkandī traveled as a pilgrim from Istanbul and tried to "regenerate" the tariqa along the way, another Naqshbandī who would soon become more successful in a similar endeavor traveled to Mecca. Tāj al-Dīn b. Zakariyā al-ʿUthmānī (d. 1051/1640) came from India after the death of his spiritual master, Muḥammad al-Bāqī, in 1012/1603.[29] In Mecca, he established at the foot of the Jabal Quʿayqiʿān a Sufi lodge (*ribāṭ*), supported by *waqf*, which offered accommodation for disciples and visiting Sufis and scholars.[30] From this Meccan base, where he was in time buried, he built in the following few decades an extensive network of disciples and *khalīfa*s that spanned the Ḥaramayn, Yemen, Hadhramawt (Ḥaḍramawt), and Hasa (al-Aḥṣāʾ) in eastern Arabia (and that reached far beyond Arabia via a number of individuals who "took the tariqa" to Egypt and as far-off as Indonesia).[31] Unlike any previous Naqshbandī presence in Arabia, that created by Tāj al-Dīn was also self-perpetuating, though it could not hold its ground for long after the coming of the Mujaddidīs, by whom it was superseded in the eighteenth century.

Accounts of Tāj al-Dīn's early career in India and the circumstances of his move to the Hijaz differ. The *Tuḥfat al-sālikīn fī dhikr tāj al-'ārifīn*, a hagiography written by Maḥmūd b. Ashraf al-Ḥusaynī, relates that initially he had received multiple initiations from the spirits of several tariqa founders (sing. *ra'īs*), then began a live training with a Shaṭṭārī shaykh, Ilāhbakhsh, who was known for his harsh ascetic exercises and powerful states of ecstasy (*jadhba*). After the death of Ilāhbakhsh, of whom he had become a *khalīfa*, he started anew as a disciple of the Naqshbandī shaykh Muḥammad al-Bāqī, who authorized him as his first *khalīfa* within a mere three days. He remained in Muḥammad al-Bāqī's *ṣuḥba* for ten years, during which the two were so intimately bonded that "it was impossible to know who was the lover and who the beloved; they ate together and slept in the same bed."[32]

From Mujaddidī sources used by S. A. A. Rizvi it appears that the author of the *Tuḥfa* may have tried to gloss over some conflict. According to this version of the story, jealous fellow disciples complained of Tāj al-Dīn's stern handling of initiates (by subjecting them to harsh ascetic exercises?), and Muḥammad al-Bāqī himself (as the *Tuḥfa* also acknowledges) admonished him to stop initiating disciples into other than Naqshbandī *silsila*s on the authority of past masters.[33] Moreover, Rizvi's sources suggest that upon the death of Muḥammad al-Bāqī, Tāj al-Dīn sought to assert his leadership over the Indian Naqshbandiyya, but was frustrated by the ascendance of a fellow *khalīfa*, Aḥmad Sirhindī, who would soon become known as the eponym of the Mujaddidiyya. It was this disappointment that led the would-be successor to leave India and move to the Hijaz.[34]

A number of points about Tāj al-Dīn's conduct as a propagator of the tariqa deserve attention. Unlike Aḥmad Ṣādiq Ṭāshkandī, who also left his birthplace (in Transoxania) after the death of his shaykh and perhaps in connection with competition over succession, Tāj al-Dīn is not portrayed by his biographer as having proclaimed any grand vision of expansion. Yet from the circumstances of his move to Mecca when Aḥmad Sirhindī's star was beginning to rise, and from the manner in which he went about building his extensive Arabian network, he emerges as an ambitious shaykh and an energetic Naqshbandī transmitter. As a *murshid*, one thing that distinguished him from others was his insistence on initiating disciples exclusively into the Naqshbandiyya. As we have seen, his biographer explained this departure from what had been the shaykh's own experience with multiple affiliations (among others, with the Shaṭṭāriyya, Chishtiyya, and Qādiriyya) as the result of a command from his spiritual master, Muḥammad al-Bāqī; but perhaps the insistence was also a response to a common or growing practice of subscribing to multiple affiliations that Tāj al-Dīn could not but notice among Sufis in seventeenth-century Arabia.[35] In turn, the exclusivity that he demanded must have reinforced the identity and cohesiveness of the spiritual line that emanated from him, even though not all of his disciples obliged. We know, for example, that Mūsā b. Aḥmad Ibn 'Ujayl practiced the Naqshbandī *dhikr* that he received from Tāj al-Dīn along with non-Naqshbandī formulas acquired elsewhere.[36] Another spiritual descendant, Muhannā b. 'Awaḍ al-Ḥaḍramī, also experienced with several *dhikrs*—for example, a Khalwatī formula that he imparted to Ibn al-'Ujaymī.[37] Nor was refraining from multiple initiations necessarily the only or most effective way of transmitting a tariqa. This much is illustrated by the fortunes of a second non-Mujaddidī Naqshbandī line (associated especially with Aḥmad al-Qushāshī and Ibrāhīm al-Kūrānī) that was implanted in Medina at about the time of Tāj al-Dīn's Meccan career.

In devotional matters, Tāj al-Dīn was at one with other Naqshbandīs of this time, combining an insistence on sobriety and fidelity to the *sunna* with confidence in the superiority of the Naqshbandī mystical way.[38] Like other Naqshbandīs, he was a reader and disseminator of the teachings of Ibn al-'Arabī, while acknowledging the dangers that indulging in mystical speculation posed to the unfit or beginner Sufi.[39] He particularly valued the Naqshbandī spiritual technique of *murāqaba* (involving fixing the meaning of the name Allāh in the heart) as well as the ability of the Naqshbandī shaykhs to lead disciples to a state of ecstasy or "spontaneous attraction to God" (*jadhba*) quickly and without harsh ascetic exercises—by "purifying the heart" rather than "breaking the lower soul," as his biographer put it.[40] Tāj al-Dīn himself appeared publicly (during the rites of the pilgrimage in 1037/1628) in a highly ecstatic condition, a state that we are told caused leading Meccan Sufis and *'ulamā'* to flock to become his disciples.[41]

Like Naqshbandīs elsewhere Tāj al-Dīn had a penchant for attracting *khalīfas* from among the ranks of the *'ulamā'*. His foremost Meccan disciple, Aḥmad Ibn 'Allān (d. 1023/1624), was an author and respected teacher of *fiqh* and *ḥadīth*. A biographer described him as one of the city's "objects of pride" (*mafākhir*). Once he was authorized as a *khalīfa*, he initiated numerous disciples and held daily sessions of silent *dhikr* at the city's Great Mosque.[42] In Hasa, Tāj al-Dīn authorized Ibrāhīm b. Ḥasan al-Aḥsā'ī, a jurist, author, poet, and grammarian, who in turn initiated Yaḥyā b. 'Alī Bāshā, a son of Hasa's ruler and also a student of *fiqh* and *ḥadīth*.[43] In the Yemen, Tāj al-Dīn's *khalīfas* hailed from some of the most prominent local families. The Ibn 'Ujayls were pillars of the town of Bayt al-Faqih, a prosperous center of the coffee trade established some three centuries earlier around the tomb of one of their ancestors. Tāj al-Dīn initiated several members of this family during a visit to Zabid. Later the most prominent among them, Aḥmad Ibn 'Ujayl, came to train with him in Mecca before returning to the Yemen and there "training a group of *khalīfa*s and benefiting the people."[44] Another Yemenite *khalīfa*, 'Abd al-Bāqī al-Mizjājī (d. 1074/1663), was the scion of well-known shaykhs and *'ulamā'* from Tuḥayta, near Zabid and himself a jurist and teacher of *ḥadīth*; in time he came to have "countless" disciples.[45] Aḥmad Ibn 'Ujayl and 'Abd al-Bāqī al-Mizjājī (along with Aḥmad al-Qushāshī, one of the central figures of a second Arabian Naqshbandī line of this period) trained two visiting disciples who proceeded to "take the tariqa" back to their native lands. The first, Aḥmad al-Dimyāṭī, originally from Egypt, returned to have numerous students, initiate disciples, teach the *dhikr*, and "benefit many, especially in the Naqshbandī way."[46] The second, Yūsuf al-Jāwī, from Makassar in south Celebes, traveled upon his return from the Hijaz to Banten in Java, where he propagated the tariqa through a combination of Sufi training, teaching, writing, and various political dealings.[47]

Like Aḥmad Ṣādiq Ṭāshkandī, and with greater vigor, Tāj al-Dīn set out to make inroads in local society and reach Arabic speakers by producing Naqshbandī literature in Arabic. Through translations of two Persian classics, Jāmī's *Nafaḥāt al-uns* and Kāshifī's *Rashaḥāt-i 'ayn al-ḥayāt*, he made available in Arabic both the history of the emergence of the Naqshbandiyya out of the Ṭarīqat-i Khwājagān and the models of behavior that such hagiographic literature is meant to inculcate. He also produced two treatises in Arabic that were in time copied by numerous hands: an exposition of the Naqshbandī devotional regimen entitled the *Risāla fī bayān sulūk al-Naqshbandiyya* (and sometimes called after him the *Tājiyya*), and a discussion of the etiquette of the relationship between shaykh and disciples, the *Risāla fī ādāb al-mashyakha wa'l-murīdīn*.[48] There is some uncertainty about how, technically, these treatises came into being. 'Abd al-Ghanī al-Nābulusī notes in the introduction to his famous commentary on the *Tājiyya* that the work was a translation from Persian,[49] and Ḥamawī, along with several copies of the *Tājiyya* itself, suggest that the writer or translator may have been Ibn 'Allān.[50] Perhaps Tāj al-Dīn—who was not madrasa-educated and who hailed from a family originally from Shiraz in Iran—had his prominent Meccan disciple Ibn 'Allān transcribe and edit his oral discourse or translate some works from the original Persian because his own written Arabic was inadequate for the task. However that may be, what matters is that he appreciated the importance of writing and translation and set out to place at the disposal of *khalīfa*s, and put within reach of Arabic speakers, some of the core texts that he deemed necessary for facilitating widespread Naqshbandī transmission.

How does the career of Tāj al-Dīn reflect on the significance of *madhhab* affiliation in attracting Naqshbandī disciples? Our sources are not usually forthcoming on this issue and allow no more than limited comments. As Shāfiʿīs, *khalīfa*s such as Ibn ʿAllān and Ibn ʿUjayl were well-placed to serve as agents of the Naqshbandī transmission among Arabic speakers, and at the same time their very emergence as Tāj al-Dīn's disciples is a testimony that the Naqshbandī devotional regimen was not always unappealing to followers of this legal rite. But it is noteworthy that Ibrāhīm b. Ḥasan al-Aḥsāʾī and ʿAbd al-Bāqī al Mizjājī were both Ḥanafī jurists, given that in Arabia Ḥanafīs were a minority. That Tāj al-Dīn was led to recruit some of his most prominent *khalīfa*s from among this minority reinforces our impression that Ḥanafīs were indeed more hospitable to the Naqshbandiyya than Shāfiʿīs.[51]

Geographically and culturally, the line of Tāj al-Dīn was oriented south and east—toward the Yemen, Hadhramawt, Hasa, and beyond to India. No relations were established with the emerging Indian Mujaddidiyya; given his early history, keeping his inedpendence vis-à-vis the Mujaddidīs would have been a matter of some significance for Tāj al-Dīn. Nor do we hear of new immigrants from India continuously replenishing the ranks of this line in Arabia, as was the case with immigrants from Transoxania coming to Istanbul. Still, the pilgrimage from India to the Hijaz served as a reasonably constant channel of communications, and there was also travel in the other direction: the shaykh himself had left a family in Sambhal, east of Delhi, and during one of his visits back home, he authorized his son as *khalīfa*.[52] By contrast, this line had little to do with the Naqshbandiyya of Istanbul or with the Ottoman cultural orbit, even though it was centered in nominally Ottoman Mecca, and despite the easy communications that the imperial pilgrimage route from Istanbul facilitated. Tāj al-Dīn himself is not known to have traveled north of the Ḥaramayn. He had one Syrian disciple, the Damascus-born Mīrzā al-Surūjī, who read Ibn al-ʿArabī with him; but this individual had been resident in the Hijaz for many years.[53] If Naqshbandīs from the Ottoman capital can be said to have been uninterested in Arabia, the reverse was probably true of Tāj al-Dīn and his disciples.[54] In turn, this meant that this Naqshbandī line could not serve as the medium through which Naqshbandīs from India and the Ottoman lands might become cognizant of or involved with each other, as Mujaddidī immigrants to the Ḥaramayn did less than a century later.

TEACHING IN MULTIPLE TARIQAS

While Tāj al-Dīn was establishing his Naqshbandī community in Mecca and the Yemen, and before the first Mujaddidīs began coming from India in mid-century,[55] the Naqshbandiyya was taught and disseminated in the Hijaz by a second, Medina-based line of Sufi shaykhs, one that combined Naqshbandī with other tariqa affiliations. Its central figures were Aḥmad al-Shinnāwī (d. 1028/1619), Aḥmad al-Qushāshī (d. 1071/1661), and somewhat later Ibrāhīm al-Kūrānī (d. 1101/1690).[56]

This was not simply a Naqshbandī spiritual line. Qushāshī, Kūrānī, and their associates made much of their reputation not as Sufi shaykhs but as scholars of mysticism, *ḥadīth*, theology, and Shāfi'ī jurisprudence. Along with writing—the first two alone produced well over a hundred works—they taught, participated in scholarly debates, and facilitated interaction among diverse visitors to the Ḥaramayn.[57] It is, in fact, as links in a Medina-centered scholarly network whose influence radiated far beyond Arabia that these individuals have become most appreciated. John Voll, in particular, has called attention to this group and identified it as an intellectual community of considerable influence (though his reading into it of a reformist impulse that may have inspired the eighteenth-century revivalist Muḥammad Ibn 'Abd al-Wahhāb is problematic).[58]

In their pursuits as Sufi shaykhs, as in scholarship, Qushāshī, Kūrānī, and their predecessors catered more to a broad Muslim network than to any local Arabian community. Unlike Tāj al-Dīn, who made his impact primarily among local Arabic speakers in the Hijaz and the Yemen, they found their principal audience and following among the large foreign community (the *mujāwirūn*) of Medina, and through them outside Arabia. With the exception of Qushāshī, who was born in the Hijaz of a family originally from a village near Jerusalem, the central figures of this line were all immigrants to Arabia: their spiritual ancestor, Ṣibghatullāh Barwajī, was from Gujarat, Shinnāwī was from the Gharbiyya province of Egypt, and Kūrānī (along with his student Muḥammad b. 'Abd al-Rasūl al-Barzanjī), from Shahrazūr in Kurdistan.[59] A number of Barwajī's immediate disciples were also foreigners, as is evident from *nisbas* (in this case, names indicating geographic origin) such as Ajamī, Balkhī, Hindī, Kurdī, and Sindī.[60] Qushāshī and Kūrānī had a string of returning pilgrims and pious residents who had been their students or associates (most notably the Sumatran 'Abd al-Ra'ūf Singkilī) carry their fame and teachings, especially in the Shaṭṭārī Sufi tradition, to far-flung Muslim communities.[61] Joseph Fletcher has traced to Kūrānī (via the Yemenite son of 'Abd al-Baqī al-Mizjājī, Zayn) one Ma Mingxin (d. 1195/1781), who took the tariqa to China and there established a Naqshbandī faction that came to be known primarily for its insistence on practicing the vocal *dhikr.*[62]

There has been some confusion concerning the Sufi identity of shaykhs of this line. Some have called them Shaṭṭārīs, others Naqshbandīs. But they are probably best defined by the very multiplicity of tariqa affiliations that they imparted to disciples. Multiple affiliations were, of course, hardly unusual among Sufi shaykhs of this time, though they were less common among Naqshbandīs, and especially a far cry from the practice of Tāj al-Dīn in Mecca. In the line of Qushāshī and Kurānī multiple affiliations went back all the way to Ṣibghatullāh Barwajī, the Indian spiritual master who had come to Medina on the pilgrimage in 1005/1597. Barwajī was primarily a Shaṭṭārī shaykh in the line of Muḥammad Ghawth and Wajīh al-Dīn Gujarātī, and in Arabia he became a principal disseminator of the teachings of the Shaṭṭāriyya, among others translating into Arabic the *Jawāhir-i khamsa* of Muḥammad Ghawth, which became a staple reading among his spiritual descendants.[63] Yet we learn from the *Al-Simṭ al-majīd* of Qushāshī that on the authority of his Shaṭṭārī master, Wajīh al-Dīn, Barwajī himself, and in turn his *khalīfa*s, routinely gave secondary initiations into some ten tariqas, including the Naqshbandiyya.[64] This may help explain how several of Barwajī's immediate disciples in Arabia—individuals such as As'ad al-Balkhī, Niẓām al-Dīn Sindī, and the future Ḥanafī *muftī* of Damascus 'Abd al-Raḥmān al-'Imādī—became Naqshbandīs.[65]

The Naqshbandī connection assumed an even greater significance in this line when Barwajī's *khalīfa*, Aḥmad al-Shinnāwī, received two discreet Naqshbandī initiations. One was from an Egyptian by the name Muḥammad al-Bahnāsī who was initiated (probably in the Hijaz) by a nephew of 'Abd al-Raḥmān Jāmī, and the second from a Bukharan immigrant via India, Ghaḍanfar al-Nahrawālī, who had "acquired" the tariqa initially in his native Transoxania and then again in Arabia from the said nephew of Jāmī and from an Indian spiritual descendant of 'Ubaydullāh Aḥrār, Zakariyā al-Bihārī.[66] According to one source, Barwajī himself also "took from" (*akhadha 'an*) Nahrawālī, though the terms of precisely what he "took" are not spelled out.[67] Be that as it may, while the Shaṭṭārī affiliation continued to be central in this line all along—as the *Al-Simṭ al-majīd* makes abundantly clear—henceforth the Naqshbandiyya became more than just one of a series of secondary affiliations conferred symbolically by a Shaṭṭārī shaykh. One of Shinnāwī's spiritual descendants, the Meccan Sālim Ibn Shaykhān, authored a Naqshbandī manual in Arabic, the *Al-Maqā'id al-'indiyya bi-mashāhid al-Naqshbandiyya*.[68] Even clearer is the pride of place that in his roster of teaching credentials, the *Al-Amam li-īqāẓ al-himam*, Ibrāhīm al-Kūrānī gives to the Naqshbandī symbolic garment (*khirqa*) and to the silent *dhikr* that his shaykh, Qushāshī, had conferred on him on the authority of Bahnasī and Nahrawālī.[69] All these must be the clues to how several Arab and Ottoman biographers, including Muḥibbī, came to identify Kūrānī and even Barwajī as Naqshbandī shaykhs and nothing else. Elsewhere, especially in Indonesia, Kūrānī became known exclusively as a Shaṭṭārī shaykh, apparently because his associate (and Qushāshī's disciple) 'Abd al-Ra'ūf Singkilī, who returned from the Hijaz in 1071/1661, found it most congenial to disseminate in the name of these two masters Shaṭṭārī rather than Naqshbandī teachings and devotional practices.[70]

How were the devotional practice and Sufi teachings that Kūrānī and his associates imparted to their disciples affected by all this mix? One thing that clearly permeated this line was a devotion to the mystical teachings of Ibn al-'Arabī. Qushāshī and Kūrānī each became known as his generation's "foremost proponent" of the doctrine of *waḥdat al-wujūd*, and several of their teachers, associates, and students wrote and taught in a similar vein.[71] In Bruinessen's assessment, this expertise goes a long way toward explaining the success of Qushāshī and Kūrānī among Indonesian students, since Indonesians would have been unresponsive to any Sufi branch that rejected Ibn al-'Arabī's metaphysics.[72] As we will see in chapter 5, however, Qushāshī and Kūrānī did not have to draw for their interest or expertise in the Andalusian mystic's thought on their Shaṭṭārī connection: numerous of their Naqshbandī fellows, both in Central Asia and in the Ottoman lands, were similarly devoted to his teachings.

What separated shaykhs of the Qushāshī and Kūrānī line most visibly from other Naqshbandīs was their practicing of the vocal *dhikr* along with the distinctive Naqshbandī silent method.[73] Our sources are not always explicit about this matter, but even a few references are sufficient to illustrate this point. Aḥmad al-Shinnāwī taught and authorized his *khalīfa*s to teach both the silent and vocal methods.[74] Qushāshī taught the author of the *Khabāyā al-zawāyā*, Ibn al-'Ujaymī, a number of *dhikr* methods involving beating drums or playing musical instruments (*al-ḍarb wa'l-daqq*).[75] 'Abd al-Ra'ūf Singkilī devoted several of his works in Malay to the mode of performing a vocal Shaṭṭārī *dhikr* that he had learned from Qushāshī and Kūrānī.[76] And Kūrānī himself not only imparted a vocal *dhikr* to his disciples, but also defended the legitimacy and benefits of this method in his writings and in public debate, pronouncing it to be particularly well-regarded by Shāfi'īs.[77]

On this as well as on several other issues, Kūrānī and his associates were easily drawn into controversy, whether as critics or as the target of criticism. On one occasion, ignoring the advice of well-wishers, Kūrānī entered into an argument about the *dhikr* with a visiting tutor of the Ottoman sultan who informed him of his own campaign to uproot the vocal *dhikr* from the mosques of the capital. This must have been Vānī Meḥmed Efendi, the private tutor and confidant of Sultan Meḥmed IV, whom we shall meet in chapter 6 as the last leader of the puritanical Ḳāḍīzādeli movement in the years before the movement was banished in the aftermath of the abortive siege of Vienna in 1094/1683.[78] On another occasion, Kūrānī himself was targeted by detractors, in this case a group that sought, albeit unsuccessfully, to condemn him for his defense of Ibn al-'Arabī's teachings.[79]

In yet another controversy, Kūrānī and a number of his associates—now on the accusing side—proclaimed as heretical some theories of the eponym of the Mujaddidiyya, Aḥmad Sirhindī, who had died several decades before. When Sirhindī's *khalīfa* Ādam Bānūrī first came to the Hijaz in mid-century, Aḥmad al-Qushāshī not only wrote a treatise in refutation of some of his shaykh's ideas, but also challenged Bānūrī personally in the Prophet's Mosque to retract his defense of these ideas. When Bānūrī refused—reports Ibn al-'Ujaymī—Qushāshī "pointed a finger to his stomach, causing him to fall into the illness [of which], soon after, he died."[80] A few years later, in 1068/1658, Sirhindī's son Muḥammad Ma'ṣūm came as pilgrim to the Hijaz, and again some of Qushāshī's disciples challenged him and clashed with his entourage over his father's theories.[81] Finally, when in 1093/1682 Indian critics requested the *'ulamā'* of Mecca and Medina to issue a legal opinion (*fatwā*) on Sirhindī's controversial theories, Kūrānī and a number of his followers emerged yet again as some of the shaykh's most outspoken Arabian detractors. One student, Muḥammad b. 'Abd al-Rasūl al-Barzanjī, quickly authored the *Qadḥ al-zand wa-qadaḥ al-rand fī radd jahālat ahl Sirhind* (soon followed by a second anti-Sirhindī treatise), stating in the introduction that he and his shaykh, Kūrānī, had been specifically asked to put to use their knowledge of the Qur'ān and *ḥadīth* in countering Sirhindī's theories.[82]

At the center of the accusations against Sirhindī as they emerge from the *Qadḥ al-zand* was the shaykh's representation of the Millennial Renewal and the implication that, as the "Renewer of the Second Millenium" (*mujaddid-i alf-i thānī*) he was himself destined to play a central role in this imminent cosmic event. Barzanjī took particular issue with Sirhindī's assertion of the superiority of the reality of the Ka'ba to that of the Prophet Muḥammad and with the notion that a thousand years after the death of the Prophet, the Muḥammadan reality would achieve perfection and unite with the reality of the Ka'ba, creating a new reality designated "Aḥmadī." This, he argued, was an allusion to Sirhindī's own name, and a preposterous claim to prophethood.[83] Without delving into the merits of Barzanjī's criticism, what is clear is that on different occasions Kūrānī and his associates found themselves on different ends of various controversies, both as accused and accusers. That in this particular case they were lined as accusers against the individual who in time would be cast as the very epitome of orthodoxy within the Naqshbandī tradition is, of course, ironic. It is also a reminder of the premise of the present study that if we are to gain a proper understanding of the Naqshbandiyya, we must approach this tariqa as a historical phenomenon, exploring it as it unfolded over time. What became an unassailable truth in the nineteenth or twentieth century (in this case the casting of Sirhindī as an epitome of orthodoxy) was not necessarily such in the seventeenth. As I argue in the following chapters, later representations of this tariqa (whether as militantly orthodox, highly politicized, or hostile to Ibn al-'Arabī) may be powerful, but it is anachronistic and misleading to project them back in time in the belief that they can illuminate earlier historical phases.

CONCLUSION

How does the evolution of the two spiritual lines that a series of pre-Mujaddidī Naqshbandīs from India established in the Ḥaramayn in the seventeenth century reflect on our quandary at the beginning of this chapter—namely, the question of whether and why the Naqshbandiyya was less easily disseminated in Arabic-speaking environments than in Istanbul or in Anatolia and the Balkans?

The two spiritual lines discussed here differed from each other in important respects. Tāj al-Dīn al-'Uthmānī initiated disciples exclusively into the Naqshbandiyya, recruited local luminaries as *khalīfas*, produced Naqshbandī literature in Arabic translation, taught a series of devotional practices that had become the accepted core of the Naqshbandī way almost everywhere, and was generally intent on addressing Arabic speakers and making inroads in local society in Mecca and the Yemen. Qushāshī, Kūrānī, and their associates represent not simply a Sufi line, but also a community of scholars whose interests spawned such diverse areas as *taṣawwuf*, theology, *ḥadīth*, and jurisprudence. As Sufis they were especially distinguished by the espousal (and polemical defense) of the vocal method of *dhikr* and by their multiplicity of tariqa affiliations, all of which they conferred on disciples. At first they exhibited a primary affiliation with the Indian Shaṭṭāriyya along with secondary, mostly symbolic connections to a number of other tariqas. Then, through a series of later initiations, a more discreet and significant Naqshbandī connection developed, though the erstwhile Shaṭṭārī affiliation always remained central in this line. Finally, these Sufi teachers found their principal audience less in local society than among Medina's foreign residents (the *mujāwirūn*), and through them in much broader Muslim networks.

Several aspects of the evolution of these admittedly rather different spiritual lines may help elucidate the question of the Naqshbandiyya's attractiveness (or lack thereof) in Arabic-speaking environments. In both lines the institution of the pilgrimage and the practice of *mujāwara* were central. Even Tāj al-Dīn, who catered to locals at least as much as to visitors, relied heavily on the communication networks of the *ḥajj*, for example, in his dissemination of the tariqa to Yemen and in the way that his *ribāṭ* in Mecca became a place of accommodation for pilgrims from Hadhramawt. Thus the vitality of these two lines may testify to the sui generis nature of Mecca and Medina as the Holy Cities, more than to the attractiveness of the Naqshbandiyya among Arabic speakers in general. We also get the impression that *madhhab* affiliation and perhaps cultural predilections of the kind mentioned at the beginning of this chapter did play a role in shaping the Naqshbandī dissemination. In Arabia we do not hear about Naqshbandī shaykhs building reputations as Persian linguists or poets or recruiting disciples via public reading of the *Masnavī*—perhaps evidence, albeit negative, that here such pursuits were not much in demand and could not be used as a tool of dissemination. As for *madhhab*, we have seen Tāj al-Dīn al-ʿUthmānī attracting a number of important Shāfiʿī *khalīfas*, yet his recruitment of several Ḥanafī ones in what was primarily a Shāfiʿī environment seems to underscore Kūrānī's caveat that Shāfiʿīs were less interested in the silent *dhikr* (and thus less likely to have been responsive to the Naqshbandī devotional regimen with its distinctive silent *dhikr*). Kūrānī himself resolved this problem in his own way—namely, by teaching the vocal method of *dhikr*, which he proclaimed acceptable in every *madhhab* and particularly suitable for Shāfiʿīs.

On the issue of Ibn al-ʿArabī our evidence remains less clear. Many Naqshbandī shaykhs mentioned in this chapter engaged in disseminating his mystical teachings, both to foreign visitors to the Ḥaramayn and to locals. In the following chapter, we will meet the Damascene Naqshbandī and scholar ʿAbd al-Ghanī al-Nābulusī as another of his prominent devotees and defenders. Whatever other sources may suggest about the respective attitudes of Arab and Ottoman *ʿulamāʾ* toward the teachings of the Andalusian mystic, on the basis of the evidence available to us here it seems best not to conclude that the devotion of Naqshbandīs of our period to these teachings made this tariqa less attractive in Arabic- than in Turkish-speaking environments.

Part II

The Politics and Culture of a Tariqa

5

Devotional Practice and the Construction of Orthodoxy

That the Naqshbandiyya is a tariqa of rigorous fidelity to the *sharī'a*, or rigorous orthodoxy, is a commonplace. Naqshbandīs have always stressed their *sharī'a*-abidance, and observers everywhere have followed in highlighting this point as one of the hallmarks of the tariqa. What precisely this entailed for Naqshbandīs at different phases of their history is not always clear, however. Depictions of the Naqshbandī orthodoxy in the secondary literature seem to have been often the product of circumstances that, as elaborated in the introduction to this study, led to Mujaddidī and Khālidī realities and literature (as well as broader nineteenth-century paradigms and images) dominating scholars' understanding of this tariqa. As a result of such circumstances it has been common, for example, to associate the Naqshbandī orthodoxy with staunch Sunnism and hostility to Shī'īs, which practitioners presumably adopted in consequence of their distinctive Bakrī spiritual genealogy (one that passes through the Prophet's companion and first caliph, Abū Bakr, rather than through 'Alī, as in most other tariqas).[1] Others have associated the Naqshbandiyya with a stark orthodoxy that precludes central aspects of mystical practice and thought, including the teaching of Ibn al-'Arabī and especially the dissemination of ideas surrounding the notion of *waḥdat al-wujūd* (the "Unity of Being").

It has been especially common to understand the Naqshbandī orthodoxy in political terms or to imagine the Naqshbandiyya as a rigorously orthodox tariqa whose concern with securing the implementation of the *sharī'a* in society has made it prone to public and political involvement or activism. In the words of one scholar, two prominent characteristics have determined the role and impact of this tariqa throughout its history: first, strict adherence to the *sharī'a* and to the Prophet's *sunna*; and second, a "determined effort to influence the life and thought of the ruling classes and to bring the state closer to religion."[2] Other scholars have pointed, in this regard, especially to the involvement of practitioners (most typically of the Mujaddidī and Khālidī periods) in various instances of activism in defense of Muslim rule and the *sharī'a*-based order against non-Muslim rulers, foreign encroachment, or religious syncretism. Modern Turkish observers have emphasized especially Naqshbandīs' opposition to modernizing and secularizing projects of the state (though others have focused on the Naqshbandiyya as a foe of "heterodoxy," at times in collaboration with the state). Hamid Algar, a foremost (and sympathetic) observer, has objected to the reduction of Naqshbandī history to a "simple matter of political militancy." Yet he too has portrayed a tariqa whose "emphatic interest in the *sharī'a* as the fundamental substance of Islam" has "inevitably disposed Naqshbandīs to political action."[3] In a way, this is a mirror image of the negative view advanced by the tariqa's foes: to some, it has been a fanatic enemy of secularism and religious accommodation; to others, a staunch defender against challenges to the *sharī'a*-based order.

An exploration of early Ottoman Naqshbandīs and their understanding of orthodoxy or *sharī'a*-abidance is potentially instructive in several ways, then. First, it provides a window into the ways in which these and other early modern Sufis might configure their mystical pursuits and adherence to the *sharī'a*. Second, it addresses a central aspect of this tariqa during its little-known "middle phase"—after the first dissemination out of Transoxania and before the dramatic proliferation of the "reformed" Mujaddidiyya from India. Third, it is a way of drawing attention to, and developing, this book's thesis that scholars' understanding of the Naqshbandiyya has been unequally and unduly informed by Mujaddidī, Khālidī, and more generally modern, realities and images.

"ACTING WITH STRICTNESS"

Like fellow Naqshbandīs at other times and in other places, early Ottoman Naqshbandīs were apt to identify rigorous adherence to the *sharī'a* and to the Prophet's *sunna* as central to their way. Formulations such as "obeying the *sharī'a*," "unadulterated observance of the *sunna*," "avoiding innovation" (*bid'a*), and "following in the footsteps of the pious ancestors" (*al-salaf al-ṣāliḥ*) were stock phrases in their literature, used time and again in expounding the Naqshbandī way to disciples and in portraying it to the larger society. The image of the Naqshbandiyya as a tariqa rigorously committed to the *sharī'a* became also a public one. As we recall, a sixteenth-century observer, the poet and biographer Laṭīfī, commented that the Naqshbandiyya was a tariqa of unusual appeal among the Ottoman religious hierarchy, and one that was particularly likely to draw those men of religion who sought to relinquish their learned careers and immerse themselves in the devotional life. More unequivocal was Laṭīfī's explanation of what lay behind this affinity. Of all the ways of the Sufi shaykhs, as he put it, it was in particular the Naqshbandī way that was considered by *sharī'a*-abiding men of religion to be "in conformity with the Prophet's practice and the Holy Law" (*mesnūn ve meşrū'*).[4]

Such statements are not sufficient, however, if we are to try to flesh out what fidelity to the *sharī'a* meant or what it entailed in terms of Naqshbandīs' personal observance, devotional practice, involvement in society, view of other Muslims, or attitudes toward various Islamic traditions. For this we must explore more nuanced and potentially instructive language, as well as evidence concerning the behavior of individual Naqshbandī practitioners.

Remaining in the realm of the tariqa's devotional and doctrinal literature, as we will in the present chapter, let us consider, for example, the language of a treatise used by the Istanbul circle of Ḥekīm Çelebi, the *Risāle-i şerīfe-i maǧrūbe fī uṣūl-i ṭā'ife-i 'aliye-i Nakşbendiye*, where the Naqshbandī way is described as committed not simply to following the *sunna*, but also to its revival (*iḥyā'*).[5] Such language—in some ways resembling the rhetoric of the Khālidiyya of the nineteenth century—suggests a public and potentially activist agenda, one that could be understood as summoning Naqshbandīs to participate in upholding the *sharī'a* in the larger society, or in enforcing *shar'ī* behavior on others. This particular formulation is unusual, however. Rather than invoking an agenda of seeking to revive the *sunna*, the Naqshbandī literature of our period was more likely to define fidelity to the *sharī'a* through the formulaic dichotomy of *al-'amal bi'l-'azīma* ("acting with "strictness") versus *al-'amal bi'l-rukhṣa* ("practicing that which is permitted by way of special dispensation").[6] Naqshbandīs were said to be distinguished from other Sufis by patterning their daily behavior on the former and shunning any activity that fell under the latter.[7]

How was the *'amal bi'l-'azīma/'amal bi'l-rukhṣa* dichotomy understood and how can it help illuminate Naqshbandīs' construction of orthodoxy? For one, it was apparently applied to matters of behavior, not to questions of mystical journeying or doctrine. Naqshbandīs of our period did not view the *'amal bi'l-'azīma* as a commitment that obliged them to shun any mystical doctrine or concept, and they were comfortable subscribing to a host of ideas and beliefs that drew the ire of some critics, including the mystical vision advanced in the teachings of Ibn al-'Arabī, the notion of a cosmic hierarchy of the "friends of God" (*awliyā'*), and the belief in Sufis' access to the paradigmatic mystical guide, Khiḍr, or to the spirits (or spiritual presence, *rūḥāniyya*, in the singular) of deceased Sufi masters.

Secondly, the *'amal bi'l-'azīma* versus *'amal bi'l-rukhṣa* dichotomy was typically framed as an issue of private behavior, even though potentially it could be understood in public terms as well. As an example of the latter we may note one Naqshbandī who described the agenda of Meḥmed Birgili (in time the intellectual mentor of the puritanical Ḳaḍizādeli movement) as a summons to *'azīma* in an environment where people were routinely allowing themselves to fall into *rukhṣa*.[8] But generally *'azīma* emerges from our sources as having a rather different sense—that of the rigorous and punctual observance of *shar'ī* duties by the individual Naqshbandī practitioners. Aḥmad Ṣādiq Ṭāshkandī taught that the Naqshbandī mystical quest began with following the Qur'ān and the *sunna* in the sense of observing with "genuine strictness" (*ṣidq al-'azīma*) the obligations of prayer, ritual purity, pilgrimage, and almsgiving, as well as the rest of the *farā'iḍ* (prescribed religious duties) and examples of the Prophet.[9] Other authors emphasized especially the proper and punctual performance of the five daily prayers, along with the Naqshbandī practitioners' duty to preserve continuously a state of ritual purity.[10] Such religious obligations were seen as the foundation for progress on the Naqshbandī mystical path. On their scrupulous and punctual observance there could be no compromise.

Beyond marking a commitment to the strict and punctual observance of individual religious duties, the *'azīma* versus *rukhṣa* dichotomy came to be associated with the Naqshbandī devotional regimen, and in particular with the silent mode of *dhikr*. The connection was made by one of the tariqa's foremost foundational stories (appearing in the *Rashaḥāt-i 'ayn al-ḥayāt* and still older sources), which several Ottoman sources later reproduced and disseminated. According to this account, Bahā' al-Dīn was a disciple of the Bukharan Khwājagānī master Amīr Kulāl, whose circle practiced a vocal form of the *dhikr*. Then Bahā' al-Dīn adopted a silent form of recollection and began to dissociate himself from his master's vocal *dhikr* after he had been instructed by the spirit of 'Abd al-Khāliq Ghujduvānī to follow the *'amal bi'l-'azīma*.[11] What this story established and disseminated, then, was the notion that the Naqshbandī devotional regimen was set apart from those of other tariqas by shunning not only behavior that was expressly forbidden, but also those practices—common among many other Sufis—that were permitted only by way of dispensation (*rukhṣa*). Thus, devotional practice was made to be the center of the Naqshbandī commitment to the *'amal bi'l-'azīma*. It was primarily through its distinctive devotional regimen that the Naqshbandiyya became the tariqa of *'amal bi'l-'azīma* and by extension that of rigorous fidelity to the *sharī'a*.

SOBRIETY IN DEVOTIONAL PRACTICE

There were two sides—one positive and one negative—to the Naqshbandī devotional regimen as it emerges from tariqa literature of our period. The positive side consisted of a series of sober and interiorized techniques that enabled practitioners to seek God continuously, in an introverted and inconspicuous manner, and while outwardly immersed in society. On the negative side, Naqshbandīs may be said to have defined themselves in opposition to other Sufis and a number of their common practices, which they shunned—though did not prohibit—as ostentatious, unduly emotive, incompatible with rigorous observance of the *sharī'a*, or otherwise inferior.

Observers everywhere have pointed to the silent method of *dhikr* (the quintessential Sufi ritual of repeating the Divine Names or related formulas in order to fill one's consciousness with the "remembrance" of God) as the hallmark of the Naqshbandī devotional practice. In this view, it is clearly silent *dhikr* that sets apart this tariqa from its counterparts, with their acceptance of vocal and emotive communal *dhikr* rituals, including *samā'* ceremonies involving musical accompaniment and dance.[12] From the period examined here we can mention three individuals—Ṣarı 'Abdullāh Efendi, Nev'īzāde 'Aṭā'ī, and Evliyā Çelebi—who all used the yardstick of silent versus vocal *dhikr* to distinguish between two categories of Ottoman tariqas, with the Naqshbandiyya and its silent *dhikr* on one side and the Khalwatiyya and its vocal one on the other.[13]

The Naqshbandī literature makes it evident that there was more to the silent *dhikr* (*al-dhikr al-khafī*, literally "hidden") than the shunning of singing, musical accompaniment, dance, and bodily movements. In its formula, it consisted of what Naqshbandīs called "negation and affirmation" (*nafy wa-ithbāt*)—that is, the phrase "There is no god but God, Muḥammad is the Messenger of God" (*lā ilāh illā Allāh Muḥammad rasūl Allāh*). Especially valued was the recitation *Muḥammad rasūl Allāh* (prized as a form of defense against religious syncretism by some other Sufis), which Naqshbandīs held to be a legacy from the Prophet's companion and their spiritual ancestor, Abū Bakr.[14] In its mode of performance, too, the silent *dhikr* entailed more than the shunning of musical accompaniment or dance. It involved a distinct method of holding the breath (*ḥabs al-nafas*). And it was to be enunciated in the heart, with the tongue attached to the roof of the mouth, so that the recitation would be inaudible and imperceptible even to a person standing next to the reciter.[15] Furthermore, rather than simply a silent or inaudible recitation, this was to be an individual, interiorized, and continuous technique.[16]

This is not to say that Naqshbandīs gave up communal *dhikr*. Even if we lack actual descriptions of such ceremonies—probably because travelers and other observers found little in this sober and interiorized technique to merit attention—we can infer their existence from casual references. Tāj al-Dīn al-'Uthmānī mentioned a Naqshbandī *dhikr* performed in a group (*dhikr bi'l-khalqa*), and Ḥasan Ibn al-'Ujaymī told of wondrous happenings that occurred in Mecca's Great Mosque once when Aḥmad Ibn 'Allān was leading one of his early-morning sessions of silent *dhikr*.[17] Rather, the point is that the Naqshbandī adepts were called upon to perform the *dhikr* at all times, "whether coming or going, standing or sitting, speaking or listening, going to bed or rising up," and not least "when . . . in the marketplace." What they strove to achieve was a continuous state of recollection (*dawām al-dhikr*) or, in another formulation, the transformation of the *dhikr* into a natural disposition (*malaka*) that even the reciter's heart would cease to sense, so as to become oblivious of anything that was not God, including the very act of remembrance.[18]

While Naqshbandī authors routinely elaborated and emphasized the importance of the silent *dhikr*, in the manuals this method was not made to be the central element, let alone the sine qua non of the tariqa's devotional regimen; instead, it was cast as part of a triad of spiritual techniques that were all prized for their interiorized character and all envisioned as ideally turning into "natural dispositions." The first was the method called *murāqaba* (or sometimes *tawajjuh*), also a kind of *dhikr* in which a practitioner strove to "fix in the heart the meaning of the Name of the Essence [Allāh]" as a means of progressing toward "witnessing" the divine power.[19] The second was the *rābiṭa* (or *rābiṭa-i pīr*), a technique of fixing in the imagination the visual form (*ṣūra*) of one's shaykh, which would then operate as a channel for the transmission of divine energy or effulgence (*fayḍ*). The third was the silent *dhikr* itself.

Some authors celebrated especially the *murāqaba* for its superior effectiveness in leading to progress on the mystical path,[20] while for others it was the *rābiṭa* that offered Naqshbandīs the most excellent means of mystical advancement. The latter opinion is particularly interesting both because of the potential for abuse inherent in a technique that made one's shaykh so utterly indispensable, and because of the view that only nineteenth-century Khālidīs elevated the *rābiṭa* to a particularly prized, or even distinct, spiritual technique.[21] In his thorough examination of the *rābiṭa* of nineteenth-century Khālidīs, Abu-Manneh suggests that "among the hard core orthodox Muslims" the legitimacy of this practice was never accepted; what 'Ubaydullāh Aḥrār meant by the term *rābiṭa* was not a distinct spiritual technique but rather a facet of *ṣuḥba* (the companionship and bond between shaykh and disciple that was the basis of spiritual guidance in the Naqshbandī way).[22] Indeed, nineteenth-century Naqshbandīs argued heatedly over the *rābiṭa*, largely, it appears, as a result of the recasting that Shaykh Khālid introduced by decreeing that not only his own disciples but also later spiritual descendants of his line were to link in *rābiṭa* with his own visual form.[23] Others had raised reservations about this technique even before the changes decreed by Shaykh Khālid, however. The Damascene 'Abd al-Gahnī al-Nābulusī had warned a century earlier that a novice practitioner of the *rābiṭa* might fall into imagining the visualized form of the shaykh as though it was his Lord. To prevent any ambiguity about the magnitude of such offense, he made it clear that it would constitute nothing but idolatry (*kufr*).[24]

Reverting to what early Ottoman Naqshbandīs made of the *rābiṭa*, we may begin with the following description by Muṣṭafā al-Ṣādiqī:

> *Rābiṭa* requires that the practitioner attach himself in obedient service (*khidma*) to a shaykh who has reached [the station of witnessing], and that he keep the shaykh's company (*ṣuḥba*) continually, fill himself with utmost attentiveness to him, cement his love for him in his heart, and [learn to] preserve the shaykh's visual form (*ṣūra*) in his imagination. Thus is generated between them such bond and union that the emanation of divine energy (*fayḍ*) reaching the shaykh can pour forth to the disciple without a need for a great deal of ascetic exercises (*mujāhada wa-ijtihād*). When the *rābiṭa* occurs and [the practitioner] feels its effect in his heart, he should strive to preserve it. Whenever there is a slackening of that [effect] he should return to companionship with the shaykh, time after time, until the effect returns to him and becomes a natural disposition (*malaka*).[25]

For Ṣādiqī the *rābiṭa* was clearly a distinct spiritual technique (described here from the perspective of the disciple, but in fact reciprocal). Moreover, like several other of his colleagues, he proclaimed it superior to any other method available to Naqshbandīs. Granted, the *rābiṭa* was cast as particularly precious or rare, both because it was difficult to perform and because as the apex of *ṣuḥba* it could not but depend on the availability of superior shaykhs, whose likes were said to have become "rarer than red sulphur." For this reason, even enthusiasts for this technique called on every Naqshbandī disciple to become adept at least in one other spiritual method, no matter whether it was the silent *dhikr* or the *murāqaba*. But rather than implying that the *rābiṭa* was dispensable, let alone suspect, this caveat was meant to underscore its very superiority. For proponents it was the most effective or "closest" of all the spiritual methods (*aqrab ṭuruq al-wuṣūl*). It might even enable shaykhs to lead their disciples to "witnessing" in one *ṣuḥba* (here probably in the sense of "session"); and it was the method that allowed practitioners to dispense with the rigorous austerities or ascetic exercises known generically as *mujāhadāt* and *riyāḍāt*, which were so common in other tariqas, but toward which Naqshbandīs were at best ambivalent.

Much as this may seem paradoxical if one is informed by the controversies that surrounded the *rābiṭa* in the nineteenth century, the earlier manuals not only deemed this technique "superior," but also celebrated it as one of the very pillars of the Naqshbandī claim to *sharī'a*-abiding sobriety. Along with the silent *dhikr* and the *murāqaba*, the *rābiṭa* itself was cast as an instrument of the tariqa's sobriety, both by dint of its interiorized character and because it enabled practitioners to dispense with the superfluous and inferior *mujāhadāt*.[26]

On the negative side, the Naqshbandī devotional regimen was distinguished by shunning more than prohibiting. The vocal *dhikr* was portrayed as inferior, rather than banned. The insistence of the *Tüḥfet eṭ-ṭālibīn* that Naqshbandīs held only the silent *dhikr* acceptable, or that vocal recollection simply had "no benefit," was unusually blunt.[27] Other authors might argue that Naqshbandīs adopted the silent *dhikr* because it was the "original way" (*al-ṭarīq al-aṣlī*), or the method most conducive to the mystic's goal of attaining "presence with God" (*ḥuḍūr*), or the *dhikr* most consistent with the *'amal bi'l-'azīma*.[28] Another way of casting the silent *dhikr* as the best and quintessential Naqshbandī method was to invoke one or another of three paradigmatic stories from the history of the Naqshbandī *silsila*. The first story related how the Prophet Muḥammad, while hiding in a cave during the emigration to Medina, taught the silent *dhikr* to his companion Abū Bakr in a dramatic moment that was graced by the presence of God.[29] The second described how Khiḍr, the paradigmatic spiritual guide of Qur'ān 18: 60–82, instructed the Khwājagānī master 'Abd al-Khāliq Ghujduvānī to recite the *dhikr* silently while submerged in water.[30] The third was the account of how, having been instructed by the spirit of Ghujduvānī to pursue the *'amal bi'l-'azīma*, Bahā' al-Dīn Naqshband abandoned the vocal *dhikr* that had been the norm among the Khwājagān for five generations and reestablished instead the silent *dhikr* of Ghujduvānī, and by implication the Naqshbandī tradition.[31] By casting the silent method of recollection as the "original" form of *dhikr* taught by the Prophet and renewed by Khiḍr, and by reminding practitioners that it was through the adoption (or readoption) of this method that Bahā' al-Dīn established the Naqshbandī way out of the Ṭarīqat-i Khwājagān, these stories made a double point: first, they portrayed the silent *dhikr* as the method of recollection most consistent with rigorous adherence to the *sharī'a*; second, they emphasized that it was the Naqshbandī *dhikr* par excellence, at least by dint of its ancient and illustrious pedigree.

Some Naqshbandī groups did practice vocal methods of recollection, either alone or along with the silent *dhikr*. Especially known for such ceremonies were the seventeenth-century Urmavī Naqshbandīs of Kurdistan, whom we have seen inheriting a vocal and dramatic form of "saw *dhikr*" from a spiritual ancestor who had been affiliated with other Sufi traditions. Evliyā Çelebi witnessed this dramatic *dhikr* on his visit to the Urmavī *tekke* of Diyarbakır in 1065/1655, and, as mentioned, he described it as inducing in practitioners a state of "intoxication and bewilderment."[32]

Other Naqshbandīs ventured to defend the vocal *dhikr* against critics. We recall that the seventeenth-century Medinese shaykh Ibrāhīm al-Kūrānī entered into an argument about this issue with a prominent Ottoman visitor known for his opposition to music and vocal *dhikr* ceremonies (probably the Ḳāḍīzādeli leader Meḥmed Vānī Efendi).[33] Kūrānī also produced two treatises in defense of the vocal method, the *Nashr al-zahr fī'l-dhikr bi'l-jahr* and the *Itḥāf al-munīb al-awwāh bi-faḍl al-jahr bi-dhikr Allāh*. In the *Itḥāf*, written in response to Transoxanian foes of vocal recollection, he marshaled numerous Qur'ānic verses and Prophetic traditions to prove that this method was licit. Moreover, Kūrānī made the point that Shāfi'īs—most of his own disciples—held the vocal *dhikr* superior. For followers of this legal school, vocal rather than silent *dhikr* was the "original" method and indeed a "key to the religion of Islam."[34]

In Damascus the prolific scholar 'Abd al-Ghanī al-Nābulusī took up the issue of music in his *Iḍāḥ al-dalālāt fī samā' al-ālāt*—according to a recent study also in response to critics associated with the Ḳāḍīzādeli movement.[35] In the *Iḍāḥ*, Nābulusī pointed out that all singing and musical accompaniment, whether by Sufis or other Muslims, was licit, if only by special dispensation (*rukhṣa*). Music was prohibited only when it positively distracted listeners from the recollection of God or from the observance of religious duties.[36] Finally, a student of Kūrānī by the name Ibn al-Mīmī held the silent method of recollection undeniably superior and the one that Naqshbandīs specifically adopted; yet in view of the high emotions that apparently continued to surround controversies about the *dhikr*, and perhaps because of the insistence or audacity of the opposition (be it Ḳāḍīzādeli or other), Ibn al-Mīmī too found it necessary to challenge the opponents of vocal *dhikr*. In a treatise devoted to the Naqshbandī way, he insisted that those who called for eliminating the vocal method were nothing but "ossified," "ignorant," and "pigheaded."[37]

Even more qualified was the Naqshbandī shunning of the rigorous austerities or ascetic exercises known as *mujāhadāt*—fasting, night vigils, and the practice of ritual seclusion in a cell. Some shaykhs clearly performed such exercises as part of their own spiritual training, or taught them to disciples. Aḥmad Ṣādiq Ṭāshkandī performed *mujāhadāt* during his training in Transoxania before coming to Istanbul, as had Maḥmūd Urmavī before he was authorized to train disciples.[38] A manual elaborating the devotional practice of the Urmavīs placed considerable emphasis on regulated fasting during certain periods of the year.[39] 'Abdullāh Ilāhī spent nine consecutive periods of *arba'īn* or *chilla*, the forty-day ritual seclusion, at the tomb of Bahā' al-Dīn Naqshband, and recommended in his *Meslek eṭ-ṭālibīn* ascetic exercises, ritual seclusion, fasting, and a "relinquishing of ties" (*tark al-'alā'iḳ*), which he suggested could be achieved by moving constantly from town to town.[40] The way of Ilāhī's successor, Aḥmad Bukhārī, included "retreat from people (*'üzlet 'an'il-anām*), eating and talking exiguously, performing night vigils, and fasting during the day."[41] The Meccan Tāj al-Dīn al-'Uthmānī recommended that disciples perform ritual seclusion in preparation for the *dhikr* and the *murāqaba*, or whenever they experienced a disruption (*tafriqa*) of their mystical journey.[42]

At the same time, we find tariqa literature portraying Naqshbandīs as uniquely privileged in that they were able to dispense with ascetic exercises, and specifically with the *khalwa* in its double sense of ritual seclusion in a cell and a more general ascetic withdrawal from society.[43] Muṣṭafā al-Ṣādiqī suggested that the whole complex of ascetic exercises was made unnecessary by the method of *rābiṭa*, which enabled a Naqshbandī disciple to concentrate instead on the visual form of the shaykh as a vehicle for the transmission of divine emanation.[44] As we have seen in an earlier chapter, Tāj al-Dīn al-'Uthmānī, and more explicitly his biographer Maḥmūd b. Ashraf al-Ḥusaynī, offered a somewhat different explanation. In this view, Naqshbandīs were set apart from other Sufis by beginning their mystical journey with "purifying the heart" (*taṣfiyat al-qalb*) rather than "cleansing" or "breaking" the human soul (*tazkiyat* or *inkisār al-nafs*) through exercises of self-mortification. Once they reached the distinctly superior level of "purifying the heart," they were able to attain quickly and without fail, by way of spontaneous divine attraction (*jadhba*), the less advanced "cleansing of the soul" that for other Sufis even years of ascetic exercises would not guarantee. According to Tāj al-Dīn's biographer, it was this reversal of the normal order of the mystical journey that was implied in the adage *al-nihāya fi'l-bidāya*, "the end [of other Sufis' mystical journey] is [encapsulated] in the beginning [of ours]," which Naqshbandīs often invoked in asserting the superiority of their tariqa.[45]

Other authors expressed their reservations by invoking the old refrains (known from the early Naqshbandī literature of Transoxania) of "*khalwa* is fame and fame is evil" (*al-khalwa shuhra wa'l-shuhra āfa*), or "ours is a tariqa of *ṣuḥba*, not *khalwa*." These were meant to convey the sense that *khalwa* (in its double meaning) was suspect, was inconsistent with the Naqshbandī way, or was superfluous.[46] Yet especially the last refrain was more than simply a rejection of either ritual seclusion in a cell or the more general ascetic withdrawal from society. Rather, it went to the very heart of the unique Naqshbandī way of seeking God—what the manuals called, after 'Abd al-Khāliq Ghujduvānī, *khalvat dar anjuman*, that is, "solitude within society" or seeking God while immersed in society. Naqshbandīs taught that mastering the interiorized techniques of silent *dhikr*, *murāqaba*, and *rābiṭa*, ideally to the point of turning them into a "natural disposition," would enable practitioners to embark on seeking God continuously, inconspicuously, and in the thick of society, without any need for ascetic withdrawal from the world or for the extroverted and inferior rituals of other Sufis.[47] A "solitude within society" of sorts was, of course, the common reality for Ottoman Sufis of diverse affiliations, who pursued their devotional regimens while living among the larger community, raising families, and being engaged in gainful occupations. But Naqshbandīs made of the continuous seeking of God "within society" a deliberate and superior endeavor.[48] Moreover, they claimed that unlike other Sufi ways, with their potentially distracting devotional practices, the Naqshbandī way provided the uniquely sober and interiorized techniques that made this endeavor feasible and effective.

The Naqshbandī ambivalence toward ascetic exercises and the whole shunning of Sufi practices that Naqshbandīs cast as unduly emotive, ostentatious, inferior, or inconsistent with rigorous observance of the *sharī'a* constituted the other side of their insistence on the centrality of the three interiorized techniques of silent *dhikr*, *murāqaba*, and *rābiṭa*. All of these were aspects of the casting of this tariqa, via its devotional regimen, as uniquely sober and superior—both in its fidelity to the *sharī'a* and as a way of mystical progress.

COMMUNICATING WITH THE "FRIENDS OF GOD"

Neither fidelity to the *sharī'a* nor insistence on devotional sobriety turned the early Ottoman Naqshbandiyya into a demysticized, despiritualized, or "starkly orthodox" tariqa, as nineteenth-century-based paradigms might suggest.[49] Naqshbandīs prided themselves on both devotional sobriety and mystical excellence, which they viewed as not only compatible but also as very much intertwined.[50] As we will see in the two following sections, they understood mystical journeying and excellence to include various forms of interaction between the living and the "world of the unseen." They also viewed as an integral part of their mystical quest their taste for and devotion to the study and dissemination of the enormously influential, if controversial, mystical teachings of Muḥyī al-Dīn Ibn al-'Arabī.

As was common among Sufis of all persuasions as well as the larger society of the time, Ottoman Naqshbandīs took for granted the ability of humans to interact with the "world of the unseen" (*'ālam al-ghayb*). They knew of many individuals who communed with the inhabitants of that world—prophets, the "friends of God," the paradigmatic mystical guide Khiḍr, deceased tariqa masters—via the latter's spiritual presence (*rūḥāniyya*), and routinely described these "friends of God" intervening when their human interlocutors were in danger, dispatching them on missions, or conferring on them guidance, mystical insights, or formal Sufi initiations. Communication with the "world of the unseen" and its inhabitants might occur during sleep or in a state of wakefulness. Often it was experienced as an "unsolicited gift" (*fatḥ*, pl. *futūḥ*) bestowed by divine grace, but Naqshbandīs also learned from no other than their eponym that the more advanced among them could evoke or bring forth such contacts through intense spiritual concentration.[51]

The issue might be one of physical closeness. Naqshbandīs shared a common belief that the spiritual presence of the "friend of God" (*walī*) was most accessible at his tomb, hence their tradition of paying visits to the tombs of their tariqa's spiritual masters.[52] 'Abdullāh Ilāhī spent nine consecutive periods of forty days communing with the spiritual presence of Bahā' al-Dīn Naqshband at his tomb in Bukhara,[53] and Aḥmad Ibn 'Allān is said to have had the spirit of Bahā' al-Dīn revealed to him as an "unsolicited gift" after merely seven days of spiritual training under Tāj al-Dīn al-'Uthmānī.[54] Of Zakariyā al-Bihārī, an Indian initiated in Mecca into the line of 'Ubaydullāh Aḥrār, it was said that he routinely communed with the Prophet "in wakefulness."[55] Aḥmad Ṣādiq Ṭāshkandī traveled from his native Transoxania all the way to the Ottoman capital in response to a "command from the world of the unseen" to spread the tariqa far and wide.[56] Years later, during a sojourn in Damascus on his return from the pilgrimage of 991/1583, Aḥmad Ṣādiq had another dramatic encounter with that world. As his disciple and biographer has it, he had just presided over a ceremonial recital in celebration of the Prophet's birthday near the tomb of the Prophet Yaḥyā in the Umayyad Mosque when he was overtaken by a powerful "spiritual state" (*ḥāl*). At his side the tomb itself went into several violent convulsions, its locked door falling open and almost breaking. The shaykh was picked up and carried home by his bewildered disciples, who later found out that the prophet Yaḥyā had been revealed to him and had bestowed on him "a precious robe, a large turban and . . . a glistening cup."[57]

Naqshbandīs took special pride in the practice of nonphysical Uwaysī transmission (so called after the Yemenite contemporary of the Prophet, Uways al-Qaranī), in which the spiritual presence of a deceased master, or the figure of Khiḍr, or the Prophet himself conferred initiations on living seekers: Bahā' al-Dīn and before him 'Abd al-Khāliq Ghujduvanī were celebrated as the recipients of such initiations.[58] Generally it was agreed that an Uwaysī initiation was no substitute for one by a living shaykh even when the Uwaysī master was most exalted. Aḥmad Ṣādiq Ṭāshkandī was an Uwaysī by dint of initiations that he had received from the spirits of the *awliyā'* before he was born, but in time he proceeded to have a live shaykh initiation with a spiritual descendant of 'Ubaydullāh Aḥrār, Makhdūm-i A'ẓam Aḥmad Kāsānī.[59] The spiritual master of Tāj al-Dīn al-'Uthmānī, Muḥammad al-Bāqī, was initiated in the Uwaysī way by the spiritual presence of Aḥrār, then proceeded to seek a link "in the outward way" (*bi-ḥasb al-ẓāhir*) from Khwāja Imkanagī.[60] Yet, the Uwaysī method was revered as extremely meaningful, and it featured prominently in the sacred history of the tariqa.

Two early links in the Naqshbandī *silsila*, Abū Ḥasan al-Kharaqānī (d. 425/1034) and Abū Yazīd Bisṭāmī (d. 261/875), were celebrated as Uwaysīs, Kharaqānī having been initiated by the spiritual presence of Bisṭāmī, and Bisṭāmī by that of Ja'far al-Ṣādiq (d. 148/765).[61] Even more central to the *silsila*, and to the construction of the Naqshbandī identity, were two later Uwaysī encounters: that in which 'Abd al-Khāliq Ghujduvānī received the silent *dhikr* from Khiḍr, and a second one in which Bahā' al-Dīn Naqshband was instructed by the spiritual presence of Ghujduvānī to follow the principle of "acting with strictness," upon which he adopted the silent *dhikr*.[62] We have seen before how critical these two stories were to practitioners' understanding of the manner in which the Naqshbandiyya emerged out of the Ṭarīqat-i Khwājagān and gained its distinctive character. What is important in the present context is how they conferred legitimacy and importance on the concept and practice of Uwaysī transmission: both Ghujduvānī and Bahā' al-Dīn went through live shaykh initiations into the Ṭarīqat-i Khwājagān, the first with Yūsuf Hamadānī and the second with Amīr Kulāl. But in each of the two cases, it was the Uwaysī transmission that was cast as most definitive, both for the recipient's own spiritual training and for the development of the Naqshbandī identity and tradition.

There was a certain similarity between Naqshbandīs' view of the Uwaysī mode of transmission and their view of the *rābiṭa*, the technique of fixing the visual form of the shaykh in the imagination as a vehicle for the flow of divine energy, which also involved a nonphysical form of spiritual transmission.[63] Naqshbandīs might acknowledge that such forms of spiritual transmission were difficult to master, or risky, or rare; and they might suggest that disciples bolster them by mastering additional, less extravagant techniques. It will be recalled that 'Abd al-Ghanī al-Nābulusī was concerned that a novice practitioner of the *rābiṭa* might fall into the idolatry of imagining the visualized form of the shaykh as though this was his Lord.[64] With regard to the Uwaysī mode, Tāj al-Dīn al-'Uthmānī argued on the authority of his spiritual master, Muḥammad al-Bāqī, that while Uwaysī transmissions were both possible and acceptable, they did not exempt one from live shaykh initiation, since a *dhikr* acquired without training and authorization by a living shaykh did not confer *baraka* on the practitioner.[65] Still, the upshot of such statements was not that these forms of spiritual transmission were suspect, or inconsistent with the *sharī'a*, or better avoided. Rather, it was that they were highly prized and reserved for advanced Sufis, as Naqshbandīs believed themselves to be. As with the *rābiṭa*, which a number of authors considered the "closest" of all spiritual methods or the most conducive to mystical progress, the Uwaysi mode, too, was seen as a mark of superiority.

Only one aspect of the world of the *awliyā'*—the ability to perform the "wondrous deeds" or "miracles" known as *khawāriq* or *karāmāt*—elicited ambivalence from our sources. Granted, we hear of many Naqshbandīs performing *karāmāt*. When the body of Aḥmad Bukhārī was lowered into his tomb in Istanbul, he is said to have opened his eyes several times, then turned himself to the right, so as to face the *qibla*, the direction of the Ka'ba in Mecca to which Muslims turn in prayer.[66] Saçlı Muṣṭafā Dede of Istanbul, who instead of water drank a glass of pomegranate juice daily, was celebrated for such purity of body that in a lifetime spanning over eighty years he never had to wash himself.[67] Of Tāj al-Dīn al-'Uthmānī we are told that he could make himself invisible to those surrounding him and that once he sent forth a ray of light that filled a bare pomegranate tree with leaves and fruit, and on another occasion he had his daughter recover from illness by making her drink the water in which he had washed his feet.[68] Tāj al-Dīn's *khalīfa*, Aḥmad Ibn 'Allān, used to conduct early-morning sessions of Qur'ān-reading and silent *dhikr* at Mecca's Great Mosque, just across from the Ka'ba's door. A disciple recounted that once he was wondering why the shaykh did not include in the ritual a circumambulation of the Ka'ba (*ṭawāf*), at which point the Ka'ba itself "advanced from its place and [instead] circumambulated the shaykh."[69]

Conceptually, the *karāmāt* were understood as gifts of divine energy bestowed by God on his "friends," as the literal meaning of *karāma*, "generosity," suggests. But unlike the *rābiṭa*, or Uwaysī transmissions, or the practice of visiting spiritual masters at their tombs, they did not become a prized aspect of Naqshbandī spirituality, and might even be shunned, if discreetly. Tāj al-Dīn, for all his celebrated excellence in such deeds, declared that performing them was not indispensable for a "friend of God" (*walī*). Instead, the real sign of the latter was the quality of being "turned away" (*munṣaraf*) from anything that was not God.[70] Tāj al-Dīn's disciple, Ibn al-Mīmī, made the point in his *naẓm al-sumūṭ al-zabrajiyya* that one who performed *karāmāt* while neglecting the *sunna* or the observance of religious duties was nothing but "an enchanter and liar."[71] Granted, even this formulation shied away from criticizing the *karāmāt* as such. Still, the bluntness of Ibn al-Mīmī's last words made the Naqshbandī ambivalence toward this aspect of the world of the "friends of God" all too clear.

TEACHING IBN AL-'ARABĪ

No lingering criticism could deter Naqshbandīs of our period from studying and disseminating the mystical teachings of the *shaykh al-akbar* (the "Greatest Master"), as Ibn al-'Arabī had come to be known to his admirers. Despite harsh criticism from some quarters, by the time the Naqshbandiyya was being introduced into the Ottoman lands in the second half of the fifteenth century, Ibn al-'Arabī had become tremendously influential in Ottoman society (among mystical writers, he was matched only by Jalāl al-Dīn Rūmī). Offering mystical insights and perceptions that were freshly articulated yet steeped in the Islamic mystical and intellectual tradition, as well as a massive technical vocabulary that had become virtually indispensable for engaging in any mystical discourse, his teachings not only permeated mysticism and poetry but were taught in madrasas and influenced the main body of scholarship.[72] Many viewed him as a "patron saint" of the Ottoman dynasty due to the (probably spurious) *Al-Shajara al-nu'māniyya fī'l-dawla al-Uthmāniyya* in which he allegedly predicted the rise of the Ottomans and their conquest of the Arab lands.[73] He was given an indubitable official recognition when upon the Ottoman conquest of Damascus in 922/1516, the *ḳāżī'asker* of Anatolia and future *şeyhülislām* Kemālpaşazāde issued a *fatwā* exonerating him, and Sultan Selīm ordered the rebuilding of the mystic's tomb in Ṣāliḥiyya and the construction of a nearby mosque complex carrying the sultan's name.[74]

Going back to the virulent attacks of the Ḥanbalī jurist and theologian Aḥmad Ibn Taymiyya in the early fourteenth century, there was a countercurrent of detractors who accused Ibn al-'Arabī of propagating monistic ideas highly threatening to the *sharī'a*. Ibn Taymiyya criticized him especially for authoring the doctrine of *waḥdat al-wujūd* (the "Unity of Being"), which in his eyes asserted nothing but the identity of God and creation. Granted, recent scholarship has dismissed the notion of Ibn al-'Arabī as the author of a "new" doctrine; according to William Chittick he did not use the term *waḥdat al-wujūd* to designate a distinct position—though his writings marked "Ṣūfism's massive entry into the theoretical discussions of *wujūd* that before him had been the almost exclusive preserve of the philosophers and [speculative theologians]". Still, both the association and accusations made by Ibn Taymiyya took hold. Critics denounced the *waḥdat al-wujūd* as a reprehensible innovation (*bid'a*) and even heresy, accusing Ibn al-'Arabī of propagating a monism that contravened Islam's understanding of the transcendence of God and of leading followers to believe that attaining a superior mystical understanding would exempt them from observance of the Holy Law.[75] Among sixteenth-century Ottoman refutations one may mention the *Ni'mat al-dharī'a fī nuṣrat al-sharī'a* of Ibrāhīm al-Ḥalabī[76] and a *fatwā* of the *şeyhülislām* Ebüssu'ūd Efendi that was invoked in the execution of the Khalwatī shaykh Muḥyiddīn Ḳaramānī.[77] Later pronouncements were more often of an explanatory or apologetic nature. But there were renewed attacks, including the particularly hard-hitting one that the puritanical Ḳāḍīzādeli movement launched in the seventeenth century.

Continuing a trend that their Central Asian spiritual ancestors had begun, Ottoman Naqshbandīs defied the criticism. They became some of the very transmitters of that greater interest in Ibn al-'Arabī that had developed within Persian, earlier than in Arab, or Ottoman, Sufism.[78] In turn, their reputation as the devoted students and disseminators of his teachings became an integral part of their appeal. It has been suggested that what propelled Sultan Meḥmed II to build the first Naqshbandī *tekke* of the capital for Isḥaq Bukhārī-i Hindī was precisely the association of Naqshbandī shaykhs and their Central Asian mentors with expertise in the *waḥdat al-wujūd*.[79] 'Abdullāh Ilāhī has been described as a principal propagator of the *waḥdat al-wujūd* in Anatolia and the Balkans through his teaching in Istanbul and Yenice-i Vardar and through his extensive use of terminology and concepts derived from Ibn al-'Arabī in a series of works of prose and poetry.[80] Muḥyiddīn Halīfe, a native of the Black Sea region and in time the prayer leader of the Sultan Murād Mosque of Bursa, distinguished himself as an expert on the *Fuṣūṣ al-ḥikam*.[81] And Bābā Ni'matullāh b. Maḥmūd Nakhchivānī, a Naqshbandī from the Caucasus who settled in Akşehir in Central Anatolia, wrote a commentary on the *Fuṣūṣ* and a treatise on *waḥdat al-wujūd* along with a Qur'ānic exegesis, the *al-Fawātiḥ al-ilāhiyya wa'l-mafātiḥ al-ghaybiyya*, through which he disseminated numerous concepts and terms developed by the "Greatest Master."[82]

The same holds true for Naqshbandīs in seventeenth-century Arabia. Tāj al-Dīn al-'Uthmānī held reading sessions in the *Fuṣūṣ*, even though he opposed the reading of all mystical literature (the *kutub al-qawm*) by the uninitiated.[83] One of those who read Ibn al-'Arabī with him was the Damascus-born Muḥammad Mīrzā al-Surūjī.[84] The teaching and defending of Ibn al-'Arabī became even more distinctive of the Medinese Naqshbandī line of Aḥmad al-Qushāshī and Ibrāhīm al-Kūrānī.[85] Qushāshī gained a reputation as his generation's "foremost proponent" (*imām al-qā'ilīn*) of the *waḥdat al-wujūd*,[86] and Kūrānī argued with critics of Ibn al-'Arabī in several polemical treatises and set out to prove that his teachings were consistent with the Holy Law and did not encourage antinomian behavior.[87] In Damascus, only a short time later, 'Abd al-Ghanī al-Nābulusī emerged as another major transmitter, exponent, and defender of Ibn al-'Arabī's Sufism. As a recent study has shown, Nābulusī was not simply the transmitter of an intellectual corpus. No less significantly, he was a passionate devotee of Ibn al-'Arabī the saint—dreaming of him frequently, "drawing upon [his] words" at all times, and even imagining himself to be the shaykh's son or "suckling child."[88]

For a tariqa so taken with its claim to superiority, part of the allure of Ibn al-'Arabī must have been the very extravagance and elusiveness of his teachings and the belief that they were intelligible only to advanced seekers. But Naqshbandīs of our period also insisted that engaging with his thought was entirely consonant with fidelity to the *sharī'a*—in this they could rely on weighty Central Asian Naqshbandī authorities, from 'Ubaydullāh Aḥrār, to 'Abd al-Raḥmān Jāmī, to Muḥammad Pārsā. Aḥrār was known as an expert on Ibn al-'Arabī, and Jāmī not only belonged to a Naqshbandī circle in late-Tīmūrid Herat in which studying the *waḥdat al-wujūd* was a common pursuit,[89] but also defended the mystic in public debates and wrote a number of Persian and Arabic commentaries devoted to the *Fuṣūṣ* and related literature. Much of Jāmī's poetry, too, was infused with "Akbarian" ideas, concepts, and terminology, so much so that Algar views him as perhaps the "most eminent and influential representative" of the Ibn al-'Arabī school, at least in the Persian-speaking world.[90] In addition, it may be that an even earlier Naqshbandī enthusiast for the *shaykh al-akbar* was Bahā' al-Dīn's *khalīfa* Muḥammad Pārsā, who compared the *Fuṣūṣ* and the *Futūḥāt al-makkiyya* to a "soul" and "heart" whose study would encourage observance of the Prophet's *sunna.* Whether Pārsā was also the author of a commentary on the *Fuṣūṣ* remains unresolved.[91]

All this fits with the much more extensive evidence that Algar has unearthed for the Naqshbandiyya more generally and with his conclusion that this was not—as has been alleged[92]—a tariqa "hostile to Ibn al-'Arabī." Ottoman Naqshbandī shaykhs of our period were clearly insistent on incorporating the study, interpretation, and dissemination of the teachings of the "Greatest Master" as part of their mystical fare; and the combination that they offered followers—namely, access to some of the most illuminating and exciting mystical insights available, along with a seal of legitimacy and "orthodoxy"—appears to have had considerable appeal in the Ottoman governing and scholarly elite. Furthermore, the enthusiasm of Naqshbandīs of our period for Ibn al-'Arabī lends credence to Algar's argument that the notion of the Naqshbandiyya's hostility toward him must originate in later (and, in his view, exaggerated) readings of the criticism of Aḥmad Sirhindī, and more generally in a later sensibility that casts observance of the *sharī'a* as inconsistent with theosophical speculation.[93] In this regard, it seems that what we have here is another example of the kind of historiographical anachronism that I have tried to challenge elsewhere in this book, whereby instead of being examined in their historical context and on the basis of appropriate sources, earlier phases in the history of the Naqshbandiyya have been explained through a projection back of modern realities, images, or sensibilities.

BAKRĪ GENEALOGY: FROM A SPIRITUAL TO A POLITICAL MARKER?

Followers of tariqa Sufism not only associated themselves with particular mystical ways, each with its distinctive spiritual methods and devotional regimen. They were also affiliated with *silsilas*, the unbroken chains of spiritual descent that connected living Sufis to past masters of a tariqa, and ultimately to the Prophet Muḥammad. The *silsilas* had several functions. At one level, they were conduits of *baraka*, the power of grace or blessing that past spiritual masters were deemed capable of bestowing on the living. On another, they were akin to the chains (*isnāds*) used in the transmission and authentication of Prophetic traditions. In other words, they served to connect certain devotional or doctrinal emphases of a tariqa to eminent figures from early Islamic history, and thus highlight these emphases as the tariqa's hallmark and confer on the whole tariqa authenticity and legitimacy.[94]

Studies on the history of Sufism have commonly classified the Naqshbandī *silsila* as "Bakrī" since it passes through the Prophet's companion and first caliph, Abū Bakr, rather than through his cousin and son-in-law, 'Alī b. Abi Ṭālib, as is typical of many other *silsilas*. Moreover, by dint of professing a Bakrī rather than 'Alid *silsila* the Naqshbandiyya has been cast as a quintessentially Sunnī tariqa, and Naqshbandīs as harboring hostility to Shī'īs.[95] The present section begins with a discussion of how Naqshbandīs came to subscribe to the notion of Bakrī descent, and how they used it as a "spiritual marker" that defined the tariqa's character and bolstered its legitimacy.[96] I then take up the issue of Bakrī descent and Sunnī identity. In particular, I ask whether and how—especially against the background of the Ṣafavid takeover of Iran at the beginning of the sixteenth century and the heightened conflict between Sunnīs and Shī'īs that surrounded it—the notion of Bakrī descent was transformed from a spiritual to a political marker, one that would identify the Naqshbandiyya as a Sunnī and perhaps anti-Shī'ī tariqa.

The historical origins of the Naqshbandī Bakrī descent remain elusive. Practitioners assigned to this issue little relevance, since they perceived the *silsila* as an objective reality that their tradition simply recorded, not a construct that was introduced at some point in history in a bid to confer on the tariqa legitimacy or to forge for it a distinctive spiritual identity. Algar has accepted the notion of the authenticity of the *silsila* on psychological and historical grounds, and has consequently ignored the question of the historical origins of the Naqshbandī Bakrī *silsila.*[97] In a recent study on the emergence of the Naqshbandiyya out of the Khwājagānī tradition, Yürgen Paul has explored the historical roots of several of this tariqa's devotional, doctrinal, and organizational features, but he too has left the question of the origins of the Bakrī *silsila* unexamined.[98]

It may be tempting to trace the earliest mention of the Khwājagānī or proto-Naqshbandī notion of Bakrī descent to the *Risāla-yi ṣāḥibiyya*, the hagiography of Yūsuf Hamadānī (d.535/1140) commonly thought to have been written by his disciple 'Abd al-Khāliq Ghujduvānī. As the author of this work put it, the way (*ravish*) of Hamadānī was "that of *ḥażrat* Abū Bakr."[99] Because Hamadānī appears as the last shared initiatic link of the Naqshbandī and Yasavī *silsila*s, singling him out as subscribing to a Bakrī spiritual descent can help "explain" the shared Bakrī *silsila* of Naqshbandīs and Yasavīs as a concept that had won acceptance in these two traditions before they crystallized, so to speak, into separate *silsila*s upon his death.[100] But if we accept the notion of *silsila*s as later reconstructions or representations of earlier developments, then tracing the notion of the Naqshbandī Bakrī descent to the *Risāla-yi ṣāḥibiyya* emerges clearly as ahistorical.[101] In any case, several peculiarities in this work's depiction of Hamadānī's life cast serious doubt on its date and authorship. In Wilfred Madelung's view, it may well represent Ghujduvānī's fictionalized account of the life of a master whom he did not know,[102] while DeWeese has argued that it is an altogether later work, whose attribution to Ghujduvānī must be mistaken.[103]

Perhaps the most that we can say at the present state of our knowledge is that the notion of Bakrī descent developed gradually as the Naqshbandiyya emerged from the earlier Khwājagānī tradition, and that this notion became established among Naqshbandīs in the generation after Bahā' al-Dīn, though even then, and indeed for some time later, it continued to be less than exclusive.[104]

In the *Qudsiyya*, the book of dicta by his spiritual master, Bahā' al-Dīn, Muḥammad Pārsā traced the tariqa's spiritual descent through three parallel lines—one leading through Abū Bakr, another through 'Alī, and a third through 'Alī and several of his descendants in the line of the Shī'a *imāms*—yet there is little doubt that he considered the Bakrī ancestry the most privileged. For Pārsā, Abū Bakr was "the most perfect, most excellent, most splendid, and best knowing of the friends of God." Indeed, it was he who, after the death of the Prophet, gave 'Alī himself a second spiritual initiation.[105]

An even clearer statement of the notion of the Naqshbandī Bakrī descent may appear in Pārsā's encyclopedic work, the *Faṣl al-khiṭāb*. According to several Ottoman sources, it was a story in the *Faṣl* (or was it another of Pārsā's works?) that depicted the Prophet Muḥammad instructing Abū Bakr in the performance of the silent *dhikr* and thus, by implication, making him the first Naqshbandī disciple-practitioner. We shall come back to this story later in this section. Even after Pārsā's time the notion of Abū Bakr as the fountainhead of the Naqshbandī *silsila* continued to be less than exclusive or definitive, however. An important example comes from Kāshifī's *Rashaḥāt*, completed in Herat in 909/1503–4. Here the author replicated Pārsā's three-pronged *silsila* of parallel Bakrī, 'Alid, and *imāmī* lines; but, unlike Pārsā he did not attach to his three-pronged *silsila* any qualifier that would indicate Abū Bakr's primacy.[106]

While a few early Ottoman *silsila*s traced exclusively through Abū Bakr have come down to us,[107] generally early Ottoman Naqshbandīs followed Pārsā's model of tracing the *silsila* through the triad of parallel Bakrī, 'Alid, and *imāmī* lines.[108] These Naqshbandīs also did not shy away from highlighting the unique quality of the line leading through the Shī'a *imāms*. Several of them labeled this line the "Chain of Gold" (*silsilat al-dhahab*), and this despite the fact that the rationale underlying this designation—viz., that this was a particularly powerful line because its links were the biological progeny of the Prophet—ran counter to the Naqshbandī privileging of spiritual over genealogical succession.[109]

But whether authors charted exclusive Bakrī *silsila*s or ones that passed through parallel Bakrī and 'Alid lines, they made their privileging of the Bakrī ancestry unambiguous.[110] Time and again Abū Bakr was identified as the source of the tariqa's central devotional emphases, and thus made into a source of legitimacy and the acknowledged fountainhead of the Naqshbandī tradition, alongside the Prophet. One author described the Bakrī ancestry as providing a complete or perfect connection (*nisbet-i kulliye*) to the Prophet (and through him to God), in contrast with the partial or incomplete connection (*nisbet-i cuz'iye*) leading through 'Alī.[111] Another quoted Pārsā's assertion that after the death of the Prophet 'Alī himself sought initiation or spiritual mentoring (*tarbiyet*, Ar. *tarbiya*) from Abū Bakr.[112] Yet others identified Abū Bakr's love for the Prophet as the origin of the method of *rābiṭa*, or declared that Naqshbandīs adopted the two-fold *dhikr* formula *lā ilāh illā Allāh*

Muḥammad rasūl Allāh "because their way is founded on the *ṣiddīq*" (Abū Bakr's common epithet, believed to have been conferred by the Prophet).[113]

Of particular import was the story attributed to the *Faṣl al-khiṭāb* according to which the Prophet gave Abū Bakr the instruction (*talqīn*) in the performance of the silent *dhikr.*[114] The basis of the *talqīn* story was a Qur'ānic verse, 9:40, which already the medieval exegetes interpreted as describing a moment of special grace that the Prophet shared with his companion Abū Bakr while the two were hiding in a cave near Mecca during the Hijra:

> If you do not help him, yet God has helped him
> already, when the unbelievers drove him forth
> the second of two, when the two were in the Cave,
> when he said to his companion, "Sorrow not; surely
> God is with us." Then God sent down on him His [*sakīna*],
> and confirmed him with legions you did not see. . . .[115]

The Naqshbandī interpreters invested the scene described in the Qur'ānic verse with crucial significance, among other things by reinforcing it through two Prophetic traditions, one in which God was said to have revealed himself to Abū Bakr "personally" (*khāṣṣatan*), and another in which the Prophet proclaimed that he had poured into Abū Bakr's breast everything that God had poured into his own.[116] Most importantly, these interpreters understood the episode portrayed in the Qur'ānic verse as the moment when, at the time the two were hiding in the cave near Mecca during the Hijra, the Prophet imparted the formula of the silent *dhikr* to Abū Bakr, thereby allowing God to be manifested to him in the form of his "quiescence" or "divine presence" (*sakīna*). As Algar has noted, it is this moment that Naqshbandīs consider the paradigmatic archetype for the transmission of the silent *dhikr*, and hence for initiation into their *silsila.*[117] From the present perspective, the story portraying Abū Bakr as the first trainee in silent *dhikr* had several functions: it emphasized the centrality of the silent *dhikr* in the Naqshbandī devotional regimen, highlighted the stature of Abū Bakr as the fountainhead of the Naqshbandī *silsila*, and conferred on the *silsila* and the tariqa superior legitimacy and antiquity.

All this leaves no doubt that early Ottoman Naqshbandīs followed Pārsā in privileging their Bakrī descent and in viewing it as a spiritual marker that served to embody and lend authority to core Naqshbandī practices and, by extension, to the Naqshbandī way as a whole. But did they view the

Bakrī *silsila*, in addition, as a political marker that conferred on the Naqshbandiyya a Sunnī as opposed to a Shī'ī identity? Did they understand it as making their tariqa quintessentially Sunnī or even an enemy of Shī'īs? And can we determine when or under what historical circumstances this significance emerged?

As we shall see in chapter 6, a number of scholars have proposed that it was already in Tīmūrid Transoxania that some Naqshbandīs (or proto-Naqshbandīs), beginning with Bahā' al-Dīn's spiritual master, Amīr Kulāl, understood their Bakrī spiritual descent as one that conferred on them an emphatic Sunnī identity, and became involved in instances of active hostility to Shī'īs. However, evidence suggests that this reading of the protohistory of the tariqa is based not on Tīmūrid realities, but instead on a projection back into the Tīmūrid period of sectarian antagonisms that would not come to the fore until after the Ṣafavid takeover of Iran at the turn of the sixteenth century and the ensuing effort to convert that country to Shī'ism.

By contrast, much of the period during which Naqshbandīs were establishing their presence in Ottoman society fell after the Ṣafavid rise to power in Iran and the heightened Shī'ī-Sunnī divide that ensued throughout the region stretching from Central Asia to India to Anatolia. As we have seen in chapter 1, Naqshbandīs living under Ṣafavid rule were now subject to various forms of harassment and persecution, leading many of them to seek refuge in Ottoman territory or in other of Iran's Sunnī neighbors. Others assumed a quiet or underground existence, ever suspect in the eyes of hostile rulers who, among other things, made cursing the first three caliphs of Islam an official ritual and a test of loyalty to the regime. The Ṣafavid takeover roiled the Ottoman state and society, too, in powerful ways. From an Ottoman perspective, the Shī'ī Ṣafavids not only posed a challenge to the dynasty's claim to Sunnī legitimacy and leadership; they also threatened to "conquer the Ottoman Empire from within" through the responsive audiences that their messianic propaganda found in much of Anatolia. The Ottomans retaliated with a combination of military expeditions against the newly established Ṣafavid state, along with campaigns of surveillance, imprisonment, and deportations of their Ḳızılbaş adherents throughout Anatolia.[118] A host of scholars, jurists, and authors joined in a campaign of polemics, branding the Ṣafavids and Ḳızılbaş as infidels and apostates against whom it was lawful to launch holy war.[119] For Ottoman Naqshbandīs, it would have been difficult not to be caught up in this mighty conflict and these heightened Sunnī-Shī'ī antagonisms.

These were circumstances under which Naqshbandīs might be expected to have reconfigured the Bakrī *silsila* on which they prided themselves from a spiritual marker into a political emblem of Sunnī and, indeed, anti-Shīʿī identity. But our sources provide little evidence for such change. Interestingly, we have evidence for such reconfiguration in a Khalwatī *silsila*—recorded in the *Ḥadāʾiḳ ül-ḥaḳāʾiḳ* of Nevʿīzāde ʿAṭāʾī—from which the names of five Shīʿī *imāms* were omitted without explanation. Apparently some Ottoman Khalwatīs took to adjusting their *silsila* in an attempt to make their tariqa less vulnerable to criticism for Shīʿī affinities or doubtful political loyalties; or perhaps they were seeking to enhance the tariqa's Sunnī image in order to benefit from official approval and its concomitant patronage.[120] By contrast, we do not see Naqshbandīs seeking to confer on their Bakrī *silsila* a new exclusivity by expunging or otherwise underplaying their ʿAlid lines of descent. As we have seen, most of them continued to trace their own *silsila* through the familiar parallel Bakrī, ʿAlid, and *imāmī* lines. Nor did they shy away from highlighting the superior quality of the line going through ʿAlī and the Shīʿa *imāms* by designating it the *silsilat al-dhahab*.[121] Another public demonstration that Naqshbandīs did not feel constrained to underplay potential ʿAlid connections or sentiments comes from Bursa. There, some ten years into Sultan Süleymān's reign, the poet and Naqshbandī *khalīfa* Lāmiʿī Çelebi recited in front of the city's packed Great Mosque his martyrdom narrative, *Maḳtel-i imām Ḥüseyn*, in which he commemorated the death of the third Shīʿī *imām* in Karbala at the hands of Umayyad troops.[122]

All this can be taken to have been nothing but predictable. Khalwatīs felt the need to expunge the names of the *imāms* from their *silsila* because of their shaky Sunnī credentials; by contrast, Naqshbandīs simply did not require such adjustment. Similarly, a less highly credentialed reciter of a eulogy for the *imām* Ḥusayn than Lāmiʿī Çelebi could have been accused of Shīʿī leanings and even disloyalty at this time of intense Sunnī-Shīʿī rivalry; but Lāmiʿī Çelebi's impeccable reputation and confidence allowed him to do just that and meet with acceptance on the part of a distinguished audience, including some of Bursa's leading *ʿulamāʾ*. There was, after all, a long history to the veneration of the family of the Prophet among Sunnīs—especially, but by no means only, in popular religion. Robert McChesney talks of "*ahl al-baytism*", a strand in which the descendants of the Prophet were revered for their power of intercession and hope of salvation and served as the most visible icon of daily religious life irrespective of one's adherence to legal rite or doctrine.[123] Among Naqshbandīs, none other than

'Abd al-Raḥmān Jāmī lavished praise on the *imāms* in his poetry and made the pilgrimage to the shrine of Ḥusayn b. 'Alī in Karbala and that of the eighth Shī'ī *imām*, 'Alī al-Riḍā, in Mashhad.[124] Several decades before Lāmi'ī Çelebi, the father of the author of the *Rashaḥāt* and himself a Naqshbandī disciple, Ḥusayn b.'Alī Vā'iẓ Kāshifī (d. 910/1504–5), wrote the ever-popular *Ravżat-i shuhadā'*, another martyrdom narrative in commemoration of the *imām* Ḥusayn.[125]

Still, since the time of Ḥusayn b.'Alī Vā'iẓ much had changed, as the Ṣafavid rise to power and the unusually intense sectarian antagonism that was ushered in by it recast the political meaning of Shī'ism and could not but affect sectarian attitudes everywhere, including among Naqshbandīs.[126] Under the new circumstances, Lāmi'ī Çelebi's recital of his eulogy for the *imām* Ḥusayn in public—and even the less public stance that other Naqshbandīs exhibited in continuing to praise their 'Alid lines of descent—had themselves assumed some political significance, if only as a negative sign of *not* hastening to remake the Naqshbandī Bakrī descent into an anti-Shī'ī emblem.[127]

We have one story of a Naqshbandī shaykh who took an extreme stand by not only praising the Bakrī *silsila* but also strongly rejecting the notion that 'Alid *silsila*s were conducive to real knowledge of God. This was Ḥasan Efendi, who was killed by Celālis at his Incirlice *tekke* in Bursa in 1016/1607–8. When Ḥasan had tried to impress upon the preacher of Bursa's Sultan Murād Mosque, 'Abdullāh Efendi, the unique quality of the Naqshbandī Bakrī *silsila*, which alone led to "real knowledge of God" (*ma'rifet-i ḥakīkī*), 'Abdullāh retorted that while the first four caliphs were all perfect, most Sufi *silsila*s were 'Alid, and it was through these 'Alid *silsila*s that real knowledge of God was to be achieved. To this Ḥasan responded by declaring that both 'Abdullāh and his spiritual master, Eşrefzāde 'Abdullāh er-Rūmī, were infidels.

> Alas, you have elevated the exalted 'Alī above the *ṣiddīḳ* [Abū Bakr], hence you are nothing but an infidel, as are all Eşrefīs. It is lawful to kill them and to take their crown and crush it under the feet. Anyone who salutes them is himself an infidel.[128]

Even coming from the sharp-tongued and controversy-prone Ḥasan, this was an extreme position. Still, here too the issue was framed as one of devotion or mystical superiority. Not even this story is indicative of a Naqshbandī agenda of reconfiguring the Bakrī *silsila* from a spiritual marker into a political emblem.

CONCLUSION

Early Ottoman Naqshbandīs viewed themselves and were viewed by contemporaries as belonging to a tariqa of rigorous fidelity to the *sharī'a*. Doctrinally they did not understand this commitment as a political or public one, but instead emphasized the principle of "acting with strictness" (*al-'amal bi'l-'azīma*), which they construed in terms of personal observance of religious duties and sobriety in devotional matters.

At the center of the tariqa's sober devotional regimen was a series of spiritual techniques—silent *dhikr* being only one—that were geared toward enabling practitioners to seek God inconspicuously and continuously while immersed in society, and to dispense with the more emotive, ostentatious, or otherwise "inferior" rituals employed in other tariqas. Generally, other Sufis' practices were not categorically prohibited. Rather, Naqshbandīs viewed them with condescension, taking pride in their own privileged and "superior" devotional regimen that, practitioners were told, rendered these other rituals unnecessary. In the face of particularly strident opponents, some Naqshbandīs actually defended practices such as the vocal *dhikr*.

While rigorously sober in devotional practice and rigorously committed to the *sharī'a*, this was not in any way a tariqa stripped of mystical insights, experiences, or aspirations. Along with sobriety and *sharī'a*-abidance, Naqshbandīs prided themselves on the superiority of their way of mystical progress. They taught a potentially extravagant yet much prized technique, the *rābiṭa*, in which the picture of one's shaykh was fixed in the imagination and turned into a vehicle for the flow of divine energy. They were proud of a spirituality that included nonphysical Uwaysī initiations and communing with the spirits of deceased masters at their tombs. And they demonstrated a remarkable expertise in, and devotion to, the study and propagation of the mystical teachings of Ibn al-'Arabī. It was apparently the very combination of promising to guide practitioners in a regimen of sobriety and *sharī'a*-abidance while at the same time encouraging them to aspire toward advanced mystical experiences and insights that made this tariqa and its carriers attractive, particularly among the Ottoman governing and scholarly elite.

New circumstances of heightened Sunnī-Shī'ī conflict in the sixteenth century did not drive Naqshbandīs to transform their notion of Bakrī descent from a spiritual into a political marker. As a whole they clung to the old modes of celebrating their Bakrī descent as a spiritual symbol, and they routinely continued to acknowledge and even praise parallel 'Alid and *imāmī* lines of descent as part of their *silsila*. Likewise, even at a time of great

Ottoman-Ṣafavid antagonism under Sultan Süleymān, a prominent Naqshbandī, the Bursan Lāmi'ī Çelebi, did not find it necessary to refrain from reciting publicly in front of the city's packed Great Mosque his eulogy for the *imām* Ḥusayn.

Thus, the early Ottoman Naqshbandīs' rigorous fidelity to the *sharī'a* did not entail the fixed dichotomies and dividing lines suggested by nineteenth-century paradigms, but instead allowed for considerably more fluidity on a number of issues. This is another testimony that Islamic orthodoxy was more complex or variegated than is sometimes assumed, and that it allowed Sufis, in particular, to aspire to mystical excellence or to engage in a rich and even extravagant spirituality. Exploring this fluidity can also add a valuable perspective to the project of challenging the dualistic paradigm that divides Sufism and tariqas sharply into popular and orthodox strands. Others have pointed especially to the dubiousness of characterizing the first pole of this divide as "popular" or "unorthodox." From its own vantage point, the present chapter suggests that characterizing the second pole simply as "orthodox" is also unsatisfactory, as this does not take sufficiently into account the variegated nature of orthodoxy itself.

6

Politics of Sunnism, Battles over Orthodoxy

We have seen that doctrinally Naqshbandīs did not view their fidelity to the *sharī'a* as a public or political commitment, but rather understood it to entail sobriety in devotional practice and personal observance of religious duties. In the present chapter, we go beyond doctrine to explore the involvement of some individual Naqshbandīs in two actual political battles that were both launched—though in different ways and under different circumstances—in the name of Sunnī orthodoxy. The first is the campaign that the Ottomans conducted throughout most of the sixteenth century against the Anatolian Ḳızılbaş adherents of the new Shī'ī-Ṣafavid state in Iran. It has been suggested that, staunch orthodox and Sunnīs that they were, Naqshbandīs were enlisted and gave the Ottoman authorities crucial assistance in this campaign, in turn being rewarded with valuable patronage that helped them consolidate their presence in Ottoman society.

The second battle to draw our attention is one that, for a good part of the seventeenth century, a group of Istanbul imperial mosque preachers—known after their first leader as the Ḳāḍīzādelis—waged in the name of a militant and vigilant orthodoxy, targeting above all Sufis and a host of their doctrines and practices. As we shall see, a Naqshbandī shaykh, the incumbent of the Ḥekīm Çelebi Tekke, 'Osmān Bosnevī, was intimately involved with the Ḳāḍīzādeli leadership in his other capacity as the Friday preacher of the Süleymāniye Mosque.

The chapter's main focus will be on what these two particular instances of Naqshbandī activism in the name of Sunnī orthodoxy amounted to, how they evolved, how they related to Naqshbandīs' understanding of their orthodoxy, and how they fit with the tariqa's larger identity. But first, in the way of introduction, it is useful to offer some comments about Naqshbandī shaykhs and politics more generally, and especially about the political paradigm that 'Ubaydullāh Aḥrār created in Tīmūrid Transoxania (and that other Naqshbandīs in Central Asia later inherited) and its possible relevance to Ottoman realities.

AḤRĀRIAN POLITICS AND THE OTTOMAN ENVIRONMENT

Despite varying readings of the chronicles and the biographical literature from which much of our picture of Aḥrār's career is derived, there is a general agreement that his political influence and economic ventures in late Tīmūrid Transoxania were sizable.[1] Studies by Gross and Paul have shown him accumulating vast landed property, mediating among warring rulers, paying off conquerors in efforts to prevent the enslavement of local populations, extending advice to the Tīmūrid sultans Abū Sa'īd and Aḥmad on matters of politics and war, and prevailing on the first to abolish the *damgha* tax in Bukhara and Samarkand.[2] In the analysis of Paul, his economic ventures and his political involvement with the Tīmūrid rulers of his day are best understood as an extensive "system of patronage" that bound to him large numbers of tenant-cultivators along with craftsmen and merchants in the towns; through this system he sought to protect the interests of the townspeople and the settled rural population of Transoxania against pillaging nomads, and especially against the military class of Turkish-Mongol *amīrs*, whose capriciousness and oppression the Tīmūrid rulers had difficulties restraining. Some of this was articulated as demands that rulers "institute the *sharī'a*" or "abolish non-Islamic customs"—the latter especially a reference to the Mongol *damgha* tax that Aḥrār's clientele found particularly oppressive because it was collected in cash. Another part of the same system of protection involved mediating among warring rulers in efforts to secure the peaceful resolution of conflicts.[3]

However we evaluate Aḥrār's motivations, his political style and effectiveness were clearly the product of an unusual political acumen, but also of the prevailing political dynamics in Transoxania under the late Tīmūrids. Scholars' analysis shows much of the shaykh's dealings to have been dependent on local conditions of political instability, warfare, tribal incursions, conflicts between nomads and the settled population, and the fragile balance between the Tīmūrid sultans and the Turkish-Mongol *amīrs*.[4] In that regard, Aḥrārian politics was also Central Asian politics, and we should be little surprised that it was among Central Asian Naqshbandīs that the pattern of political involvement and influence begun by Aḥrār continued after the demise of the Tīmūrids and the establishment of Shībānid rule.[5]

The Ottoman political environment and culture—imperial, bureaucratic, seeking to assert centralized control, and averse to the accumulation of independent power—were fundamentally different from those of late Tīmūrid or Shībānid Central Asia; and thus, while Aḥrār was the spiritual ancestor of many early Ottoman Naqshbandīs and perhaps the source of a number of doctrinal, devotional, and organizational emphases that they adopted, anything resembling Aḥrārian politics would have been unwelcome in this environment. We have seen that some Ottoman Naqshbandī shaykhs, especially in the capital, established relationships with members of the dynasty and court, high officialdom, and the learned-religious hierarchy. They served as tutors, shared their expertise in Ibn al-ʿArabī and in Rūmī's *Masnavī*, gave initiations and mystical training, intervened with advice and solace at times of crisis, and in a few cases became the lifelong confidants and spiritual advisers of certain individuals. For their expertise and spiritual services, they might be rewarded with access to the court, gifts of cash and real estate, and the establishment and endowment of Naqshbandī *tekkes*.

A few Naqshbandī shaykhs cultivated relations with Ottoman sultans. We recall Isḥaq Bukhārī-i Hindī, for whom Sultan Meḥmed II built the first Naqshbandī *tekke* of the capital shortly after the conquest.[6] Uzun Muṣliḥüddīn, a *khalīfa* of Aḥmad Bukhārī from the area of Kastamonu near the Black Sea, had Sultan Bāyezīd II remove an "injustice" (*ẓulm*) against the local population, having informed the sultan that local "pious people" had seen the Prophet "saddened" in their dreams.[7] Aḥmad Ṣādiq Ṭāshkandī and Ṣaʿbān Efendi were both close to Sultan Murād III, the first perhaps initiating him into the tariqa and the second having him visit his *tekke* in the Fātiḥ district on several occasions. When Aḥmad Ṣādiq died in the plague of 994/1586, the sultan is said to have suspended the work of the Imperial Council for three days.[8] However, the relations that all these individuals established with members of the Ottoman dynasty and governing elite were squarely within the traditional mold of Sufi shaykhs extending spiritual advice, guidance, and sustenance to the powerful in exchange for patronage. Not one of these individuals was involved in dynastic or factional conflicts or influenced crucial political decisions. In other words, none of this amounted to anything close to Aḥrārian politics.[9]

The one exception to this pattern among Naqshbandīs occurred in the distant frontier region of Kurdistan, where, under unique circumstances of war with Shīʿī-Ṣafavid neighbors in the early seventeenth century, Shaykh

Maḥmūd Urmavī engaged in a political style resembling that of Aḥrār, though in a provincial context and on a much smaller scale. As we have seen in chapter 3, from his base in Diyarbakır the shaykh brought to its height a family tradition of exercising leadership over large communities throughout Kurdistan and beyond. At several moments in the ongoing war with the Ṣafavids, he accompanied the imperial army in campaigns, participated in peace negotiations, or petitioned the Ottoman authorities on behalf of war-weary local populations. For a number of years he was deemed sufficiently serviceable to the Ottoman state for his political involvement to be allowed. But the Ottoman authorities did not view this political style as one to be easily tolerated, and once the military balance in the east had changed as a result of the Ottoman takeover of Baghdad in 1048/1639, he was put to death at the sultan's orders. It seems that even in a distant frontier province of the empire, there was little room for Aḥrārian politics of sorts, except temporarily and under unusual circumstances.

"BRINGING THE HETERODOX TO HEEL"

There were other Sufi shaykhs, especially Khalwatīs, who wielded more political influence than their Naqshbandī counterparts in the Ottoman environment of our period.[10] This brings up the question of whether, and in what ways, the Ottoman political environment of this time did, after all, allow, encourage, or promise to reward the political involvement of Sufi shaykhs—and of how Naqshbandīs, specifically, responded to such opportunities.

A number of scholars, most notably İrfan Gündüz in his *Osmanlılarda Devlet-Tekke Münasabetleri*, have proposed that a mobilization of Naqshbandīs against the newly established Ṣafavid regime in Iran and its Ḳızılbaş adherents throughout Anatolia underlay and facilitated the establishment of this tariqa in Ottoman society at the turn of the sixteenth century. The assumption is that Naqshbandīs' firm Sunnī credentials and anti-Shīʿī, hence anti-Ṣafavid, sentiments, along with their rigorous commitment to the *sharīʿa*, both conditioned them and enabled them to play an instrumental role in the Ottoman struggle against the Ṣafavids, and in particular in efforts to tame the Ḳızılbaş of Anatolia. In return for their participation in one of the most critical Ottoman campaigns of the time, Naqshbandīs were given generous official patronage that in turn facilitated and underpinned their expansion and consolidation within the empire.[11] In Gündüz's view, Naqshbandīs had already become distinguished by their firm Sunnī credentials and hostility to the Shīʿa in Central Asia, where they had been favored by the Tīmūrids, who had had their share of Shīʿī uprisings to contend with.[12] The rise of the Ṣafavids to power in Iran and their proselytizing inside Anatolia around the turn of the sixteenth century led to a replay of the same dynamics, once again bringing to the fore and endearing to the (now Ottoman) ruling authorities all Sunnī shaykhs and men of religion, the Naqshbandīs in particular.

With regard to the Tīmūrid period, the notion of the Naqshbandiyya's "anti-Shīʿī" stance appears to be based on three specific episodes: one in which shortly before his death in 772/1370, Bahāʾ al-Dīn Naqshband's spiritual master, Amīr Kulāl, was involved in the expulsion of Shāh Niʿmatullāh from Tīmūr's Transoxania; another in which, half a century later, Naqshbandīs helped Sultan Shāhrukh in undermining the messianic claims of Muḥammad Nūrbakhsh; and a third in which, half a century after that, ʿAbd al-Raḥmān Jāmī, or his friend ʿAlī Shīr Navāʾī, prevailed upon Sultan Ḥusayn Bāyqarā of Herat to refrain from minting the names of the Shīʿī *imāms* on his coinage and from inserting them into the formula of his Friday sermons.[13] There is good reason to believe, however, that what we have here is a projection back into Tīmūrid times of heightened sectarian antagonisms that would not come to the fore (for either Naqshbandīs or the larger society) until after the Ṣafavid takeover of Iran at the beginning of the sixteenth century and the ensuing effort to convert that country to Shīʿism. The two stories concerning Shāh Niʿmatullāh and Muḥammad Nūrbakhsh originated in later sources that could not but be colored by the more developed sectarian antagonisms of their time.[14] The often-repeated story of Ḥusayn Bāyqarā's flirting with the idea of including the names of the *imāms* in his symbols of sovereignty does appear in a source from Bāyqarā's time.[15] But what this story seems most to reflect is not a clear-cut conflict between Sunnīs and Shīʿīs in which figures such as Jāmī, and through him the Naqshbandiyya, were involved; instead, it is more reflective of the "climate of ambiguity" that obtained in Transoxania and Khorasan at the time—one that allowed for a kind of sectarian fluidity that would become less imaginable only after the Ṣafavid takeover.[16]

As Gündüz has it, after the rise of the Ṣafavids to power the Naqshbandīs again distinguished themselves as uniquely prepared to rise to the challenge, this time not in Transoxania or Khorasan, but instead in Anatolia and on the side of the Ottoman state. The new dynamics emerged during the reigns of Bāyezīd II and Selīm I, then continued under Sultan Süleymān, who "arduously endeavored to maintain the unity of Anatolia by extending his patronage to the Naqshbandīs—distinguished as they were by their Sunnism and their antagonism towards the Shīʿī creed—as well as to the followers of other Sunnī tariqas."[17]

Moreover, the thesis of the Naqshbandiyya's instrumentality in the anti-Shīʿī, anti-Ṣafavid campaign of the Ottomans, which may have originated among scholars sympathetic to the tariqa, has made strides within modern Turkish scholarship more generally, as the following succinct formulation of Şerif Mardin suggests:

> Indeed, the Ottomans relied on the Nakshibendi as one part of their policy of establishing law and order in the empire, especially in Anatolia. During the early years of their rise to power, the Ottomans were confronted by the heterodox beliefs and practices of the Turkic tribes that had entered Anatolia in great numbers from the thirteenth century onward. Ottoman hegemony depended on the pacification of tribes, and one way to achieve this was to integrate them with Sunni orthodoxy. From the fifteenth century onward, the Ottomans found in the Nakshibendi an excellent ally in achieving this goal. They were given the task of bringing the heterodox to heel. The order achieved considerable prestige in the empire [though] the revival of its energies came somewhat later and from outside the empire [presumably under the aegis of the Mujaddidīs].[18]

Mardin invokes a broader context of the Ottoman endeavor of "bringing the heterodox to heel," one reflecting the thesis of a series of scholars who over the years have explained Anatolia's syncretistic religious culture as one that originated in Central Asia in the process of the conversion of Turkish tribesmen to Islam. From there—both before and increasingly after the Mongol invasion of the thirteenth century—this culture is said to have been carried westward by migrating seminomadic Turcoman tribesmen, who in time became not only politically disaffected in the face of restrictive Ottoman administrative and tax policies, but also responsive to millenarian propaganda. It was from among their ranks that in the second half of the fifteenth century emerged the Ḳızılbaş, responding to Ṣafavid propaganda that combined the old millenarian themes with new, specifically Shīʿī symbols.[19]

A THESIS REVISITED

It is not possible to do justice here to recent criticism of the whole idea that Anatolia's heterodox culture originated in Central Asian shamanism carried west by Turcoman tribesmen; for this, one should consult Ahmet Karamustafa's *God's Unruly Friends.*[20] Rather than the origins of the challenge facing the Ottomans in Anatolia, what is central from our perspective is the idea that, confronted with that challenge, the Ottomans relied on Naqshbandīs to lend them assistance, or that Naqshbandīs became uniquely instrumental in the Ottoman campaign against Anatolia's heterodox. For such a picture, there is little evidence in sixteenth-century sources. Rather, this picture seems to be based on a projection backward of much later realities; it thus both originates in and reinforces a misreading of the character and fortunes of the Naqshbandiyya in its pre-Mujaddidī phase.

Sixteenth-century sources tell of one Naqshbandī disciple, the poet from Filibe Baba Maḥmūd Riżā'ī, who was involved with the struggle over Anatolia through his association with Süleymān's grand vezir, Rüstem Paşa. According to 'Āşık Çelebi, Riżā'ī became a lifelong confidant of Rüstem, having served as his tutor when the latter was the chief equerry (*mīrāhūr-i evvel*) of the palace. In time, the poet and confidant emerged as the driving force behind various building projects that Rüstem undertook on behalf of various Sufis and *'ulamā'*. At the same time, he became the "guidance and inspiration" behind Rüstem's efforts "to eliminate the men of fallacious beliefs and destroy the heretics" of his day (*irmā'-i erbāb-i sū'-i i'tiḳād ve ifnā'-i ehl-i zandaḳa ve ilḥād*).[21] 'Āşıḳ Çelebi does not explain what specific aspects of a career that is not usually associated with the anti-Ḳızılbaş struggle inform his depiction of Rüstem as the enemy of the *ehl-i zandaḳa ve ilḥād.*[22] Probably he had in mind the series of investigative and punitive measures that were taken against *tekke*s and groups of "*ışıḳ*s" in Anatolia and the Balkans in the late 960s/1550s, when Rüstem was serving his second tenure as grand vezir. A role in inspiring these measures (which are known to us through a series of imperial orders published by Ahmet Refik) would have indeed made the Naqshbandī disciple (though not a shaykh), Riżā'ī, a participant in the critical Ottoman struggle over Anatolia.[23]

Gündüz and before him Kasım Kufralı have based their thesis concerning the Naqshbandiyya's role in the anti-Ḳızılbaş struggle on another individual and another specific incident—also from the years of Rüstem's second tenure as grand vezir. This was a Naqshbandī from Bursa, Enverī or Enverī Dede (d.973/1565–66), who, according to the biographical notice that Nev'īzāde 'Aṭā'ī devoted to him, began his learned pursuits as a student of *'ilm*, then left this path to become a Naqshbandī disciple and eventually shaykh. When the Seyyid Ǧāzī Tekke near Eskişehir had been "cleansed of the filth of the men of dissent and heresy" (*levs-i erbāb-i rafż ve-ilḥāddan tenzīh olunup*), Enverī was made its shaykh, presumably with the task of reestablishing it as a respectable institution and of preventing the return of its former occupants.[24] It was this role of Enverī in the purge of Seyyid Ǧāzī and its Kalenderī (Per. *qalandar*) inhabitants, as they refer to them, that in the eyes of Kufralı and Gündüz points to Sultan Süleymān's reliance on the Naqshbandiyya in the struggle against Anatolia's Ḳızılbaş.[25]

Other accounts of the purge and rehabilitation of Seyyid Ǧāzī beside this piece concerning Enverī suggest, however, that the involvement of the Naqshbandiyya in this affair was quickly frustrated, and only of minor or secondary importance. The principal instrument that the central Ottoman authorities used to prevent the complex from falling back into suspicious hands appears to have been a madrasa that was assigned to one Muṣṭafā 'Işretī, a professor and judge who was the protégé of Prince Bāyezīd. Several biographies of 'Işretī relate that in 962/1555, shortly after the return of Sultan Süleymān from his last Ṣafavid campaign, this recently appointed judge of Eskişehir informed the sultan of objectionable goings-on in the *tekke*, whose clean-shaven occupants paid no heed to the *sharī'a*, failed to take ablutions and perform the five daily prayers, and turned the whole site into an "abode of decadence and moral depravity." The resident *abdal*s or *qalandar*s were expelled from Seyyid Ǧāzī, and once they were banished, a madrasa was established in the complex and assigned to 'Işretī. Işretī himself fell from favor some three years later, but the madrasa continued to function under his replacement, Sinān Çelebi Aḳyazılı. According to Nev'īzāde 'Aṭā'ī, it was still functioning in his time, some three-quarters of a century after its establishment, though a document published by Ahmet Refik suggests that by 980/1572 the former occupants were again living at the complex alongside the students of the madrasa, having brought back with them their old objectionable practice of using drums in processions.[26] When Evliyā Çelebi visited the site in the mid-seventeenth century, he encountered a large Bektaşī *tekke* with two hundred resident dervishes.[27]

Enverī's tenure as shaykh in Seyyid Ǧāzī must have been short, at best. According to Nev'īzāde 'Aṭā'ī, he left the *tekke* sometime after his appointment and spent the rest of his life in the Orhān Ǧāzī Tekke in his native Bursa. The identity of his replacement as shaykh—if there was one—remains unknown.[28] In sixteenth-century Naqshbandī sources there is no mention of the shaykh or his spiritual genealogy, nor any reference to the role of the tariqa in the Seyyid Ǧāzī purge. Apparently Enverī was not an important personality, nor was his incumbency in Seyyid Ǧāzī, or indeed the tariqa's role in its rehabilitation, of much significance.

In itself, then, the story of Enverī has little in it to support the argument that the Naqshbandiyya was instrumental in the Ottoman struggle over Anatolia. Following a connection first made by the nineteenth-century Ottoman scholar and historiographer Es'ad Efendi in his *Üss-i ẓafer*, Kufralı and Gündüz apparently came to read this story in light of the tariqa's history in the nineteenth century, and especially of the incident in which after the suppression of the Bektaşī order in 1241/1826 the Ḥācci Bektaş Tekke in Kırşehir was turned over to a Naqshbandī shaykh.[29] Finding a parallel between the two incidents helped create a paradigm of Naqshbandī shaykhs stepping in to help the Ottoman authorities reestablish respectable Sunnī orthodoxy wherever heterodox challenges appeared.

Even putting aside the precise nature of the particular incident, there are reasons for doubting the premise that Naqshbandīs were in an advantageous position to lend support to the anti-Ḳızılbaş or antiheterodox campaign of the Ottomans by winning over heterodox elements or otherwise bringing them under tighter state control. Scholars have associated other Sufis, especially the Bektaşīs and Khalwatīs, with efforts to discipline heterodox elements in Anatolia and elsewhere. Mélikoff has proposed that it was the Bektaşīs to whom early Ottoman sultans, and later Bāyezīd II, assigned the task of "channeling and bringing under the state's control the heterodox currents that proliferated . . . in Anatolia." As she sees it, in the process the Bektaşīs not only restrained the heterodox, but were themselves influenced and transformed by them.[30] In Karamustafa's recent revision, early sixteenth-century Bektaşīs were one of a series of "deviant dervish groups" operating in Anatolia that would soon be driven by official pressure or persecution to surrender their independent existence. When others surrendered, the Bektaşīs were able to capitalize on their Janissary connection and transform themselves into a full-fledged tariqa. In the process they absorbed a number of the other groups, and subsequently preserved some of these groups' legacy.[31] Fuad Köprülü has pointed to a Khalwatī role in aiding the Shirvānshāhs of the Caucasus contain a local Ḳızılbaş outbreak in the later years of the fifteenth century; what allowed these Khalwatīs to play that role, he argued, was their considerable local standing, together with their ability to exhibit "'Alawī tendencies" while staying within the "Sunnī fold."[32] As we have seen, Nathalie Clayer has recently argued that during the sixteenth and seventeenth centuries some Khalwatī branches enlisted in the Ottoman campaign of "Sunnitization" (targeting both Christians and heterodox populations); for their services they were awarded official patronage, becoming the favorites of many Ottoman sultans.[33]

There is a common rationale to these analyses. It is that those best equipped to assist the Ottoman authorities in co-opting the Ḳızılbaş or other heterodox elements were Sufis who were in some ways related or congenial to the latter, and at the same time sufficiently connected to the apparatus of the state, or resigned to its brand of Sunnī Islam, or—in the case of sixteenth-century Khalwatīs—convinced that it was now time to erase the memory of their own mixed beginnings and transform themselves into an instrument of "Sunnitization" on behalf of the state.[34] The Bektaşīs would have been particularly well equipped for the task, given their heterodox sensibilities along with their long-standing ties with the Ottoman dynasty and close association with the backbone of the Ottoman army, the Janissary corps. The Khalwatīs were in the process of transforming themselves as they moved from the Caucasus to Amasya, and then to Istanbul and the Balkans. In the Shirvan area in the Caucasus they may have relied on their ability to combine 'Alawī tendencies with "great care not to leave the Sunnī fold," as Köprülü had it. Later on, some Khalwatī branches transformed themselves into a tool of "Sunnitization" in collaboration with the state. By contrast, it would be difficult to imagine the sober, elitist, emphatically Sunnī, and deliberately *sharī'a*-minded Naqshbandiyya playing a similar role in appealing to, disciplining, or absorbing the heterodox of sixteenth-century Anatolia.

In addition, any battle to win over or discipline the heterodox of the sixteenth century would have had to be launched primarily in the Anatolian countryside, and largely among a recently or incompletely settled population.[35] This was precisely a region in which the Naqshbandiyya did not establish a solid presence at this time, and indeed not until the nineteenth century. Imagining pre-Mujaddidī Naqshbandīs as significant players in this area appears to be yet another projection backward from the fortunes of the nineteenth-century Khālidiyya, which was the first to construct in large parts of rural Anatolia an impressive Naqshbandī network of shaykhs and *tekkes*.[36] As we have seen, in pre-Khālidī and pre-Mujaddidī times, the Naqshbandī presence in this region was modest: apart from Bursa—and, of course, Istanbul—Naqshbandīs were most active among the Kurds, a Sunnī and Shāfi'ī constituency whose relations with the Ḳızılbaş were generally antagonistic.[37]

That Naqshbandīs were not particularly suited to winning the hearts and minds of the Ḳızılbaş should not have precluded them from contributing to the Ottoman anti-Ṣafavid struggle in other ways. Disposed, as they were, not only toward Sunnism and fidelity to the *sharī'a*, but also toward literary production, Naqshbandī shaykhs could easily become involved in the anti-Ṣafavid, anti-Ḳızılbaş propaganda campaign that others conducted through polemical tracts, *fatwās*, and mosque preaching. Drawing on an old and rich tradition of Islamic heresiography, numerous polemicists branded the Ṣafavids as infidels and apostates, declared them a fitting target for *jihād*, and accused them of insulting the companions of the Prophet or deceitfully claiming descent from his family.[38] Yet for Naqshbandī participation in this extensive propaganda campaign, we find exceedingly slim evidence, at best.

It may be illuminating to consider here in some detail one piece, the *Silsilanāma-yi khwājagān-i Naqshband*, written in Damascus in 978/1570 by the Naqshbandī refugee from Iran Muḥammad Qazvīnī.[39] The *Silsilanāma* reflects on the issue at hand in a number of ways. First, through biographical notices on scores of Naqshbandī shaykhs of the lines of Aḥrār and Sa'd al-Dīn Kāshgharī, it made available outside Iran an account of the fate of the tariqa and its followers under the Ṣafavids. What Qazvīnī covered was not only his native city of Qazvin, but also other Naqshbandī centers such as Herat and Tabriz. And while he did not intend the *Silsilanāma* simply as an indictment of the Ṣafavids for their persecution of the tariqa, what resulted was a clear, if subtle, picture of "disorders" and "meddling," richly detailing various instances of ill-treatment of Naqshbandīs, along with victims' efforts to seek refuge outside Iran. Moreover, for Qazvīnī the Ṣafavids were reprehensible not only in their ill-treatment of Naqshbandīs, but also in their general character. Usually he referred to them as Ḳızılbaş ("redheads," the common epithet referring to their distinctive red headgear with its twelve gourds commemorating the Shī'ī *imāms*). But at times he resorted to less-neutral designations, such as *ravāfiż* (Ar. *rawāfiḍ*), the "opponents of the way of certitude" (*mukhālifān-i ṭarīq-i yaqīn*), and "the redheads who forbid right and command wrong" (*amr-i munkar va nahy-i ma'rūf-i qizilbāsh*, an allusion to the description of the "hypocrites" in Qur'ān 9: 67).[40]

Second, Qazvīnī was one of those few Naqshbandīs known to us who chose to identify themselves by an unambiguous Bakrī ancestry. 'Alid lines are mentioned in the narrative introduction to the *Silsilanāma*. But the diagrammatic *silsila* that forms the core of the work is traced exclusively through Abū Bakr, omitting any 'Alid line, even the potentially less objectionable one that leads through 'Alī but not through any other of the Shī'a *imāms*.[41] Qazvīnī must have chosen this construction of the *silsila* out of political considerations, albeit ones different from those that drove the authors of the abridged Khalwatī *silsila* that we discussed in chapter 5. Unlike his Khalwatī counterparts, he was under no pressure to enhance the respectability of the Naqshbandiyya in the eyes of the Ottoman public or governing elite. Rather—like Shaykh Maḥmūd Urmavī, another refugee from Ṣafavid territory—he must have chosen to underscore his Bakrī descent because of the strong antipathy that he harbored toward those from whose persecution his family had fled to Ottoman territory.

Third, a series of extant manuscripts of the *Silsilanāma* in Istanbul and elsewhere sheds light on the process through which Qazvīnī's work was disseminated and made available to an apparently eager circle of readers. In the decades following its completion in Damascus in 978/1570, the work was copied by a number of hands, made its way to the Ottoman capital, and was there translated into Ottoman Turkish. I do not have the dates of copies found in several collections of the Süleymaniye Library, but two manuscripts from the Bibliothèque Nationale and the Topkapı Palace Library are dated 993/1585 and 1000/1591, respectively.[42] In 1008/1599, Muṣṭafā b. Hayreddīn, a Naqshbandī devotee and madrasa professor with close palace connections, undertook the Turkish translation-adaptation of which there is a copy from 1033/1623–24 or shortly afterward in the Hüsrev Paşa collection of the Süleymaniye Library.[43] According to Muṣṭafā's own testimony, he undertook this task in response to repeated requests from his pupil in the Palace Service, Mışırlı 'Osmān Ağa, who convinced him that numerous readers who could not benefit from the Persian original were awaiting a translation. Once completed, the translation was dedicated to another Palace official, the veteran chief white eunuch (*bāb üs-sa'ādet ağası*), Ğażanfer Ağa.[44]

Still, Qazvīnī's *Silsilanāma* was not strictly speaking an anti-Ṣafavid polemical tract, nor did it come close in the severity of its reproach to works of this genre. We also have little evidence for other Naqshbandī refugees from Iran who expressed strong hostility to the Ṣafavids in writing or preaching (the latter, in particular, could have been an effective medium). One anti-Ṣafavid polemical tract from the late seventeenth century has been attributed to the Naqshbandī and Shaṭṭārī devotee from Medina, Muḥammad b.'Abd al-Rasūl al-Barzanjī. But this work, a summary of an earlier tract by a Shāfi'ī *'ālim* and refugee from Iran, is itself of debated authorship.[45] Other than that, the one interesting piece that we have is a chronogram that the poet and Naqshbandī shaykh Açıḳbaş Maḥmūd Resmī (who was the descendant of refugees from Iran) composed in scorn of the death of Shāh 'Abbās and the advent of Shāh Ṣāfī in 1038/1629.

> Shāh 'Abbās, degenerate and vile of faith,
> Has settled in the vale of Hell.
> With the damned one gone, in his place
> The miserable Ṣāfī has now become king.

A chronogram that befits them both is
Shāh-e now ("New King"), as he has fallen off the throne (*takht*).[46]

Finally, our sources do not single out the Naqshbandiyya from among other established Ottoman tariqas in terms of the nature or extent of the official patronage conferred on it, nor do they suggest that the Ottoman governing elite was unusually keen on promoting this tariqa, as one would expect had it been singularly instrumental in the struggle over Anatolia. For sure, Naqshbandīs enjoyed elite and official patronage that manifested itself in gifts of cash and equipment, access to the Ottoman court and governing elite, and the establishment or endowment of some *tekkes*. But such official patronage did not surpass that given to other established tariqas. In terms of access to the Ottoman court, *tekkes* founded, endowments, and other material support, it is the Khalwatiyya rather than the Naqshbandiyya that was favored by the Ottoman governing elite of our period, perhaps, as Clayer has argued, because Khalwatīs, or at least some Khalwatī branches, were more politically useful to the Ottomans. We may recall in this regard that some of the Naqshbandī *tekkes* of the capital were sustained economically not by the upper echelons of the Ottoman learned and governing elite, but instead through cumulative patronage of followers from more modest backgrounds—what the Istanbul *waqf* register of 953/1546 called "disciples' endowments" (*evḳāf ül-mürīdīn ve'l-muḥibbīn*).[47]

What are we to conclude? The Ottoman struggle to wipe out or coopt the Ḳızılbaş and other heterodox elements might indeed offer a Sunnī and orthodox tariqa, especially one that could appeal to the heterodox in some ways, an opportunity to become politically active, in the process ingratiating itself with the Ottoman authorities. Yet we have seen that if read in its appropriate context—without projecting onto it images based on nineteenth-century realities—the evidence that has been invoked to suggest a Naqshbandī role in this struggle is of minor significance. Naqshbandīs were not intimately involved in disciplining Ḳızılbaş followers in Anatolia, nor were they particularly well suited for participating in this endeavor. They also did not participate in the literary propaganda campaign against the Ṣafavids, nor used the whole Ṣafavid-Ḳızılbaş affair to ingratiate themselves with the Ottoman authorities in ways that could earn them unusual political patronage or underlie their consolidation in Ottoman society.

The issue here is not doctrinal. Naturally, the extent of Naqshbandīs' involvement in the campaign that the Ottomans conducted in Anatolia throughout the sixteenth century would have been predicated on a number of factors. The Naqshbandī construction of orthodoxy, or practitioners' understanding of the significance of their Sunnī-Bakrī spiritual descent under new political circumstances, could well have played a role in their conduct; but there were surely other factors at play, including the extent of Naqshbandīs' physical presence in the Anatolian "battleground," their ability to attract and hence incorporate "heterodox" populations, and the proclivities of individual shaykhs.

One interesting point that the presumed involvement of Naqshbandīs in the anti-Ḳızılbaş, anti-Ṣafavid campaign of the sixteenth century suggests is a historiographic one. What is instructive is our ability to relate the *idea* of their unique instrumentality in this campaign to certain nineteenth-century realities, and thus to trace the historiographic dynamics through which this idea developed. We should not be misled by the fact that in this case Naqshbandīs are said to have resorted to activism in support of the Ottoman state and status quo rather than in opposition to it, as might be the case in the nineteenth century (though not in the Kırşehir incident). Conceptually the two belong in the same category. What is important, and what seems to be a projection back of nineteenth-century realities or images, is the very notion of tariqas as networks of political activism, and specifically of the Naqshbandiyya as a staunchly orthodox and staunchly Sunnī tariqa, always ready to take political action against challenges to the *sharīʿa*-based order.

A NAQSHBANDĪ ḲĀḌĪZĀDELI

A rather different instance of Naqshbandī involvement in a campaign launched in the name of militant orthodoxy comes from mid-seventeenth-century Istanbul. There we find ʿOsmān Bosnevī, the incumbent of one of the tariqa's oldest and most active *tekke*s, turning out to be, in his other capacity as an imperial mosque preacher, one of the principal spokesmen of the Ḳāḍīzādeli movement.

The Ḳāḍīzādeli affair, which raged in the Ottoman capital and reverberated in a number of Ottoman cities for much of the seventeenth century, originated in the 1030s/1620s with the appointment of Ḳāḍīzāde Meḥmed Efendi as preacher in several of the capital's imperial mosques (the ten or so major Friday mosques that had been endowed over the centuries by Ottoman sultans).[48] He was inspired by the teachings of the puritanical scholar and preacher Meḥmed Birgili (d. 981/1573), but also—as Madeline Zilfi has shown—spurred by disparities within the *ʿilmiye* hierarchy and competition (often with Sufi shaykhs) over lucrative preacher positions in Istanbul's imperial mosques. Along with fellow imperial mosque preachers he set in motion a movement that drew its following from the Palace Service and the wider mosque-going urban population. Its rhetoric called for the imposition of a strictly defined orthodoxy on the public. Followers denounced as *bid'a*, and set out to uproot, a host of beliefs, rituals, customs, and social practices, from the use of music and dance in the Sufi ritual to supererogatory prayers performed in congregation, visits to saints' tombs in search of intercession, dissemination of the teachings of Ibn al-'Arabī, belief in the immortality of the legendary figure of Khiḍr, the consumption of tobacco and coffee, and intercommunal prayers organized in time of crisis. While not all of these were specifically associated with Sufis, clearly Sufi practices were at the center of the Ḳāḍīzādeli agenda. Especially Khalwatīs bore the brunt of the movement's anger, but Mevlevīs, Bektaşīs, and Celvetīs were also harassed, and indeed the whole tenor of the Ḳāḍīzādeli rhetoric and actions was a threat to any tariqa whose public *dhikr* ceremonies involved music and dance.

Invoking the age-old Islamic doctrine of "commanding right and forbidding wrong" (*al-amr bi'l-ma'rūf wa'l-nahy 'an al-munkar*), to which they gave a decidedly activist and political bent,[49] the Ḳāḍīzādeli leaders did not stop with simply denouncing certain practices; instead, they called upon their followers to actively confront those who engaged in the proscribed behavior, and on several occasions actually led them in physical attacks on Sufi shaykhs and *tekkes*. Those who shunned participation in this kind of vigilantism were denounced as no better than the perpetrators of the reprehensible innovations themselves. Much criticism was reserved for the official guardians of the *sharī'a*, the *'ilmiye* hierarchy, whom the Ḳāḍīzādelis often accused of tolerating popular religious practices and other *bid'as*.[50] At the same time, leaders of the movement were keenly aware of the importance of mobilizing behind their cause the support of senior men of religion and the coercive power of the state. And while the governing and learned elite generally sought to restrain the movement and to foster some balance between it and the Sufis, on a number of occasions the Ḳāḍīzādelis were able to gain official sanction for their demands. Thus, they had Sultan Murād IV issue a decree outlawing tobacco and wine and his grand vezir, Melek Aḥmed Paşa, sanction the destruction of the Khalwatī *tekke* near Demir Ḳapı (in 1061/1651). At one point the *şeyhülislām*, Bahā'ī Efendi, issued a legal opinion censoring Sufi music and dance, though before long he apparently reversed himself and instructed the *qāḍī* of Istanbul to punish preachers who used their pulpits to incite their listeners against the Sufis.

The role of the Naqshbandī shaykh 'Osmān Bosnevī as one of the principal propagators of the Ḳāḍīzādeli agenda emerges from Na'īmā's account for the year 1061/1651, which introduces the then leader of the movement, Meḥmed Üsṭüvānī, and a group of his mosque preacher-collaborators. It was these individuals, we are told, who from their pulpits mounted the campaign of disapprobation and rebuke against the Sufis, even resorting to accusation of unbelief (*takfīr*). And it was around them that there gathered the corps of vigilantes—many of them guardsmen of the Palace Service—who actually took to attacking *tekke*s and their visitors.[51] One of the group of Üsṭüvānī associates was "the teacher of the pages in the Palace [and] preacher of the Süleymāniye [Mosque], Şeyh 'Osmān."[52] The *nisba* Bosnevī is not mentioned in Na'īmā's text, but the identity of the shaykh is beyond doubt. We know from the *Zeyl-i şaḳā'iḳ* of 'Uşāḳīzāde that concurrently with his tenure at the Ḥekīm Çelebi Tekke, Bosnevī served as preacher in a series of the capital's major imperial mosques—Sultan Meḥmed, Bāyezīd, Süleymāniye, and finally Aya Sofya. The year 1061/1651 was his tenth as the preacher of the Süleymāniye Mosque, whence he would soon move to Aya Sofya, to be replaced at Süleymāniye by a Khalwatī shaykh.[53]

It may be that Bosnevī's involvement with the Ḳāḍīzādelis was short-lived. Na'īmā does not mention him in accounts of later incidents surrounding the movement, nor in the description of the banishment of Üsṭüvānī and his associates from Istanbul after the appointment of Köprülü Meḥmed as grand vezir in 1066/1656.[54] In fact, we know that Bosnevī was not exiled from Istanbul with Üsṭüvānī, since he continued to serve as both a *tekke* incumbent and an imperial mosque preacher at Aya Sofya for close to another decade, until his death in 1074/1664.[55] Perhaps he was moved to restrain his rhetoric or distance himself from the other Ḳāḍīzādeli preachers in response to the *şeyhülislām*, Bahā'ī Efendi, who, having become angered by the Ḳāḍīzādelis' increasing boldness, summoned Üsṭüvānī's preacher-collaborators to appear before him "one by one" and apparently warned them that their inciting rhetoric was unacceptable.[56]

Still, even a short involvement in a campaign of such vituperative anti-Sufi rhetoric and such a militant approach to "forbidding wrong" would have been striking. In voicing the militant Ḳāḍīzādeli rhetoric to the public from the pulpit of the Süleymāniye, Bosnevī might well alienate not only Sufis, but also members of the capital's religious and scholarly elite, many of whom were associated with Sufi leaders and ritual, and not particularly sympathetic to the Ḳāḍīzādeli discourse or constituency. The Ḳāḍīzādeli rhetoric was also quite removed from the common Naqshbandī attitude of treating Sufi practices such as *samā'* recitals with condescension rather than seeking to ban them. (In addition, Naqshbandīs themselves engaged proudly in some of the practices that the Ḳāḍīzādelis sought to proscribe, such as visiting deceased spiritual masters at their tombs, or disseminating the teachings of Ibn al-'Arabī.) Questions thus naturally arise as to how someone like Bosnevī became involved in this campaign. Was his a lone case, or were there other Naqshbandīs with Ḳāḍīzādeli connections: were his Ḳāḍīzādeli sympathies somehow related to his Naqshbandī spiritual upbringing? Was his rhetoric distinguished from that of the other Ḳāḍīzādeli preachers by some specific Sufi bent or agenda?

Although Bosnevī's role as a Ḳāḍīzādeli campaigner was no doubt unique, several other Naqshbandīs had had connections with the puritanical preacher Meḥmed Birgili, in whom, posthumously, the Ḳāḍīzādelis found their intellectual mentor. Birgili's first patron, the *ḳāżī'asker* of Rūmeli Ḳızıl 'Abdurraḥmān Amasyalı, was a Naqshbandī devotee and benefactor, as was the tutor of Sultan Selīm II, Aṭā'ullāh Efendi, who established him in his madrasa in Birgi.[57] Another Naqshbandī follower, the translator of the *Rashaḥāt-i 'ayn al-ḥayāt* into Turkish, Ma'rūf Ṭrābzūnī (d. 1002/1594), who served as *qāḍī* of Izmir, not far from Birgi, shortly after Birgili's death, was described by Nev'īzāde 'Aṭā'ī as a "commander of right"—perhaps an indication that he too was inspired by the puritan from Birgi.[58]

Particularly intriguing is a story according to which Bosnevī's own Naqshbandī preceptor (and long-serving predecessor at the Ḥekīm Çelebi Tekke), Aḥmed Tirevī (d. 1034/1624–25), had been at some point close to Birgili. The story appears in a biographical notice appended to the *Silsile-i hōcagān* of Muṣṭafā b. Hayreddīn, and must have been authored by one of Tirevī's disciples. Tirevī is said to have come to know and admire Birgili while serving as *muftī* in Tire near Birgi in his youth. He referred to him as "beloved" or "saintly" (*'azīz*) and "most worthy of companionship" (*aḥaḳḳ-ı ṣoḥbet*), and he approved of his summoning people to '*azīmet*,' or "[acting with] strictness" (a notion that Naqshbandīs themselves emphasized, as we have seen in chapter 5).[59] However, the credibility of this source is weakened not only by unknown authorship, but also by ambiguous writing and apparent inaccuracies. Ultimately there does not seem to be enough in this single account to establish that it was Bosnevī's spiritual master, Tirevī, who—inspired by his acquaintance with Birgili years before—nurtured in his disciple the activist attitude that in time would lead him to become one of the capital's principal Ḳāḍīzādeli preachers. Granted, it may be that Bosnevī himself was the anonymous Tirevī disciple who wrote this piece, perhaps in an attempt to make the Ḳāḍīzādeli agenda more acceptable to Naqshbandīs by describing his Naqshbandī preceptor, the respected Tirevī, as an admirer of Birgili's activism in his time. But this is only a speculation.

Other than this, we have no evidence of Bosnevī seeking to justify or bequeath his Ḳāḍīzādeli agenda to his Naqshbandī disciples, nor of other Naqshbandī shaykhs-cum-mosque preachers who used their pulpits in the service of the movement's rhetoric. Of another mosque preacher and *khalīfa* of Tirevī, Ya'ḳūb Ḳayṣeriyeli, we are told that his sermons at the Sultan Selīm and Bāyezīd Mosques brought him much fame and were written down, perhaps an indication that they were of a more learned bent.[60] One prominent individual, the *şeyhülislām* Feyżullāh Efendi (d.1115/1703), did, in time, combine Naqshbandī and Ḳāḍīzādeli connections. Feyżullāh began his learned career in his native Erzurum under the patronage of Vānī Efendi (d.1096/1685), who soon left for Istanbul, where he became the imperial tutor and the leader of the last wave of Ḳāḍīzādeli activism. It was Vānī who brought the future *şeyhülislām* to the capital in 1074/1663, gave him his daughter in marriage, helped his speedy advance along the *'ilmiye* career, and nurtured him as a lifelong confidant.[61] Some twenty years and many political upheavals later, Feyżullāh was initiated into the Naqshbandiyya, not by Bosnevī (by that time long deceased), but by a newcomer from Bukhara via India and the first propagator of the Naqshbandiyya-Mujaddidiyya in the Ottoman capital, Shaykh Murād al-Bukhārī (d.1132/1720). Of the extent of Feyżullāh's involvement with the tariqa we know little. All that we have is the account of a great-grandson of Shaykh Murād, the historian Khalīl al-Murādī, according to which during two lengthy sojourns in the Ottoman capital beginning in 1092/1681 the shaykh initiated into the tariqa and instructed in the Naqshbandī *dhikr* many of the city's high-ranking *'ulamā'*. Among them was Feyżullāh, who is said to have conferred with him and paid him "special reverence."[62] By that time, Feyżullāh's old patron, Vānī Efendi, had died or was about to die, and the whole Ḳāḍīzādeli movement was petering out. Clearly, in Feyżullāh's case, the convergence of Naqshbandī and Ḳāḍīzādeli connections was nowhere as direct or significant as in the case of Bosnevī.

It may be of some significance that while other Naqshbandīs beside Bosnevī (and less directly, Feyżullāh) did not become involved with the Ḳāḍīzādeli campaign, Naqshbandīs also did not become engaged in opposition to the Ḳāḍīzādelis, whether in efforts to exonerate fellow Sufis, or in a bid to defend denounced practices and beliefs that they themselves held dear.

Among the Sufis, the Khalwatīs stood out in their outspoken ripostes to the Ḳāḍīzādelis,[63] but shaykhs of other tariqas also criticized their rhetoric and action. The Bayramī shaykh Ḥüseyn Lāmekānī took on Münīrī Belğradī's attack against Sufi music and dance; such practices, he asserted, had been sanctioned by many religious authorities, including the Prophet.[64] The Celvetī shaykh-cum-preacher Zākirzāde Efendi declared the same from the pulpit of the Sultan Meḥmed Mosque.[65] And two other Celvetī shaykhs, Cennet Efendi and Ǧafūrī Maḥmūd Efendi, brought the case of the Ḳāḍīzādelis' anti-Sufi militancy before the *şeyhülislām* Ḥanefī Efendi.[66] Among Istanbul Naqshbandīs, by contrast, there is no evidence for such challenges.

A number of Naqshbandīs in Arabia and Damascus did become sufficiently scandalized by the Ḳāḍīzādelis to mount criticism, though this came rather late, and was sometimes less than explicit.[67] As we have seen, the Naqshbandī and Shaṭṭārī shaykh from Medina Ibrāhīm al-Kūrānī at one point became embroiled in an argument over vocal *dhikr* with a prominent visitor from Istanbul, probably the last Ḳāḍīzādeli leader, Vānī Efendi. One of Kūrānī's students, Ibn al-Mīmī, also ventured into the debate, calling the opponents of vocal *dhikr* (though without naming them) "ignorant" and "pigheaded." In Damascus, somewhat later, it was the Ḳāḍīzādeli rhetoric and action that, according to a recent study, sent ʿAbd al-Ghanī al-Nābulusī, however subtly, on his "ideological mission" of defending Sufism.[68]

Was Bosnevī's Ḳāḍīzādeli involvement an aberration, then, or was his militant Ḳāḍīzādeli rhetoric indicative of attitudes that were more common among Naqshbandīs, or even implicit in their formation? Our sources do not indicate that as a group, by dint of commitment to rigorous orthodoxy, Naqshbandīs were prone to condoning or participating in activism of the Ḳāḍīzādeli brand—which was indeed extreme. And yet, it is perhaps possible to understand Bosnevī's activism as an extension—however farfetched—of the attitude of defining the Naqshbandiyya in opposition to the "inferior" practices of other Sufis. Here a text of Bosnevī's teachings or preaching could have been of much value in that it could reveal the precise substance of his rhetoric and perhaps shed light on his motive or strategy. But unfortunately we do not possess such a text, nor do we have any indication that Bosnevī's sermons were written down—like those of his Naqshbandī colleague, the imperial mosque preacher Yaʿḳūb Ḳayṣeriyeli—and thus we are reduced again to speculating.

It may be that Bosnevī was trying to deliver a particular message, perhaps pushing for and proving the feasibility of a "correct Sufism" embodied in the Naqshbandiyya as a countermodel to the Sufism that the Ḳāḍīzādelis were denouncing. For such anti-Sufi criticism by Naqshbandīs (or rather proto-Naqshbandīs) there is a precedent from Tīmūrid Transoxania, which Devin DeWeese has analyzed in "Khojagānī Origins." There, a proto-Naqshbandī group had criticized the "corrupt Sufism" of its time, with its "fraudulent shaykhs" and privileging of external symbols of piety and affiliation, in order to highlight its own superiority and to score points in competition for disciples.[69] Similarly Bosnevī may have adopted the Ḳāḍīzādeli rhetoric (in some recast fashion?) as a tool in the competitive struggle among tariqas, a way of emphasizing the Naqshbandī devotional probity and superiority, and perhaps a means of defending or drawing attention away from Naqshbandīs' own "weaknesses," such as the practice of visiting tombs or the devotion to Ibn al-'Arabī.

Finally, how does the story of Bosnevī bear on this chapter's earlier discussion of Naqshbandīs and the anti-Ḳızılbaş campaign—or does it? Here we do have positive evidence of one Naqshbandī's intimate involvement in a campaign of imposing a strict *shar'ī* behavior on others. But this evidence is not, I would argue, of the kind or strength that would call for a revision of my earlier point—namely, that the notion of the Naqshbandiyya as a tariqa perpetually ready to take public and political action against challenges to the *sharī'a*-based order owes more to nineteenth-century images than to earlier realities.

7

Organizational and Cultural Modes

Avoiding explanations centered on politics and patronage—which have been, along with missionary paradigms, a staple of modern images of tariqas—this chapter explores a series of more subtle and little-studied cultural and organizational patterns that Naqshbandīs of our period exhibited, some in continuation of older Islamic and Sufi habits, others in new ways. Such modes—a privileging of the role of the shaykh as *murshid*, the practice of "spiritual" as opposed to hereditary family succession, the sense of belonging to an unbroken vertical tradition going back to the Prophet, shaykhs' ability to operate from outside specialized institutions, linguistic adaptability, a propensity for long-distance travel, or a knack for the dissemination of Persian culture—together underlay and gave a distinct texture to the Naqshbandī dissemination into and establishment within Ottoman society. Paying attention to these and related modes is crucial for understanding the Ottoman Naqshbandiyya and other premodern tariqas as networks and as instruments of cultural transmission and integration. It also serves in some ways as a fitting conclusion to this study.

"THE SHADOW OF THE SHAYKH IS BETTER THAN *DHIKR*"

Ottoman Naqshbandīs were avowed practitioners of an *irshādī* mode of Sufism in which the shaykh as *murshid*, the intimate guide of disciples in the transformative process of progressing toward mystical union, was at center stage. It was this kind of shaykh, along with the spiritual training (*irshād* or *tarbiya*) that he imparted and the companionship (*ṣuḥba*) that disciples (*murīds*) established with him, that underlay the superiority of the mystical way taught to Naqshbandīs. To dramatize this point the shaykh might be proclaimed as even more pivotal than *dhikr* in making this mystical way what it was, and in conferring on it its superiority. In one formulation attributed to ʿUbaydullāh Aḥrār, the "shadow of the shaykh" was itself "better than *dhikr*."[1]

Granted, shaykhs were pivotal to Sufism in all its modes whether they were viewed primarily as preceptors in a transformative mystical journey or as conduits of divine blessing (*baraka*), as was the case in the more intercessionary types of *zāwiya-* and shrine-based Sufism. No type of Sufism was possible without the mediation of living shaykhs.[2] Old and well-known Sufi adages underscored this point, proclaiming that a Sufi who did not have a shaykh was liable to have "Satan become his leader," or that "a tree that grows by itself without anyone planting it produces leaves but no fruit."[3] Naqshbandīs nevertheless stand out in the emphasis that they put on both the centrality of shaykhs to their mystical way and the superiority of their model of *irshādī* Sufism.

The Naqshbandī manuals portrayed the shaykh as the quintessential *murshid*. Rather than simply a teacher of a mystical doctrine or a guide in the performance of prescribed spiritual techniques, he also supervised the disciple's every state, regulated his breathing and movements, stood ready to extricate him whenever he encountered a complication or retreated in his mystical journeying, and watched over his changing spiritual disposition like a "spy of the heart." An even more distinctive Naqshbandī formulation required shaykhs to reach the realm of "remaining" in God after the "annihilation" of the lower self (*baqā'* after *fanā'*) and to be constantly in a state of "presence" (*ḥuḍūr*) with God. Without these, the shaykh could not become both "perfect" and "perfection-bestowing" (*kāmil* and *mukammil*), and would not be endowed with the power of *taṣarruf*, the ability to bring about changes in the trainee's spiritual disposition and thus kill the whims of his lower soul and turn his heart to the "ultimate desire."[4]

Some authors were more explicit than others about the special inflection that the superior quality of the Naqshbandī shaykh and *ṣuḥba* gave to the whole devotional regimen of this tariqa. As Muṣṭfā al-Ṣādiqī had it, the Naqshbandī *ṣuḥba* and *rābiṭa* made unnecessary the ascetic exercises (*mujāhadāt*) that were the cornerstone of the devotional regimen of Khalwatīs and other Sufis.[5] As we have seen, a similar idea was expressed in the adage "ours is a tariqa of *ṣuḥba*, [not] *khalwa*," that is, a tariqa whose center was companionship with and training under a shaykh rather than seclusion, particularly of the ritual kind in a cell.[6] For Tāj al-Dīn al-'Uthmānī, the superiority of the Naqshbandī shaykh and *ṣuḥba* had another crucial aspect to it: it meant that shaykhs were able to lead their disciples to experience "divine attraction" (*jadhba*) at the very beginning of the *sulūk*, the disciplined progress along the mystical path under a shaykh's supervision.[7] The point was not that for Naqshbandīs the *sulūk* itself became in any way less important, let alone expendable. Rather the possibility of experiencing "divine attraction" at the very beginning of the process of *sulūk* was seen as lending this process added significance and effectiveness.

In the eyes of Naqshbandīs there was nothing paradoxical about the Uwaysī mode of transmission, in which seekers gained initiation and mystical guidance in a nonphysical manner from the spiritual presence (*rūḥāniyya*) of a deceased shaykh, or from the paradigmatic Sufi guide, Khiḍr. In fact, they held the Uwaysī mode in particularly high esteem, not the least because it was associated with Bahā' al-Dīn Naqshband, and before him 'Abd al-Khāliq Ghujduvānī. Both were the recipients of Uwaysī transmissions, and it was through this mode that they were taught the silent *dhikr* that in time became the defining spiritual method of the tariqa.[8] Granted, Tāj al-Dīn proclaimed on the authority of his Indian preceptor that an Uwaysī initiation did not exempt one from training under a living shaykh: "The need for a living shaykh continues to exist [even when one has received a nonphysical initiation]. The teaching and conferring of the *dhikr* without authorization from a perfection-bestowing shaykh is devoid of any grace (*baraka*) or advantage."[9] This caveat apart, however, it is important to remember, as J. G. J. ter Haar has observed, that in the eyes of Naqshbandīs the nonphysical nature of the Uwaysī mode did not render it fundamentally different from a disciple's *ṣuḥba* with, and guidance under, a living shaykh: in both Uwaysī and live shaykh relationships it was the spiritual rather than the bodily presence of the shaykh that was viewed as the important agent of communication.[10]

The epitome or apex of the Naqshbandī *ṣuḥba* was the *rābiṭa*, the practice of fixing the visual form of the shaykh in the imagination as a prelude to taking on his qualities and to making him the conduit for the flow of divine energy.[11] The *rābiṭa* endowed shaykhs with exceptional importance: as disciples were cautioned, any slackening in their love to the shaykh, or behaving in ways that he would find distasteful, or even speaking unnecessarily in his presence could block the flow of divine energy through him.[12] One may even think of the *rābiṭa* as turning into a regulated technique the concept of annihilation in the shaykh as a step toward annihilation in God. Tāj al-Dīn al-'Uthmānī quoted the view that "annihilation in the shaykh *is* annihilation in God" (*qīla al-fanā' fī'l-shaykh fanā' fī'llāh*).[13] Indeed, this idea was so extravagant that he felt constrained to warn disciples against the pitfall of imagining the shaykh as though he was himself the journey's ultimate goal. Metaphorically, he suggested, the shaykh may be imagined as a drainpipe without which water could not flow; he was not, however, the water's source.[14]

Perhaps the importance of the *rābiṭa* among Naqshbandīs of our period also helps explain why our sources do not convey the understanding that Arthur Buehler found in the eighteenth-century Indian Mujaddidiyya, where the import of the shaykh as a conduit to God was more than anything else a function of his role as heir and exemplar of the Prophet.[15] Naqshbandīs of our period, too, held emulating the *sunna* of the Prophet as a foundation of their mystical endeavor; and they too viewed shaykhs as links between living practitioners and a *silsila* leading all the way back to the Prophet. But more than a "functional embodiment of the Prophet," the shaykh that our sources depict was an unfailing guide and supervisor of the mystical journey, an exemplar of behavior to be imitated and internalized, and a conduit to God by means of the *rābiṭa*. In comparison with the Mujaddidī paradigm identified by Buehler—one in which the shaykh's importance inhered first and foremost in his ability to replicate the Prophet—the model shaykh depicted by Tāj al-Dīn, for example, was an even more direct channel to God, and a more independently central agent or facilitator of the Naqshbandī mystical journey.

How did the view of the manuals translate into practice and manifest itself in the ways in which individual shaykhs initiated and trained disciples? Naqshbandī shaykhs naturally varied in their temperament and proclivities, but as a rule they put a premium on the intimate training of small groups while shunning anonymous or mass initiations. Apart from the Urmavīs of Kurdistan, who departed from other Naqshbandīs in a number of devotional and organizational practices, shaykhs had little use for the mass initiation of large crowds or for exercising leadership over whole communities. Perhaps this had deep roots going back to Central Asian Khwājagān-Naqshbandīs of the Tīmūrid period, with their polemics against fellow Yasavīs and the communal style of leadership that the latter employed in effecting the (nominal) conversion of whole communities.[16]

We have only a few descriptions of actual sessions in which individual shaykhs trained disciples. One account by Lāmi'ī Çelebi depicts a *majlis* (in this case, "seating") of 'Abdullāh Ilāhī and an intimate group of his disciples at the Zeyrek Mosque, where the shaykh was imparting to disciples the Naqshbandī devotional and mystical discipline. Everybody assumed a highly focused manner that enabled disciples to make great strides in their mystical journeying. The shaykh treated these disciples with utmost care and gentleness. He interpreted dreams that they related, supervised exercises of ritual seclusion, and noticed and responded whenever a stray thought interfered with someone's concentration.[17] Of course, only a limited number of followers would have been devoted disciples of this kind, who took a shaykh's *ṣuḥba*, paid him the proverbial unquestioning obedience, and became trainees in a spiritual regimen of seeking mystical ascent. Many others would have been more casual followers, who received initiation from a shaykh, visited his *tekke* on occasion, practiced the *dhikr* along with his other followers, attended his sessions of reading the *Masnavī* or explicating Ibn al-'Arabī, sought spiritual advice from him, or hoped to benefit from his *baraka*.[18] Many of the prominent followers that 'Abdullāh Ilāhī and Aḥmad Bukhārī attracted were probably of this more casual kind.[19] Of Ilāhī we know that he was annoyed with these casual followers, preferring to devote himself to the "real" disciples with whom he could pursue the *irshādī* mode.[20] Bukhārī seems to have been more comfortable with casual followers. Later his *khalīfa* Maḥmūd Çelebī made an explicit case for taking on such casual followers—what his biographer called "those who have come to appreciate [Sufism] but have not embarked on the process of *sulūk*" (sing. *al-mu'tarif al-ghayr sālik ilā ṭarīqihim*). As Maḥmūd Çelebi saw it, what began as general appreciation would ultimately bring these followers to the *ṭarīq al-ḥaqq*, the "path of God" and presumably a specialized devotional course.[21]

Even more than committed disciples, it was shaykhs of superior quality that were always difficult to come by, or at least there was a common refrain among Naqshbandīs lamenting the fact that the ideal or highly qualified shaykhs were becoming increasingly rare.[22] But whatever the reality, the ideal of *irshādī* Sufism—or, in other words, the expectation that in this tariqa shaykhs were to function as superior guides in a superior regimen of mystical progress—was central to Naqshbandīs' view of their way. In turn this was part of the allure of the tariqa, and not only in the eyes of those who would themselves become committed disciples. Many of the more casual followers, too, were apparently attracted to a tariqa whose shaykhs were guides in a superior mystical regimen, just as they found appealing the reputation of this tariqa for rigorous fidelity to the *sharī'a*, or the reputation of its shaykhs as experts in Ibn al-'Arabī or in a much-sought-after Persian literary culture.

BEQUEATHING SPIRITUAL AUTHORITY AND SENDING OFF *KHALĪFAS*

Naqshbandīs of our period practiced a nonhereditary style of bequeathing spiritual authority as a matter of routine. Shaykhs would designate as *khalīfas* (deputies or successors authorized to confer initiations and to give spiritual guidance in the Naqshbandī path) prized disciples who were not family members and who may have come to train with them from afar. In the case of a particularly close *khalīfa*, such transfer of authority, and sometimes of *zāwiya* tenure, might involve also receiving the shaykh's daughter in marriage.[23]

The Naqshbandī predilection for nonhereditary succession (in the double sense of bequeathing spiritual authority and *zāwiya* tenures) emerges from *silsilas*, biographical literature, and lists of *zāwiyas* and their successive incumbents. In a variety of these sources Naqshbandīs are set apart from their counterparts in other tariqas, where a hereditary family succession had become much more accepted and common.[24] There were exceptions in which not only individual shaykhs but whole Naqshbandī lines adopted a hereditary mode of succession. The Urmavīs of Kurdistan (unusual also in their mixed devotional regimen, their Shāfi'ī following, and the geopolitical setting in which they operated) are the first to come to mind as practicing a hereditary mode of succession along with a highly successful style of communal leadership.[25] In the capital, too, there was a Naqshbandī hereditary-family line—that which Aḥmad Ṣādiq Ṭāshkandī established (perhaps unwittingly) before his death in the plague of 994/1586, and which coalesced around the premier Emīr-i Bukhārī Tekke of Fātiḥ. Members of the same family were the incumbents of the *tekke* for two and a half centuries.[26]

Interestingly, Aḥmad Ṣādiq's move to the Ottoman capital—which his biographer Muṣṭafa al-Ṣādiqī depicted as the fulfillment of a missionary dream—may itself have been a response to an attempt to transform the line of his Transoxanian shaykh, Makhdūm-i A'ẓam Aḥmad Kāsānī, into a family patrimony. According to one source, when Kāsānī died in 949/1542, his son Muḥammad Amīn first became the overall spiritual leader (*shaykh al-kull*) of this circle, with authority over fellow *khalīfas* and their disciples. Then he was prevailed upon to step down in favor of Muḥammad Islām Jūybārī, who used antihereditary rhetoric to justify his claim to Kāsānī's succession, but later built his own hereditary shaykh and *sayyid* family line, that of the Jūybārīs of Bukhara.[27] In the rendition of Muṣṭafā al-Ṣādiqī the story of Kāsānī's succession was quite different, with the shaykh's younger son,

Khwāja Isḥāq, instructing all the *khalīfa*s of the *silsila* to accept the authority of Aḥmad Ṣādiq as the new *shaykh al-kull.*[28] While it is difficult to sort out these and additional versions of precisely what happened after Kāsānī's death, what is clear is that in sixteenth-century Transoxania the issue of hereditary succession and the old Naqshbandī distaste for this mode were in some flux.

This brings up the question of how Naqshbandīs adopted the nonhereditary mode of succession to begin with, and how they rationalized it (or whether they felt that it needed rationalizing, either because they lived in societies in which sons commonly assumed their fathers' occupations, or because tenure in a *zāwiya* and hence material resources were at stake). Clearly, the rejection of hereditary succession had had old and venerable roots in the Naqshbandī tradition. Bahā' al-Dīn Naqshband is said to have characterized himself in opposition to the hereditary model (though among his immediate successors both Muḥammad Pārsā and 'Alā' al-Dīn 'Aṭṭār authorized sons as *khalīfas*).[29] Devin DeWeese has shown how other Transoxanian Khwājagānīs of the fourteenth and fifteenth centuries tried to gain an advantage vis-à-vis competing Sufi groups—and in the process better define their own identity and distinctiveness—by resorting to polemics against a Yasavī style of leadership that combined hereditary succession, communal Sufi affiliation, and the Islamization, or "bringing into the fold," of whole communities.[30] It seems that in those early days of the emergence of the Naqshbandiyya out of the Ṭarīqat-i Khwājagān, the adoption of the nonhereditary mode of succession was also connected to an attitude of ambivalence toward, or even a frowning upon, the construction of *zāwiya*s (or *khānqāh*s). That attitude is epitomized in the testament attributed to 'Abd al-Khāliq Ghujduvānī: "Do not build *khānqāh*s and do not live in them."[31] It is easy to see how shaykhs who were not invested in *zāwiya*s would have been more accepting of the possibility of nonhereditary succession than those for whom such institutions were central.

Although fitting arguments could be easily marshaled to that effect, there is no evidence in sources from the Ottoman period of Naqshbandīs engaging in antihereditary polemics. For example, we do not find criticism of the hereditary mode of succession as one that was unlikely to generate those "perfect and perfection-bestowing" shaykhs that Naqshbandīs so prized. Nor do we encounter another seemingly ready-made argument: that of justifying the bequeathing of spiritual authority to nonrelatives as replicating the paradigmatic model of Abū Bakr's succession to the Prophet. In his *Khulāṣat al-athar*, the historian Muḥibbī reports the use of precisely this argument by some Khalwatīs in seventeenth-century Aleppo. He tells of two

Khalwatī circles in that city, one (of Ikhlāṣ al-Khalwatī) in which a shaykh's authority was routinely bequeathed to nonrelatives (*ajānib*, literally "foreigners"), and a second one in which the opposite practice of bequeathing authority exclusively to sons, brothers, or other relatives was preferred. According to Muḥibbī,

> The first [of these two circles] used as its proof (*dalīl*) the fact that the Prophet chose the Friend [Abū Bakr] as a *khalīfa* even though he was a non-relative and although a paternal uncle, al-ʿAbbās, and a paternal cousin, ʿAlī b. Abī Ṭālib, were available. The second [circle] had its proof in the claim that disciples were likely to put their trust in relatives and not to look down on them lest the [shaykh's] blessing be cut off from [his] progeny.[32]

In an inversion of the rationale used by the first of these two Khalwatī groups, we hear of modern Shādhilīs who have branded the practice of hereditary succession a "Shīʿī custom."[33] Such arguments could have fit well with the Naqshbandī notion of Bakrī descent and with the practice of rationalizing various Naqshbandī devotional emphases by identifying them as a legacy of Abū Bakr.[34] But we do not have evidence for Ottoman Naqshbandīs applying this rationale to the issue of succession, either in a positive way or in the negative anti-Shīʿī form used by the above-mentioned Shādhilīs. Perhaps all this indicates that by the period examined here the nonhereditary mode had become sufficiently established among Naqshbandīs, so much so that it could be treated as a routine matter needing little defense or polemicizing.

Whatever the manner or rationale of its adoption, a nonhereditary, "spiritual" mode of succession could affect a tariqa's expansion and endurance in several ways. Both encouraging spiritual masters to bequeath their authority to their most distinguished disciples and offering the prospect of succession to disciples who were not sons or close family members could militate against the drying up of spiritual lines, the exhaustion of charisma, or the incidence of unimpressive or unqualified shaykhs. The prospect of nonhereditary succession could also create around many a shaykh pools of eager disciples who came from diverse backgrounds and locales, and who could in time be dispatched without qualms to new venues, where they might take up *irshād*, establish new *zāwiyas*, or spread the tariqa through other means. It was surely easier and more natural for ʿUbaydullāh Aḥrār, to cite the most obvious example, to send 'Abdullāh Ilāhī back to Anatolia or 'Alī Kurdī (originally from Amadiyah in Kurdistan) to Qazvin than it would have been to send off a son or close family member.

Here the issue of *zāwiyas*, too, may be of some relevance. Early Ottoman Naqshbandīs no longer frowned on such institutions as 'Abd al-Khāliq Ghujduvānī is said to have done. But as we have seen, Naqshbandī shaykhs were able to operate comfortably with a variety of institutional arrangements. Perhaps this was so because of some continued ambivalence toward *zāwiyas*, or because the sobriety of the Naqshbandī devotional regimen freed shaykhs from any dependence on paraphernalia.[35] Perhaps it was in connection with a mode of succession that was antithetical to the creation of hereditary families of shaykhs (which elsewhere have been often shrine- or *zāwiya*-based).

But while a nonhereditary or "spiritual" mode of succession (as well as shaykhs' ability to operate independently of *zāwiyas* and especially of a central *zāwiya*) could certainly enhance widespread geographic expansion, it did not lead to such expansion automatically, let alone guarantee it. In the case of Aḥrār there was undoubtedly a connection between the use of the nonhereditary mode of succession, the attraction of disciples from far away, and the setting in motion of widespread geographic expansion. But as we have seen, Aḥrār's dispatching of *khalīfas*, which was so central to the dissemination of the Naqshbandiyya to the Ottoman lands, was predicated on much more than nonhereditary succession: his training and authorization of a number of "foreign" disciples, his dispatching of *khalīfas* to multiple destinations, and his continued communication with *khalīfas* who settled in new locations bespoke a deliberate effort to establish a widespread Naqshbandī network, which was apparently fueled by a unique missionary vision.[36] Early Ottoman Naqshbandīs—whether those who were spiritually descendant from Aḥrār or others—did not necessarily replicate this whole complex. Most of them practiced a nonhereditary mode of succession as a matter of routine, and not a few demonstrated a commitment to the training of multiple *khalīfas* in ways that encouraged the development of enduring lines. But generally they were not highly invested in expansion to new geographic regions through the dispatching of multiple *khalīfas* far off, and they certainly did not replicate Aḥrār's practice of sending *khalīfas* far off in an orchestrated fashion (perhaps Tāj al-Dīn al-'Uthmānī, in Mecca, came closest to this mode of operation).[37] Instead, they set out to spread the tariqa in a variety of more subtle ways, for example through the production and dissemination of texts.

TARIQA, *SILSILA*, AND PRIDE OF AFFILIATION

The Naqshbandiyya was a quintessential *silsila*-tariqa, a tariqa whose authenticity was expressed and ensured through a *silsila* or genealogical chain leading from the living practitioners to the eponym and all the way back to the Prophet Muḥammad. It may be that the concept of the *silsila* was established definitively in this tariqa only after Bahā' al-Dīn, who still thought of himself primarily as an Uwaysī.[38] But by our period—regardless of Naqshbandīs' continued acceptance and celebration of the possibility of nonphysical Uwaysī transmission—the concept of an unbroken *silsila* going back to the Prophet had clearly become central.

In a manner resembling the *isnād*s used in the transmission and authentication of Prophetic traditions, the *silsila* served to connect a tariqa to the Prophet, the ultimate fountainhead of Sufism, and to tie its devotional and doctrinal emphases to eminent figures from early Islamic history, thus highlighting particular devotional and doctrinal emphases as its hallmark. In chapter 5 we saw how in this regard the most crucial link in the Naqshbandī *silsila* was Abū Bakr, to whom Naqshbandīs traced several of the most distinctive devotional emphases of their way. At a second level, *silsila*s were conceived as initiatic power-lines that connected living practitioners ritually to spiritual masters who were deemed capable of bestowing on them not only particular mystical or devotional rites, but also *baraka*, the power of blessing that these masters possessed as *silsila*-links and as "friends of God" (*awliyā'*).

The *silsila* was a concept and artifact in which practitioners were greatly invested, and with which they developed a keenly felt bond. *Silsila*s were committed to memory, written down, and read aloud as part of a tariqa's communal ritual.[39] They could take the form of a separate document organized as a list or diagram (sometimes with attached biographical notices) that individual practitioners copied for safekeeping. They were conceived as badges of identity, displayed in *tekke*s, and appeared routinely in biographies and treatises, where they identified and located authors within a tariqa's initiatic network. By extension, as can be seen throughout this book, *silsila*s also provide the historian of Sufism with an indispensable source, one that helps establish the spiritual descent and interconnections of a tariqa's affiliates from a variety of generations and locales.

Naqshbandīs of our period might use the terms tariqa and *silsila* interchangeably. They conceived of their Naqshbandī "connection" or "ascription" (*nisba*) as one with a mystical and devotional way and with a vertical tradition, the *silsila*: only derivatively, through these, did it tie them with a large group or horizontal network, a brotherhood. This was illustrated in the vocabulary that practitioners used when speaking about initiation and mystical training. A seeker might "take" or "complete" the way from a preceptor, or "travel" on the way supervised by him (as expressed in the phrases *takmīl al-ṭarīqa, akhdh al-ṭarīqa,* and *sulūk 'alā al-ṭarīq*). He might become "affiliated" with the tariqa or the *silsila* (as in *kāna muntasab li'l-silsila*). By contrast, we do not find in our sources language that connotes becoming a "member" in a group, let alone a large network.

How is the keenly felt bond with the *silsila* that the Naqshbandī literature reveals compatible with the matter of multiple tariqa affiliations? We are often reminded that tariqa affiliations tended to be nonbinding during the period with which we are concerned.[40] Sufis went about casually obtaining double or multiple tariqa and *silsila* affiliations in the belief that this would augment their access to *baraka*; they did not need to invest much to acquire such affiliations, which might be conferred wholesale, in writing, without much training, and even on a child or a future child. Indeed, we know of individual Naqshbandīs who had multiple affiliations, and generally we do not have evidence that Naqshbandīs challenged the practice of seeking them—at least not openly. Yet outside the Arabian line of Aḥmad al-Qushāshī and Ibrāhīm al-Kūrānī, which was virtually defined by its multiplicity of affiliations, it is rare that we meet Naqshbandī shaykhs *giving* initiations into multiple tariqas.[41] It seems that while exclusivity of affiliation was not mandated in this tariqa, it was much encouraged by the crucial importance that Naqshbandīs assigned to their *nisba* with the tariqa (as both vertical tradition and system of mystical guidance) and by their belief that this bond was critical to the quality of their mystical journeying.

Naqshbandīs were taught that theirs was a superior tariqa, whose devotional sobriety, rigorous fidelity to the *sharī'a*, continuous *dhikr*, companionship with and intimate training by shaykhs (*ṣuḥba* and *irshād*), and facilitation of "solitude within society" all made it more effective than its counterparts in leading toward the mystic's goal.[42] For the more committed disciples, the emphasis placed on the uniqueness of the Naqshbandī *ṣuḥba* and *rābiṭa*—which made one's shaykh into a conduit of divine energy—would have made any casual wavering among shaykhs, let alone tariqas, highly risky. Granted, pride of affiliation had little to do with formal or external markers of identity, which Naqshbandīs cast as superfluous and even suspect. As we learn from the *Manāqib* of 'Alī 'Azīzān Rāmītanī, Naqshbandīs or proto-Naqshbandīs of the early fifteenth century (or before) were already criticizing the wearing of a Sufi robe (*khirqa*), along with the building of Sufi lodges (*khānqāhs*) and the handing over of formal documents (*shajaras*) authorizing disciples to give Sufi training.[43] In time, the core of the Naqshbandī initiation came to consist in the *talqīn*, the teaching of the formula and manner of performing the *dhikr*, rather than in a ceremonial investiture with robes, as was common in many other tariqas. According to Ibn al-'Ujaymī, Naqshbandīs (like Shādhilīs) were known for "having no interest in donning the *khirqa*"; instead, their way was "that of *dhikr* and companionship [with the shaykh]."[44] It should be apparent by now that this shunning of external markers was itself a symbol of the very pride of tariqa affiliation on which Naqshbandīs insisted.[45]

Outside the line of Qushāshī and Kūrānī (and to some extent there, too), the impression is that when Naqshbandī shaykhs subscribed to multiple affiliations, they felt compelled to make the Naqshbandī one preeminent. In the biography of Tāj al-Dīn al-'Uthmānī there is a story of how at the beginning of his career as a Naqshbandī shaykh (still in India) he would initiate disciples into the 'Ishqiyya and other tariqas on the authority of earlier masters. Then his preceptor, Muḥammad al-Bāqī, having been informed by the spiritual presence of Aḥrār that Tāj al-Dīn was "eating from our kitchen" and then "excluding us from his *nisba*," instructed him to stop initiating disciples into any but the Naqshbandī tariqa; and he obliged.[46] Tāj al-Dīn later became adamant about exclusivity of tariqa affiliation, and, indeed, exclusivity of attachment to one's shaykh—perhaps in response to the growing popularity of seeking multiple affiliations among Sufis in seventeenth-century Arabia, as emerges from the *Khabāyā al-zawāyā* of Ibn al-'Ujaymī.[47] In his treatise on the behavior of shaykhs and disciples, he criticized the practice of switching shaykhs and called upon shaykhs to prevent their disciples not only from taking the companionship of another, but even from associating with another's disciples, lest such an association, and the comparisons that it was bound to generate, might cause a disciple to be left devoid of a shaykh altogether. For Tāj al-Dīn such behavior would be nothing but an "abomination," if only because of the ease with which an unattached disciple could fall prey to Satan. This explains his harshness in labeling the tendency of Sufis of his time to waver among shaykhs *irtidād*—literally, "falling back," but by dint of its most common historical connotation more properly "apostasy."[48]

In the case of Aḥmad al-Nakhlī, another naturalized Meccan whose Naqshbandī affiliation passed through a Balkhī line descendant from 'Ubaydullāh Aḥrār and Aḥmad Kāsānī, the dilemma of a triple affiliation and a triple authorization to give Sufi training in the Naqshbandiyya, Shaṭṭāriyya, and Khalwatiyya was resolved through a dream in which the Prophet instructed him to choose the Naqshbandiyya. As he relates the story in his *Bughyat al-ṭālibīn*, when his Khalwatī shaykh 'Īsā Ibn Kinnān asked him to become his *khalīfa* in Mecca, Nakhlī was much dismayed, since his "heart was strongly inclined to the tariqa of the Naqshbandī masters [with its practice of] anonymity (*khumūl*) and silent *dhikr*." Still, he was upset with the thought of disobeying shaykh 'Īsā and repeatedly solicited God's advice, until a visit to Medina was facilitated. While there, in the Prophet's Mosque, he had a dream in which the Prophet instructed him to sit on a prayer rug (*sajjāda*) belonging to "Shaykh Tāj." This, Nakhlī quickly understood, was a sign that his real charge was to be a *khalīfa* of Tāj al-Dīn al-'Uthmānī, who had died in Mecca some decades before, and of whom Nakhlī had been made aware by his father when he was a young boy of six or seven, shortly before Tāj al-Dīn's death.[49] Thus, he too was made to "choose" between different affiliations and become exclusively a shaykh in the Naqshbandī tariqa.

TRAVEL, LANGUAGE, AND THE TARIQA AS INTERREGIONAL NETWORK

Early Ottoman Naqshbandīs did not exhibit the kind of missioinary organizing that lay at the root of the original expansion of the tariqa west from Transoxania at the hands of 'Ubaydullāh Aḥrār and his *khalīfa*s. The Naqshbandī presence that developed in the Ottoman capital as of the late fifteenth century, while distinguished by its vitality and endurance, did not become the engine of vigorous expansion to Anatolia or the Balkans—and certainly not to Arabia—through the well-orchestrated dispatching of *khalīfa*s (though something more akin to this pattern developed in Arabia itself, in the seventeenth century).

Nor do we find in the early Ottoman Naqshbandiyya the centralized or hierarchical organization that modern images of geographically widespread and tight-knit tariqas might lead us to expect. The Naqshbandī network of our period was as loose, uninstitutionalized, and decentralized as it was widespread. What we normally encounter in areas where Naqshbandīs established themselves is an array of circles that were crystallized around individual shaykhs and their *zāwiya*s and were anchored in personal bonds along with vertical *silsila* ones. Such circles were typically independent of each other, not only throughout the the vast area extending from Transoxania to the Balkans, but also within more restricted geographic regions and even in individual cities.

When an incumbent of a *tekke* died, he was commonly succeeded in his role by a prized *khalīfa*, while other *khalīfa*s, if there were such, went off to train disciples in other locales or from other venues (a *zāwiya*, mosque, or private residence) or established other careers as mosque preachers, prayer leaders, or private tutors. Those who succeeded their spiritual masters as *zāwiya* incumbents did not assume authority over fellow *khalīfa*s in some hierarchical fashion. We do not meet successors who turned themselves into "supershaykhs"—for example, by requiring fellow-*khalīfa*s to receive from them a renewed initiation or a renewed authorization to engage in Sufi training,[50] or by using the *rābiṭa*, as Shaykh Khālid would do in the nineteenth century, to subject to their own spiritual authority not only their immediate disciples but also those of their *khalīfa*s.[51] Nor were shaykhs moved from one Naqshbandī institution to another as a measure of promotion, as might happen among contemporary Khalwatīs or Mevlevīs.[52] And there was no equivalent among Naqshbandīs of the Bektaşī or Mevlevī practice of maintaining a central *tekke* whose incumbent presided over a large network of institutions and made decisions about their respective shaykhs.[53] Overall, the Naqshbandiyya of our period clearly does not support common modern images of tariqas as tight-knit, let alone centralized or hierarchical organizations.

The point here is not to underplay the extent to which geographic expansiveness was at the heart of this tariqa as it developed from the second half of the fifteenth century, once it spread throughout Transoxania and Khorasan, and was then disseminated far beyond Transoxania, including to central and western Iran, Arabia, and the Ottoman lands. The Naqshbandiyya was, from that time on, a quintessentially interregional or universal tariqa, whose mystical teachings and devotional regimen were directed at and deemed relevant to all Muslims, across linguistic, ethnic, social group, and *madhhab* (though not necessarily gender) boundaries. Rather the point is that we can better understand this expansiveness not by focusing on the notion of a missionary project or on tight-knit organization, but instead by exploring also a variety of more subtle means (or modes), such as the privileging of nonhereditary succession, or shaykhs' ability to operate from nonspecialized sites, or (as we will see below) a propensity for travel and linguistic and cultural adaptability.

Some of these modes had roots in the early days of the tariqa in Transoxania. For example, the Naqshbandī propensity for long-distance travel appears to have been born during the very early Naqshbandī or Khwājagānī period, perhaps out of the circumstances of a tariqa that was Transoxanian-based and at the same time strongly invested in "living the proper Muslim life." Committed to the latter, Naqshbandīs were always ready to travel, whether it was to various centers of Islamic learning or as pilgrims to the Holy Places in the Hijaz, as Bahā' al-Dīn Naqshband is said to have done twice. Little surprise, then, that the issue of travel from Central Asia, along with the various logistical and geopolitical considerations that attended it, continued to be central throughout the generations. We have seen, for example, how once the Ottomans had annexed the Arab lands, become the "Protectors of the Ḥaramayn," and established a well-attended imperial pilgrimage route from Istanbul in the early sixteenth century, Central Asian Naqshbandīs began to follow a new itinerary, traveling to Arabia via a northern detour leading through Istanbul (whether first through Iran or on the alternative northern route around the Caspian and Black Seas). Elsewhere we have seen how Mecca and Medina—being, as they were, the hub of the pilgrimage and the locus of various communities of "pious residents"—were for a long time the only place in the Arab lands where Naqshbandīs were able to build a sustained presence.[54] Clearly, these Sufi travelers, while serving to integrate the Islamic world through their travel and networks, also benefited from a physical (and conceptual) infrastructure for travel that had been put in place by others, mostly in connection with the institution of the *ḥajj*, the annual pilgrimage to Mecca.

But Naqshbandīs not only benefited from existing infrastructures; they also established their own. As we have seen, the route or routes of the pilgrimage from Central Asia via Istanbul were dotted with a series of Bukharan Naqshbandī *tekke*s that Central Asian benefactors established and endowed for the accommodation of Transoxanian pilgrims, and whose shaykhs were routinely Bukharans. Pilgrims would camp here on their way to the Hijaz, or would take the opportunity of the lengthy and arduous trip to spend a more extended period of time in one of these sites. In Bursa there was one such *tekke* from the mid-sixteenth century and another from sometime in the seventeenth. In Greater Istanbul there were two (one in Sulṭānaḥmed and the other in Bülbül Dere in Üsküdar) from the last years of the seventeenth century and another two (one in Sulṭāntepe in Üsküdar and the other in Eyüp) from the mid-eighteenth. Edirne in Thrace and Cizre in

Kurdistan had Naqshbandī *tekkes* of Central Asians (and in Cizre "Indians" or perhaps Afghans) when Evliyā Çelebi visited in the second half of the seventeenth century, and perhaps long before.[55] Jerusalem had the Zāwiya al-Uzbakiyya, established by one Uthmān al-Bukhārī in the early seventeenth century, where the right of residence was reserved to non-Arab and especially Transoxanian Naqshbandīs.[56]

Related to the Naqshbandī propensity for long-distance travel was an apparent knack for bridging over linguistic and cultural differences. This too seems to have had its origins very early on, with the first Naqshbandī and Khwājagānī shaykhs of Transoxania. Active in both urban and rural (albeit settled) milieus, and among Turkish as well as Persian speakers, these early shaykhs developed an ability to work across linguistic barriers and to appeal to diverse groups;[57] in time their spiritual descendants apparently internalized this ability and carried it with them to new venues. How this played out was evident, for example, in the ways in which Naqshbandī shaykhs drew adherents from different *madhhabs*. The majority of Naqshbandīs were Ḥanafīs (the tariqa's strongholds being the mostly Ḥanafī regions of Central Asia, the Indian subcontinent, Anatolia, and the Balkans). By contrast Shāfi'īs are said to have been less inclined toward this tariqa, at least partially because they assigned a high value to the vocal mode of *dhikr* and thus had difficulties obliging the Naqshbandī privileging of the silent *dhikr*.[58] Yet we have seen Naqshbandī shaykhs making important inroads in Shāfi'ī populations. Such was the situation with the Urmavī shaykhs of Kurdistan in the late sixteenth and early seventeenth century or with the line of Qushāshī and Kūrānī, and to some extent that of Tāj al-Dīn al-'Uthmānī, in seventeenth-century Arabia. Similar instances would occur later—for example, in Indonesia and again in Kurdistan, both under the aegis of the nineteeeth-century Khālidiyya.[59]

The ability of Naqshbandīs to bridge over linguistic and cultural difference can be seen also in the way in which, in the Ottoman world, they routinely acted as the carriers, disseminators, and perpetuators of a Perso-Islamic literary culture (whose origins had been in a number of Iranian and Central Asian cultural centers between the tenth and fifteenth centuries, among them Tīmūrid Bukhara and the Herat of Sultan Ḥusayn Bāyqarā). Numerous Naqshbandī shaykhs—immigrants from the east as well as Anatolian born—composed verse in Persian, wrote commentaries on Persian grammar and language, or exhibited expertise in Persian literature in other ways.[60] Others began a long and proud tradition of reading, teaching, and interpreting the *Masnavī* of Jalāl al-Dīn Rūmī, which continued all the way into the nineteenth century.[61] Because of all these activities and expertise, Naqshbandīs were often sought out by members of the Ottoman governing and intellectual elite (certainly in the capital and among Turkish speakers, if less so in Arabic-speaking environments), who coveted and held this Perso-Islamic literary culture in much esteem.[62]

At the same time that they distinguished themselves as the purveyors of a certain Persian literary culture, Naqshbandī shaykhs also understood the crucial importance of producing literature in Turkish and Arabic if they were to make inroads among many Turkish and Arabic speakers who otherwise would have had no access to the foundational texts of the tariqa, all written in Persian. This they set out to do both by writing original works in Turkish and Arabic and through translations or adaptations from Persian. To realize the extent to which Naqshbandī shaykhs surpassed their counterparts from other tariqas in their commitment to this endeavor of writing, copying, and translation, one need only leaf through catalogs of numerous Istanbul manuscript libraries, with their unequaled number of copies of Naqshbandī treatises, manuals and related works—though the real torrent of Naqshbandī writings in these libraries seems to date from the later, Mujaddidī and Khālidī, periods.

Among the most important translations-adaptations from Persian produced during the period studied here were those of Jāmī's *Nafaḥāt al-uns* and Kāshifī's *Rashaḥāt-i 'ayn al-ḥayāt* by Lāmi'ī Çelebi, Ma'rūf Ṭrābzūnī, and Tāj al-Dīn al-'Uthmānī (or his Meccan *khalīfa* Ibn 'Allān), along with that of Qazvīnī's *Silsilanāma-yi khwājagān-i Naqshband* by Muṣṭafā b. Hayreddīn. Works written directly in Turkish or Arabic include 'Abdullāh Ilāhī's *Meslek eṭ-ṭālibīn* and *Ervāḥ ül-müştāḳīn*, Şa'bān Efendi's *Merātib-i sülūk ve-keşf*, Muṣṭafā al-Ṣādiqī's *Al-Manhaj al muwaṣṣil ilā al-ṭarīq al-abhaj* (written in Arabic at the instructions of Ṣādiqī's shaykh, Aḥmad Ṣādiq Ṭāshkandī), and two much-copied *Risālas* by Tāj al-Dīn al-Uthmānī (or again his *khalīfa* Ibn 'Allān), one on the Naqshbandī devotional regimen and the other on the etiquette of shaykhs and disciples. Some authors—for example, the Bursan Aḥmad Ilāhī in his treatise on *sulūk*—ventured to produce works simultaneously in "the three languages": Arabic, Turkish, and Persian.[63] Together these and fellow writers created as of the sixteenth century and certainly by the seventeenth a corpus of tariqa literature that was intelligible to local Naqshbandīs and prospective Naqshbandīs. It included devotional manuals and mystical treatises as well as the biographical and hagiographical literature that was crucial both for establishing models of behavior to be emulated and for connecting new practitioners to the tariqa's history. In the process, they demonstrated a commitment to making the tariqa available to new audiences through the production and dissemination of texts, if not in more explicitly missionary or activist Aḥrārian ways.

A window into the manner and pace at which such written materials were used and diffused can be had from a manuscript copy of a lesser-known work entitled the *Risāle-i şerīfe-i mağrūbe fī uṣūl-i ṭā'ife-i 'aliye-i Nakşbendiye*, now part of a bound volume of Naqshbandī writings at the Süleymaniye Library.[64] The original Persian, treating the Naqshbandī *silsila* and the series of principles known as the *kalimāt-i qudsiyya*, is said to have been written by a son or descendant of Muḥammad Pārsā. Travelers from Bukhara brought it to Istanbul, where it began to be copied and used despite the fact that for some time the identity of the author remained unknown.[65] The Persian text was reproduced in the Ottoman capital at least once before 1000/1591–92, and sometime later a Turkish translation-adaptation was written by one 'Abdülkerīm Efendi, a spiritual descendant of Ḥekīm Çelebi's *khalīfa* Şa'bān Efendi. The copy now in the Süleymaniye Library consists of that translation, with the Persian original on the margin. It was made in 1008–9/1600 by Ibrāhīm b. Meḥmed Sīvāsī, a resident of the Rüstem Paşa Madrasa. He was a disciple of Şa'bān Efendi, and a prolific copier of Naqshbandī texts, several of which are included in the same volume. From a number of comments added on the margin of the *Risāle*, we learn of the existence of at least four other copies of the same work from the two decades before and two decades after the preparation of Sīvāsī's manuscript. Two of the copiers were well-known individuals: Meḥmed Ḳavaḳlızāde, shaykh of the Emīr-i Bukhārī Tekke in Fātiḥ for seven years, and Aḥmed Tirevī, described here simply as "Aḥmed Efendi," an "interpreter and transmitter of the *kalimāt-i qudsiyya*," but easily identifiable as Aḥmed Tirevī, the prominent shaykh and long-serving incumbent of the Ḥekīm Çelebi Tekke in Fīl Dāmī.

We may note that all the individuals associated with the *Risāle* through translation or copying had in common spiritual descent from Ḥekīm Çelebi (though except for Tirevī they all came to reside or officiate in institutions other than the Ḥekīm Çelebi Tekke). More significant, however, is the very involvement of prominent shaykhs and *tekke* incumbents such as Ḳavaḳlızāde and Tirevī in copying. This illustrates the central importance that Naqshbandīs assigned to the work of disseminating texts, and by extension their conviction that what they were offering disciples was relevant across linguistic and ethnic (and at least to some extent, social and *madhhab*) boundaries. Even more than the privileging of nonhereditary succession or the ability of shaykhs of this tariqa to operate independently of *zāwiyas*, the Naqshbandī commitment to the production and dissemination of literature was at the center of the expansiveness and the universal appeal of this tariqa, and thus a reminder that such expansiveness can be understood in terms other than the tight-knit organization or missionary paradigms that modern scholarship has been wont to emphasize.

Conclusion

Naqshbandīs established a presence in various parts of the Ottoman world, and within Ottoman society, long before the introduction of the Mujaddidiyya from India at the turn of the eighteenth century. The process began over two centuries earlier as an integral part of a larger historical moment during which this tariqa was being disseminated from its birthplace in Transoxania, most notably by *khalīfa*s of 'Ubaydullāh Aḥrār. While various changes later occurred in geopolitics and communications, most notably those wrought by the Shī'ī-Ṣafavid takeover of Iran, immigrants, visitors, and pilgrims from Transoxania continued to travel west for generations, in the process refurbishing the ranks of the Ottoman Naqshbandiyya and keeping very much alive the memory of the tariqa's historical center in Central Asia. Except for the Holy Cities of the Hijaz, where two Naqshbandī lines of Indian origin were introduced at the beginning of the seventeenth century, the Ottoman Naqshbandiyya was of direct Transoxanian origin until the vigorous Mujaddidī expansion from India changed things in the eighteenth century.

This is important in more than one way. It not only puts to rest the notion that Naqshbandī expansion equals Mujaddidī expansion. The very direction in which the Naqshbandī influence flowed at this time—from late Tīmūrid and Uzbek Transoxania west to Arabia and to the newly expanded imperial and Islamic state that was the Ottoman Empire—is itself significant. Again, we are reminded here of the complex and dynamic workings of core and periphery in the Islamic world, and of the careful thought that must always be given to the use of these twin terms in Islamic contexts.

In comparison with the later and better-known Mujaddidī and Khālidī phases, the phase of Naqshbandī history examined here exhibited little drama. Both the missionary impulse and the intensity of movement associated with the first *khalīfa*s of Aḥrār subsided in later generations. Nor did early Ottoman Naqshbandīs distinguish themselves through political activism or through grand doctrinal or devotional shifts or innovations. Rather than drama, what marked this Naqshbandiyya was its ability to develop and deploy a distinct devotional identity, build a reputation, attract disciples and followers, carve a presence for itself in various locales, establish lasting structures, become integrated into society, and adapt to a social and political climate that was profoundly different from that of the tariqa's birthplace in Tīmūrid Central Asia.

The issues of becoming integrated into society and of adapting to a new social and political climate are particularly significant inasmuch as they bear on the question of whether Naqshbandīs of our period are best seen as the legatees of a universal Sufi tradition who came to inhabit the Ottoman environment (or environments), or whether the Naqshbandiyya of this time became an Ottoman as well as a universal tariqa—and how. In some ways the first proposition seems more apt. Ottoman Naqshbandīs were far from a unified or cohesive group, not the least because the various locales where they established themselves—Istanbul, Bursa, Kurdistan, the Balkans, or the Holy Cities of the Hijaz—offered rather different opportunities and obstacles and encouraged different strategies of propagating the tariqa. Naqshbandīs throughout this area also were not bound together by any institutional framework—as opposed to sharing an awareness that they all subscribed to a universal tariqa and *silsila*, with its historical center in Transoxania.

Naqshbandīs of our period also appear less than eager to take advantage of a number of opportunities that could have had the effect of "Ottomanizing" them, including the availability of abundant state and elite patronage in the newly established Ottoman capital, and opportunities to become active along still-expanding imperial and Islamic frontiers. Here the thesis that they were uniquely instrumental in the sixteenth-century campaign of the Ottoman state against the Ṣafavids and Ḳızılbaş is obviously appealing. Such a role not only would have underscored the adamantly Sunnī and orthodox character of this tariqa; it could also have Ottomanized it by making it a player in one of the most critical Ottoman battles of the time. As we have seen, however, there is not enough evidence to support the whole anti-Ḳızılbaş thesis or to show a significant Naqshbandī involvement in this critical battle. More than a careful reading of the relevant sixteenth-century sources, what appears to drive this thesis is a projection back into history of nineteenth-century realities and images.

Still, one may think of this Naqshbandiyya as having become an Ottoman tariqa, at least to an extent, if only because Naqshbandīs' success in establishing and sustaining a presence in various parts of the empire bespeaks a willingness and an ability to adapt to new circumstances and to remake themselves accordingly. Here was a state with a well-organized central government and an increasingly bureaucratic and hierarchical religious establishment, a political system that sought to limit or co-opt independent power, and a polity with a claim to both the implementation of the *sharī'a* and the protection and representation of Sunnī Islam. With few exceptions, most notably in Kurdistan during protracted and indecisive wars with Shī'ī-Ṣafavid neighbors, Ottoman Naqshbandī shaykhs could not hope to build themselves up by taking advantage of a fragmented or weakened state or central government, as 'Ubaydullāh Aḥrār had done in Samarkand. Nor could they easily cast themselves as the champions of the *sharī'a*-based order, since the state and its religious establishment already assumed that role. But Naqshbandīs adapted and found effective ways to function in the new environment, or environments. Among other things, they staked a double claim to *sharī'a*-abidance and mystical superiority, encouraged their followers to live "within society," devised new ways of mobilizing material patronage from the wealthy as well as more humble, and developed a reputation as the purveyors of a mystical tradition and a broader Persian literary culture, for which there was much demand among Ottoman elites.

In the introduction to this book, I argued that phenomena belonging to pre- or early-modern Islamic history, as is the pre-Mujaddidī Naqshbandiyya, ought to be studied in their proper historical context and on the basis of proper sources; moreover, their study ought to be informed by an awareness of the potential of powerful modern paradigms to obscure our understanding when they are retrojected into history and employed as prisms through which such earlier phenomena are viewed. Three broad aspects of Naqshbandī history in the Ottoman world have become better illuminated through the application of these caveats: the Naqshbandiyya as an "orthodox" tariqa, Sufi expansion, and the relationship of Naqshbandīs with political involvement and activism.

Early Ottoman Naqshbandīs declared repeatedly and routinely their rigorous fidelity to the *sharī'a*, but the manner in which they configured this commitment was at odds with common images of the Naqshbandiyya's orthodoxy and with more general nineteenth-century-based paradigms—be they colonial, modernist, or Salafī—that assume a highly politicized view of Islamic orthodoxy, or place great emphasis on the inherent tension between *sharī'a*-abidance and mystical journeying. For one thing, the Naqshbandī identity that was inculcated in disciples during our period had at its heart not simply rigorous fidelity to the *sharī'a* but rather a more complex regimen. It combined devotional sobriety and *sharī'a*-abidance along with the shunning of common Sufi practices that Naqshbandīs cast as ostentatious or inferior, a call for adepts to engage in their Sufi discipline while leading lives fully immersed in society, a claim to superior mystical journeying, and a vision of an *irshādī* Sufism in which shaykhs were intimate guides of individual mystical seekers along a path of spiritual transformation. It was around this whole edifice, and not simply around the rigorous fidelity to the *sharī'a* that is the staple of modern views of this tariqa, that Naqshbandīs of this period built their appeal and developed their pride.

Second, *sharī'a*-abidance, or what tariqa literature might call *al-'amal bi'l-'azīma* ("acting with strictness"), was understood primarily as a matter of personal observance and devotional sobriety (the notion of *al-'amal bi'l-'azīma* having been associated from the very early Naqshbandī days in Transoxania with the silent form of *dhikr*). Neither a public or political stance of battling to protect the *sharī'a*-based order nor the rejection of mystical speculation or journeying (as opposed to some devotional *practices* employed in other tariqas) were implied. This meant that Naqshbandīs could combine comfortably two claims (to rigorous *sharī'a*-abidance and to mystical superiority), teach a potentially dangerous spiritual exercise such as the *rābiṭa*, entertain a keen sense of being immersed in the world of the "friends of God," and study and propagate with enthusiasm the mystical teachings of Muḥyī al-Dīn Ibn al-'Arabī. S*harī'a*-abidance was not and did not have to be the mark of a demysticized Sufism, as modern sensibilities might suggest.

The issue of Sufi expansion, its motives, and its means also becomes more subtly appreciated once we approach the early Ottoman Naqshbandiyya with due awareness of the power of modern paradigms to obscure our understanding. The Naqshbandiyya was from sometime in the late fifteenth century a universal tariqa rather than one confined to a particular region or a particular linguistic, ethnic, social, or cultural group. In that sense, its expansion out of Transoxania was natural. Yet after the generation of Aḥrār's *khalīfas*—those who were at the heart of the original Naqshbandī dissemination to Arabia and the Ottoman lands—we no longer encounter anything like the well-orchestrated sending off of *khalīfa*s that Aḥrār apparently put in motion. No such wave of missionary-*khalīfa*s "took" the tariqa from Istanbul to the towns of Anatolia or the Balkans, let alone the Arab lands. We also do not find the Naqshbandiyya of this period exhibiting the tight-knit or hierarchical organization built around "supershaykhs" and central *zāwiya*s that nineteenth-century paradigms would suggest; instead, we meet a remarkable looseness and an array of independent and institutionally unconnected circles based primarily in personal and vertical *silsila* bonds. The point is not whether any individual Naqshbandī can be labeled a "missionary" (even leaving aside the Christian connotations of this term). It is that we are more likely to gain a complex understanding of the expansion of this and other tariqas if instead of expecting Sufi dissemination to be the work of missionaries and their well-organized networks—as modern scholars often have—we would set out to explore a series of less dramatic organizational and cultural modes or preferences related to travel, writing, succession, the use of *zāwiya*s, the deployment of patronage, or the production and dissemination of texts.

For example, Naqshbandī shaykhs employed and made into something of a tariqa hallmark, with roots going back all the way to the eponym Bahā' al-Dīn Naqshband, a mode of bequeathing spiritual authority (and, when relevant, *zāwiya* tenures) to prized disciples who were not sons or family members. This was not only conducive to a continued renewal and reinvigoration of spiritual lines. Combined, as it often was, with the training as *khalīfa*s of nonfamily members who had come to seek a shaykh's guidance from afar, it could also encourage the very sending of these *khalīfa*s far off, be it back to their native lands or to new destinations.

Another very old Naqshbandī or Khwājagānī attitude—this one attributed to 'Abd al-Khāliq Ghujduvānī—was one of ambivalence toward *zāwiya*s. By Ottoman times there were many specialized Naqshbandī *zāwiya*s (or *tekke*s). Such sites naturally attracted local or official patronage, provided space for conducting the tariqa's ritual and for training and sometimes housing disciples, and became the nucleus around which shaykhs prospered and spiritual circles and lines coalesced. They might become integrated into the life of local communities by drawing on local patronage or by extending charity to the local poor via their *waqf*s. Still, the old ambivalence apparently did not die out completely, perhaps because *zāwiya*s were not absolutely critical for the survival of a tariqa whose adamantly sober devotional regimen made it independent of paraphernalia, and whose shaykhs did not seek to create family patrimonies. Numerous Naqshbandī shaykhs—most notably in Bursa—operated from nonspecialized "generic" spaces such as madrasas or, especially, public or neighborhood mosques where they were the appointed preachers or prayer leaders. While such institutions and arrangements rarely supported spiritual lines that lasted beyond one or two generations, they served individual shaykhs effectively in their efforts to build public reputations and to introduce the tariqa to the larger society.

With regard to material resources, we have seen that early Ottoman Naqshbandīs were the recipients of far less (though by no means negligible) patronage from the state or the governing elite than is often assumed. Khalwatīs and others clearly surpassed them in that regard. But when we look beyond such obvious sources, we find more subtle ways of mobilizing patronage. For example, there was the distinctive mode labeled "disciples' endowments" (*evḳāf ül-mürīdīn*), which a comprehensive *waqf* register from mid-sixteenth-century Istanbul associated specifically with Naqshbandī institutions. A series of Naqshbandī disciple-patrons, almost none of them hailing from the Ottoman governing elite and certainly not from its high echelons, created these *waqf*s through cumulative efforts.

In a similar vein, Naqshbandīs emerge as effective agents of cultural transmission and facilitators of interregional and intergroup integration without being given to "missionary organizing." We routinely encounter them traveling long distances in search of spiritual guides and audiences, propagating the tariqa while on the pilgrimage, establishing *zāwiya*s to accommodate travelers, translating and copying texts, sharing linguistic and literary expertise, and attracting followers from different social groups, linguistic backgrounds, and *madhhab* affiliations; granted, some of these (Turkish speakers, Ḥanafīs, educated elites, city dwellers) were more easily attracted than others (Arabic speakers, Shāfi'īs, peasants). Much of this may have been inherited from ancestors in Central Asia, where the tariqa had been active from its very inception among different linguistic and ecological groups, and where remoteness from the Hijaz and from other centers of Islamic learning had made long-distance travel expected, taken for granted, and internalized, if not always routine. In traveling across long distances, Naqshbandīs continued old Islamic habits and made use of existing logistical structures. They especially used structures related to the institution of the pilgrimage to Mecca, whose importance in affecting the history of this tariqa emerges from our examination time and again. But they also set up their own logistical structures, like the series of Naqshbandī Bukharan *tekke*s that Transoxanian benefactors founded specifically to provide accommodations for Central Asian pilgrims on their way to the Hijaz; these ranged from Istanbul, Bursa, Jerusalem, and Edirne to Cizre in Kurdistan. Like other

Sufis, Naqshbandīs were in this regard both the beneficiaries and facilitators of structures of cultural integration and transmission within and among Muslim societies.

Along with long-distance travel, an instrument of cultural transmission and integration that Naqshbandīs employed repeatedly was the production and dissemination of texts via writing, translating, copying, and conducting public reading sessions. They particularly developed a reputation as the purveyors of a Persian literary culture whose elegance and sophistication made it much sought after in some Ottoman circles; we know of a number of prominent Ottomans who became drawn to the tariqa having heard a Naqshbandī shaykh read the *Masnavi* in a *tekke* or a public mosque. At the same time, these shaykhs were committed to the production and the dissemination of tariqa literature in Turkish and Arabic for the use of the less-well-heeled—we have seen prominent Naqshbandī shaykhs and *tekke* incumbents engage not only in writing or translating such materials but also in copying and disseminating them.

The potential of nineteenth-century realities and images to obscure our understanding of the early Ottoman Naqshbandiyya, and by extension of other early-modern tariqas, is perhaps most explicit in the area of politics or political activism. It is sometimes argued that the establishment of the Naqshbandiyya in the Ottoman Empire at the turn of the sixteenth century was facilitated by official patronage that Naqshbandīs received as a reward for their help in the critical Ottoman battle against the Ṣafavids and Ḳızılbaş. However, an examination of sixteenth-century sources suggests that Naqshbandīs played at best a minor role and were not particularly well equipped to take part in this drama. By the time the Naqshbandī presence was being established in various parts of the empire, the Ṣafavids had already come to power in Iran, and Sunnī-Shī'ī relations had become newly politicized and embittered; yet the adamant Sunnism that would later become a hallmark of the Naqshbandīs is not yet apparent. Sources of this period show their Sunnism as rather mild and not yet particularly politicized—for one thing, the Naqshbandī Bakrī *silsila* was not yet transformed from the spiritual marker that it had always been into a political or anti-Shī'ī one.

Nor were Naqshbandīs the recipients of the kind of official patronage that one would expect to have been bestowed on important collaborators in one of this period's major battles; it is rather the Khalwatīs on whom ample patronage of this kind was bestowed. The idea that rigorous orthodoxy and an adamant Sunnī and anti-Shī'ī identity conditioned Naqshbandīs to be particularly hostile toward the Ṣafavids and Ḳızılbaş, and that consequently they played a prominent role as an ally of the Ottoman state in trying to tame the latter, thus finds little support in sixteenth-century sources. There is evidence that it may have been inspired, rather, by the early nineteenth-century turning over of Bektaşī institutions to Naqshbandī shaykhs, and more generally by modern notions of tariqas as networks of political activism, and of the Naqshbandiyya as a tariqa militantly devoted to the protection of the *sharī'a*-based order, be it in support of the state or in opposition to it. (That early Ottoman Naqshbandī shaykhs also did not replicate, or attempt to replicate, the system of political and economic involvement and influence that 'Ubaydullāh Aḥrār had constructed in late Tīmūrid Transoxania is a different matter, for which there is a practical explanation. What Aḥrār did in Central Asia was made possible by particular circumstances, especially of political fragmentation. None of this would have been tolerated in the Ottoman environment, except, as we have seen, temporarily and during special circumstances, such as those in faraway Kurdistan, on the Ṣafavid frontier, for some years during the early seventeenth century.)

In conclusion, one would want to note that the temptation to view the past via nineteenth-century prisms may be particularly strong in the Naqshbandī case because of the unusual vigor of the Mujaddidī and Khālidī phases and of Mujaddidī and Khālidī spiritual lines, which together have caused earlier phases in this tariqa's history to become marginalized and earlier spiritual Naqshbandī lines of direct Transoxanian origins to be eclipsed. But the understanding of other early-modern aspects of Islamic history, and especially other early-modern tariqas, must also be at stake. They, too, are better approached and more likely to be appreciated in their complexity if keen attention is paid to the potential of modern paradigms to obscure our understanding when they are projected uncritically back into the past.

Notes

INTRODUCTION

1. "Tariqa" is commonly translated as meaning a Sufi brotherhood or order. The latter is particularly problematic because of its evocation of the rather different institution of Christian monastic orders; but both terms emphasize organizational aspects unduly while failing to convey the sense of tariqa as a mystical system or way, which Sufis themselves held central. To preserve the complex meaning that the word tariqa held in the eyes of practitioners, in what follows I try as much as possible to use the original term rather than resort to translations. For the tendency of Naqshbandīs of our period to think of their tariqa first and foremost as a mystical system and vertical tradition, and only then, derivatively, as a horizontal network, see chap. 7.

2. Trimingham, *Sufi Orders in Islam*. In Trimingham's schema, the term tariqa was more properly applied to the "schools of mysticism" that characterized Sufism's "second stage" in about 1100–1400. For the full-fledged "orders" of the "third stage" he proposed the term *ṭā'ifa*; however, he was himself inconsistent in following this terminological schema.

3. Ibid., chap. 4.

4. Ibid., 102-4.

5. O'Fahey, *Enigmatic Saint*; Elias, *Throne Carrier of God*; Gross, "Khoja Ahrar."

6. Cornell, *Realm of the Saint*; Buehler, *Sufi Heirs of the Prophet*.

7. Ernst, *Eternal Garden*.

8. Eaton, *Sufis of Bijapur*; Jong, *Ṭuruq and Ṭuruq-Linked Institutions*; Winter, *Society and Religion*.

9. Faroqhi, *Bektaschi-Orden in Anatolien*; Clayer, *Mystiques, état et société*; Mélikoff, *Hadji Bektach*; Gaborieau, Popovic, and Zarcone, *Naqshbandis*; Popovic and Veinstein, *Bektachiyya*; Clayer, Popovic, and Zarcone, *Melâmis-Bayrâmis*.

10. On the Mujaddidiyya and Khālidiyya in the Ottoman lands, see Abu-Manneh, "Rise and Expansion," "Naqshbandiyya-Mujaddidiyya in the Early Nineteenth Century," "Naqshbandiyya in the Early Tanzimat Period," and "Shaykh

Ahmed Ziyā'üddīn el-Gümüşhanevi" (articles partially revised from "Naqshbandiyya-Mujaddidiyyya in the Ottoman Lands"); Algar, "Devotional Practices"; Algar, "Naqshbandī Order in Republican Turkey"; Gündüz, *Gümüşhânevî Ahmed Ziyâüddîn*. On Transoxania, see Babad anov, "On the History of the Naqšbandīya Muǧaddidīya." On the Indian subcontinent, Buehler, *Sufi Heirs of the Prophet*. On Indonesia, Bruinessen, "Origins and Development."

11. For the history of this Naqshbandī phase we are still dependent essentially on Kufralı, "Nakşbendliğin Kuruluş ve Yayılışı"; and Kufralı, "Molla İlâhî." Others, especially Hamid Algar, have examined specific individuals or aspects of this period in various venues; references to these works are given separately below.

12. On the great lacuna concerning the "middle Ottoman centuries," see Kafadar, "New Visibility of Sufism," 309–10. For the debate over and a critique of the paradigm of post-Süleymānic decline, see Faroqhi, "Crisis and Change," 552–56; Abou-El-Haj, *Formation of the Modern State*. For a study that makes use of the career of the seventeenth-century Damascene shaykh 'Abd al-Ghanī al-Nābulusī to counter the decline paradigm, see Schlegell, "Sufism in the Ottoman Arab World."

13. For a critical analysis of what R. S. O'Fahey and Bernd Radtke term the *littérature de surveillance*, see their "Neo-Sufism Reconsidered," 61–64. Cf. Triaud, "Thème confrérique"; Harrison, *France and Islam in West Africa*, 19–23, 31.

14. See Merad, "Iṣlāḥ."

15. See, for example, Voll, *Islam: Continuity and Change*, 36–39; Voll, "Linking Groups," 83–87; Levtzion and Voll, introduction to *Eighteenth-Century Renewal and Reform in Islam*, 10–11. For a critique of these ideas, see O'Fahey, *Enigmatic Saint*, 1–9; O'Fahey and Radtke, "Neo-Sufism Reconsidered." Cf. two responses: Levtzion, "Eighteenth Century Sufi Brotherhoods"; and Voll, foreword to *The Sufi Orders in Islam*, ix–xiii.

16. Karamustafa, *God's Unruly Friends*. For general comments on the two-tiered model of religious and cultural history that still reigns in Islamic studies, and on the contribution that studies of Sufism can make in this regard, see Kafadar, "Self and Others," 121–22; and Kafadar, "New Visibility of Sufism," 307–9.

17. See Schlegell, "Sufism in the Ottoman Arab World."

CHAPTER 1

1. This concept informs, for example, the discussion in Trimingham, *Sufi Orders in Islam*, chaps. 2 and 3.

2. See esp. Paul, *Doctrine and Organization*, 2–3, and references there.

3. For the later Naqshbandī practice of designating the *silsila* "Khwājagānī" from the generation of Ghujduvānī to that of Bahā' al-Dīn and "Naqshbandī" thereafter, see [Üsküdarī], *Menāḳib-i Aḥmed Yekdest*; Khānī, *Al-Ḥadā'iq al-wardiyya*, 8; Nev'īzāde 'Aṭā'ī, *Ḥadā'iḳ*, 61.

4. See the story of Bahā' al-Dīn's adoption of the silent *dhikr* in Kāshifī, *Rashaḥāt* (ed. Mu'īniyān), 1:95. For a succinct rendition of the Naqshbandī tradition, see Algar, "Silent and Vocal *Dhikr*," 42–43; Algar, "Brief History," 8–12. For an older but still valuable discussion, see Molé, "Autour du Daré Mansour."

5. Algar, "Silent and Vocal *Dhikr*," 43.

6. Florian Schwarz argues that in Transoxania, as opposed to Iran and the Ottoman lands, the term in use throughout the sixteenth century was Khwājagān. See his *Unser Weg*, 124–25.

7. Paul, *Doctrine and Organization*, passim.

8. DeWeese, *"Uvaysī" Sufi*; DeWeese, "Yasavī Šayẖs"; DeWeese, "Masha'-ikh-i Turk"; DeWeese, "Khojagānī Origins."

9. On Bahā' al-Dīn's immediate successors, see Kāshifī, *Rashaḥāt* (ed. Mu'īniyān), 1:101–205; Jāmī, *Nafaḥāt*, 389–403; Qazvīnī, *Silsilanāma*, 12b–14a; Kufralı, "Nakşbendiliğin Kuruluş ve Yayılışı," 55-63; Paul, *Doctrine and Organization*, passim.

10. On Kāshgharī's circle see Kāshifī, *Rashaḥāt* (ed. Mu'īniyān), 1:205–361; Jāmī, *Nafaḥāt*, 403–5; Qazvīnī, *Silsilanāma*, 14b–18a; Kufralı, "Nakşbendiliğin Kuruluş ve Yayılışı," 64–67. On 'Alī Shīr Navā'ī, see Barthold, "Mīr 'Alī Shīr"; Togan, "Ali Şîr Nevai"; Subtelny, "Mīr 'Alī Shīr Nawā'ī." On Jāmī, Ḥikmat, *Jāmī*; Huart, "D̲j̲āmī." On Bāyqarā's Herat as a cultural center, Frye, "Harāt"; Gandjeï, "Ḥusayn (Mīrzā B. Manṣūr B. Bayḳara)"; Subtelny, "Arts and Politics"; Subtelny, "Scenes from the Literary Life of Timurid Herat"; Subtelny, "Socioeconomic Bases of Cultural Patronage."

11. See Paul, *Politische und soziale Bedeutung*; Gross, "Khoja Ahrar"; Rogers, "Aḥrār"; Algar, "Aḥrār." The notion of Aḥrār's "system of patronage" is Paul's (for this see the discussion in chap. 6).

12. Jamī, *Nafaḥāt*, 388, 392-95, 405; Kāshifī, *Rashaḥāt* (ed. Mu'īniyān), 1:97, 109–10, 206–10. The next few paragraphs of our discussion offer a skeletal account on the basis of which we can pose some questions about the circumstances and motivations of the early Naqshbandī transmitters to the Ottoman lands. For more details, see chaps. 2, 3, and 4.

13. For Rukn al-Dīn, see 'Abdīzāde, *Amasya ta'rīhī*, 1:243–44. See also Gündüz, *Osmanlılarda Devlet-Tekke Münasabetleri*, 40, 48.

14. Ayvānsarāyı, *Ḥadīḳat ül-cevāmi'*, 1:219.

15. Baldırzāde, *Revżat el-evliyā'* 28a; Belīğ-i Bursevī, *Güldeste-i riyāż*, 143–44.

16. Ćehajić, *Derviški redovi*, 35–36.

17. See the discussion in chap. 2.

18. Ṭaşḳöprüzāde, *Shaqā'iq*, 2:162–63; *Silsilenāme-i ṭuruḳ-i 'aliye*, 17; *Silsilet eṭ-ṭuruḳ*, 60b; Ayvānsarāyı, *Ḥadīḳat ül-cevāmi'*, 1:285.

19. Ṭaşḳöprüzāde, *Shaqā'iq*, 1:549-50; *Silsilet eṭ-ṭuruḳ*, 60b; Bursalı, *'Osmānlı mü'ellifleri*, 1:40–41; Kufralı, "Molla İlâhî," 147.

20. Ṭaşḳöprüzāde, *Shaqā'iq*, 1:374; Lāmi'ī Çelebi, *Terceme-i nefaḥāt*, 462; 'Āşıḳ Çelebi, *Meşā'ir üş-şu'arā*, 35b.

21. Ṭaşḳöprüzāde, *Shaqā'iq*, 1:568; *Silsilenāme-i ṭuruḳ-i 'aliye*, 18.

22. Ṭaşḳöprüzāde, *Shaqā'iq*, 1:548-49, 551-53; Qazvīnī, *Silsilanāma*, 18b; *Silsilenāme-i ṭuruḳ-i 'aliye*, 17.

23. Kāshifī, *Rashaḥāt* (ed. Mu'īniyān), 2:638-41; Qazvīnī, *Silsilanāma*, 17b; Lāmi'ī Çelebi, *Terceme-i nefaḥāt*, 459; *Silsilenāme-i ṭuruḳ-i 'aliye*, 17.

24. Ṭaşḳöprüzāde, *Shaqā'iq*, 1:550-53; Lāmi'ī Çelebi, *Terceme-i nefaḥāt*, 450-60; *Silsilenāme-i ṭuruḳ-i 'aliye*, 17.

25. Qazvīnī, *Silsilanāma*, 18a; Karbalā'ī Tabrīzī, *Ravżat al-jinān*, 1:214–17, 416–18, 582–83.

26. Qazvīnī, *Silsilanāma*, 19b–20b.

27. See Gross, "Khoja Ahrar," 47–48, quoting Kāshifī's *Rashaḥāt.*

28. See esp. Paul, *Politische und soziale Bedeutung.*

29. Paul, *Doctrine and Organization*, 65 ff.

30. On Ilāhī's move to the capital, see Ṭaşḳöprüzāde, *Shaqā'iq*, 1:374; Lāmi'ī Çelebi, *Terceme-i nefaḥāt*, 462; and the discussion in chap. 2.

31. Kāshifī, *Rashaḥāt* (ed. Mu'īniyān), 1:262–63. This was a few years after Uzun Ḥasan had become the master of most of Iran and had secured Ḥusayn Bāyqarā's acceptance of his suzerainty. To Jāmī, he would have been much more relevant than the Ottomans, at least until the major defeat that they inflicted on him later that summer. See Woods, *Aqquyunlu*, 110–14, 125–26, 131–34.

32. Though he did end up in Istanbul at the invitation of the grand vezir, Rüstem Paşa. See Nev'īzāde 'Aṭā'ī, *Ḥadā'iḳ*, 207–8; 'Alī Mınıḳ, *'Iqd*, 2:403–4.

33. See the biographical notices in Qazvīnī, *Silsilanāma*, 14b–18b.

34. On Maktabdār, see Qazvīnī, *Silsilanāma*, 18a. I thank Professor Devin DeWeese of Indiana University for alerting me to the endurance of his line in Central Asia (where it was the only non-Aḥrārian Naqshbandī line to survive past the mid-sixteenth century). On Kūzakunānī, see Qazvīnī, *Silsilanāma*, 18b; Karbalā'ī Tabrīzī, *Ravżat al-jinān*, 1:98–105; and the biography of his son in Nev'īzāde 'Aṭā'ī, *Ḥadā'iḳ*, 207–8 and 'Alī Mınıḳ, *'Iqd*, 2:402–6. Another *khalīfa* of Kāshgharī, 'Alā' al-Dīn Kirmānī, traveled to Mecca and there had at least one disciple in 'Abd al-Ghafūr Sāwijī (see Qazvīnī, *Silsilanāma*, 16a).

35. On the dissemination of Kūzakunānī's line in Anatolia, see below and chap. 3. The connection of Bābā Ni'matullāh to this line emerges from Shirvānī, *Silsilanāma.* I thank Dr. Necdet Tosun of Marmara University, Istanbul, for sharing with me this information.

36. On Makhdūm-i A'ẓam Aḥmad Kāsānī and his line, see Schwarz, *Unser Weg*, 169-75, 188-97; Algar, "Dahbīdīya."

37. The Istanbul line that ensued from him became, however, a hereditary family line. On Aḥmad Ṣādiq, see Ṣādiqī, *Manhaj*, 10a–13a, and the discussion in chaps. 2 and 4.

38. Sālim Efendi, *Tezkere*, 293–94; Ayvānsarāyı, *Ḥadīḳat ül-cevāmi'*, 2:240-41; Meḥmed Tevfīḳ, *Mecmū'at üt-terācim*, 66a. Ḥaydar Rasā's successor seems to be the

Muḥammad Niyāz who appears in several *silsilas* as a fifth-generation spiritual descendant of Kāsānī. See, for example, Niyāzī, *Sülūk-i ḳavīm*, 19b–20a; and Meḥmed 'Aṭā'ullāh, *Silsile-i şerīfe*, 20a–b.

39. On Khwāfī, see Ibn al-'Ujaymī, *Khabāyā*, 116b–118a. On Balkhī, Schlegell, "Sufism in the Ottoman Arab World," 143–44, quoting Nābulusī's great-grandson and biographer, Kamāl al-Dīn Ghazzī.

40. Ṣādiqī, *Manhaj*, 11b.

41. Another, less explicit, expression of the same may have been the boasting of a later spiritual descendant of Kāsānī and transplant to Istanbul, 'Abdullāh Nidā'ī (d.1174/1760), that Kāsānī had "twelve accomplished sons and seventy-two perfected *khalīfas*" (quoted in Algar, "From Kashghar to Eyüp," 2).

42. I am indebted to one of the anonymous readers for SUNY Press for raising this question.

43. Arjomand, *Shadow of God*, 109–21 (quotes from 112, 113 respectively); Algar, "Naqshbandi Order: A Preliminary Survey," 139.

44. Qazvīnī, *Silsilanāma*, 15a-b; Ṭaşköprüzāde, *Shaqā'iq*, 1:392.

45. Qazvīnī, *Silsilanāma*, 16a–17a, 18a–19a.

46. Ibid., 19a; Yazıcı, "Safī."

47. Subtelny, "Art and Politics," 137.

48. Dickson, "Shāh Tahmāsb and the Ūzbeks," passim (and, for an invasion by 'Abdullāh Khān II that led to a decade-long Uzbek takeover of Herat toward the end of the century, see pp. 390–91).

49. Ibid., 46 (including quote), 191–93, 320–24.

50. Qazvīnī, *Silsilanāma*, 19b.

51. Ibid., 20a–20b.

52. Ibid., 21a.

53. In 955/1548 or 962/1555. See Savory, "Ṣafawids"; Lambton, "Ḳazwīn."

54. Qazvīnī, *Silsilanāma*, 6a, 21a, 21b.

55. On these Ottoman-Ṣafavid battles, see Roemer, "Safavid Period," 211–12, 225, 241–44, 257–61, 266–68; Parry, "Reign of Sulaimān," 85–86, 93–95; and Parry, "Successors of Sulaimān," 114–16, 131. On the Ottoman conquests of 1578–88, see Kütükoğlu, *Osmanlı-İran Siyasi Münasabetleri*.

56. Nev'īzāde 'Aṭā'ī, *Ḥadā'iḳ*, 207; 'Alī Mınıḳ, *'Iqd*, 2:401–2. *Ḥubb al-waṭan*—"patriotism" in nineteenth-century usage—was naturally employed here in a premodern sense (for the range of meanings of this term, see Lewis, "*Watan*").

57. Qazvīnī, *Silsilanāma*, 19a. According to the (late eighteenth-century) *Silsilet eṭ-ṭuruḳ*, 59b, Ilyās Bādāmyārī died in Orumiyeh. This mistake must have originated in Muṣṭafā b. Hayreddīn's Turkish translation of Qazvīnī's *Silsilanāma*, in which Ilyās Bādāmyārī's biography is erroneously replaced by that of his relative and *khalīfa* Muḥammad Bādāmyārī. See Muṣṭafā b. Hayreddīn, *Silsile-i hōcagān*, 15a.

58. Qazvīnī, *Silsilanāma*, 19a; Muṣṭafā b. Hayreddīn, *Silsile-i hōcagān*, 15a; *Silsilet eṭ-ṭuruḳ*, 59b.

59. Nev'īzāde 'Aṭā'ī, *Ḥadā'iḳ*, 207–8; 'Alī Mınıḳ, *'Iqd*, 2:402–5. Neither Qazvīnī nor his translator, Muṣṭafā b. Hayreddīn, mention these events or, for that matter, include Abū Sa'īd in the *silsila*. The anonymous (nineteenth-century) *Silsilenāme-i ṭuruḳ-i 'aliye* shows him to be a disciple of Aḥrār, but this is impossible if he died in 980/1572, at "over eighty years," as that same source claims. Most likely, he was born in Tabriz around 900/1495 and was initiated there by his father.

60. Qazvīnī, *Silsilanāma*, 19b; *Silsilenāme-i ṭuruḳ-i 'aliye*, 21. The latter work introduces him as Meḥmed Baba, also known as 'Ācizī and Urmavī, the author of the *Tezkere-i Baba*.

61. Shaykh Maḥmūd's career is treated in detail by several Ottoman chroniclers and biographers (see the following note). Some of them identify his father as a *seyyid* Aḥmed from Orumiyeh, known as Ḳoç Baba; but none connects the father to the Kūzakunānī line. The affiliation is provided by the *Şerā'iṭ ve naṣā'iḥ-i meşā'ih*, a Naqshbandī manual written by an anonymous disciple of Shaykh Maḥmūd, where the shaykh's *silsila* is traced through his brother Aḥmed; his father, Baba Bādāmyārī; then Ilyās Bādāmyārī, Darvīsh Akhī Khusrawshāhī, and Ṣun'ullāh Kūzakunānī (see *Şerā'iṭ*, 73b). This *silsila* was reproduced by the nineteenth-century *Silsilenāme-i ṭuruḳ-i 'aliye* (pp. 20–21) without explanation.

62. On his early life and his escape to Diyarbakır, see 'Uşāḳīzāde, *Zeyl-i şaḳā'iḳ*, 48; Na'īmā, *Ta'rīh*, 3:386; Evliyā Çelebi, *Seyāḥatnāme*, 4:53; 'Alī Emīrī, *Tezkere-i şu'arā'*, 1:20; Şeyhī, *Zeyl*, 77b. See also the discussion of the shaykh's career in chap. 3.

63. This was one Bāyezīd Efendi (d.1061/1651), who became a mosque *imām* in Bursa for several decades (see Belīğ-i Bursevī, *Güldeste-i riyāż*, 441). On Bāyezīd's possible connection to the spiritual line of Muḥammad Bādāmyārī and his son Maḥmūd, see chap. 3.

64. After the campaigns of Shāh 'Abbās at the turn of the seventeenth century, there would be no known Naqshbandī presence throughout the Ṣafavid realm. Algar's statement that in the east the extirpation of the tariqa was never "complete" is based on the establishment of a Naqshbandī *khānqāh* in Karrūkh near Herat in the early nineteenth century (see "Naqshbandī Order: A Preliminary Survey," 142). In the west, too, Naqshbandīs reappeared in the late eighteenth and especially the nineteenth century, and then only in the northern, non-Iranian side of the Caucasus mountain range (see the discussion of Shaykh Shāmil and Muslim resistance to the Russian conquest of the Caucasus in Knysh, "S̲h̲āmil").

65. Some repercussions of the other two developments affecting geopolitics and communications at this time are discussed in chap. 4.

66. On the basis of late seventeenth-century sources, Robert McChesney has shown that Ṣafavid rule did not entail a breakdown in either travel or other forms of social and cultural contact, and thus did not create the "barrier of heterodoxy" that nineteenth-century observers made into a trope of later scholarship. See his "'Barrier of Heterodoxy'."

67. See Bacqué-Grammont, "Études turco-safavides," esp. 75; Bacqué-Grammont, "Notes sur une saisie de soies"; İnalcık, "Ottoman Economic Mind,"

210, 213–14. Another traditional trade route between Iran and Anatolia—that going from the Gulf via Baghdad and Aleppo—also suffered a serious setback during this period as a result of the Portuguese grand design of shifting maritime travel to the Cape of Good Hope; but here, too, the trade never stopped completely. On this issue, see Savory, *Iran under the Safavids*, 192–202; Issawi, "Decline of Middle Eastern Trade," 263; and Kissling, "Šâh Ismâ'îl 1er," 93, 96.

68. Dickson has documented how the obstruction of travel and its repercussions for would-be Transoxanian pilgrims were often an issue in Uzbek diplomacy. See his "Shāh Ṭahmāsb and the Ūzbeks," 163–64.

69. On some of these realities, see Parry, "Successors of Sulaimān," esp. 130–32; Parry, "Period of Murād IV," esp. 143–47; Savory, "Ṣafawids."

70. Another alternative sometimes chosen by Central Asian pilgrims to the Hijaz involved travel south to India and from there by sea. For some of the difficulties faced by such travelers, especially on the last leg of their trip, see chap. 4.

71. See especially Bennigsen and Lemercier-Quelquejay, "Grande Horde Nogay," 211–13.

72. Documents quoted ibid., 224–28.

73. Ibid., 227-28; Dickson, "Shāh Ṭahmāsb and the Ūzbeks," 129–30; Sīdī ['Alī] Re'īs, *Mir'āt ül-memālik*, 64–65, 88–89.

74. Sīdī ['Alī] Re'īs, *Mir'āt ül-memālik*, esp. 71–75; Bennigsen and Lemercier-Quelquejay, "Grande Horde Nogay," 232-34; Soucek, "Sīdī 'Alī Re'īs."

75. Document quoted in Bennigsen and Lemercier-Quelquejay, "Grande Horde Nogay," 224.

76. Nev'īzāde 'Aṭā'ī, *Ḥadā'iḳ*, 72. The author does not confirm the account of Sīdī 'Alī Re'īs (pp. 88–89) according to which the shaykh and his entourage traveled along with the three hundred Janissaries mentioned above (perhaps in an attempt to give the dispatch of the Janissaries a civilian rationale?).

77. See references in note 67.

78. See, for example, Kāshifī, *Rashaḥāt* (ed. Mu'īniyān), 1:110–11, 163, 174, 254–64, 2:582–83 (biographies of Muḥammad Pārsā, Ḥasan 'Aṭṭār, Darvīsh Aḥmad Samarqandī, 'Abd al-Raḥmān Jāmī, and Muḥammad Yaḥyā).

79. See chaps. 2 and 3, and, for the phenomenon of these *tekke*s and places of accommodation for Transoxanian pilgrims, chap. 7.

80. Smith, "Özbek Tekkes," 131.

CHAPTER 2

1. See Kufralı, "Molla İlâhî," 130.

2. Kāshifī, *Rashaḥāt* (ed. Mu'īniyān), 1:262–63.

3. Some have attributed this commentary to the more famous 'Abdullāh Ilāhī (e.g., Bursalı, *'Osmānlı mü'ellifleri*, 1:91), but Kufralı disagrees, especially given

evidence contained in a manuscript copy from Konya (see Kufralı, "Molla İlâhî," 131). For the Bursan Aḥmad Ilāhī, see chap. 3.

4. Ayvānsarāyı, *Ḥadīḳat ül-cevāmi'*, 1:219.

5. E.g., MS Süleymaniye Library (Istanbul), Pertev Paşa 616, 218b. The work has been published as *Risāle-i molla Ilāhī* (Istanbul, 1261/1845).

6. Kara, "Molla İlâhî," 305, 315–16. At the same time, he draws attention to a statement in one of Ilāhī's works, the *Zād ül-müştākīn*, according to which the shaykh was present in the capital in 882/1477–78, that is, a few years before the sultan's death.

7. See the biographies of Ilāhī and Bukhārī in Lāmi'ī Çelebi, *Terceme-i nefaḥāt*, 460–65, 465–70. All later biographers apparently based their accounts on Lāmi'ī. For example, see Ṭaşköprüzāde, *Shaqā'iq*, 1:373–77, 553–59; Laṭīfī, *Tezkere*, 50–51; Kefevī, *Kitāb al-a'lām*, 650b–651b; and Eyyūbī, *Hediyet ül-aṣdiḳā'*, 173a–76a.

8. The date can be inferred from Lāmi'ī Çelebi's account; he states that Bukhārī spent at least six years in Simav, one in Mecca, and some time in Istanbul before Ilāhī's move to the capital in 886/1481.

9. Mağnısalı Çelebi was no longer *ḳāżī'asker* when Ilāhī settled in Simav, but was later reinstated under Sultan Bāyezīd and held the position until his death (see Ṭaşköprüzāde, *Shaqā'iq*, 1:293–96).

10. *zīn miyān khāṭir-i āsūde kasī rāst ke u/ dāman-i yār gereftast va kinārī dārad* (Lāmi'ī Çelebi, *Terceme-i nefaḥāt*, 468–69). In Mustafa Kara's reading, the meaning of this coded line was rather different; it was in fact this message from Bukhārī that convinced Ilāhī to move to the capital (see Kara, "Molla İlâhî," 304).

11. Lāmi'ī Çelebi, *Terceme-i nefaḥāt*, 462. Kara believes that Ilāhī's reluctance to move to the capital derived from his association with the fourteenth-century rebel Bedreddīn Simāvī, on whose *Vāridāt* he in time composed a commentary (see Kara, "Molla İlâhî," 305).

12. Ṭaşköprüzāde, *Shaqā'iq*, 1:374. Like all other accounts of Ilāhī's life, Ṭaşköprüzāde's is based on Lāmi'ī Çelebi. Here the Arabic rendering (*wa-ẓaharat al-fitan fī waṭanihi*) is particularly useful, however, because it eliminates a certain ambiguity in Lāmi'ī's original formulation: *waṭan* would not have been used in reference to the capital, and thus the whole reference must be to disorders occurring in the vicinity of Simav, perhaps in connection with the capture of Bursa by Prince Cem's forces in the spring of that year. Curiously, in his Turkish translation of Ṭaşköprüzāde, Mecdī Efendi introduced a new confusion by identifying the disorders that prompted Ilāhī's move to the capital with the Shāh Ḳūlī incident of 917/1511, when Ilāhī had long been dead. See Mecdī Efendi, *Terceme-i şaḳā'iḳ*, 263. In turn, Mecdī's mistake did not die out, or perhaps it was later resurrected because it tallied with a view of the Naqshbandiyya as a distinctly anti-Shī'ī, anti-Ḳızılbaş tariqa (on this view, see the discussion in chap. 6).

13. On Muṣliḥüddīn, see Ṭaşköprüzāde, *Shaqā'iq*, 1:561-63; Baldırzāde, *Revżat el-evliyā'*, 37a–b; Beliğ-i Bursevī, *Güldeste-i riyāż*, 180 (the latter identifying

him as a disciple of Aḥmad Ilāhī from Bursa). On ʿĀbid Çelebi, see Ṭaşköprüzāde, *Shaqā'iq*, 1:564; Ayvānsarāyı, *Ḥadīḳat ül-cevāmiʿ*, 1:152. On Üskübī, Ṭaşköprüzāde, *Shaqā'iq*, 1:565-57.

14. Lāmiʿī Çelebi, *Terceme-i nefaḥāt*, 462.

15. Ibid.

16. On Ilāhī's sojourn at the tomb of Bahā' al-Dīn and his acquaintance with Jāmī, see his biography in Lāmiʿī Çelebi, *Terceme-i nefaḥāt*, 461.

17. Ilāhī, *Meslek eṭ-ṭālibīn*, passim.

18. Ibid,. 54a–57a.

19. Ibid., 23b.

20. On these works, see Algar, "Bo<u>k</u>ārī, Amīr Aḥmad."

21. Lāmiʿī Çelebi, *Terceme-i nefaḥāt*, 468. For the significance of the two concepts of "acting with strictness" (*al-ʿamal bi'l-ʿazīma*) and continuous recollection (*dhikr dā'imī*) in the Naqshbandī devotional regimen, see chap. 5; for that of close companionship (*ṣuḥba*) between shaykh and disciple, see chap. 7.

22. Ibid.

23. Prominent *khalīfa*s such as Maḥmūd Çelebi, Ḥekīm Çelebi, and Muṣliḥüddīn Muṣṭafā were madrasa students, and some other major benefactors of the shaykh (discussed below in the section on *tekke*s) apparently came from modest backgrounds. He had two more prominent disciples in Necmeddīn b. Meḥmed Necmī, in time a well-known madrasa professor, and in Hıżır Beğ, a madrasa professor and the son of the *müftī* of Istanbul Aḥmed Paşa. On Necmī, see Nevʿīzāde ʿAṭā'ī, *Ḥadā'iḳ*, 139–40; and Belīğ-i Bursevī, *Güldeste-i riyāẓ*, 512–13. On Hıżır Beğ, Ṭaşköprüzāde, *Shaqā'iq*, 2:37; Baldırzāde, *Revżat el-evliyā'*, 59b–60a; Belīğ-i Bursevī, *Güldeste-i riyāż*, 463. On the office of *müftī* of Istanbul at this time, before it was absorbed into and became the apex of the Ottoman learned hierarchy, see Repp, *Müfti of Istanbul*, esp. xix–xx, 297–307.

24. See Lāmiʿī Çelebi, *Terceme-i nefaḥāt*, 467 (for the Fātiḥ and Ayvānsarāy *tekke*s), and Ayvānsarāyı, *Ḥadīḳat ül-cevāmiʿ*, 1:42–44, 45–47, 297–98 (for the Fātiḥ, Ayvānsarāy, and Edirne Ḳapı *tekke*s, respectively). On all three, see also the discussion below in the section on *tekke*s.

25. On Bālī Efendi's tenure at Zeyrek, see Zâkir Şükrî, *Istanbuler Derwisch-Konvente*, 19. His immediate successors there remain unknown; we are only told that in the mid-sixteenth century his *khalīfa* Muṣliḥüddīn Nūrüddīnzāde (who was called to Istanbul under unclear circumstances) stayed at the *tekke* "anonymously." On this incident and on Bālī Efendi's later career in Sofia, see Clayer, *Mystiques, état et société*, 70–84.

26. Kissling, "Aus der Geschichte des Chalvetijje," 244–45, 250–51, 256–57; Martin, "Short History," 281–82. On the formation of the district of Koca Muṣṭafā Paşa, cf. İnalcık, "Istanbul," 231.

27. Clayer, *Mystiques, état et société*, chap. 2, esp. 106–12.

28. Martin, "Short History," 282-83; Jong, "<u>Kh</u>alwatiyya."

29. The notion of "line" is how, looking back, living practitioners view their spiritual affiliation with eminent tariqa ancestors: they ignore all those branches that also ensue from the same tree trunk, so to speak, but lead to other than their own shaykhs. This is what normally appears in one's *silsila* (though there are some *silsilas*, for example Qazvīnī's, that show trees, not only lines).

30. On Maḥmūd Çelebi, see Ṭaşköprüzāde, *Shaqā'iq*, 2:152–54; Kefevī, *Kitāb al-a'lām*, 617a–618b. On his place in the line of Ilāhī and Bukhārī and on his successors in the Fātiḥ and Edirne Ḳapı *tekkes*, see Şeyhī, *Zeyl*, 72a–b; *Silsilet eṭ-ṭuruḳ*, 27b, 60b; Zâkir Şükrî, *Istanbuler Derwisch-Konvente*, 54, 68; Ayvānsarāyı, *Ḥadīḳat ül-cevāmi'*, 1:43, 297. On his *waqf* in support of the Edirne Ḳapı *tekke*, see Barkan and Ayverdi, *Istanbul Vakıflan Tahrîr Defteri*, entry 1167. I discuss the significance of this source (always followed by entry rather than page number) in the following section.

31. Belīğ-i Bursevī, *Güldeste-i riyāż*, 152; Baldırzāde, *Revżat el-evliyā'*, 83b–84a, 110a.

32. On 'Abdüllaṭīf's career and his place in the *silsila*, see Nev'īzāde 'Aṭā'ī, *Ḥadā'iḳ*, 84–85, 230–32; 'Alī Mınıḳ, *'Iqd*, 2:272–73; 'Āşıḳ Çelebi, *Meşā'ir üş-şu'arā*, 257a; *Silsilet eṭ-ṭuruḳ*, 27b, 60b; Ayvānsarāyı, *Ḥadīḳat ül-cevāmi'*, 1:43; Zâkir Şükrî, *Istanbuler Derwisch-Konvente*, 68. On Cemālzāde, see Nev'īzāde 'Aṭā'ī, *Ḥadā'iḳ*, 361; Şeyhī, *Zeyl*, 72b; Ayvānsarāyı, *Ḥadīḳat ül-cevāmi'*, 1:303; *Silsilet eṭ-ṭuruḳ*, 27b, 29a; Zâkir Şükrî, *Istanbular Derwisch-Konvente*, 27–28, 68; Muṣṭafā b. Hayreddīn, *Silsile-i hōcagān*, 15b (Muṣṭafā b. Hayreddīn presents a different tradition according to which Cemālzāde was a former madrasa professor, a disciple of Aḥmad Bukhārī's *khalīfa* Ḥekīm Çelebi, and a shaykh at the Ḥekīm Çelebi Tekke in Fīl Dāmī). On Sürūrī, see 'Āşıḳ Çelebi, *Meşā'ir üş-şu'arā*, 153a–155b; Nev'īzāde 'Aṭā'ī, *Ḥadā'iḳ*, 23–25; 'Alī Mınıḳ, *'Iqd*, 2:215–20; Bursalı, *'Osmānlı mü'ellifleri*, 2:225–26. Cf. Fleischer, *Bureaucrat and Intellectual*, 28–29, quoting Muṣṭafā 'Ālī.

33. Şeyhī, *Zeyl*, 72a-b; *Silsilet eṭ-ṭuruḳ*, 27b, 60b; Zâkir Şükrî, *Istanbuler Derwisch-Konvente*, 54, 68; Ayvānsarāyı, *Ḥadīḳat ül-cevāmi'*, 1:43, 297.

34. Nev'īzāde 'Aṭā'ī, *Ḥadā'iḳ*, 216–17; 'Alī Mınıḳ, *'Iqd*, 2:307; 'Āşıḳ Çelebi, *Meşā'ir üş-şu'arā*, 234a–37a; Peçevī, *Ta'rīh*, 1:465. According to Peçevī, Rüstem gave the shaykh an oath of allegiance (*bay'a*) and "for twenty years never disobeyed his words."

35. Nev'īzāde 'Aṭā'ī, *Ḥadā'iḳ*, 216; Ayvānsarāyı, *Ḥadīḳat ül-çevāmi'*, 1:89–90; Kürkçüoğlu, *Süleymaniye Vakfiyesi*, 191–98 (modern Turkish transcription, 50–51). There were several places by the name Fīl Dāmī in Istanbul. According to Ayvānsarāyı, the one in which the Ḥekīm Çelebi Tekke was established was near Ḳoşḳa, roughly between Bāyezīd and Aḳsarāy.

36. See the lists of incumbents in Ayvānsarāyı, *Ḥadīḳat ül-çevāmi'*, 1:90, and Zâkir Şükrî, *Istanbuler Derwisch-Konvente*, 64–65. On the spiritual descent of these individuals (about which there are several disagreements), see Muṣṭafā b. Hayred-

dīn, *Silsile-i hōcagān*, 15a-b; *Silsilet eṭ-ṭuruḳ*, 28a, 60b; Şeyhī, *Zeyl*, 72b; Nev'īzāde 'Aṭā'ī, *Ḥadā'iḳ*, 204, 360, 759–60.

37. On Tirevī's career, see Nev'īzāde 'Aṭā'ī, *Ḥadā'iḳ*, 759–60. For a list of his spiritual descendants, see *Silsilet eṭ-ṭuruḳ*, 28a.

38. On Bosnevī, see 'Uşāḳīzāde, *Zeyl-i şaḳā'iḳ*, 551, and the discussion in chap. 6. On Esīrī Damadı, see Muṣṭafā b. Hayreddīn, *Silsile-i hōcagān*, 16a; Zâkir Şükrî, *Istanbuler Derwisch-Konvente*, 65.

39. Thus according to Nev'īzāde 'Aṭā'ī, *Ḥadā'iḳ*, 372; and *Silsilet eṭ-ṭuruḳ*, 29a. Acccording to Ayvānsarāyı, *Ḥadīḳat ül-çevāmi'*, 1:43, and Zâkir Şükrî, *Istanbuler Derwisch-Konvente*, 68, they were not among this *tekke*'s incumbents. On Ḳavaḳlızāde, see also Nev'īzāde 'Aṭā'ī, *Ḥadā'iḳ*, 372; Na'īmā, *Ta'rīh*, 1:76. On Şa'bān Efendi, see Muṣṭafā b. Hayreddīn, *Silsile-i hōcagān*, 14b; Nev'īzāde 'Aṭā'ī, *Ḥadā'iḳ*, 295–96, 371–72, 380; Na'īmā, *Ta'rīh*, 1:115; Peçevī, *Ta'rīh*, 2:36; Bursalı, *'Osmānlı mü'ellifleri*, 1:98.

40. On Simkeşzāde, see ' Uşāḳīzāde, *Zeyl-i şaḳā'iḳ*, 650; Şeyhī, *Zeyl*, 72b, 74a–b; Bursalı, *'Osmānlı mü'ellifleri*, 1:139; Meḥmed Tevfīḳ, *Mecmū'at üt-terācim*, 60b. On Şeyhī, Sālim Efendi, *Tezkere*, 399–402; Bursalı, *'Osmānlı mü'ellifleri*, 3:74.

41. Ayvānsarāyı, *Ḥadīḳat ül-çevāmi'*, 1:45–46; Zâkir Şükrî, *Istanbuler Derwisch-Konvente*, 66; *Silsilet eṭ-ṭuruḳ*, 28a; ' Uşāḳīzāde, *Zeyl-i şaḳā'iḳ*, 554.

42. See chap. 1.

43. See the discussion on his residence-*tekke* in the following section.

44. Nev'īzāde 'Aṭā'ī, *Ḥadā'iḳ*, 215–16.

45. On an apparent attempt by Aḥmad Bukhārī's *khalīfa*, Maḥmūd Çelebi, to establish himself as a kind of "supershaykh" over two Naqshbandī circles of the capital, see the following section.

46. Ṣādiqī, *Manhaj*, esp. 9b–11b. See a fuller quote in chap. 1.

47. Ibid., 11b–12a; Nev'īzāde 'Aṭā'ī, *Ḥadā'iḳ*, 362; Selānīkī, *Ta'rīh-i Selānīkī* (Freiburg reprint), 211–12.

48. Ṣādiqī, *Manhaj*, 12a–13a; Nev'īzāde 'Aṭā'ī, *Ḥadā'iḳ*, 362; Evliyā Çelebi, *Seyāḥatnāme*, 1:373. On the shaykh's work of disseminating the tariqa in the Arab lands, see the discussion in chap. 4.

49. According to the lists in Ayvānsarāyı, *Ḥadīḳat ül-çevāmi'*, 1:43–44, and Zâkir Şükrî, *Istanbuler Derwisch-Konvente*, 68, Aḥmad Ṣādiq was the first of his family to have held this position. Earlier sources give the shaykhs of the *tekke* as 'Abdüllaṭīf, followed by Meḥmed Cemālzāde, Meḥmed Ḳavaḳlızāde, Şa'bān Efendi, and Aḥmad Ṣādiq's son, Ḍiyā' al-Dīn Aḥmad. See Nev'īzāde 'Aṭā'ī, *Ḥadā'iḳ*, 361, 371–72; Şeyhī, *Zeyl*, 72b; and a later source, *Silsilet eṭ-ṭuruḳ*, 29a. For Faḍlallāh Efendi, see Şeyhī, *Zeyl*, 77a; ' Uşāḳīzāde, *Zeyl-i şaḳā'iḳ*, 47-48.

50. See the discussion on succession in chap. 7.

51. See Fernandes, *Evolution of the Sufi Institution*; Geoffroy, *Soufisme en Égypte*, 165–75. However, in sources from early Ottoman Cairo, according to Behrens-Abouseif and Fernandes, "Sufi Architecture," 103–14, terminology was less

likely to reflect a site's functions. Chabbi also maintains that *khānqāh*, *ribāṭ*, *zāwiya*, and *tekke* all generally referred to institutions similar in aims (see Chabbi, "Khānḳāh").

52. See Doğan, cited in Ocak and Farûkî [Faroqhi], "Zâviye."

53. For the use of *zāwiya/zāviye* in reference to urban institutions of different sizes, see, for example, Ṭaşköprüzāde, *Shaqā'iq*, 1:556; Nev'īzāde 'Aṭā'ī, *Ḥadā'iḳ*, 84, 205, 359, 606, 671; Şeyhī, *Zeyl*, 72a–76b; Barkan and Ayverdi, *İstanbul Vakıflar Tahrîr Defteri*, passim. For the description of the Emīr-i Bukhārī Tekke with its component *zāwiya*, see Ayvānsarāyı, *Ḥadīḳat ül-çevāmi'*, 1:42–43.

54. For the network of Naqshbandī *tekkes* in mid-nineteenth-century Istanbul, see *Āsitāne-i 'aliyede tekyeler.*

55. See Nev'īzāde 'Aṭā'ī, *Ḥadā'iḳ*, 24–25; Ayvānsarāyı, *Ḥadīḳat ül-çevāmi'*, 2: 4–5; 'Āşıḳ Çelebi, *Meşā'ir üş-şu'arā*, 153a–b.

56. See Ṭaşköprüzāde, *Shaqā'iq*, 1:564; Ayvānsarāyı, *Ḥadīḳat ül-çevāmi'*, 1:152; Barkan and Ayverdi, *İstanbul Vakıfları Tahrîr Defteri*, entries 1679–85.

57. Nev'īzāde 'Aṭā'ī, *Ḥadā'iḳ*, 362; Ayvānsarāyı, *Ḥadīḳat ül-çevāmi'*, 1:100; Evliyā Çelebi, *Seyāḥatnāme*, 1:373; Meḥmed Tevfīḳ, *Mecmū'at üt-terācim*, 11a; Zâkir Şükrî, *Istanbuler Derwisch-Konvente*, 66–67.

58. See the discussion of this spiritual line in the previous section.

59. On the early ambivalence, see Kāshifī, *Rashaḥāt* (ed. Mu'īniyān), 1:37; Paul, *Doctrine and Organization*, 60–63; and the discussion in chap. 7, where this attitude is related also to the Naqshbandī preference for nonhereditary succession.

60. See the discussion of the spiritual line of Ḥekīm Çelebī in the previous section.

61. See 'Uşāḳīzāde, *Zeyl-i şaḳā'iḳ*, 570; Nev'īzāde 'Aṭā'ī, *Ḥadā'iḳ*, 601; Peçevī, *Ta'rīh*, 2:360, respectively.

62. For the first, see Ayvānsarāyı, *Ḥadīḳat ül-çevāmi'*, 1:219; for the second, ibid., 1:89–90, and Kürkçüoğlu, *Süleymaniye Vakfiyesi*, 191–98 (modern Turkish transcription, 50–51).

63. On the first, see Smith, "Özbek Tekkes," 137-39; *Āsitāne-i 'aliyede tekyeler*, 4. On the second (which should not be confused with another Bukharan *tekke* established in the Sulṭāntepe neighborhood of Üsküdar in 1166/1752–53), see Ayvānsarāyı, *Ḥadīḳat ül-çevāmi'*, 2:240–41; Sālim Efendi, *Tezkere*, 293; *Āsitāne-i 'aliyede tekyeler*, 3; Konyalı, *Abideleri ve Kitabeleriyle Üsküdar Tarihi*, 1:162. For the phenomenon of Bukharan *tekkes* and instances of such *tekkes* outside the capital, see chaps. 3 and 7.

64. Barkan and Ayverdi, *İstanbul Vakıfları Tahrîr Defteri*, entries 1167–97 and 1433. For the *waqfs* of the shaykh and his wife, see entries 1167 and 1180.

65. Ibid., entries 1149–66, 1204, 1210, 1216, 1220, 1223, 1225, 1234, 1322, 1614, and 2514. For the *waqf* of Pirinçci Sinān Ağa, whose primary beneficiary was the Pirinçci Sinān Mosque in the neighborhood of the same name, see entry 1223.

66. Ibid., entries 1679–85.

67. Ayvānsarāyı, *Ḥadīḳat ül-çevāmi'*, 1:42, 297.

68. It has been suggested that the Emīr-i Bukhārī Tekke in Edirne Ḳapı may have been the beneficiary of income generated from *waqf* villages (see Faroqhi, "Tekke of Hacı Bektaş," 193). This is not borne out by the 953/1546 register, which records several other Istanbul institutions (e.g., entries 395, 1037, 1631, 2354, 2491, 2496), but not the two Emīr-i Bukhārī Tekkes, as beneficiaries of *waqf* villages. Note, however, that the register covers only *waqfs* established before midcentury and excludes sultanic endowments.

69. Kürkçüoğlu, *Süleymaniye Vakfiyesi*, 195-98 (modern Turkish transcription, 50–51).

70. On such great *waqfs* see, for example, Barkan and Ayverdi, *İstanbul Vakıflan Tahrîr Defteri*, entries 269, 2045, 2167, 2491, 2496. For the income of the *waqf* of the Fātiḥ complex in 895/1490 (amounting to some 1.5 million *aḳçe*), and for that of all of Sultan Süleymān's *waqfs* during the reign of Murād III (amounting to 5,277,759 *aḳçe*), see İnalcık, "Istanbul," 229 and 232, respectively.

71. See the diagram in İnalcık, *Ottoman Empire*, 170. Cf. the discussion in Repp, *Müfti of Istanbul*, chap. 2 and diagram on p. 28.

72. Barkan and Ayverdi, *İstanbul Vakıflan Tahrîr Defteri*, entries 12, 226, 1554, 1626, 1807, 1808, 1810, 1811, 2080, 2175.

73. Ibid., entries 116–24, 2252–56, 2438, 2502.

74. Ibid., entries 395, 764, 906, 916, 1037, 2167, 2208–15, 2499. The Mevlevīhānes of Galata, Ḳāsım Paşa, and Üsküdar, located outside Istanbul *intra muros*, do not appear as beneficiaries in the 953/1546 register. On the annual income of the Ḥāccı Bektaş Tekke in central Anatolia, amounting to some 100,000 *aḳçes*, see Faroqhi, "Tekke of Hacı Bektaş," 193.

75. Barkan and Ayverdi, *İstanbul Vakıflan Tahrîr Defteri*, entries 1167–97, 2433. On the establishment of the *tekke*'s congregational mosque by Sultan Süleymān, see Ayvānsarāyı, *Ḥadīḳat ül-çevāmi'*, 1:297. On the physical configuration of *tekkes* in Ottoman times and earlier, cf. Ocak and Farûkî, "Zâviye," esp. 473–75.

76. Barkan and Ayverdi, *İstanbul Vakıfları Tahrîr Defteri*, entry 1679.

77. Ayvānsarāyı, *Ḥadīḳat ül-çevāmi'*, 1:43.

78. Barkan and Ayverdi, *İstanbul Vakıfları Tahrîr Defteri*, entry 1164.

79. Ayvānsarāyı, *Ḥadīḳat ül-çevāmi'*, 1:46–47.

80. But to the contrary, see the account concerning the Özbek Tekke of Sulṭāntepe, Üsküdar, in Ayvānsarāyı, *Ḥadīḳat ül-çevāmi'*, 2:240. According to this account, in 1166/1752–53 the founder of the *tekke* (and a supervisor of the Istanbul mint), 'Abdullāh Paşa, gave it as private property (*mulk*) to a Naqshbandī shaykh, who several years later "gave the *tekke* in *waqf* to the Naqshbandī tariqa."

81. While the state was involved in the appointment of shaykhs of the more hierarchical networks of the Bektaşī and Mevlevī *tekkes* (see Ocak and Farûkî, "Zâviye," 471–72), in *tekkes* of other tariqas such involvement would become common practice only in the nineteenth century. Only shaykhs who doubled as mosque

preachers were, in this second capacity, government employees whose appointment required the approval of the *şeyhülislām*. On the state's efforts to bureaucratize Sufi shaykhs and tariqas in this way, see the discussion about shaykhs as mosque preachers in the following section.

82. Some of Ḥekīm Çelebi's spiritual descendants who trained in the Fīl Dāmī *tekke* and then officiated in several of the Emīr-i Bukhārī Tekkes are discussed above. On the Mevlevī practice of transferring shaykhs among various institutions and especially of appointing *tekke* incumbents at the decision of the tariqa's central institution in Konya, see Ocak and Farûkî, "Zâviye."

83. Barkan and Ayverdi, *İstanbul Vakıfları Tahrîr Defteri*, entry 1167.

84. See İnalcık, "Istanbul," esp. 229–34.

85. On Koca Muṣṭafā Paşa in Samaṭya and the Mevlevīhānes of these four locations, see Ayvānsarāyı, *Ḥadīḳat ül-çevāmi'*, 1:161–66, 228–30, 2:10–12, 42–47, 104–9.

86. Of the fifty-three *zāwiya*s listed in the *Āsitāne-i 'aliyede tekyeler*, twenty-two were located in these two areas (or between Fātiḥ and Edirne Ḳapı), nine in Galata or along the Bosphorus, eight in Üsküdar, seven in the Cerrāḥ Paşa-Samaṭya area, and only three in the area between Bāb-ı 'Ālī and Bāyezīd. The location of another four *tekke*s cannot be determined.

87. See Algar, "Naqshbandi Order: A Preliminary Survey," 140.

88. Lāmi'ī Çelebi, *Terceme-i nefaḥāt*, 467; Muṣṭafā b. Hayreddīn, *Silsile-i hōcagān*, 14b.

89. On those identified as Naqshbandīs, see Nev'īzāde 'Aṭā'ī, *Ḥadā'iḳ*, 8–11, 17, 21–22, 23–25, 38, 139–40, 228, 230–32, 294–95, 321, 722.

90. On the distinction between these echelons and the "subhierarchy" of the *'ilmiye*, see Zilfi, *Politics of Piety*, 24–26. Cf. Fleischer, *Bureaucrat and Intellectual*, 17.

91. See the biographical notices in Nev'īzāde 'Aṭā'ī, *Ḥadā'iḳ*, 8–11, 230–32; Ṭaşköprüzāde, *Shaqā'iq*, 1:294–96; Meḥmed Tevfīḳ, *Mecmū'at üt-terācim*, 94a; and 'Uşāḳīzāde, *Zeyl-i şaḳā'iḳ*, 77–78, respectively.

92. Nev'īzāde 'Aṭā'ī, *Ḥadā'iḳ*, 230-32; Ayvānsarāyı, *Ḥadīḳat ül-çevāmi'*, 1:43.

93. Cf. Fleischer, *Bureaucrat and Intellectual*, 17, on this type.

94. Nev'īzāde 'Aṭā'ī, *Ḥadā'iḳ*, 23-25; 'Āşıḳ Çelebi, *Meşā'ir üş-şu'arā*, 153a–55b; 'Alī Mınıḳ, *'Iqd*, 2:215–20. On the downfall of the immensely popular Prince Muṣṭafā, see Peirce, *Imperial Harem*, 79–90. On Muṣṭafā 'Ālī's study with Sürūrī during these last years, see Fleischer, *Bureaucrat and Intellectual*, 28–29.

95. Laṭīfī, *Tezkere*, 52.

96. On the "sense of cultural inferiority, vis-à-vis the older Persian tradition" and a related glorification of Ḥusayn Bāyqarā's court in Herat, see Fleischer, *Bureaucrat and Intellectual*, 141, 149, respectively.

97. See Ṭaşköprüzāde, *Shaqā'iq*, 2:153; Nev'īzāde 'Aṭā'ī, *Ḥadā'iḳ*, 25, 216, 321, 372; 'Āşıḳ Çelebi, *Meşā'ir üş-şu'arā*, 153b–154b; 'Alī Mınıḳ, *'Iqd*, 2:215; Bursalı, *'Osmānlı mü'ellifleri*, 1:139, 2:20–21, 225; Na'īmā, *Ta'rīh*, 1:74.

98. Ṭaşköprüzāde, *Shaqā'iq*, 2:153.

99. Nev'īzāde 'Aṭā'ī, *Ḥadā'iḳ*, 216.

100. On the first, see Ṣādiqī, *Manhaj*, 11b–12a; Selānīkī, *Ta'rīh-i Selānīkī* (Freiburg reprint), 1:211–12; Nev'īzāde 'Aṭā'ī, *Ḥadā'iḳ*, 362. On the second, Nev'īzāde 'Aṭā'ī, *Ḥadā'iḳ*, 371–72; Na'īmā, *Ta'rīh*, 1:115; Muṣṭafā b. Hayreddīn, *Silsile-i hōcagān*, 14b. Cf. the discussion about the political involvement of Naqshbandī shaykhs in chap. 6.

101. The first was the eponym of the 'Uşşāḳī branch of the Khalwatiyya, the second a follower of Ümmī Sinān, the eponym of the Sināniye. See Clayer, *Mystiques, état et société*, 106–7; and, on the popular Şuccā', Fleischer, *Bureaucrat and Intellectual*, 72–75.

102. Clayer, *Mystiques, état et société*, esp. chap. 2. See also the list of Ottoman sultans and their shaykhs in Şapolyo, *Mezhepler ve Tarikatlar Tarihi*, 448–49.

103. On the Naqshbandiyya of Kurdistan, see chap. 3. In Istanbul, it is only in connection with the arrival of the first Khālidī shaykhs in the nineteenth century that we hear of unconventional techniques of recruiting a large following—and of the resentment that this aroused. See Abu-Manneh, "Naqshbandiyya in the Early Nineteenth Century," 47–48.

104. See Muḥibbī, *Khulāṣat al-athar*, 1:389, 4:313.

105. Ilāhī, *Meslek eṭ-ṭālibīn*, 23b; Ilāhī, *Ervāḥ ül-müştāḳīn*, 3b; Muṣṭafā b. Hayreddīn, *Silaile-i hōcagān*, 1b.

106. On the career of Friday mosque preachers and its apex in the capital's imperial mosques, see Zilfi, *Politics of Piety*, 129–31. On efforts to bureaucratize the Sufi orders by combining the position of Sufi shaykhs with that of mosque preachers (whose appointment was subject to the approval of the *şeyhülislām*), see Kafadar, "Self and Others," 140.

107. See 'Uşāḳīzāde, *Zeyl-i şaḳā'iḳ*, 551, 554, 650; and Nev'īzāde 'Aṭā'ī, *Ḥadā'iḳ*, 601, respectively.

108. See Ṭaşköprüzāde, *Shaqā'iq*, 1:56–57; Baldırzāde, *Revżat el-evliyā'*, 53a; and 'Uşāḳīzāde, *Zeyl-i şaḳā'iḳ*, 570, respectively.

109. Barkan and Ayverdi, *İstanbul Vakıfları Tahrîr Defteri*, entry 1223. Cf. Ayvānsarāyı, *Ḥadīḳat ül-çevāmi'*, 1:63.

110. Barkan and Ayverdi, *İstanbul Vakıfları Tahrîr Defteri*, entries 1153, 1154, 1183, 1184.

111. Ibid., entry 1197.

112. I have considered "small" those *waqfs* that were based on a single residential house or urban commercial asset (such as a shop or garden) or those that were based on a sum of money expected to yield at most 2,000 *aḳçe* annually.

113. Barkan and Ayverdi, *İstanbul Vakıfları Tahrîr Defteri*, entries 1149, 1164, 1167, 1180, 1679, 1685 (*waqfs* of Aḥmad Bukhārī; his wife, Ziyāde Hātūn, his *khalīfa* Maḥmūd Çelebi; Maḥmūd's wife and Bukhārī's daughter, Fāṭima Hātūn; 'Ābid Çelebi; and his wife, Sittişāh Hātūn, respectively).

114. Ibid., entries 1164, 1166, 1175, 1176, 1177, 1180, 1183, 1184, 1186, 1190, 1191, 1195, 1210, 1216, 1682, 1684, 1685. Gabriel Baer used the data provided by this register in his pioneering "Women and Waqf."

115. Kāshifī, *Rashaḥāt* (ed. Mu'īniyān), 1:326, 330. In nineteenth-century Kurdistan, we hear of a female mystic, poetess, and spiritual master, Zamzam Hanım, who belonged to a mixed Naqshbandī-Qādirī line going back to Shaykh Ismā'īl Faḳīrullāh (see 'Alī Emīrī, *Tezkere*, 1:421-23).

116. See Buehler, *Sufi Heirs of the Prophet*, 161. Critical circumstances might call for critical means, however, as we learn from the story of Tāj al-Dīn al-'Uthmānī's healing of a near-dead female disciple. The Meccan shaykh is said to have saved the woman by "holding her onto him" (*fa-akhadhaha fī ḍimnihi*) in a practice (apparently not simply metaphorical) that his biographer described as "well established among the Naqshbandī great masters." For this story, see Ḥusaynī, *Tuḥfat al-sālikīn*, 629.

117. Kafadar, "Mütereddit bir Mutasavvif."

118. Lāmi'ī Çelebi, *Terceme-i nefaḥāt*, 463–64.

119. On the Naqshbandī practice of *rābiṭa* and concept of a continuous *dhikr*, see chap. 5, and on *ṣuḥba*, chap. 7. Buehler describes Indian Mujaddidī shaykhs imparting the Naqshbandī *dhikr* to female disciples by focusing spiritual energy on them as these disciples were visualizing the name of God written on their heart (see Buehler, *Sufi Heirs of the Prophet*, 161).

120. Kissling, "Sociological and Educational Role."

121. See Nev'īzāde 'Aṭā'ī, *Ḥadā'iḳ*, 357, 362, and 'Alī Mınıḳ, *'Iqd*, 2:218 on the bachelors Baba Maḥmūd Riżā'ī, Aḥmad Bukhārī (Unḳapanılı), and Muṣṭafā Sürūrī, respectively. The latter, we are told, was "disinclined towards procreation," since children would complicate the "severance of attachments" (*ḳaṭ' ül-'alā'iḳ*) on which a serious commitment to the tariqa would have to be based. On the Naqshbandī concept of *khalvat dar anjuman*, see chap. 5.

122. In contrast to the practice of *khalīfa*s marrying their shaykhs' daughters, we do not hear of such individuals "inheriting" the wives of deceased shaykhs as a form of authenticating spiritual authority. For such form of inheritance as practiced by Egypt's Mamlūk *amīrs*, see Fay, "Women and *Waqf*," 41–45.

123. See Bueler, *Sufi Heirs of the Prophet*, 161. As these sources had it, women also would have to give up singing and dancing, as well as the non-Muslim customs of resorting to magic, sacrificing animals on shaykhs' tombs, and fasting on auspicious days determined by astrology.

124. Ṭaşköprüzāde, *Shaqā'iq*, 1:564. Cf. chap. 3 for an account from Yenice-i Vardar, suggesting that because of the lingering spirituality of 'Abdullāh Ilāhī, many of the town's male inhabitants were Sufis or Naqshbandīs, while the women were all pious, virtuous, and reluctant to venture into the public sphere.

125. See the list of entries in note 113. The *waqf*s of Ziyāde Hātūn, Fāṭima Hātūn, and Sittişāh Hātūn appear in entries 1164, 1180, and 1685, respectively.

126. In addition to Baer, "Women and Waqf," see Meriwether, "Women and *Waqf* Revisited," and bibliographic references there, n. 3.

CHAPTER 3

1. Ṭaşköprüzāde, *Shaqā'iq*, 1:549–50; Bursalı, *'Osmānlı mü'ellifleri*, 1:40–41.
2. Nev'īzāde 'Aṭā'ī, *Ḥadā'iḳ*, 371–72; 'Uşāḳīzāde, *Zeyl-i şaḳā'iḳ*, 557.
3. Muṣṭafā b. Hayreddīn, *Silsile-i hōcagān*, 15a.
4. Evliyā Çelebī, *Seyāḥatnāme*, 3:187, 189.
5. 'Abdīzāde, *Amasya ta'rīhi*, 1:243–4, 253–4.
6. Barkan, "Osmanlı İmparatorluǧunda bir İskân ve Kolonizasyon Metodu."
7. On the nineteenth-century Khālidī campaign of dissemination, see Algar, "Brief History," 32; Kufralı, "Nakşbendiliǧin Kuruluş ve Yayılışı," 182; Gündüz, *Osmanlılarda Devlet-Tekke Münasabetleri*, 242–43; Abu-Manneh, "Rise and Expansion," 18.
8. With regard to Sufis as agents of conversion, DeWeese has shown that in fourteenth- and fifteenth-century Central Asia, it was the Yasavīs, with their hereditary and communal modes of leadership, who were the principal agents of the (nominal) conversion of whole communities; for this they drew much criticism from Khwājagānī (or "proto-Naqshbandī") quarters (see his "Yasavī Šayḫs," and "Khojagānī Origins").
9. On this role of the Khalwatīs and the official patronage they were given, see Clayer's arguments in *Mystiques, état et société*, esp. chap. 2.
10. See the analysis of the Naqshbandī construction of orthodoxy in chap. 5.
11. For a similar notion concerning the Naqshbandiyya in the western Balkans, especially Bosnia and Herzegovina, see the following section.
12. Faroqhi, *Bektaschi-Orden in Anatolien*, 7–8.
13. See Muḥibbī, *Khulāṣat al-athar*, 1:152–53, 2:277.
14. For the situation in Transoxania, where Naqshbandīs were active among both urban and settled rural groups, see Paul, *Politische und soziale Bedeutung*, chaps. 3, 6, and 7.
15. Some of this has been done (for individual tariqas) in the two studies mentioned above: Faroqhi, *Bektaschi-Orden in Anatolien*, and Clayer, *Mystiques, état et société*. Faroqhi has made use in particular of archival material, including *waqf* documents and registers of imperial decrees (*mühimme*) and population and revenue (*tapu*). Clayer has relied primarily on narrative sources written in the capital, whose effectiveness and deficiencies she discusses in the introduction, pp. 55–61. Concerning the presence of multiple tariqas in the western Balkans (modern Yugoslavia), substantial Ottoman archival material has been incorporated in Ćehajić, *Derviški redovi*. For reading with me parts of this monograph, I am indebted to Dr. Nenad Filipovic of Princeton University.

16. Lāmi'ī Çelebi, *Terceme-i nefaḥāt*, 462; Ṭaşköprüzāde, *Shaqā'iq*, 1:374; 'Āşıḳ Çelebi, *Meşā'ir-i şu'arā*, 35b; Mecdī, *Terceme-i şaḳā'iḳ*, 263.

17. Evliyā Çelebi, *Seyāḥatnāne*, 8:176.

18. See Ṭaşköprüzāde, *Shaqā'iq*, 1:568; *Silsilenāme-i ṭuruḳ-i 'aliye*, 18.

19. Ṭaşköprüzāde, *Shaqā'iq*, 1:565–67.

20. Laṭīfī, *Tezkere*, 194; Bursalı, *'Osmānlı mü'ellifleri*, 2:231; Kiel, "Prizren."

21. Evliyā Çelebi, *Seyāḥatnāme*, 3:454–55. For Central Asian Naqshbandī *tekkes* in these other locations, see the sections on Kurdistan and Bursa below and chaps. 2 and 7.

22. Nev'īzāde 'Aṭā'ī, *Ḥadā'iḳ*, 369–70; Na'īmā, *Ta'rīh*, 1:75–76.

23. Ćehajić, *Derviški redovi*, 35–37.

24. Ibid., 35–39; Ćehajić, "Socio-Political Aspects," 664.

25. Ćehajić, *Derviški redovi*, 48–50.

26. Evliya Çelebi, *Seyāḥatnāme*, 6:433; Ćehajić, *Derviški redovi*, 62–63.

27. Ćehajić, *Derviški redovi*, 67.

28. Ćehajić, "Socio-Political Aspects," 663–64.

29. See chap. 6 for a critique of this view as it has been applied to the Ottoman campaign against the Ṣafavids and Ḳızılbaş and the Naqshbandī role therein.

30. As Clayer has made clear, Khalwatīs were always more active in these areas. According to Ćehajić, while in Kosovo and Macedonia Naqshbandīs were secondary not only to Khalwatīs but also to Bayramī-Melāmīs, Bektaşīs, and Rifā'īs, in Bosnia and Herzegovina their presence was central (see *Derviški redovi*, 68, and "Socio-Political Aspects," 664).

31. Bruinessen, "Religious Life in Diyarbekir," 51–52.

32. Others, apart from Kurds, also lived in this area. For some data, see the sections on population in Bois, "Kurds, Kurdistān."

33. For this observation, see chap. 4.

34. Bruinessen, "Economic Life in Diyarbekir," 36–38.

35. Narrative accounts such as Evliyā Çelebi, *Seyāḥatnāme*, and Ṭabbākh, *A'lām al-nubalā'* suggest that the tariqa did not spread from here to adjacent non-Kurdish areas in central Anatolia or south to Aleppo (for Evliyā's account of two recently deceased shaykhs in Kayseri, see above). As we see below, in time one Kurdish Naqshbandī line was carried from Diyarbakır to Bursa, however.

36. On his training with Aḥrār and activities in Qazvin, see chap. 1.

37. Bruinessen, "Naqshbandī Order in Kurdistan," 351, quoting the original manuscript of the *Seyāḥatnāme* from the Topkapı Palace Library. This was perhaps one of those Naqshbandī Bukharan *tekkes* that were built to provide accommodations for Central Asian pilgrims on their way to the Hijaz (for more details, see the sections on Bursa and the Balkans in this chapter, and chaps. 2 and 7).

38. On Shaykh Ismā'īl and his ancestors, see [Erżurūmī], *Ma'rifetnāme*, 504–28; and Bursalı, *'Osmānlı mü'ellifleri*, 1:33–36 (Ibrāhīm Ḥaḳḳı's biography). On

the later history of this line, see 'Alī Emīrī, *Tezkere-i şu'arā'*, 1:421–23 (biography of Zamzam Hanım).

39. Evliyā Çelebi, *Seyāḥatnāme*, 4:9; Evliyā Çelebi, *Evliya Çelebi in Bitlis*, 68–69.

40. Evliyā Çelebi, *Seyāḥatnāme*, 2:327.

41. Ibid., 4:139.

42. Tabbākh, *A'lām al-nubalā'*, 6:418–19.

43. On his escape, see chap. 1.

44. For Sīvāsī's note, see *Risāle-i şerīfe*, 159a (folio prefixed to the *Risāle*). For the copier and the circumstances under which the work was copied and disseminated see chap. 7. Shirvan was occupied by the Ṣafavids in 906/1500 and incorporated fully into their state after the defeat of the last Shīrvānshāh in 944/1538; it then came under Ottoman control, before reverting again to Ṣafavid control at the turn of the seventeenth century (see Barthold, "Shīrwān"; and Barthold, "Shīrwān Shāh").

45. See references below, n. 60.

46. The *Şerā'iṭ* is the first of three related pieces that appear consecutively in the same volume, MS Süleymaniye Library (Istanbul), Fātiḥ, 2658. The *Şerā'iṭ* itself (fols. 71a–76a) includes a discussion of the series of Naqshbandī principles known as the *kalimāt-i qudsiyya*, an account of the devotional regimen of Shaykh Maḥmūd's circle, and a *silsila* that allows us to locate this spiritual line within the broader Naqshbandī spiritual network. The second piece, *Silsile-i hōcagān-i nakşbendiye nisbet-i kulliye-i bekriye* (fols. 76b–78a), offers a spiritual chain of the same line that is traced via an exclusive Bakrī descent. The third, *Faṣl fi'l-kalimāt al-qudsiyya* (fols. 78b–80a), explains again the *kalimāt-i qudsiyya*, now in Arabic. A reference (fol. 78a) to Shaykh Maḥmūd as "the martyr" (*al-shahīd*) indicates that at least the second of the three pieces was written or copied after his death.

47. *Şerā'iṭ*, 71a–73b; Qazvīnī, *Silsilanāma*, 14b–19b.

48. *Şerā'iṭ*, 73b; *Silsilenāme-i ṭuruḳ-i 'aliye*, 21.

49. Qazvīnī, *Silsilanāma*, 19b.

50. Peçevī, *Ta'rīh*, 2:461–62.

51. Na'īmā, *Ta'rīh*, 3:385;

52. Evliyā Çelebi, *Seyāḥatnāme*, 4:33.

53. For Bursa, see Meḥmed Şemseddīn, *Bursa Dergâhları*, 561–69; Belīğ-i Bursevī, *Güldeste-i riyāż*, 155; Bursalı, *'Osmānlı mü'ellifleri*, 1:14. A nineteenth-century Naqshbandī-Khālidī source (*Silsilenāme-i ṭuruḳ-i 'aliye*, 21) identified several other works written by the Urmavī shaykhs: a *Tezkere-i baba* by Ḳocağa; a *Menāḳib-i çāhāryār güzin* by his great nephew, Ebvābī 'Ācizī; and a *Kitāb-i güzide* by "Şeyh Maḥmūd" (either Kocağa's son or his later descendant in Bursa, Açıḳbaş Maḥmūd, known as Resmī). Perhaps the last mentioned work is the same as Maḥmūd b. Seyyid Meḥmed en-Naḳşbendī el-Urmavī, *Tecvīd-i güzide*, MS Staatsbibliothek (Berlin), or. 4685. I am indebted to the late Dr. Klaus Schwarz of the Staatsbibliothek for this reference.

54. According to the *Şerā'iṭ* (fol. 72b) the Naqshbandī *dhikr* itself may be recited either in the heart or with the tongue: "*Yād kardan* means that the wayfarer, aware / says continuously "there is no god but God" / from the bottom of his consciousness, in either of two ways / with the tongue or in the heart." (*Yād kardan ke sālikī āgāh / har zamān lā ilāha illā 'llāh / Bi-zabān yā bi-dil bi-har du ṭarīq / muttaṣil gūyad az sar-i taḥqīq.*)

55. Ibid., 71a–72b. On the "saw *dhikr*," which elsewhere has been associated primarily with Yasavīs, see Trimingham, *Sufi Orders in Islam*, 197; Algar, "Brief History," 8. From Qazvīnī, *Silsilanāma*, 19a, it appears that Molla Ilyās could have received the vocal *dhikr* also from his Naqshbandī preceptor, Khusrawshāhī, who had been a disciple of Muḥammad Nūrbakhsh in his youth and later practiced both a silent and vocal *dhikr*. Given the clarity of the *Şerā'iṭ* (though less so Qazvīnī), there is no need to speculate, as does Bruinessen, that the vocal *dhikr* of the Urmavīs may have originated in the contemporary Gulshanī tradition of *dhikr* accompanied by music (see "Naqshbandī Order in Kurdistan," 347).

56. On this Medinese line, associated primarily with Aḥmad al-Qushāshī and Ibrāhīm al-Kūrānī, see chap. 4. On nineteenth-century Naqshbandī Khālidīs professing a secondary Kubravī affiliation, see Irbīlī, *Al-Risāla al-as'adiyya*, 29.

57. The *silsila* contained in the *Şerā'iṭ* has a common three-pronged structure, with one line passing through Abū Bakr, a second through 'Alī, and a third through 'Alī and several of his descendants; but the Bakrī line is dubbed "perfect" or "complete" (*nisbet-i kulliye*), and that passing through 'Alī "incomplete" (*nisbet-i cuz'iye*). Only a Bakrī line appears in the piece immediately following, the *Silsile-i hōcagān-i nakşbendiye nisbet-i kulliye-i bekriye* (fols. 76b–78a). For Bakrī and 'Alawi ('Alid) configurations and their role in the Naqshbandī *silsila*, see the discussion in chap. 5.

58. See Na'īmā, *Ta'rīh*, 3:385; 'Uşāḳīzāde, *Zeyl-i şaḳā'iḳ*, 48; Şeyhī, *Zeyl*, 77b.

59. Bruinessen, "Naqshbandī Order in Kurdistan," 341–42.

60. The story has been told, among others, by Na'īmā, *Ta'rīh*, 3:385–92; Evliyā Çelebi, *Seyāḥatnāme*, 4:53–55; Peçevī, *Ta'rīh*, 2:461–62; 'Uşāḳīzāde, *Zeyl-i şaḳā'iḳ*, 48–49; Şeyhī, *Zeyl*, 77b–78a; and Kātib Çelebi, *Fezleke*, 2:207. Bruinessen, "Naqshbandī Order in Kurdistan" offers a pioneering account in English.

61. Na'īmā, *Ta'rīh*, 3:385, 389–90; 'Uşāḳīzāde, *Zeyl-i şaḳā'iḳ*, 48; Şeyhī, *Zeyl*, 77b.

62. Quote from Evliyā Çelebi, *Seyāḥatnāme*, 4:53. Cf. Na'īmā, *Ta'rīh*, 3:389–90.

63. For the vicissitudes of the Ottoman-Ṣafavid struggle in the region stretching from Lake Van to Azerbaijan and the Caucasus during this period, see Parry, "Successors of Sulaimān"; and Parry, "Period of Murād IV."

64. For these circumstances, see Bruinessen, "Naqshbandī Order in Kurdistan," 343.

65. 'Uşāḳīzāde, *Zeyl-i şaḳā'iḳ*, 48; Şeyhī, *Zeyl*, 77b.

66. Evliyā Çelebi, *Seyāḥatnāme*, 4:54; Na'īmā, *Ta'rīh*, 3:386.

67. Na'īmā, *Ta'rīh*, 3:385.

68. Evliyā Çelebi, *Seyāḥatnāme*, 4:53–54; Na'īmā, *Ta'rīh*, 3:386–89; 'Uşāḳīzāde, *Zeyl-i şaḳā'iḳ*, 48; Şeyhī, *Zeyl*, 77b.

69. Evliyā Çelebi, *Seyāḥatnāme*, 4:54.

70. Na'īmā, *Ta'rīh*, 3:385.

71. Peçevī, *Ta'rīh*, 2:462. On this meaning of *al-mulk 'aqīm*, see Mottahedeh, *Loyalty and Leadership*, 190; Lane, *Arabic-English Lexicon*, s.v. *'aqīm*. Bruinessen has taken it to mean "the lands are barren" ("Naqshbandī Order in Kurdistan," 343).

72. Evliyā Çelebi, *Seyāḥatnāme*, 4:54.

73. Na'īmā, *Ta'rīh*, 3:387–89; Evliyā Çelebi, *Seyāḥatnāme*, 4:54–55. Peçevī makes the sultan's consort (*ḫāṣṣeki*), who was in Diyarbakır during the campaign, especially instrumental in indicting the shaykh (see Peçevī, *Ta'rīh*, 2:462).

74. Na'īmā, *Ta'rīh*, 3:390–91; 'Uşāḳīzāde, *Zeyl-i şaḳā'iḳ*, 49; Şeyhī, *Zeyl*, 77b–78a.

75. Cf. Bruinessen, "Naqshbandī Order in Kurdistan," 343.

76. Na'īmā, *Ta'rīh*, 3:386; 'Alī Emīrī, *Tezkere-i şu'arā'*, 1:20–21; Evliyā Çelebi, *Seyāḥatnāme*, 4:36; *Silsilenāme-i ṭuruḳ-i 'aliye*, 21.

77. *Silsilenāme-i ṭuruḳ-i 'aliye*, 21.

78. Na'īmā, *Ta'rīh*, 3:386; Evliyā Çelebi, *Seyāḥatnāme*, 4:182.

79. Bruinessen, "Naqshbandī Order in Kurdistan," 353, referring to an anonymous Turkish *silsila*, but noting that this line must have been extinguished by the early eighteenth century.

80. Baldırzāde, *Revżat el-evliyā'*, 28b; Belīğ-i Bursevī, *Güldeste-i riyāż*, 143–44.

81. Nev'īzāde 'Aṭā'ī, *Ḥadā'iḳ*, 360; Belīğ-i Bursevī, *Güldeste-i riyāż*, 145; Muṣṭafā b. Hayreddīn, *Silsile-i hōcagān*, 15a.

82. Belīğ-i Bursevī, *Güldeste-i riyāż*, 335–38, 432–33. According to Belīğ, the last family member to have been buried in the compound was a *qāḍī* of Iznikmid, Yūsuf Ilāhīzāde (d. 1037/1627–28).

83. Meḥmed Şemseddīn, *Bursa Dergâhları*, 601.

84. Ibid., 321–22. In the account of Meḥmed Şemseddīn, the brigands asked Ḥasan to surrender to them his good-looking and sweet-voiced son, whom they had heard reciting the call to prayer at the *tekke*. Alarmed at the sexual transgression that might ensue, he killed his son, sending to them his severed head. In rage the brigands then surrounded the *tekke*, and in the melee that followed Ḥasan was killed. On another incident, in which the "iron-tongued" Ḥasan pronounced as "infidel" (*kāfir*) a local *'ālim* who claimed that 'Alid *silsila*s were just as spiritually effective as the Naqshbandī Bakrī one, see chap. 5.

85. Meḥmed Şemseddīn, *Bursa Dergâhları*, 299–302. Cf. Aḥmed Muhtār, *Brusa sergisi rehberi*, 56.

86. Meḥmed Şemseddīn, *Bursa Dergâhları*, 447–48.

87. Baldırzāde, *Revżat el-evliyā'*, 83b–84a, 110a; Belīğ-i Bursevī, *Güldeste-i riyāż*, 152.

88. Baldırzāde, *Revżat el-evliyā'*, 53a.

89. Ibid., 79a–b; Belīǧ-i Bursevī, *Güldeste-i riyāż*, 167–68.

90. Baldırzāde, *Revżat el-evliyā'*, 120b; Belīǧ-i Bursevī, *Güldeste-i riyāż*, 180–82.

91. Baldırzāde, *Revżat el-evliyā'*, 104b–5b; Belīǧ-i Bursevī, *Güldeste-i riyāẓ*, 168–69.

92. Belīǧ-i Bursevī, *Güldeste-i riyāẓ*, 160–61.

93. On Lāmi'ī Çelebi, see Ṭaşköprüzāde, *Shaqā'iq*, 2:38–39; 'Āşıḳ Çelebi, *Meşā'ir üş-şu'arā*, 108b–11a; Baldırzāde, *Revżat el-evliyā'*, 96a–97a; Laṭīfī, *Tezkere*, 290–94; Belīǧ-i Bursevī, *Güldeste-i riyāż*, 176–80; Bursalı, *'Osmānlı mü'ellifleri*, 2:492–95. See also Flemming, "Lāmi'ī." On his translation and sequel to Jāmī's *Nafaḥāt al-uns* and on the incident in which he recited a eulogy commemorating the death of Ḥusayn b. 'Alī in Karbala in 61/680, see chaps. 2 and 5 respectively.

94. Belīǧ-i Bursevī, *Güldeste-i riyāẓ*, 169–70.

95. 'Alī Emīrī, *Tezkere-i şu'arā'*, 1:380–86; Belīǧ-i Bursevī, *Güldeste-i riyāż*, 154–59; Meḥmed Şemseddīn, *Bursa Dergâhları*, 561–63; Bursalı, *'Osmānlı mü'ellifleri*, 1:14.

96. 'Alī Emīrī, *Tezkere-i şu'arā'*, 381–82. For a chronogram that Açıḳbaş Maḥmūd wrote in scorn of the death of Shāh 'Abbās and the advent of Shāh Ṣāfī in 1038/1629, see chap. 6.

97. According to Bursalı, *'Osmānlı mü'ellifleri*, 1:14, the author was the first; according to Meḥmed Şemseddīn, *Bursa Dergâhları*, 564, he was the second. Bursalı attributes to Açıḳbaş Maḥmūd a number of other works, including a collection of poems in Arabic, Persian, and Turkish, a work that describes and categorizes twelve branches of knowledge, and a work entitled *Güzide* on an unknown subject (but see above, note 53, for a *Kitāb-i güzide* whose author may have been Açıḳbaş's uncle and spiritual master, Shaykh Maḥmūd Urmavī).

98. Meḥmed Şemseddīn, *Bursa Dergâhları*, 566.

99. Ibid., 567. Bāyezīd Efendi (d. 1061/1651), a Naqshbandī refugee from Yerevan who was the prayer leader of the Reyḥān Paşa Mosque in Bursa for some five decades, also built a reputation as a reciter of the *Awrād-i fatḥiyya* (see Belīǧ-i Bursevī, *Güldeste-i riyāż*, 441). Although his biographer does not identify Bāyezīd's spiritual ancestry, perhaps he too was an early follower of the Urmavīs, or perhaps the devotional mixture that they practiced was shared by other groups in the area between Azerbaijan and the Caucasus.

100. Meḥmed Şemseddīn, *Bursa Dergâhları*, 565. 'Abdülkerīm Müfīd was a *khalīfa* of the first carrier of the Mujaddidiyya to Istanbul, Shaykh Murād al-Bukhārī. On 'Abdülkerīm's poetry and expertise in Persian, see Sālim Efendi, *Tezkere*, 624–25.

101. Meḥmed Şemseddīn, *Bursa Dergâhları*, 565–69.

102. Evliyā Çelebi, *Seyāḥatnāme*, 2:17–18. Deficient orthography makes the distinction between Khalwatī and Celvetī uncertain. In addition, as is always the

case, this information must be regarded as tentative because of the traveler's sometime cavalier attitude toward historical accuracy (on this, see Bruinessen, "Evliya Çelebi and His Seyahatname," esp. 8–12).

103. By comparison, an account from early twentieth-century Bursa counted altogether thirty-six *tekkes* (or *dergāhs*), seven of them Naqshbandī. Of these (Münzevī 'Abdullāh, Hālidī, Özbekiye, Ğār-ı 'Āşıḳān, and three institutions appearing simply as Naḳşbendī), at least the first two were eighteenth- and nineteenth-century Mujaddidī and Khālidī *tekkes* (see Aḥmed Muhtār, *Brusa sergisi rehberi*, 56–57).

CHAPTER 4

1. For the practice of "pious residence," see Ende, "Mudjāwir."

2. Jāmī, *Nafaḥāt*, 388, 392–95; Kāshifī, *Rashaḥāt* (ed. Mu'īnyān), 1:97, 109–11.

3. Jāmī, *Nafaḥāt*, 405; Kāshifī, *Rashaḥāt* (ed. Mu'īnyān), 1:254–64, 310–11, 345–47.

4. Qazvīnī, *Silsilanāma*, 18b; Ṭaşköprüzāde, *Shaqā'iq*, 1:548–49.

5. Kāshifī, *Rashaḥāt* (ed. Mu'īnyān), 2:641; Qazvīnī, *Silsilanāma*, 17b; Ṭaşköprüzāde, *Shaqā'iq*, 2:162; Lāmi'ī Çelebi, *Terceme-i Nefaḥāt*, 459.

6. Qazvīnī, *Silsilanāma*, 16a.

7. Qazvīnī, *Silsilanāma*, 16a, 19a; Ṭaşköprüzāde, *Shaqā'iq*, 1:550–53; Lāmi'ī Çelebi, *Terceme-i Nefaḥāt*, 460.

8. Ibn al-'Ujaymī, *Khabāyā*, 23b–24a, 128b–29a. For Nahrawālī's involvement with the Medina-based Naqshbandī and Shaṭṭārī line of Aḥmad al-Qushāshī and Ibrāhīm al- Kūrānī, see below.

9. See Lāmi'ī Çelebi, *Terceme-i Nefaḥāt*, 465–67; and Nev'īzāde 'Aṭā'ī, *Ḥadā'iḳ*, 216, 84–85, 24, respectively.

10. See Ṣādiqī, *Manhaj*, 1b–2b for the author, title, and circumstances under which the work was written. The *Manhaj* remains little known to scholars.

11. Ibid., 10a–12a. For Aḥmad Ṣādiq's career in Istanbul, see chap. 2.

12. See the description in Ṣādiqī, *Manhaj*, 12a–13b.

13. See Qudsī's biography in Muḥibbī, *Khulāṣat al-athar*, 2:433.

14. Ṣādiqī, *Manhaj*, 12a.

15. In India, a Naqshbandī presence of Transoxanian origin had emerged by the late sixteenth century. For this Naqshbandiyya, see Rizvi, *History of Sufism*, 2:174–96; Rizvi, "Sixteenth Century Naqshbandiyya Leadership," 153–65.

16. Ibn al-'Ujaymī, *Khabāyā*, 84b–85a, 116b–118a. Ibn al-'Ujaymī was initiated into the tariqa through several other channels, as is indicated later in this chapter.

17. See the fascinating biography by Schlegell, "Sufism in the Ottoman Arab World." For Nābulusī's Naqshbandī *silsila*, see his *Al-Ḥaqīqa wa'l-majāz*, 146.

18. Even in the nineteenth century, and indeed when Shaykh Khālid, the eponym of the Khālidiyya, lived in Damascus (where he died prematurely in the plague of 1242/1827), the spread of the tariqa in Syria, as opposed to Kurdistan and Anatolia, was rather limited (confined, as it were, to Damascus and Tripoli). For this, see Abu-Manneh, "Rise and Expansion," 21.

19. Farooqi, "Moguls, Ottomans, and Pilgrims."

20. Francis Robinson notes that precisely thanks to its position in the Indian Ocean trade along with its role as the center of the pilgrimage, the Arabian peninsula became a focus of growing importance for Islamic scholarship in India from the sixteenth century. See his "Ottoman-Safawids-Mughals," 223–24.

21. On Sufism in early Ottoman Egypt, see Winter, *Society and Religion*, esp. chaps. 3–5; Winter, *Egyptian Society under Ottoman Rule*, chap. 5.

22. Martin, "Short History," 290–97; Winter, *Society and Religion*, 105–12.

23. Winter, "Sheikh 'Alī Ibn Maymūn."

24. On the Naqshbandī penchant for writing, copying, and translating, see the discussion in chap. 7.

25. See Bruinessen, "Agha, Shaikh and State"; Bruinessen, "Origins and Development." Note also 'Abdülbaki Gölpınarlı's assertion that when the Khālidiyya spread to Istanbul in the nineteenth century, it found most of its followers there in the ranks of Shāfi'īs from the east (though this assessment might be influenced by political overtones, "Shāfi'īs from the east" being a euphemism for Kurds). See Gölpınarlı, *100 Soruda Türkiye'de Mezhepler ve Tarikatlar*, 220–21.

26. Kūrānī, *Itḥāf al-munīb*, esp. 3b–4a, 8a.

27. See, for example, Robinson, "Ottomans-Safawids-Mughals," 228.

28. McChesney, "'Barrier of Heterodoxy'," 236.

29. Beside al-'Uthmānī (indicating his family's descent from the Caliph 'Uthmān), Tāj al-Dīn was sometimes called as al-Hindī or al-Sambhalī (having taught in Sambhal, east of Delhi, before moving to the Hijaz). On Muḥammad al-Bāqī, known in the Naqshbandī tradition as Khwāja Bāqī Bi'llāh and often presented as the "founder" of the Indian Naqshbandiyya, see Kishmī, *Zubdat al-maqāmāt*, 5–60; Rizvi, *History of Sufism*, 2:185–93.

30. Ibn al-'Ujaymī, *Khabāyā*, 23a–b; Ḥamawī, *Fawā'id al-irtiḥāl*, 2:288 (I use two copies of the *Fawā'id al-irtiḥāl* from the Dār al-Kutub Library; references with page numbers are to MS Ta'rīkh Taymūr 923, references with folio numbers, to MS Ta'rīkh 1093).

31. In addition to the preceding two references, see notes 42–47 below.

32. Ḥusaynī, *Tuḥfat al-sālikīn*, 616–40 (quote from p. 624). Though extensive parts of it were incorporated into the *Fawā'id al-irtiḥāl*, in its original form the *Tuḥfa* seems to be unknown to scholars. I use the Dār al-Kutub Library's photocopy of a manuscript from San'a in Yemen.

33. Rizvi, *History of Sufism*, 2:336–37, quoting Kishmī's *Zubdat al-maqāmāt* and the *Maktūbāt* of Muḥammad al-Bāqī. Cf. Ḥusaynī, *Tuḥfat al-sālikīn*, 625.

34. Rizvi, *History of Sufism*, 2:337. It would be some time, however, before the influence of Sirhindī and the Mujaddidiyya spread from the area around Delhi to other parts of India. See, for example, Digbi, "Naqshbandîs in the Deccan." For seventeenth-century criticism of Sirhindī in India and the Hijaz, see below.

35. For Muḥammad al-Bāqī's command, see Ḥusaynī, *Tuḥfat al-sālikīn*, 625. The common practice of holding multiple tariqa affiliations emerges from Ibn al-'Ujaymī, *Khabāyā*, passim. In this regard, see also the discussion in chap. 7.

36. See Ḥamawī, *Fawā'id al-irtiḥāl*, 3:384a.

37. See Ibn al-'Ujaymī, *Khabāyā*, 126b–27a.

38. See his pronouncements on these issues in 'Uthmānī, *Risāla fī sulūk al-Naqshbandiyya*, 162a–73a; 'Uthmānī, *Risāla fī ādāb al-mashyakha* (MS India Office Library), 125a–43a (all following references to this work are to this India Office manuscript, unless otherwise indicated).

39. See biographies of students who read Ibn al-'Arabī with him in Ibn al-'Ujaymī, *Khabāyā*, 122a, 126b. For his reservations, see Ḥusaynī, *Tuḥfat al-sālikīn*, 632.

40. 'Uthmānī, *Risāla fī sulūk al-Naqshbandiyya*, 162a, 164b–65b; Ḥusaynī, *Tuḥfat al-sālikīn*, 617. Tāj al-Dīn's early Naqshbandī disciples in India became known for the speed with which they attained *jadhba* under his supervision (see Ibn al-'Ujaymī, *Khabāyā*, 23a).

41. Rizvi, *History of Sufism*, 2:338, quoting Shāh Walīullāh, *Anfās al-'ārifīn*.

42. Ibn al-'Ujaymī, *Khabāyā*, 107b–108a; Ḥamawī, *Fawā'id al-irtiḥāl*, 1:719–20; Muḥibbī, *Khulāṣat al-athar*, 1: 157–58.

43. Muḥibbī, *Khulāṣat al-athar*, 1:19, 4:475–76.

44. Ibn al-'Ujaymī, *Khabāyā*, 48a; Ḥamawī, *Fawā'id al-irtiḥāl*, 1:722–24; Muḥibbī, *Khulaṣat al-athar*, 1:346–47; Ibn al-Buṣrawī, *Safīna farīda*, 157b. On Aḥmad's son, Mūsā, see Ḥamawī, *Fawā'id al-irtiḥāl*, 3:383b–84a; Muḥibbī, *Khulāṣat al-athar*, 4:431. On the Ibn 'Ujayl family, see Headley, "Bayt al-Faḳīh."

45. Ibn al-'Ujaymī, *Khabāyā*, 82a–b; Ḥamawī, *Fawā'id al-irtiḥāl*, 3:47a; Muḥibbī, *Khulāṣat al-athar*, 2:283. On the Mizjājī family, see Voll, "Linking Groups."

46. Ḥamawī, *Fawā'id al-irtiḥāl*, 1:587–90; Jabartī, *'Ajā'ib al-āthār*, 1:89–90.

47. On his teachers in the Hijaz, see Ibn al-'Ujaymī, *Khabāyā*, 131a–b. On his later impact in Indonesia (as reflected in Arab, Malay, and Dutch sources), see Bruinessen, "Origins and Development," 153–59. On 'Abd al-Bāqī's son, Zayn, who initiated in the Yemen a carrier of the tariqa to China, see the following section.

48. On these and other writings, see Ḥamawī, *Fawā'id al-irtiḥāl*, 2:288; Muḥibbī, *Khulāṣat al-athar*, 1:464. The two *Risāla*s are available in numerous copies in various manuscript collections in India, Europe, and the Middle East.

49. Nābulusī, *Miftāḥ al-ma'iyya*, 142a. Nābulusī's commentary itself enjoyed in time a wide circulation (see Schlegell, "Sufism in the Ottoman Arab World," 145–46).

50. Ḥamawī mentions several works by Ibn ʻAllān, including a treatise on the Naqshbandī principles and spiritual masters (see Ḥamawī, *Fawā'id al-irtiḥāl,* 1:719–20). Two copies of the *Risāla fī sulūk al-Naqshbandiyya* also suggest Ibn ʻAllān's authorship of this work. See MSS Süleymaniye Library (Istanbul), Serez 1530, fol. 158a, and Staatsbibliothek (Berlin), We. 1760, fol. 59b.

51. We also know of a Mālikī disciple or associate of Tāj al-Dīn, a visitor from Egypt by the name Abū al-Isʻād Yūsuf Ibn al-ʻAṭā ʻAbd al-Razzāq. The two are said to have "taken from" each other (see Ḥamawī, *Fawā'id al-irtiḥāl,* 2:223).

52. Ḥusaynī, *Tuḥfat al-sālikīn,* 636–37.

53. On Mīrzā al-Surūjī, see Ibn al-ʻUjaymī, *Khabāyā,* 121b–22b; Ḥamawī, *Fawā'id al-irtiḥāl,* 1:458–60; Muḥibbī, *Khulāṣat al-athar,* 4:202–3.

54. It is thus ironical that Tāj al-Dīn was sometimes known by the *nisba* al-Rūmī in reference to his move from India to what was at least nominally Ottoman territory.

55. The first Mujaddidī to have settled in Arabia, in 1052/1642–43, was Sirhindī's *khalīfa* Ādam Banūrī, who was apparently banished by the Mughal emperor because of the large Afghan following that he had attracted. Fifteen years later, Banūrī was followed by Sirhindī's son Muḥammad Maʻṣūm, who came on the pilgrimage and left a number of Mujaddidī *khalīfas* in Mecca and the Yemen. See Ibn al-ʻUjaymī, *Khabāyā,* 55a, 114b–16a; Rizvi, *History of Sufism,* 2:338–39.

56. See the biographical notices in Ibn al-ʻUjaymī, *Khabāyā,* 37a–b, 44a–47a; Ḥamawī, *Fawā'id al-irtiḥāl,* 1:572–575, 640–667, 2:46–67; Muḥibbī, *Khulāṣat al-athar,* 1:243–45, 343–46; Bursalı, *ʻOsmānlı mü'ellifleri,* 1:226–27.

57. In addition to the references in the previous note, see the biographical notices for associates of this group in Muḥibbī, *Khulāṣat al-athar,* 1:163–64, 226–29, 2:167, 3:70, 4:435; and Ḥamawī, *Fawā'id al-irtiḥāl,* 1:336–39, 3:345a–b.

58. Voll "Muḥammad Ḥayyā al-Sindī." Cf. Johns, "Ḳus͟hās͟hī"; Johns, "Kūrānī"; and Johns, "Friends in Grace."

59. On Barwajī, see Muḥibbī, *Khulāṣat al-athar,* 2:243–44.

60. See Muḥibbī, ibid., 1:402, 2:243–44, 4:435; Ḥamawī, *Fawā'id al-irtiḥāl,* 3:370a.

61. Bruinessen, "Origins and Development," 153–61; Johns, "Friends in Grace."

62. Fletcher, "'Voies' (*ṭuruq*) soufies en Chine," 19–21; Fletcher, "Naqshbandiyya in Northwest China," 24–33. On Ma Mingxin and his Chinese Naqshbandī faction, see also Lipman, *Familiar Strangers,* 86–89 (though Lipman stretches even further Voll's ideas about Kūrānī as the centerpoint of a grand wave of Muslim revivalism in the seventeenth and eighteenth centuries).

63. Ḥamawī, *Fawā'id al-irtiḥāl,* 2:682-84; Muḥibbī, *Khulāṣat al-athar,* 2:243–44; Rizvi, *History of Sufism,* 2:329–30. Kūrānī lists the *Jawāhir-i khamsa* as one of the books that his shaykh, Qushāshī, read with his spiritual master, Shinnāwī. See Kūrānī, *Amam,* 125.

64. Qushāshī, *Simṭ*, 67ff. and statement on p. 80.

65. Muḥibbī, *Khulāṣat al-athar*, 1:83, 402, 2:380, 4:451–53. Muḥibbī indicates that 'Imādī was initiated by Barwajī while in Medina during the pilgrimage season of 1014/1606 (ibid, 2:380).

66. See *silsila*s in Kūrānī, *Amam*, 108–9; Ibn al-Mīmī, *Naẓm al-sumūṭ*, 12a; Ibn al-'Ujaymī, *Khabāyā*, 23b–24a; and the biographical notice for Nahrawālī in Ḥamawī, *Fawā'id al-irtiḥāl*, 1:42b–43a.

67. Ḥamawī, *Fawā'id al-irtiḥāl*, 1:42b–43a.

68. Ibid., 2:189, 602; Muḥibbī, *Khulāṣat al-athar*, 2:201.

69. Kūrānī, *Amam*, 108–9. Interestingly, Kūrānī charted in this work only his Naqshbandī *silsila*s, albeit indicating that they were acquired "for blessing" (*tabarrukan*) rather than through a disciplined course of Sufi training.

70. Bruinessen, "Origins and Development," 154, n. 13.

71. For details, see the discussion on Naqshbandīs' devotion to Ibn al-'Arabī in chap. 5.

72. Bruinessen, "Origins and Development," 154–57. Compare Werner Kraus's suggestion that 'Abd al-Ra'ūf preferred to disseminate the teachings of the Shaṭṭāriyya because the Naqshbandiyya was tainted by the controversy that raged in the Hijaz in midcentury over some of Aḥmad Sirhindī's ideas (Kraus, "Some Notes," 691–93).

73. See chap. 3 for the vocal *dhikr* of the Urmavī Naqshbandīs of Kurdistan (whose devotional practice also had mixed origins).

74. Ḥamawī, *Fawā'id al-irtiḥāl*, 2:189, 602, 3:345a–b (biographical notices for his *khalīfa*s Sālim Ibn Shaykhān and Kamāl al-Dīn al-Shinnāwī al-Sūdānī and for Sālim's son Abū Bakr).

75. Ibn al-'Ujaymī, *Khabāyā*, 47a.

76. Voorhoeve, "'Abd al-Ra'ūf al-Siṅkilī."

77. For his pronouncements in this regard, see the first section of this chapter and note 26.

78. Rizvi, *History of Sufism*, 2:331–32, quoting Shāh Walīullāh, *Anfās al-'ārifīn*. On Vānī's career and leadership of the Ḳāḍīzādeli movement, see chap. 6.

79. Ibn al-'Ujaymī, *Khabāyā*, 37b. Nineteenth-century followers of Muḥammad al-Sānūsī in Fez would criticize Kūrānī posthumously, among other things for his views on the faith of Pharaoh and his assertion of the historicity of the so-called Satanic verses of Qur'ān 53:21 (see Johns, "Kūrānī").

80. Ibn al-'Ujaymī, *Khabāyā*, 55a-b (biographical notice for Jamāl al-Hindī al-Naqshbandī). Cf. Rizvi, *History of Sufism*, 2:339, including an account of some of Qushāshī's counterarguments.

81. Ibn al-'Ujaymī, *Khabāyā*, 114b–16a.

82. Barzanjī, *Qadḥ al-zand*, 73a–b. See also biographical notices on Barzanjī in Ibn al-'Ujaymī, *Khabāyā*, 101b–2a; Ḥamawī, *Fawā'id al-irtiḥāl*, 1:336–39; Murādī, *Silk al-durar*, 4:65–66; Bursalı, *'Osmānlı mü'ellifleri*, 2:26–27. Barzanjī (who may or

may not have been initiated specifically into the Naqshbandiyya) was more embroiled in politics than Kūrānī and his earlier associates. At one point he was sent as an envoy of the local ruler (*sharīf*) of Mecca to the Mughal emperor Awrangzīb, but was recalled midway because of disagreements over the *sharīf*'s handling of Indian charities to the Ḥaramayn. Later he became embroiled in a conflict with rivals in Medina that he resolved by traveling with a returning pilgrimage caravan to Istanbul, where he procured a sultanic decree in his defense.

83. For a detailed examination of Barzanjī's criticism and the larger seventeenth-century debate of which it was part, see Friedmann, *Shaykh Aḥmad Sirhindī*, esp. 7–9, 96–99.

CHAPTER 5

1. In Algar's formulation, hostility to Shī'ī Islam has been "a second trait" of this tariqa, along with the first trait of sobriety and *sharī'a*-abidance. This hostility derived from the tariqa's Bakrī ancestry combined with the fact of its emergence in the broader Islamic world at a time of intense Sunnī-Shī'ī rivalry. See his "Naqshbandī Order in Republican Turkey," 1–2.

2. Nizami, "Naqshbandiyyah Order," 163.

3. Algar, "Political Aspects of Naqshbandī History," esp. 151–52; Algar, "Brief History." In an article on Naqshbandīs' interest in Ibn al-'Arabī (see the penultimate section of this chapter and references there), Algar has specifically called attention to the problem of viewing this tariqa through the prism of the later Mujaddidiyya. Others have been altogether less interested in such nuanced historical analysis, often giving the impression, implicitly or explicitly, that what they have identified as aspects of the Naqshbandiyya's orthodoxy has characterized this tariqa all along.

4. Laṭīfī, *Tezkere*, 52.

5. *Risāle-i şerīfe*, 162a. Chap. 6 dwells on action, including the involvement of one Naqshbandī shaykh, 'Osmān Bosnevī, in a campaign of enforcing strict orthodox behavior on the public.

6. On the meaning of *'azīma* and *rukhṣa* in legal and Sufi discourse, see Goldziher, "'Azīma"; and Peters and Haar, "Rukhṣa." *Rukhṣa* might involve, for example, the suspension of the obligation to fast during Ramaḍān when one is ill or traveling.

7. See, for example, *Tüḥfet eṭ-ṭālibīn*, 73a, 87a; Lāmi'ī Çelebi, *Terceme-i nefaḥāt*, 468 (biography of Aḥmad Bukhārī); 'Uthmānī, *Risāla fī ādāb al-mashyakha*, 128a.

8. See the biographical notice on Aḥmed Tirevī in Muṣṭafā b. Hayreddīn, *Silsile-i hōcagān*, 15b. For the possibility that the author of this particular entry was the afore-mentioned 'Osmān Bosnevī, see chap. 6.

9. Ṣādiqī, *Manhaj*, 13b–14a.

10. 'Uthmānī, *Risāla fī sulūk al-Naqshbandiyya*, 172a; Ṣādiqī, *Manhaj*, 14a; *Tüḥfet eṭ-ṭālibīn*, 72b.

11. Kāshifī, *Rashaḥāt* (ed. Mu'īniyān), 1:95; Jāmī, *Nafaḥāt*, 384-86; Ṣalāḥ b. Mubārak al-Bukhārī, *Anīs al-ṭālibīn*, 93. For an Ottoman reproduction of the story, see the biography of 'Abdullāh Ilāhī in Ṭaşköprüzāde, *Shaqā'iq*, 1:378. For the *Anīs al-ṭālibīn* and the possibility that the author was Muḥammad Pārsā or someone of his circle, see Paul, *Doctrine and Organization*, 10–12.

12. For a general survey of the two types of recollection among Naqshbandīs, see Algar, "Silent and Vocal *Dhikr*." On the vocal ceremonies of other tariqas, see Schimmel, *Mystical Dimensions*, 167–86; Trimingham, *Sufi Orders in Islam*, 195–96, 204–7; Gardet, "Dhikr"; During, "Samā'"; Süleymān Fā'iḳ, *Mecmū'a*, 19b–20a.

13. Ṣarı 'Abdullāh, *Cevheret el-bidāye*, 142b–48a; Nev'īzāde 'Aṭā'ī, *Ḥadā'iḳ*, 60; Evliyā Çelebi, *Seyāḥatnāme*, 1:389.

14. Ṣādiqī, *Manhaj*, 16a; *Şerā'iṭ*, 73a. On the use of the formula *Muḥammad rasūl Allāh* in other Sufi traditions, see Schimmel, *Mystical Dimensions*, 214.

15. Ṣādiqī, *Manhaj*, 15a–16a; *Tüḥfet eṭ-ṭālibīn*, 78a; *Risāle-i şerīfe*, 175a; 'Uthmānī, *Risāla fī sulūk al-Naqshbandiyya*, 163b–64a. These and other sources do not bear out Buehler's conclusion from Mujaddidī literature that silent *dhikr* and the "*dhikr* of the heart" were "two different practices," each with its distinct formula (see Buehler, *Sufi Heirs of the Prophet*, 127–28).

16. Ṣādiqī, *Manhaj*, 15a–16a, 17b–20a; *Tüḥfet eṭ-ṭālibīn*, 75a–b, 77a–78b, 86a; *Risāle-i şerīfe*, 175a–b; 'Uthmānī, *Risāla fī sulūk al-Naqshbandiyya*, 163a–64b, 166a–68a; *Şerā'iṭ*, 72b.

17. 'Uthmānī, *Risāla fī ādāb al-mashyakha*, 130a; Ibn al-'Ujaymī, *Khabāyā*, 57a.

18. *Risāle-i şerīfe*, 175a; *Tüḥfet eṭ-ṭālibīn*, 73a, 75b–76a; 'Uthmānī, *Risāla fī sulūk al-Naqshbandiyya*, 164a; Ṣādiqī, *Manhaj*, 15b. The quotes are from the *Risāle-i şerīfe*, 175a and the *Tüḥfet eṭ-ṭālibīn*, 73a respectively.

19. Ṣādiqī (*Manhaj*, 16a–b) offered the following description of the *murāqaba*: "[The practitioner] observes continuously the meaning of the Name of the Essence [Allāh], . . . directing it with his full power and grasp towards his pineal heart (*qalb ṣanawbarī*), and preserving it without becoming distracted. He forces himself [to continue] to preserve that meaning until this becomes a natural disposition (*malaka*) . . . [so that] any discomfort is removed, the desired meaning takes over his heart never to disappear again, and the *murāqaba* ends in . . . witnessing (*mushāhada*)." For other descriptions, see *Risāle-i şerīfe*, 175b–76a; *Tüḥfet eṭ-ṭālibīn*, 79a; and 'Uthmānī, *Risāla fī sulūk al-Naqshbandiyya*, 164b–65a (the last two calling this technique a "*dhikr* of the Name of the Essence").

20. *Tüḥfet eṭ-ṭālibīn*, 79a; 'Uthmānī, *Risāla fī sulūk al-Naqshbandiyya*, 164b–65a; Ibn al-Mīmī, *Naẓm al-sumūṭ*, 18b. Tāj al-Dīn and Ibn al-Mīmī tied the superiority of the *murāqaba* to a preference for "divine attraction" (*jadhba*) over "disciplined traveling on the path" (*sulūk*) as the most effective way for attaining mystical progress.

21. See Algar, "Devotional Practices", 218; Abu-Manneh, "*Khalwa* and *Rābiṭa*," 289–302.

22. Abu-Manneh, "*Khalwa* and *Rābiṭa*," esp. 293–95, 299. However, he points out the primacy of the *rābiṭa* in the devotional regimen of Tāj al-Dīn al-ʿUthmānī in seneteenth-century Mecca (ibid., 294–95).

23. On these controversies over the organizational implications of the *rābiṭa*, see ibid., 297–301; Chodkiewicz, "Quelques aspects des techniques spirituelles," esp. 75–81.

24. Nābulusī, *Miftāḥ al-maʿiyya*, 206b.

25. Ṣādiqī, *Manhaj*, 16b. See also ʿUthmānī, *Risāla fī sulūk al-Naqshbandiyya*, 165b; *Şerāʾiṭ*, 76b (the latter calling this practice the *ḥifẓ-i nisbet*). The first part of Meier, *Zwei Abhandlungen* is devoted in its entirety to the Naqshbandī *rābiṭa* and points to many instances of its use by early Naqshbandīs (along with some parallels and antecedents from other Sufi traditions). See also Meier, *Meister und Schüler*, 11–16, 22–23; Paul, *Doctrine and Organization*, 36–44; and, on the use of the *rābiṭa* among Naqshbandīs more generally, Chodkiewicz, "Quelques aspects des techniques spirituelles," 75–78.

26. See Ṣādiqī, *Manhaj*, 17a; *Tüḥfet eṭ-ṭālibīn*, 79a; *Risāle-i şerīfe*, 174b–75a.

27. *Tüḥfet eṭ-ṭālibīn*, 78b.

28. Ilāhī, *Meslek eṭ-ṭālibīn*, 55b-57a; Ṣādiqī, *Manhaj*, 8b, 16a; *Tüḥfet eṭ-ṭālibīn*, 79a; Ibn al-Mīmī, *Naẓm al-sumūṭ*, 8b; ʿUthmānī, *Jāmiʿ al-fuʾād*, 19a. The last two nevertheless stated that vocal *dhikr* was compatible with the *sunna* or widely acknowledged in the *ḥadīth*.

29. *Tüḥfet eṭ-ṭālibīn*, 81a; Qazvīnī, *Silsilanāma*, 6a; Muṣṭafā b. Hayreddīn, *Silsile-i hōcagān*, 4b-5a. The author of the *Ṭüḥfet* and the copier of the *Silsilanāma* attributed the story to Muḥammad Pārsā's *Faṣl al-khiṭāb*. For a fuller discussion, see below.

30. *Tüḥfet eṭ-ṭālibīn*, 80a; *Risāle-i şerīfe*, 160b; Qazvīnī, *Silsilanāma*, 7b; [Ṣādiqī], *Risāla fī bayān ṭarīq al-Naqshband*, 159a–61b, esp. 160b (the latter being a fragment of the *Manhaj*, including a piece that is erroneously missing from the Princeton manuscript). See also Kāshifī, *Rashaḥāt* (ed. Muʿīniyān), 1:35; Jāmī, *Nafaḥāt*, 378.

31. Kāshifī, *Rashaḥāt* (ed. Muʿīniyān), 1:95; Jāmī, *Nafaḥāt*, 384–86; Ṣalāḥ b. Mubārak al-Bukhārī, *Anīs al-ṭālibīn*, 93; and Ottoman-period renditions in Ṣādiqī, *Manhaj*, 8b; and Ṭaşköprüzāde, *Shaqāʾiq*, 1:378 (biography of ʿAbdullāh Ilāhī). On the importance of this moment in Naqshbandī history, see Algar, "Silent and Vocal *Dhikr*," 43. Paul has shown on the basis of diverse Khwājagānī sources how the silent *dhikr* emerged out of a more complex process than that implied in this story. Controversies and Khwājagānī groups practicing competing styles of *dhikr* existed in the generations preceding Bahāʾ al-Dīn as well as in the period following his death. See Paul, *Doctrine and Organization*, 18–30.

32. Evliyā Çelebi, *Seyāḥatnāme*, 4:33. See also Naʿīmā, *Taʾrīh*, 3:385.

33. Rizvi, *History of Sufism,* 2:331–32, quoting Shāh Walīullāh, *Anfās al-'ārifīn*. See chap. 4 for more details.

34. Kūrānī, *Nashr al-zahr*; Kūrānī, *Itḥāf al-munīb*, esp. 3b–4a, 8a.

35. Schlegell, "Sufism in the Ottoman Arab World," 80ff. See also the discussion of the Naqshbandī involvement with the Ḳāḍīzādelis in chap. 6.

36. Nābulusī, *Iḍāḥ al-dalālāt*, esp. 15b, 27a, 28b, 51a.

37. Ibn al-Mīmī, *Naẓm al-sumūṭ*, 8b.

38. Ṣādiqī, *Manhaj*, 10b; Şeyhī, *Zeyl*, 77b.

39. *Şerā'iṭ*, 73a.

40. Lāmi'ī Çelebi, *Terceme-i nefaḥāt*, 461 (biography of Ilāhī); Ilāhī, *Meslek eṭ-ṭālibīn*, 30a-50b.

41. Lāmi'ī Çelebi, *Terceme-i nefaḥāt*, 468 (biography of Bukhārī). On *'uzla* as a lighter form of ritual *khalwa*, see Meier, *Zwei Abhandlungen*, 34.

42. 'Uthmānī, *Risāla fī sulūk al-Naqshbandiyya*, 167b; Uthmānī, *Risāla fī ādāb al-mashyakha*, 137b.

43. On the origins of this ambivalence among earlier Naqshbandīs in Transoxania, see Meier, *Zwei Abhandlungen*, 33–41; Paul, *Doctrine and Organization*, 30–34. On ascetic exercises performed by other Ottoman Sufis, see, for example, Muḥibbī, *Khulāṣat al-athar*, 1:250, 389–90, 4:16 (on Khalwatīs); Belīğ-i Bursevī, *Güldeste-i riyāẓ*, 227 (on a Zaynī disciple); Muṣṭafā b. Hayreddīn, *Silsile-i hōcagān*, 15b (on a Bayramī disciple).

44. Ṣādiqī, *Manhaj*, 16b.

45. Ḥusaynī, *Tuḥfat al-sālikīn*, 617; 'Uthmānī, *Risāla fī ādāb al-mashyakha*, 138a.

46. *Risāle-i şerīfe*, 169b; *Tüḥfet eṭ-ṭālibīn*, 86a.

47. Though the manuals routinely listed and discussed the *khalvat dar anjuman* within the series of Khwājagānī-Naqshbandī principles attributed to 'Abd al-Khāliq Ghujduvānī (the *kalimāt-i qudsiyya*), a general reading of the Naqshbandī devotional literature makes clear the centrality of this particular principle. For the technical discussion in the manuals, see Ṣādiqī, *Manhaj*, 19a; *Risāle-i şerīfe*, 169a–b; *Tüḥfet eṭ-ṭālibīn*, 73b–74a; and 'Uthmānī, *Risāla fī sulūk al-Naqshbandiyya*, 167a. Though a shunning of distinctive forms of dress would have been very much in keeping with the inconspicuousness implied in the *khalvat dar anjuman*, I have not found explicit references to this issue in the early Ottoman Naqshbandī sources. On other Naqshbandīs, see Algar, "Naḳshband, Khwādja Bahā' al-Dīn."

48. In the understanding of Aḥmad Sirhindī and later Mujaddidīs, the adage "the end is in the beginning" referred specifically to the return of advanced mystics, and hence Naqshbandīs, to the created world (outwardly behaving like ordinary pious Muslims) after having traversed the path and reached not only the annihilation of the lower self (*fanā'*) but also the "remaining" in God (*baqā'*). See Buehler, *Sufi Heirs of the Prophet*, 92, 100, 116, 123; Haar, *Follower and Heir*, 93.

49. For the notion that the Naqshbandiyya was a tariqa of "stark orthodoxy," see for example Mardin, "Nakshibendi Order," 206.

50. Some Naqshbandīs of our period portrayed *sharī'a*-observance, even more explicitly, as the means or the "external manners" (*al-ādāb al-ẓāhira*) of the mystical quest (see Ṣādiqī, *Manhaj*, 2b; 'Uthmānī, *Risāla fī sulūk al-Naqshbandiyya*, 172a). By contrast, see Aḥmad Sirhindī's description of the "Sufi path" as the "servant of religious teachings" (quoted in Haar, *Follower and Heir*, 48), though one hesitates to make much of uncontextualized statements of this kind.

51. On the elaboration of this idea by Bahā' al-Dīn, see Haar, "Importance of the Spiritual Guide," 317.

52. That this was a long-standing Naqshbandī tradition is made clear not only from tariqa literature, but also from Kātib Çelebi's singling out of Naqshbandīs for this practice in his *Mīzān ül-ḥaḳḳ*, 77.

53. Lāmi'ī Çelebi, *Terceme-i Nefaḥāt*, 461 (Ilāhī's biography).

54. Ibn al-'Ujaymī, *Khabāyā*, 108a.

55. Ibid., 128b.

56. Ṣādiqī, *Manhaj*, 11b.

57. Ibid., 13b (the first item is presumably *khirqa*, erroneously copied *ḥ. d. q. h*).

58. Haar discusses the Naqshbandī tradition of Uwaysī transmission in "Importance of the Spiritual Guide," 312–19. Schlegell examines the same phenomenon in connection with 'Abd al-Ghanī al-Nābulusī ("Sufism in the Ottoman Arab World," chap. 4). For a general treatment of the phenomenon and its namesake, see Baldick, "Uways al-Ḳaranī"; Baldick, "Uwaysiyya"; Ocak, *Veysel Karanî ve Üveysîlik*. On the possibility of Uwaysī transmission conferred by the Prophet, see *Şerā'iṭ*, 74b.

59. Ṣādiqī, *Manhaj*, 10a.

60. Ḥusaynī, *Tuḥfat al-sālikīn*, 623.

61. At least this was the accepted view concerning their dates and the nature of their initiations (see Haar, "Importance of the Spiritual Guide," 314).

62. Especially on the latter, see the discussion of the Naqshbandī silent *dhikr* in the previous section.

63. On the nature of *rābiṭa*, see the discussion in the previous section.

64. Nābulusī, *Miftāḥ al-ma'iyya*, 206b.

65. 'Uthmānī, *Risāla fī ādāb al-mashyakha*, 127a.

66. Lāmi'ī Çelebi, *Terceme-i Nefaḥāt*, 469.

67. Şeyhī, *Zeyl*, 25b; ' Uşāḳīzāde, *Zeyl-i şaḳā'iḳ*, 127-28; Ayvānsarāyı, *Ḥadīḳat ül-cevāmi'*, 1:13.

68. Ḥusaynī, *Tuḥfat al-sālikīn*, 627.

69. Ibn al-'Ujaymī, *Khabāyā*, 57a–b.

70. Ibid., 127b.

71. Ibn al-Mīmī, *Naẓm al-sumūṭ*, 33a. But cf. the much more forceful deprecation by an early Naqshbandī shaykh, Ya'qūb Charkhī, who described the *karāmāt* as "the menstrual discharge of men" (quoted in Algar, "Silent and Vocal *Dhikr*," 43).

72. On Ibn al-'Arabī's influence and on some of the qualities that underlay it, see Chittick, "Ibn 'Arabī and His School," 54–57; Chittick, "Rūmī and *waḥdat al-*

wujūd," 77–79; Chittick, *Self-Disclosure of God*, ix–xl; Chodkiewicz, "Diffusion of Ibn 'Arabi's Doctrine" (quote from p. 51). See also, for some of the best available work on Ibn al-'Arabī's teachings, Chittick, *Imaginal Worlds*; Chodkiewicz, *Ocean without a Shore*; and Chodkiewicz, *Seal of the Saints*.

73. See Chodkiewicz, *Ocean without a Shore*, 17. I thank one of the anonymous readers of my manuscript for drawing my attention to this point.

74. Ateş, "Ibn al-'Arabī." Cf. Schlegell's detailed examination of Sultan Selīm's restoration and transformation of the tomb, and her argument that more than conferring legitimacy on Ibn al-'Arabī, the rebuilding of his tomb was designed to confer religious legitimacy on the sultan and the Ottoman dynasty by tying them to the shaykh's monumental legacy and charisma (Schlegell, "Sufism in the Ottoman Arab World," 236–47).

75. On debates and criticisms during Ibn al-'Arabī's life and in the three centuries following his death, see Knysh, *Ibn 'Arabi in the Later Islamic Tradition*. On Ibn Taymiyya's criticism, see Memon, *Ibn Taymīya's Struggle*. For a recent criticism of the whole notion of *waḥdat al-wujūd* as a distinct doctrine, especially one "founded" by Ibn al-'Arabī, see Chittick, "Waḥdat al-Shuhūd" (and the quote there).

76. Ateş, "Ibn al-'Arabī."

77. Baysun, "Ebüssu'ûd Efendi."

78. On the Naqshbandī involvement with Ibn al-Arabī's thought, especially during the tariqa's formative period, see Algar, "Reflections." On the role of Persian sufism in the diffusion of his thought, see Chodkiewicz, "The *Futūḥāt Makkiyya*," 219–21.

79. Kufralı, "Molla İlâhî," 130.

80. Kara, "Molla İlâhî," 312–16, 320, 327–28; Algar, "Reflections," 58.

81. Baldırzāde, *Revżat el-evliyā'*, 120b; Beliğ-i Bursevī, *Güldeste-i riyāż*, 181.

82. Kufralı, "Molla İlâhî," 147; Algar, "Reflections," 58–59; Bursalı, *'Osmānlı mü'ellifleri*, 1:40–41.

83. Ibn al-'Ujaymī, *Khabāyā*, 122a, 126b; Ḥusaynī, *Tuḥfat al-sālikīn*, 632; Muḥibbī, *Khulāṣat al-athar*, 4:442. Algar has challenged the tradition according to which Tāj al-Dīn's spiritual master, Muḥammad al-Bāqī, abandoned the belief in *waḥdat al-wujūd* in favor of *waḥdat al-shuhūd* under the influence of his more famous disciple, the eponym of the Mujaddidiyya, Aḥmad Sirhindī (see "Reflections," 59–60.)

84. Muḥibbī, *Khulāṣat al-athar*, 4:202–3.

85. Several individuals associated with this line, apart from Qushāshī and Kūrānī, wrote or translated treatises interpreting or defending Ibn al-'Arabī's teachings, viz., As'ad al-Balkhī, Aḥmad al-Shinnāwī, 'Abd al-Karīm b. Kamāl al-Dīn al-Quṭbī, Raḍī al-Dīn b. 'Abd al-Rahmān al-Haythamī, 'Abdallāh b. Ṣalāḥ al-Yamanī, and Muḥammad b. 'Abd al-Rasūl al-Barzanjī (see Muḥibbī, Khulāṣat al-athar, 1:244, 402, 2:167, 474; Ibn al-'Ujaymī, *Khabāyā*, 68a; Bursalı, *'Osmānlı mü'ellifleri*, 2:27).

86. Muḥibbī, *Khulāṣat al-athar*, 1:345.

87. Ibn al-'Ujaymī, *Khabāyā*, 37b; Knysh, "Ibrāhīm al-Kūrānī"; Johns, "Kūrānī."

88. Schlegell, "Sufism in the Ottoman Arab World," chap. 5 (the quote, p. 221, is from the biography written by Nābulusī's great grandson, Kamāl al-Dīn Ghazzī).

89. Jāmī acquired his expertise in *waḥdat al-wujūd* from a famous local preacher, Shams al-Dīn Kūsū'ī, whose popular sessions he attended together with his Naqshbandī master, Sa'd al-Dīn Kāshgharī. Two fellow Kāshgharī disciples—Shams al-Dīn Rūjī and 'Alā' al-Dīn Ābīzī known as Maktabdār—were distinguished advocates of the doctrine of *waḥdat al-wujūd*, which they had learned from the famous Yemenite teacher 'Abd al-Kabīr al-Yamanī during a sojourn in Mecca. For these connections, see Kāshifī, *Rashaḥāt* (ed. Mu'īniyān), 244–45; Kufralı, "Nakşbendiliğin Kuruluş ve Yayılışı," 65–69.

90. Algar, "Reflections," 53-56 (quote from p. 56). On translations of Jāmī's commentaries into Ottoman Turkish, see Ṭaşköprüzāde, *Shaqā'iq*, 1:390–91; Bursalı, '*Osmānlı mü'ellifleri*, 1:24–25.

91. Kāshifī, *Rashaḥāt* (ed. Mu'īniyān), 1:244, quoting Pārsā's son, Abū Naṣr. Algar discusses at length the possibility that Pārsā was the author of a commentary on the *Fuṣūṣ* generally attributed to the Kubravī master 'Alī Hamadanī (see "Reflections," 48–50).

92. See, for example, Molé, "Autour du Daré Mansour," 62.

93. Algar, "Reflections," 45-6, 60. Sirhindī's criticism of Ibn al-'Arabī and the *waḥdat al-wujūd* are examined in Haar, *Follower and Heir*, esp. chap. 9, and Friedmann, *Shaykh Aḥmad Sirhindī*, 62-68.

94. See also the discussion on tariqa and *silsila* in chap. 7.

95. Algar has attributed the Naqshbandiyya's explicit hostility to Shī'ism to its Bakrī *silsila*, along with the fact that its first diffusion in the Sunnī world coincided with the rise of a militant Shī'ī state in Iran and the inauguration, thereby, of centuries of sectarian warfare (Algar, "Brief History," 5).

96. The notion that each of the first four caliphs represented a distinctive spiritual type appears in the *Kashf al-maḥjūb* of 'Alī al-Hujwīrī (d. 460s/1070s), where Abū Bakr is associated with the way of contemplation (*mushāhada*) and with reciting the Qur'ān in a low voice; 'Umar, with ascetic exercises and reciting the Qur'ān loudly; 'Uthmān, with resignation in time of calamity and sincere devotion; and 'Alī, with subtle understanding of the Divine Truth and severance of the heart from all things save God. See Hujwīrī, *Kashf al-maḥjūb*, 70–74.

97. Algar, "Naqshbandi Order: A Preliminary Survey," 126.

98. Paul, *Doctrine and Organization*.

99. [Ghujduvānī?], *Risāla-yi ṣāḥibiyya*, 80.

100. See the Yasavī *silsilas* cited in Trimingham, *Sufi Orders in Islam*, 149 (quoting Mouradgea D'Ohsson) and in Wāsiṭī, *Tiryāq al-muḥibbīn*, 47.

101. In a number of recent articles, Devin DeWeese has begun to recast our understanding of early Yasavī history and to draw attention to the complex Yasavī-

Naqshbandī competition (actual and rhetorical) that shaped later standard notions about the early Yasaviyya. Especially relevant to the present discussion is the "Mashā'ikh-i Turk," where DeWeese points out the retrospective reformulation of the Khwājaganī *silsila* in the later Naqshbandī tradition, and specifically in the *Rashaḥāt*. See also DeWeese, "Neglected Source"; DeWeese, *"Uvaysī" Sufi*.

102. Madelung, "Yūsuf al-Hamadānī and the Naqšbandiyya," according to which Ghujduvānī was too young to be Hamadānī's disciple and must have simply appropriated him as his master, as he did with other links in his *silsila*.

103. DeWeese, "Mashā'ikh-i Turk," 189 (and n. 22).

104. DeWeese has argued that the very notion of *silsila* was introduced in the Naqshbandiyya only after Bahā' al-Dīn. Bahā' al-Dīn presented himself as an Uwaysī whose spiritual credentials did not derive from a connection to a living shaykh or an unbroken *silsila*. It was only the later and more developed Naqshbandī hagiographical tradition that came to consider the Uwaysī status of the tariqa's eponym as an embarrassment and "found" for him established *silsila* links. See DeWeese, *"Uvaysī" Sufi*, 25–26.

105. See Pārsā, *Qudsiyya*, 12–14.

106. Kāshifī, *Rashaḥāt* (ed. Mu'īniyān), 1:12–13.

107. Qazvīnī, *Silsilanāma*, 6b (with the 'Alid lines mentioned only in the narrative introduction, 5b–6a); Muṣṭafā b. Hayreddīn, *Silsile-i hōcagān*, 6a (with parallel lines in the introduction, 4a); *Silsile-i hōcagān nisbet-i kulliye* (piece attached to the *Şerā'iṭ*), 76b–78a. In the *Risāla fī sulūk al-Naqshbandiyya* (163a), Tāj al-Dīn al-'Uthmānī traced the *silsila* through the Bakrī line, with a brief mention of the "father-to-son line" leading back from Ja'far al-Ṣādiq, "as is known." Ṣarı 'Abdullāh Efendi also charted an exclusive Bakrī line in his *Cevheret el-bidāye*, 142b–43a.

108. See, for example, *Tüḥfet eṭ-ṭālibīn*, 80b–81a; *Risāle-i şerīfe*, 161a–b; [Ṣādiqī], *Risāla fī bayān ṭarīq al-Naqshband*, 160a–61a. Cf. Nev'īzāde 'Aṭā'ī, *Ḥadā'iḳ*, 61-62.

109. Qazvīnī, *Silsilanāma*, 5b; Muṣṭafā b. Hayreddīn, *Silsile-i hōcagān*, 4a; *Risāle-i şerīfe*, 161a; *Şerā'iṭ*, 74b; *Tüḥfet eṭ-ṭālibīn*, 81b; [Ṣādiqī], *Risāla fī bayān ṭarīq al-Naqshband*, 161b. Ṣādiqī explains the uniqueness of the line designated *silsilat al-dhahab* through a Prophetic tradition proclaiming that "on the Day of Judgment all bonds and pedigrees (*al-ansāb wa'l-asbāb*) except my own [i.e., the Prophet's] will be severed." On the Naqshbandī privileging of spiritual succession, see chap. 7.

110. Indeed, this was sufficient for early Ottoman Naqshbandīs to become publicly known for their Bakrī descent. See, for example, Ṣarı 'Abdullāh, *Cevheret el-bidāye*, 142b–43a; Evliyā Çelebi, *Seyāḥatnāme*, 1:389–90.

111. *Şerā'iṭ*, 73b.

112. *Tüḥfet eṭ-ṭālibīn*, 81b, quoting Muḥammad Pārsā's *Qudsiyya* and the consensus of the "great authorities of the tariqa" (*ekābir-i ṭarīkat*). For a modern version that has 'Alī initiated by Abū Bakr and deprived of any direct initiatic connection to the Prophet, see Algar, "Brief History," 5.

113. *Risāle-i şerīfe*, 174a–b; *Şerā'iṭ*, 73a; 'Uthmānī, *Jāmi' al-fu'ād*, 19a; Ḥusaynī, *Tuḥfat al-sālikīn*, 633–34 (including the quote).

114. Qazvīnī, *Silsilanāma*, 6a; Muṣṭafā b. Hayreddīn, *Silsile-i hōcagān*, 4b-5a; *Tüḥfet eṭ-ṭālibīn*, 81a; Ṣarı 'Abdullāh, *Cevheret el-bidāye*, 142b. The *Cevheret el-bidāye* along with a copier's note in Qazvīnī's *Silsilanāma* identified the source of this account as the *Faṣl al-khiṭāb* of Muḥammad Pārsā. The story does not seem to appear in the published Turkish translation, *Tevhide Giriş*. It may feature in one of the original Persian manuscripts, to which I have had no access, or perhaps in a related work that the Ottoman informants mistook for the *Faṣl*.

115. The translation is from Arberry, *Koran Interpreted*, 186, except for *sakīna*, rendered here in transliteration from the Arabic instead of his "Schechina." For the meaning of the term, see Fahd, "Sakīna." For the interpretation of the medieval exegetes, see, for example, Muḥammad b. Ismā'īl al-Bukhārī, *Ṣaḥīḥ al-Bukhārī*, 5:204.

116. That neither of the two Prophetic traditions invoked by Naqshbandīs can be found in the standard medieval collections is not surprising. Many traditions used by later Sufis cannot be traced to these early sources (see Schimmel, *Mystical Dimensions*, 221).

117. Algar, "Naqshbandi Order: A Preliminary Survey," 129.

118. For these circumstances, see Beldiceanu-Steinherr, "Règne de Selim 1er"; Imber, "Persecution of the Ottoman Shī'ites"; Mélikoff, "Problème Ḳızılbaş," 50–52; Sohrweide, "Sieg der Ṣafaviden." The quote is from İnalcık, *Ottoman Empire*, 197.

119. For more details, see chap. 6.

120. Nev'īzāde 'Aṭā'ī, *Ḥadā'iḳ*, 62. See also the comparative table in Kissling "Aus der Geschichte des Chalvetijje," 283; Kissling, "Zur Geschichte des Bajrâmijje," 245–49; Martin, "Short History," 284–85; Jong, "Khalwatiyya."

121. According to Buehler (*Sufi Heirs of the Prophet*, 90), the *imāmī* links were ignored in later Mujaddidī *silsilas*. However, see, for example, a nineteenth-century Khālidī *silsila* that includes the *imāmī* line and the designation *silsilat al-dhahab* in Ibn Sulaymān, *Al-Ḥadīqa al-nadiyya*, 7.

122. 'Āşıḳ Çelebi, *Meşā'ir üş-şu'arā*, 110a–b; Baldırzāde, *Revżat el-evliyā'*, 97a; Belīğ-i Bursevī, *Güldeste-i riyāż*, 179–80. According to the *Güldeste-i riyāż*, 291–92, the incident took place during the tenure as *qāḍī* of Āşcızāde Ḥasan Çelebi, which puts it at between the year 934/1527–28 and that of Lāmi'ī Çelebi's death, 938/1531–32.

123. McChesney, *Waqf in Central Asia*, 33–34.

124. Kāshifī, *Rashaḥāt* (ed. Mu'īniyān), 1:255; Ḥikmat, *Jāmī*, 137–42; Huart, "Djāmī."

125. For the *Ravżat-i shuhadā'* and its author, see Yousofi, "Kāshifī."

126. McChesney notes that before the rise of the Ṣafavids and the ensuing change in the political meaning of Shī'ism, Sunnī reverence of the *ahl al-bayt* could be completely separate from politics. Even at times of political confrontation, individuals who identified themselves as defenders of the caliphal rights of the first three

caliphs saw no contradiction in going on pilgrimage to the tombs of the *imāms* (see *Waqf in Central Asia*, 34–35). After the Ṣafavid rise to power, such attitudes would presumably become less feasible.

127. Still, reverence for the *ahl al-bayt* hardly disappeared from Ottoman society even at this time. As an example, one may cite the visit that, in fulfillment of a vow he had made at sea, the Ottoman mariner Sīdī 'Alī Re'īs paid to the shrine of 'Alī al-Riḍā in Mashhad during his famous trip from Samarkand to Istanbul in the early 960s/mid-1550s. See Sīdī ['Alī] Re'īs, *Mir'āt ül-memālik*, 76. For the general circumstances of this trip via Iran, see above, chap. 1.

128. Meḥmed Şemseddīn, *Bursa Dergâhları*, 321.

CHAPTER 6

1. In Algar's view, he was the "effective ruler of much of Transoxania for four decades," driven by concern for securing the implementation of the *sharī'a* by the Tīmūrid sultans. Rogers concurs that he was politically and economically the foremost (though not only) influential Sufi shaykh of Tīmūrid Transoxania, yet he suggests that both the hagiographers and chroniclers of the time exaggerated his influence. See Algar, "Aḥrār"; Rogers, "Aḥrār."

2. Paul, *Politische und soziale Bedeutung*, passim; Gross, "Khoja Ahrar," esp. chap. 1. Both have made use of an extensive array of sources along with modern scholarship, much of it by Soviet scholars (see the review of the literature in Paul's introduction). Gross has focused on contemporaries' perceptions of Aḥrār, viewed in their social context.

3. Paul, *Politische und soziale Bedeutung*; and Paul, "Forming a Faction." Paul notes that in calling upon the Tīmūrid rulers to abolish "non-Islamic customs," the shaykh was targeting taxes, especially the *damgha*; by contrast, he did not address transgressions of Islamic public morality such as wine drinking (see *Politische und soziale Bedeutung*, 220).

4. Paul, *Politische und soziale Bedeutung*; Paul, "Forming a Faction"; Gross, "Khoja Ahrar," especially the discussion in chap. 1.

5. For the Nashbandiyya in Central Asia in the sixteenth century we now have Schwarz, *Unser Weg*, esp. 164ff. See also Babajanov [Babad anov], "Naqshbandiyya sous les premiers Sheybanides."

6. Ayvānsarāyı, *Ḥadīḳat ül-cevāmi'*, 1:219.

7. Ṭaşköprüzāde, *Shaqā'iq*, 1:561–62; Baldırzāde, *Revżat el-evliyā'*, 37a; Belīğ-i Bursevī, *Güldeste-i riyāż*, 180.

8. On the first, see Ṣādiqī, *Manhaj*, 11b–12a; Nev'īzāde 'Aṭā'ī, *Ḥadā'iḳ*, 362; Selānīkī, *Ta'rīh-i Selānīkī* (Freiburg reprint), 211–12. On the second, Muṣṭafā b. Hayreddīn, *Silsile-i hōcagān*, 14b; Nev'īzāde 'Aṭā'ī, *Ḥadā'iḳ*, 371–72, 380; Selânikî, *Tarih-i Selânikî* (ed. Mehmet İpşirli), 1:343–44.

9. On Baba Maḥmūd Rizā'ī, the Naqshbandī disciple from Filibe and lifelong confidant of the grand vezir Rüstem Paşa, who is said to have inspired Rüstem's efforts to eliminate the "heretics" of his day, see the following section.

10. See, for Khalwatīs, the analysis of Clayer, *Mystiques, état et société*, esp. chap. 2.

11. Gündüz, *Osmanlılarda Devlet-Tekke Münasabetleri*, 39–42, 63–66, drawing in part on Kufralı, "Molla İlâhî," 143–45.

12. Gündüz, *Osmanlılarda Devlet-Tekke Münasabetleri*, 41.

13. Kufralı, "Nakşbendiliğin Kuruluş ve Yayılışı," 61–62; Gündüz, *Osmanlılarda Devlet-Tekke Münasabetleri*, 41, 45–46; Ḥikmat, *Jāmī*, 4–10; Aubin, *Matériaux*, 13–14 (author's introduction). Cf. Köprülü, *Islam in Anatolia*, chap. 7.

14. Kermānī, *Manāqib*, 122–23; Shushtarī, *Majālis al-mu'minīn*, 2:143–48. Terry Graham believes that Amīr Kulāl may have used the sectarian argument with Tīmūr even though Shāh Ni'matullāh was squarely a Sunnī by background and education (see Graham, "Shāh Ni'matullāh Walī"). Algar argues that in the Naqshbandī sources there is no mention of Amīr Kulāl's role in the expulsion of Shāh Ni'matullāh (Algar, "Ni'mat-Allāhiyya").

15. See Nizāmī-i Bākharzī, *Maqāmāt-i Jāmī*, 189–90, where Jāmī is said to have saved the religion of Islam by warning the sultan that inserting the names of the *imāms* in his Friday sermon would "cause a break with tradition and bring scandal to the state." I thank Professor Jo-Ann Gross of the College of New Jersey for this reference. Several other versions of the story appear in Köprülü, *Islam in Anatolia*, 119–20, n. 235.

16. See the discussion in Amoretti, "Religion," 610–14 (quote from p. 614). See also McChesney's remarks on Sultan Ḥusayn Bāyqarā's attitude toward the "rediscovered" tombsite of 'Alī b. Abī Ṭālib near Balkh. His enthusiasm for the site was not a sign of political flirtation with Twelver Shī'ism, but rather one of spiritual devotion to the *ahl al-bayt*—granted, at a time still before the rise of the Ṣafavids to power and the consequent redefinition of the political meaning of Twelver Shī'ism (McChesney, *Waqf in Central Asia*, 35).

17. Gündüz, *Osmanlılarda Devlet-Tekke Münasabetleri*, 66.

18. Mardin, "Nakshibendi Order," 207. Similar notions inform D emal Ćehajić's description of Naqshbandīs in Bosnia and Herzegovina from the fifteenth century on as an "orthodox *ṣūfī* association" that became "a base of Ottoman ideology and Ottoman policy" and of which the Ottoman administration "made use . . . in the struggle against unorthodox dervishes." The basis of this assessment seems to be the patronage that a number of Ottoman governors extended to Naqshbandī shaykhs or *tekkes* (see Ćehajić, "Socio-Political Aspects," 663–64, and the discussion above, chap. 3).

19. These ideas go back to Mehmed Fuad Köprülü—for example, in the work now translated as *Islam in Anatolia*. For recent elaborations of this view, see Mélikoff, *Hadji Bektach*; and Ocak, "Aperçu général."

20. Karamustafa, *God's Unruly Friends*, esp. the introduction. In the author's view, Anatolia's heterodox culture did not originate in Central Asian shamanism as it was transformed by the conversion and migration westward of Turcoman tribes. Rather, it was rooted in what he calls "dervish renunciation" of the Islamic later middle period, a movement welding asceticism with deliberate and blatant forms of social deviance, whose recruits might come from the middle and high social strata.

21. 'Āşıḳ Çelebi, *Meşā'ir üş-şu'arā*, 235b.

22. On Rüstem Paşa's career, see Altundağ and Turan, "Rüstem Paşa"; and Woodhead, "Rüstem Pasha." On the persecution of the Ḳızılbaş in the sixteenth century, see Imber, "Persecution of the Ottoman Shī'ites"; and Sohrweide, "Sieg der Ṣafaviden."

23. See the decrees in Ahmet Refik, *Onaltıncı Asırda Râfizîlik*, 36, 41–42, 44–46, 49–50, and the discussion in Köprülü, "Abdal," 32–33. Mélikoff explains that the term *ışıḳs* (which Ahmet Refik translated as Ḳızılbaş and Köprülü traced etymologically to the Arabic "shaykhs") was used interchangeably with *qalandars* and *abdals* to refer to heterodox dervishes in Anatolia (see Mélikoff, *Hadji Bektach*, 55).

24. The story appears in Nev'īzāde 'Aṭā'ī, *Ḥadā'iḳ*, 86; and Belīğ-i Bursevī, *Güldeste-i riyāẓ*, 452 (the latter account apparently copied from the first, with its dating of the shaykh's death to 953/1546-7 most likely a copyist's error).

25. Kufralı, "Molla Ilâhî," 145; Gündüz, *Osmanlılarda Devlet-Tekke Münasebetleri*, 66.

26. See Nev'īzāde 'Aṭā'ī, *Ḥadā'iḳ*, 56; 'Āşıḳ Çelebi, *Meşā'ir üş-şu'arā*, 175a–b (including the quote); Ahmet Refik, *Onaltıncı Asırda Râfizîlik*, 91–94 (document no. 42). For modern analyses, see Köprülü, "Abdal," 32–33; Faroqhi, "Seyyid Gazi Revisited," 91–97.

27. Evliyā Çelebi, *Seyāḥatnāme*, 3:13.

28. Nev'īzāde 'Aṭā'ī, *Ḥadā'iḳ*, 86.

29. The turning over of the Ḥācı Bektaş *tekke* to the Naqshbandiyya was said to be predicated on the latter's orthodox credentials, along with the affinity between the Naqshbandī and Bektaşī *silsilas*. For this incident, see Meḥmed Es'ad Efendi, *Üss-i ẓafer*, 199–221; Abu-Manneh, "Naqshbandiyya in the Early Nineteenth Century," 51–55; Abu-Manneh, "Naqshbandi-Mujaddidi and Bektashi Orders," 61, 71; Faroqhi, "Tekke of Hacı Bektaş," 201–3. Meḥmed Es'ad created the connection between the Ḥācı Bektaş incident and the Seyyid Ğāzī purge of some three centuries before by including a long extract from 'Āşıḳ Çelebi's biography of Muṣṭafā 'Işretī as an appendix to his account of the suppression of the Bektaşīs (*Üss-i ẓafer*, 221–22). It is not known whether Gündüz or Kufralı were also informed by another incident in which in 1312/1894–95 Sultan 'Abdülḥamīd II had a newly established madrasa in Samarra in Iraq assigned to a Naqshbandī shaykh, Muḥammad Sa'īd, in an effort to fight Persian Shī'ī influence there. For this incident, see Sāmarrā'ī, *Ta'rīkh 'ulamā' Sāmarrā'*, 47–49. I thank Professor Itzhak Nakash of Brandeis University for this reference.

30. Mélikoff, *Hadji Bektach*, 92-103 (qoute from p.103); Mélikoff, "Problème Ḳızılbaş," 53.

31. Karamustafa, *God's Unruly Friends*, 83-84, 95.

32. Köprülü, *Islam in Anatolia*, 48.

33. Clayer, *Mystiques, état et société*, especially chap. 2.

34. For the Khalwatī transformation, see Kissling, "Aus der Geschichte des Chalwetijje," 250–57; Martin, "Short History," 282-83.

35. Though Karamustafa's work might suggest otherwise (see note 20).

36. Kufralı, "Nakşbendiliğin Kuruluş ve Yayılışı," 182–85.

37. On the Naqshbandī presence in Anatolia and more generally in provincial and rural contexts, see chap. 3.

38. On the Ottoman war of propaganda against the Ṣafavids, see Tansel, *Yavuz Sultan Selim*, 20–35; Eberhard, *Osmanische Polemik*. See also Irène Beldiceanu-Steinherr's critique of Eberhard in "À propos d'un ouvrage." On the Naqshbandī propensity for writing, copying, and translation, see chap. 7.

39. The circumstances of Qazvīnī's escape to Damascus appear in the entry on his father, Ḥusayn (Qazvīnī, *Silsilanāma*, 21a).

40. Ibid., 15a-21a. Although Shī'īs might turn the originally pejorative term *rāfiḍa* or *rawāfiḍ* ("rejecters") into an honorific, generally it was used (by their enemies) in polemical contexts. See Kohlberg, "'Rāfiḍa' in Imāmī Shī'ī Usage," 677–79; Kohlberg, "Rāfiḍa."

41. Qazvīnī, *Silsilanāma*, 6b, and the introduction, 5b. On the significance of this point, see chap. 5.

42. See MS Bibliothèque Nationale (Paris), Suppl. Persan 1418; MS Topkapı Palace Library (Istanbul), E.H. 1198. Other extant copies include MSS Süleymaniye Library (Istanbul), Laleli 1381, Es'ad Efendi 1487, Şehīd 'Alī 2893, Ḥamīdiye/Lala Ismā'īl Efendi 155, and MS, 'Ārif Ḥikmat Library (Medina), 22/106.

43. Muṣṭafā b. Hayreddīn, *Silsile-i hōcagān*, 1a–2a, 13b–16a.

44. Ibid., 1b-2a. The translation apparently remained in circulation for a long time; it is listed in Bursalı, '*Osmānlı mü'ellifleri*, 2:24. On Ǧażanfer Ağa, see Süreyya, *Sicill-i 'osmānī*, 3:619.

45. Barzanjī's authorship of the work is noted in Murādī, *Silk al-durar*, 4:65; and in Ḥamawī, *Fawā'id al-irtiḥāl*, 1:338. Brockelmann considers it uncertain: see Brockelmann, *Geschichte*, 2:587. For the original work and its author, Mu'īn al-Dīn Ashraf (known as Mīrzā Makhdūm), see Nev'īzāde 'Aṭā'ī, *Ḥadā'iḳ*, 297–99; Burīnī, *Tarājīm al-a'yān*, 2:52–56; Eberhard, *Osmanische Polemik*, 47, 56–60, 65–66; Brockelmann, *Geschichte*, 2:586–87. On Barzanjī's uncertain tariqa affiliation, see chap. 4.

46. Subtracting *shāh-e now* from *takht* yields 1038, the year of the new shāh's advent. I thank Professor Paul Sprachman of Rutgers University for his help in translating this verse from Resmī's biography in 'Alī Emīrī, *Tezkere-i şu'arā'*, 1:384. On Resmī's career in Bursa, see above, chap. 3.

47. See chap. 2.

48. The following discussion of the Ḳāḍīzādelis is based primarily on Zilfi, "Kadizadelis," and Zilfi, *Politics of Piety*, chaps. 4–5. Both emphasize the social and political as well as the intellectual aspects of the movement. For other treatments, see Çavuşoğlu, "Ḳāḍīzādeli Movement"; Öztürk, "Islamic Orthodoxy." For an account of a related incident in early eighteenth-century Cairo, see below.

49. On the evolution of this doctrine throughout Islamic history, see Cook, *Commanding Right.*

50. One *'ālim* who came under considerable criticism was the *şeyhülislām* Zekeriyāzāde Yaḥyā (d. 1054/1644), an intimate of poets and musicians; Ḳāḍīzādeli preachers declared those who recited his wine poetry to be guilty of unbelief (see Zilfi, *Politics of Piety*, 171–72.) Interestingly, while he had served as *qāḍī* in Egypt several decades earlier, Yaḥyā was initiated into the Naqshbandiyya by a Syrian shaykh, 'Abd al-Qādir al-Bān, whom he later appointed to the position of the *naqīb al-ashrāf* (head of the descendants of the Prophet) in Aleppo (Ṭabbākh, *A'lām al-nubalā'*, 6:232). We know nothing, however, of any association that as *şeyhülislām* Yaḥyā might have had with Naqshbandīs in the capital.

51. Na'īmā, *Ta'rīh*, 5:54–59.

52. Ibid., 5:55.

53. 'Uşāḳīzāde, *Zeyl-i şaḳā'iḳ*, 551, and (on Bosnevī's replacement, Ömer Efendi) 549. Incidentally, Bosnevī's career as mosque preacher partially dovetailed with that of Ḳāḍīzāde Meḥmed Efendi, whom he replaced in Bāyezīd and, at some remove, in Aya Sofya.

54. On these incidents, see Na'īmā, *Ta'rīh*, 5:54–59, 267–73, 6:227–41.

55. 'Uşāḳīzāde, *Zeyl-i şaḳā'iḳ*, 551; Ayvānsarāyı, *Ḥadīḳat ül-cevāmi'*, 1:90.

56. Na'īmā, *Ta'rīh*, 5:58.

57. On Birgili's career, and on his ties with both Ḳızıl 'Abdurraḥmān and 'Aṭā'ullāh Efendi, see Nev'īzāde 'Aṭā'ī, *Ḥadā'iḳ*, 179–81; and Kufrevî [Kufralı], "Birgewī." In time, Birgili's son Muṣṭafā "took" the Naqshbandiyya, later combining this affiliation with an *'ilmiye* career that culminated in the judgeships of Tripoli and Baghdad (Nev'īzāde 'Aṭā'ī, *Ḥadā'iḳ*, 295–96). On Birgili's interpretation of the principle of forbidding wrong, see Cook, *Commanding Right*, 323–25.

58. Nev'īzāde 'Aṭā'ī, *Ḥadā'iḳ*, 327–28; Bursalı, *'Osmānlı mü'ellifleri*, 2:22. Neither gives Ṭrābzūnī's tariqa affiliation or indicates by whom he was trained or initiated. In the introduction to his translation, Ṭrābzūnī himself does not mention his *silsila* or initiating shaykh, though he makes clear his affiliation with what he calls *aḳrab ṭarīḳat-i irşād*, the "closest" of all the ways of Sufi training. See Kāshifī, *Rashaḥāt* (trans. Ma'rūf al-Ṭrābzūnī), 5–6, 10.

59. Muṣṭafā b. Hayreddīn, *Silsile-i hōcagān*, 15b. The biographical notice on Tirevī was clearly written after his death in 1033/1623–4—i.e., some quarter of a century after Muṣṭafā b. Hayreddīn had produced the *Silsile.* Along with other material that appears toward the end of the Hüsrev Paşa manuscript, this particular entry was apparently written and appended to the *Silsile* by the work's copier, who

must have been a disciple of Tirevī in the Ḥekīm Çelebi *tekke*. I thank Hasan Karataş and Giv Nassiri of the University of California, Berkeley, for suggestions concerning ambiguous parts of this piece.

60. ʿ Uşāḳīzāde, *Zeyl-i şaḳā'iḳ*, 554.

61. On Feyżullāh's career, see Köprülü, "Feyzullah Efendi." On this final phase of Ḳāḍīzādeli activism, see Zilfi, "Kadizadelis," 263–65; and Çavuşoğlu, "Ḳāḍīzādeli Movement," 149-82.

62. Murādī, *Maṭmaḥ al-wājid*, 23b–26a; Murādī, *Silk al-durar*, 4:130. On the career and influence of Shaykh Murād, see Algar, "Brief History," 27–28.

63. On ʿAbdülmecīd Sīvāsī's clashes with Ḳāḍīzādeli Meḥmed Efendi from his mosque pulpit, and on the attempt by two Khalwatī partisans of Üsṭüvānī's time to refute the teachings of Meḥmed Birgili, see Zilfi, "Kadizadelis," 255–56, 261–62.

64. Çavuşoğlu, "Ḳāḍīzādeli Movement," 196-98, quoting Lāmekānī's letter.

65. Naʿīmā, *Ta'rīh*, 5:59.

66. Ibid., 6:240-41. On their Celvetī affiliation, see ʿUşāḳīzāde, *Zeyl-i şaḳā'iḳ*, 548, 554.

67. We know little about the reverberations of the Ḳāḍīzādeli affair outside the capital. For Cairo, see Peters, "Battered Dervishes."

68. On Kūrānī's argument, see Rizvi, *History of Sufism*, 2:331–32, quoting Shāh Walīullāh, *Anfās al-ʿārifīn*. On his student's comments, see Ibn al-Mīmī, *Naẓm al-sumūṭ*, 8b. On Nābulusī's "mission," see Schlegell, "Sufism in the Ottoman Arab World," esp. 21–22, 77–94; and the analysis of his commentary on Birgili's *Al-Ṭarīqa al-muḥammadiyya* in Cook, *Commanding Right*, 325-30. More details can be found in chap. 4.

69. DeWeese, "Khojagānī Origins," passim.

CHAPTER 7

1. For this particular formulation as reported by Sirhindī, see Haar, *Follower and Heir*, 76. For similar emphases by Aḥrār, see Paul, *Doctrine and Organization*, 35; and Paul, *Politische und soziale Bedeutung*, 77. An echo of the same idea can be found in Muṣṭafā al-Ṣādiqī's description of the *rābiṭa* (see Ṣādiqī, *Manhaj*, 16b).

2. See Buehler, *Sufi Heirs of the Prophet*, esp. chaps. 1, 2, and 6, on the pivotal role of living shaykhs in Sufism in all its forms, and on the two types of shaykhs that he calls "directing" and "mediating."

3. For these statements attributed to Abū Yazīd al-Bisṭāmī and Abū ʿAlī al-Daqqāq, see Trimingham, *Sufi Orders in Islam*, 183–84. Tāj al-Dīn al-ʿUthmānī quotes both at the beginning of his *Risāla fī sulūk al-Naqshbandiyya*, 162a.

4. See ʿUthmānī, *Risāla fī ādāb al-mashyakha*, esp. 126a, 128a, 129a, 130a, 133a, 136b. This work discusses Naqshbandī as well as more generic aspects of *irshādī* Sufism.

5. Ṣādiqī, *Manhaj*, 16b.

6. For example, see *Risāle-i şerīfe*, 169b; *Tüḥfet eṭ-ṭālibīn*, 86a.

7. 'Uthmānī, *Risāla fī ādāb al-mashyakha*, 138a; Uthmānī, *Risāla fī sulūk al-Naqshbandiyya*, 162b. See also the more explicit formulation of Tāj al-Dīn's biographer, Muḥammad b. Ashraf al-Ḥusaynī, in *Tuḥfat al-sālikīn*, 617.

8. See the discussion of Uwaysī transmission in chap. 5.

9. 'Uthmānī, *Risāla fī ādāb al-mashyakha*, 127a.

10. Haar, "Importance of the Spiritual Guide," 312.

11. For more details, see the discussion of *rābiṭa* in chap. 5.

12. 'Uthmānī, *Risāla fī ādāb al-mashyakha*, 133b–36a.

13. Ibid., 136b. In a similar vein, Tāj al-Dīn had the shaykh "take on the attributes of God" (*ittaṣafa bi-awṣāf Allāh*) and proclaimed that "seeking him was tantamount to seeking [God] the Exalted" (*ammā ṭalab al-shaykh fa-huwa ṭalabuhu ta'ālā*) (ibid., 136b and 126b, respectively).

14. Ibid., 137a.

15. Buehler, *Sufi Heirs of the Prophet*, esp. chaps. 2 and 4.

16. See DeWeese, "Yasavī Šayẖs."

17. Lāmi'ī Çelebi, *Terceme-i nefaḥāt*, 462–65.

18. A committed disciple who embarked on the process of *sulūk* under a shaykh's guidance might be designated *murīd* or *sālik*; a more casual disciple might be designated *muḥibb*, and sometimes *ṭālib*, *rāghib*, or *'āshiq*. But these were not fixed terms and certainly not formal ones expressing a graded or institutionalized system of "membership" in the tariqa.

19. On these prominent followers, see Lāmi'ī Çelebi, *Terceme-i nefaḥāt* 461–62, 467.

20. Ibid., 462.

21. Ṭaşköprüzāde, *Shaqā'iq*, 2:154.

22. Ṣādiqī, *Manhaj*, 17a; *Tüḥfet eṭ-ṭālibīn*, 79b.

23. A nice illustration of this is Ibn al-'Ujaymī's reference to the authorization of Ibrāhīm al-Kūrānī by his spiritual master, Aḥmad al-Qushāshī. As he has it, Qushāshī "gave Kūrānī his daughter in marriage and made him a *khalīfa*" (*zawwajahu bi-ibnatihi wa-istakhlafahu*) (see Ibn al-Ujaymi, *Khabāyā*, 37b).

24. A hereditary succession of some sort obtained in about three-fifths of the fifty or so pre-eighteenth-century *tekkes* (of all tariqas) listed by Zâkir Şükrî in the *Mecmu'a-ı tekaya* (published as the *Istanbuler Derwisch-Konvente*). Of the 159 *tekkes* that the *Mecmu'a* lists for the whole four centuries and more that it covers, a hereditary mode was routine in about a fifth (30 *tekkes*) and occasional in another two-thirds (99 *tekkes*). In comparison with the bequeathing of *zāwiya* tenures, that of bequeathing spiritual authority more generally is much more difficult to gauge (and impossible to quantify). The systematic survey that would be necessary to establish a Naqshbandī preference for nonhereditary succession in this sense cannot be undertaken here. Still, the impression given by the biographical dictionaries is that in this matter, too, Naqshbandī shaykhs were more likely than shaykhs of other tariqas to prefer a non-hereditary approach. Cf. the remarks of Jong, "Khalīfa."

25. Kurdistan may have been particularly welcoming of the hereditary style: in the village of Tillū near Şiirt we encounter a Naqshbandī/Qādirī line in which hereditary succession was practiced without interruption all the way into the nineteenth century. For both the Urmavīs and the Tillū Naqshbandīs, see chap. 3.

26. See chap. 2.

27. For this and other versions of the story of Kāsānī's succession, see Schwarz, *Unser Weg*, 189–94.

28. Ṣādiqī, *Manhaj*, 11a–b

29. See Paul, *Doctrine and Organization*, 65, 66–67; and Schwarz, *Unser Weg*, 141–42.

30. DeWeese, "Mashā'ikh-i Turk," esp. 187–99. Schwarz shows continued opposition to hereditary shaykhs among Transoxanian Naqshbandīs in the mid-sixteenth century (see *Unser Weg*, 141–49).

31. Kāshifī, *Rashaḥāt* (ed. Mu'īniyān), 1:37 (quoting Ghujduvānī's "spiritual testament"); Paul, *Doctrine and Organization*, 61.

32. Muḥibbī, *Khulāṣat al-athar*, 1:389.

33. Jong, "Khalīfa," quoting 'Ammār, *Abū'l-Ḥasan al-Shādhilī*, 1:31.

34. On this, see chap. 5.

35. Algar has argued that precisely this independence from paraphernalia, and hence from *tekkes*, helped Naqshbandīs survive in Turkey after the proscription of the brotherhoods in 1925 (see Algar, "Naqshbandi Order in Republican Turkey," 18).

36. On Aḥrār's endeavor of sending off *khalīfas* and its role in the introduction of the tariqa into the Ottoman lands, see chap. 1.

37. For Tāj al-Dīn and his *khalīfas* throughout the Arabian Peninsula and beyond, see chap. 4. Another seventeenth-century Arabian line discussed in chap. 4, that of Aḥmad al-Qushāshī and Ibrāhīm al-Kurānī, became even more distinguished for drawing disciples from afar, then sending them off as *khalīfas* who carried the tariqa to faraway venues such as Egypt, China, and Indonesia. Among Istanbul Naqshbandīs, Aḥmad Ṣādiq Ṭāshkandī deserves special notice for his concern (at least a rhetorical one) with spreading the tariqa widely (see the discussion of his missionary vision in chaps. 1 and 4).

38. On this, see DeWeese, *"Uvaysī" Sufi*, 25–26.

39. See Smith, "Özbek Tekkes," 134 for a ritual in which in the early twentieth century Naqshbandīs of the Sulṭāntepe *tekke* in Üsküdar used to read the *silsila* aloud to the accompaniment of a musical mode before the recitation of the *khatm-i khwājagān* and the Friday afternoon prayer.

40. See Geoffroy, *Soufisme en Égypte*, 199–201; Schlegell, "Sufism in the Ottoman Arab World," 128–31; Kafadar, "New Visibility of Sufism," 309.

41. The Urmavīs of Kurdistan practiced a mixed devotional regimen that combined Naqshbandī with Kubravī and Nūrbakhshī practices; but unlike shaykhs

of the line of Qushāshī and Kūrānī in Arabia they apparently did not initiate disciples into these other tariqas (see chap. 3).

42. See chapter 5 and the first section of the present chapter.

43. See the analysis of DeWeese in "Khojagānī Origins," esp. 503–19.

44. Ibn al-'Ujaymī, *Khabāyā*, 24a. The author was quick to add, however, that the donning of a *khirqa* was not entirely absent in this tariqa; he himself "donned a *khirqa*" received from his shaykh, Aḥmad al-Qushāshī.

45. Our sources' depiction of the Naqshbandī adherents' investment and pride in their affiliation with the tariqa and the *silsila* suggests a somewhat different reality from that which Schlegell has inferred from the experience of 'Abd al-Ghanī al-Nābulusī and some of his contemporaries. She has questioned the importance of adherents' tariqa-conciousness and subscription to uniform teachings and rituals—and even the usefulness of studying tariqas, as opposed to individual shaykhs, as a tool for gaining a better understanding of Sufism in our period (see Schlegell, "Sufism in the Ottoman Arab World," esp. chap. 2).

46. Ḥusaynī, *Tuḥfat al-sālikīn*, 625.

47. The *Khabāyā*, written in Mecca shortly after Tāj al-Dīn's death, provides ample evidence for the multiplicity of shaykhs—Naqshbandī and other—to whom the author and some of his associates were attached. Among others it tells of at least one spiritual descendant of Tāj al-Dīn, Muḥammad b. al-'Awaḍ al-Ḥaḍramī, from whom the author received a Khalwatī *dhikr* (for this, see Ibn al-'Ujaymi, *Khabāyā*, 126b-27a).

48. 'Uthmānī, *Risāla fī ādāb al-mashyakha*, 129b.

49. Nakhlī, *Bughyat al-ṭālibīn*, 78–81 (and 73–76 for Nakhlī's initiation into the Naqshbandiyya and Shaṭṭāriyya by Mīr Kālān b. Maḥmūd al-Balkhī).

50. We have seen this happening after the death of Aḥmad Kāsānī in Transoxania in 949/1542. Similarly, it is reported that upon the spread of the Khālidiyya in Anatolia during the nineteenth century, many non-Khālidī Naqshbandī shaykhs sought reinitiation from Khālidī colleagues, thus admitting the supremacy of Shaykh Khālid and his spiritual descendants (see Algar, "Brief History," 32). Outside the Naqshbandiyya, we have an example in the respected shaykh of the Gulshanī *zāwiya* in Aleppo, Ismā'īl al-Gulshanī (d. 1076/1665–66), who traveled upon the death of his shaykh to seek reconfirmation from this individual's foremost *khalīfa* in Cairo (see Muḥibbī, *Khulāṣat al-athar*, 1:419).

51. See Abu-Manneh, "*Khalwa* and *Rābiṭa*," 295.

52. Though see chap. 2 for Aḥmad Bukhārī's *khalīfa*, Maḥmūd Çelebī, who was successively the incumbent of the Emīr-i Bukhārī Tekkes in Edirne Ḳapı and Fātiḥ.

53. On the role of the central Mevlevī *tekke* in Konya, see Trimingham, *Sufi Orders in Islam*, 179. On the Bektaşī *pīr evī* in Ḥācı Bektaş, see Tscudi, "Bektāshiyya." One Naqshbandī-Nūrbakhshī *tekke*, in Akhlāṭ north of Lake Van, is said to have exercised a similar role in the regional context of eastern Anatolia and northern Syria (see Ṭabbākh, *A'lām al-nubalā'*, 6:418–19).

54. See the discussion in chaps. 1 and 4, respectively.

55. See chaps. 2 and 3; and Zarcone, "Histoire et croyances," 145–65.

56. Jong, "Sufi Orders in Palestine," 168. For similar institutions in nineteenth-century Cairo, see Jong, *Ṭuruq and Ṭuruq-Linked Institutions*, 80–82.

57. This is the picture given by Paul, *Politische und soziale Bedeutung*, for the time of Aḥrār, the second half of the fifteenth century. Half a century earlier Muḥammad Pārsā had sought to appeal to more intellectual circles by incorporating into his work ideas from pre-Mongol Sufism and Islamic thought, and by writing in Persian and Arabic (for this, see Paul, *Doctrine and Organization*, 51).

58. For this Shāfiʿī attitude, see chap. 4.

59. On nineteenth-century Kurdistan, see Bruinessen, "Agha, Shaikh and State," chap. 4; on Indonesia, Bruinessen, "Origins and Development," 161ff.

60. For details about individual Naqshbandīs and their engagement with Persian literary culture as both writers and interpreters, see esp. chaps. 2 and 3.

61. The tradition of Naqshbandīs as *Masnavī* readers was clearly established during the period studied here. It was not introduced by the eighteenth-century Mujaddidī shaykh Neccārzāde Muṣṭafā Rıżā, as Abu-Manneh has concluded on the basis of nineteenth-century sources; though it may well have been taken a step further by nineteenth-century shaykhs who gave *ijāza*s in *Masnavī* teaching or had special annexes called *dār al-Masnavī* added to their *tekke*s (see Abu-Manneh, "Naqshbandiyya in the Early Tanzimat Period," 111–12).

62. For the importance of this same high culture, expressed in Persian, as a pillar of cosmopolitan urban Muslim civilization in India between the eleventh and seventeenth centuries, see Robinson, "Perso-Islamic Culture," 9–19. Robinson also notes how the teachings of Ibn al-ʿArabī became part and parcel of this culture as they were translated into Persian and incorporated into and expressed via Persian poetry, for example by Jāmī (ibid., 17).

63. Individual works are mentioned in chaps. 2, 3, 4, and 6. Abu-Manneh examines the explosion in Naqshbandī publications in the nineteenth century, particularly in connection with editions and translations of the *Rashaḥāt* (including Ṭrābzūnī's). See Abu-Manneh, "Note on the *Raşaḥāt*," 141–47.

64. *Risāle-i serīfe* (MS Süleymaniye Library, Istanbul, Esʿad Efendi 3702, 159b–179a). Most of the following information derives from copier's notes. For a similar inquiry into the dissemination of the *Silsilanāma-yi khwājagān-i Naqshband* of Muḥammad Qazvīnī, written in Damascus in 978/1570, see chap. 6.

65. The author was identified by a Naqshbandī visitor from Bukhara during the reign of Murād III (d. 1003/1594).

Glossary

The glossary is designed to help the nonspecialist reader by providing definitions of technical and administrative terms in Arabic, Ottoman Turkish, and Persian that in the text are defined or explained only on first appearance. Many of these terms have multiple meanings, and what I provide here is generally the sense in which they appear in the study. Fuller meanings can be found in the *Encyclopaedia of Islam*, second edition.

abdals: a type of itinerant and deviant dervishes in Anatolia and the Balkans of the sixteenth century, with their center in the Seyyid Ǧāzī complex; they were scandalously dressed, showed deliberate disregard for Islamic ritual practice, and adopted a cult of ʿAlī

adab, ādāb: etiquette or behavioral norms—for example, those regulating the interaction between a shaykh and his disciples

ağa: in Ottoman usage, the title of various officers of the imperial household or government service (especially military or nonsecretarial)

akçe: the silver coin denomination that served as the chief unit of account in the Ottoman Empire

akhdh/takmīl al-ṭarīqa: literally, "taking" or "completing" the way; these phrases underscore the sense of tariqa as a system of mystical guidance of which one partakes rather than a group of which one becomes a member

ʿālam al-ghayb: literally "the world of the unseen"; especially in Ibn al-ʿArabī's thought, a concept denoting the intermediate realm inhabited by prophets and the "friends of God" that is the source of everything appearing in the visible world

ʿālim: singular of *ʿulamāʾ*

al-'amal bi'l-'azīma: literally "acting with strictness" or "observing religious duties with strictness"; tariqa manuals encouraged Naqshbandīs to take pride in their commitment to this standard of behavior

al-'amal bi'l-rukhṣa: "practicing that which is permitted by way of special dispensation"; Naqshbandīs sought to disengage themselves from this type of behavior that other Sufis tolerated

amīr: a title used to refer to various Muslim military commanders and rulers

al-amr bi'l-ma'rūf wa'l-nahy 'an al-munkar: "commanding right and forbidding wrong"; Muslims' duty, mentioned in the Qur'ān and interpreted by generations of scholars, to "put right" wrongs that they witness and to challenge offenders

'askerī: a member of the Ottoman nontaxpaying military, administrative, or learned elite

'avārıż: extraordinary Ottoman taxes levied on the *re'āyā* in times of emergency

'awāmm and *khawāṣṣ*: two terms used in juxtaposition to denote the common people, as opposed to the elite or people of distinction

baba: a Turkish and Persian honorific meaning "father"; it was applied especially to various religious and mystical leaders of tribal and peasant populations that the Ottomans cultivated in the early stages of state building

baqā': literally, "remaining" in God; the station on the mystical path that a mystic may strive to attain after having reached effacement of the self in God

baraka: divine blessing or charisma bestowed by God on a *walī* or pious individual

bid'a: an innovation in belief or practice for which there is no precedent in the Prophet's *sunna*; *bid'as* were often regarded as blameworthy

Celālis: the dispossessed *timar* holders and unemployed mercenaries who turned into rebels and bandits, terrorizing Anatolia at the turn of the seventeenth century

damgha: literally, "brand," and by extension tariff or commercial tax; under the Mongols, a tax collected in cash from the urban population and denounced by jurists as noncanonical

dawām al-dhikr: the practice of engaging in the ritual remembrance of God continuously

defter: a register or logbook

defterdār: a chief treasurer or finance director

dhikr: litterally, "recollection"; the central Sufi exercise of repeating one of the divine names or other religious formulas as a means of attaining spiritual concentration and of rendering God's presence throughout one's being

dhikr-i arra: a vocal "saw *dhikr*" producing a rasping sound; it is associated principally with Yasavī practice

dhikr jahrī: a vocal *dhikr*, often involving music and dance, that Naqshbandīs shunned as ostentatious and inferior

dhikr khafī: a silent *dhikr* shunning singing, music, and bodily movement; most Naqshbandīs adopted it as their preferred mode

du'ā': a supplicatory prayer

efendi: a title of respect given to nonmilitary men, especially to members of the Ottoman scribal or learned profession

evḳāf ül-mürīdīn: *waqfs* created by the followers of a shaykh in support of a *tekke*; they may be small endowments whose value is cumulative

fanā': the mystic's effacement of the self in God

fanā' fī'l-shaykh: effacement of the self in one's shaykh as a means to effacement in God

faqīr (pl. *fuqarā'*): literally, "a poor one"; a general term for a dervish

fatḥ (pl. *futūḥ*): "opening"; in the technical vocabulary of Sufism, a spiritual illumination attained as a grace of God rather than through a methodical discipline

fatwā: a legal opinion issued by a qualified Muslim jurist

fayḍ: the emanation of divine energy or effulgence

fiqh: the science of Islamic jurisprudence

ghāzī (Tur. *ğāzī*): a Muslim "warrior for the faith" and specifically the frontier warriors, with their distinctive frontier culture and ethos, to whom the Ottoman Empire owed much of its early expansive energies and power

grand vezir: a chief minister; the sultan's deputy in all military, administrative, and legal matters

ḥabs al-nafas: a technique of holding the breath used in performing the Naqshbandī *dhikr*

ḥadīth: a recorded tradition of a saying or deed of the Prophet or his companions; on the basis of the corpus of *ḥadīth* contained in written collections, the medieval scholars and jurists established the *sunna* of the Prophet

ḥajj: the annual pilgrimage to Mecca

ḥāl: a mystical "state" perceived as a gift from God, as opposed to *maqām*, the mystical station or stage that one attains through spiritual discipline

ḥalqa: a circle of a teacher and his students or of a spiritual master and his disciples

Ḥaramayn: literally, "the two sanctuaries"; the two Muslim Holy Cities in the Hijaz

Hijra: the emigration of the Prophet from Mecca to Medina, marking the founding of the first Muslim community and hence the beginning of the Muslim calendar

ḥuḍūr: the mystic's "presence" with God

ijāza: a license permitting a student to transmit a text; in Sufi usage, also a shaykh's authorization permitting a trainee to initiate disciples into a tariqa

ilḥād: a term used from 'Abbāsid times in the sense of heretical unbelief; in sixteenth-century Ottoman usage it was employed to describe subversive movements and doctrines, especially those with messianic or Shī'ī overtones

'ilm: knowledge or learning, especially of the religious sciences; Sufis distinguished it from *ma'rifa*, the intuitive mystical knowledge of God

'ilmiye: the Ottoman learned or religious establishment

imām: a leader of a group of Muslims in ritual prayer; in Shī'ī usage, a descendant of the Prophet and one of the series of rightful leaders of the Muslim community

'imāret: a soup kitchen commonly attached to a *waqf* complex

irshād: a spiritual master's training of a disciple in the devotional discipline of a tariqa and hence in the transformative process leading to union with God

ışık: another term for *abdal*

isnād: a chain of authorities linking a student via his teacher and teacher's teachers back to the source of a text; *isnād*s were particularly crucial in linking *ḥadīth*s back to the Prophet, and thus ensuring their authenticity

jadhba: ecstasy or spontaneous attraction to God believed to result from his abrupt intervention, in contrast with the orderly mystical progress through *sulūk*

jāmi': a congregational mosque

jihād: "struggle" in the path of God and, more specifically, holy war against infidels (which is sometimes defined as the "lesser *jihād*")

Ka'ba: the central sanctuary of Islam in Mecca, to which all Muslims direct their prayers and around which the rites of the pilgrimage are performed

kāfir: infidel, unbeliever

al-kalimāt al-qudsiyya: a set of eleven principles attributed to 'Abd al-Khāliq Ghujduvānī and Bahā' al-Dīn Naqshband that define the character and spiritual methods of the Khwājagān-Naqshbandiyya

kāmil wa-mukammil: "perfect and perfection-bestowing"; the Naqshbandī devotional manuals expected these attributes in shaykhs of the tariqa

karāmāt (sing. *karāma*): wondrous deeds or miracles performed by the *awliyā'* as a sign of the grace that God has invested in them

ḳāżī'asker: in Ottoman usage, the chief military judge of Anatolia or Rūmeli

khalīfa: in Sufi usage, a successor or deputy whom a shaykh authorizes to initiate and train disciples; the *khalīfa* may also inherit the shaykh's tenure in a Sufi lodge

khalvat dar anjuman: "solitude within society"; the Naqshbandī adage dismissing the practice of ascetic withdrawal and calling on adepts to engage in seeking God while immersed in society

khalwa: the Sufi practice of ascetic withdrawal and especially ritual seclusion in a cell

khānqāh: in our sources this term may be used interchangeably with *tekke* and *zāwiya*; in Mamlūk sources, it was generally reserved for large sultanic or amirial foundations housing "salaried" Sufis

khaṭīb (in Ottoman usage also *vā'iẓ*): a mosque preacher who delivers the sermon before the congregational Friday prayer; in the Ottoman empire, Sufi shaykhs doubling as preachers enjoyed a direct access to the public but were at the same time dependent on the state and subject in appointment to the *şeyhülislām*

khatm-i khwājagān: a Naqshbandī litany recited in congregation after some ritual prayers

khidma: the obedient "service" that a Sufi adept owes the spiritual master; hence, "discipleship"

khirqa: a Sufi robe given to a new adept as a sign of initiation into a tariqa, and by extension a term designating the initiation as such

khuṭba: a sermon delivered in a congregational mosque before the Friday noon prayer; the mention of the name of the ruler in the *khutba* was a mark of sovereignty and conferred political significance on the whole occasion

Khwājagān: "masters"; a series of Central Asian Sufi masters of the thirteenth to the fifteenth centuries from whom originated the Naqshbandī tradition

Ḳızılbaş: literally "redheads"; the Anatolian Turcomans of heterodox beliefs who from the late fifteenth century rebelled against the centralizing and orthodox Sunnī policies of the Ottomans and who became the supporters of the Shī'ī Ṣafavid cause

kufr: unbelief, infidelity

madhhab: a school of Islamic jurisprudence; among Sunnī Muslims there are four recognized schools: the Ḥanafī, Shāfi'ī, Mālikī, and Ḥanbalī

madrasa: a school offering instruction in the Islamic religious sciences, especially law

mahdī: the awaited savior who, according to a widely held Muslim belief, will restore religion and justice before the end of the world; various messianic movements in Islamic history acted in the name of declared *mahdī*s

majlis: a meeting or session where questions of law or literature may be debated, poetry recited, or teaching or Sufi guidance dispensed; the term is applied both to the occasion and the venue in which it takes place

malaka: literally, "natural disposition"; Naqshbandīs strove to turn their *dhikr* into a *malaka* in order to become oblivious of the act of remembrance, as of anything that was not God

manāqib: literally, "virtues" or "traits of character," and by extension a hagiography, for example of a Sufi master

ma'rifa: the intuitive mystical knowledge of God that is distinct from *'ilm*, religious knowledge

mashā'ikh: a plural form of shaykh; in Ottoman usage, especially Sufi masters and mosque preachers

mashyakha: the position or office of a shaykh, especially one who is the incumbent of a Sufi lodge

mawālī (Tur. *mevālī*) (pl. of *mawlā*, *mevlā*, molla): in sixteenth-century Ottoman usage, a title of senior *'ulamā'*, especially judges of the major provincial capitals

mawlid al-nabī: the Prophet's birthday and the recital or ceremony in celebration of it

mīrāhūr-i evvel: the chief equerry of the palace

mudarris: a teacher; specifically, a professor of law or its ancillary subjects in a madrasa

muftī: a jurist qualified to issue *fatwā*s, legal opinions

muḥibb: literally, "lover"; one of several words used to denote a Sufi, sometimes in the sense of a shaykh's casual follower rather than a full-fledged disciple

mühimme: in Ottoman administrative usage, registers containing copies of sultanic orders to provincial governors and other officials

mujaddid-i alf-i thānī: "the Renewer of the Second Millennium"; the epithet of Aḥmad Sirhindī, based on the tradition that at the beginning of each century God will send someone who will renew the religion

mujāhadāt: a generic term for a variety of Sufi ascetic exercises (such as fasting, ritual seclusion, or night vigils) that some Naqshbandīs shunned as inferior

mujāwir: a pious sojourner, especially in the Holy Cities of Mecca and Medina

mülāzim: in Ottoman usage, a trainee and candidate for office

mulk: a legal term denoting ownership (as distinct from mere possession), along with the piece of property that is owned; only *mulk* can be disposed of freely, for example by endowing it as *waqf*

murāqaba (sometimes called *tawajjuh*): one of the central Naqshbandī devotional methods; a kind of *dhikr* in which adepts strive to fix the name of God in the heart as a means of progressing toward mystical union

murīd: disciple, aspirant on a Sufi path

murshid: the shaykh as an intimate guide of disciples along the path of spiritual discipline and transformation

müsāfirhāne: a guesthouse, often part of a mosque complex

mushāhada: the "witnessing" of the divine power that a mystic strives to attain through contemplation

nafs: the lower soul or carnal nature, which the mystic struggles to purge and tame as a starting point in the process of purification

nafy wa-ithbāt: literally, "negation and affirmation"; the formula of the Naqshbandī *dhikr*, consisting of the phrase *lā ilāh illā Allāh Muḥammad rasūl Allāh*

nāẓir: a financial supervisor, especially of a *waqf*

al-nihāya fī 'l-bidāya: literally, "the end is in the beginning"; an adage expressing the notion of the superiority of the Naqshbandī mystical way, whose adepts can "taste" the end of the mystical journey immediately upon the beginning of the process of *sulūk*

nisba: the mystic's "connection" to God via a tariqa and a *silsila*; Naqshbandīs hold that the connection attained via their tariqa and *silsila* is superior to all others

pīr: "elder," and by extension a Sufi master

pōstnishīn: literally, "he who sits on the sheepskin," hence, a shaykh who is the incumbent of a *zāwiya*

qāḍī: a judge in a *sharī'a* court

qalandars: one of several groups of mendicant deviant dervishes in Anatolia and the Balkans of the fifteenth and sixteenth centuries, with their origins in Iran

qibla: the direction of the Ka'ba in Mecca to which Muslims turn in prayer

rābiṭa: the Naqshbandī spiritual technique of fixing the picture of the shaykh in the imagination as a vehicle for the flow of divine energy

raqṣ: dancing or rhythmical movement that some Sufis employed to help induce ecstatic states, but that Naqshbandīs eschewed

ravish: Persian for "way"

rawāfiḍ: literally, "rejecters"; a term that various enemies used to refer to Shī'īs in a pejorative sense or in polemical contexts

re'āyā: in Ottoman usage, the taxpaying subjects of the empire; used in opposition to *'askerīs*

risāla: a treatise, essay, or monograph on a particular topic; early *risāla*s were often in the form of epistles

riyāḍāt: same as *mujāhadāt*

rūḥāniyya: a spiritual presence or being; Naqshbandīs held that one can be initiated by the *rūḥāniyya* of a deceased spiritual master

sajjādanishīn: same as *pōstnishīn*

sālik: a disciple, "one who travels" the Sufi path

samā': a collective ritual of listening to chanted verses with or without musical accompaniment as a way of helping to induce ecstatic states; Naqshbandīs eschewed the *samā'*, though some of them defended others' right to engage in it

sancaḳ: in Ottoman usage, an administrative district smaller than a province

sancaḳ beği: governor of a *sancaḳ*

sayyid: one who claims descent from the family of the Prophet

şeyhülislām: the chief jurisconsult of the empire and, from the mid-sixteenth century, head of the Ottoman religious institution

sharī'a: the revealed Holy Law of Islam

shaykh: literally "old man"; a term used to refer to any figure of religious authority, and especially to a Sufi master or a head of a Sufi lodge

al-shaykh al-akbar: "the Greatest Master"; an epithet of Ibn al-'Arabī

shaykh al-kull: a *khalīfa* whose authority extends over fellow *khalīfa*s and their disciples, making him a kind of supershaykh of a tariqa or a Sufi circle

Shī'īs: those Muslims, throughout most of Islamic history the minority, who believe that the leadership of the Muslim community should have passed from the Prophet to 'Alī and thence to his descendants

al-ṣiddīq: literally "righteous"; an epithet of Abū Bakr, believed to have been conferred by the Prophet

silsila: an *isnād*-like chain of initiatic descent made up of consecutive individual links through which living Sufis are connected to eponymous founders of tariqas and all the way back to the Prophet

silsilat al-dhahab: literally, "the chain of gold"; the designation given to one of three principal lines of the Naqshbandī *silsila*—namely, that leading through 'Alī and several of the Prophet's biological progeny (and Shī'a *imāms*)

Sufi: a generic designation for a Muslim mystic

ṣuḥba: the intimate companionship between shaykh and disciple that Naqshbandīs believe facilitates their superior process of Sufi training; the *ṣuḥba* with the shaykh is further emphasized and ritualized through the practice of *rābiṭa*

sultan: literally "one who wields authority"; the title most commonly given to the Ottoman sovereign (and to various other Muslim rulers since the eleventh century)

sulūk: the orderly progress along the mystical path by means of a prescribed devotional discipline and under the guidance of a spiritual master

sunna: a term referring principally to the normative practice of the Prophet and his companions as known through *ḥadīth*; the *sunna* is a model of emulation for all Muslims and the most important source of Islamic jurisprudence after the Qur'ān

Sunnīs: the majority of Muslims, who accept the legitimacy and authority of the historical caliphate

sūra: a chapter of the Qur'ān

ṭā'ifa: a circle of a shaykh and his disciples and followers

tajallī: the manifestation of God in creation as a mystical experience *takfīr*: declaring someone an unbeliever

talqīn: instruction in the performance of the *dhikr*; in the Naqshbandiyya, the core of the compact of initiation

tarbiya: same as *irshād*

tariqa: literally, "path"; a Sufi "way" or system of mystical guidance and discipline, and by extension, one of the Sufi brotherhoods or orders

Ṭarīqat-i Khwājagān: The Sufi way of the Central Asian masters known as the Khwājagān, from which the Naqshbandiyya arose

taṣarruf: the shaykh's ability to bring about changes in the moral and spiritual disposition of a disciple as part of facilitating his mystical journey

taṣawwuf: Sufism

tawajjuh: a shaykh's concentration on the disciple as a means of facilitating progress on the mystical path

tekke: a Sufi lodge, where adepts learn a mystical discipline from a master, engage in devotional exercises, and may reside; in our sources, used interchangeably with several other terms

'ulamā' (sing. *'ālim*): scholars of the Islamic religious and legal sciences; members of the Ottoman learned religious establishment

umma: the Muslim community

Uwaysī: a mystic who is initiated in a nonphysical manner by the *rūḥāniyya* of a deceased master, a prophet, or another figure from the invisible world

vezir: a minister of the sultan and member of the imperial council; the highest rank in the Ottoman military/administrative hierarchy

waḥdat al-shuhūd: literally, "the unity of witnessing"; a doctrine developed by Aḥmad Sirhindī in response to *waḥdat al-wujūd*, which he believed contemporaries in India were using as a pretext to avoiding observance of the *sharī'a*

waḥdat al-wujūd: literally, "the unity of being"; both critics and admirers have used this term to refer to a set of ideas about the relationship betewen God and the created world that they took to be a "doctrine" and associated especially with Ibn al-'Arabī; in the eyes of critics this doctrine asserted the identity of God and creation

wā'iẓ (Tur. *vā'iẓ*): in Ottoman usage, a mosque preacher (though in earlier times *wa'ẓ*, as opposed to *khuṭba*, denoted a sermon that could be delivered at any time and place)

walī (pl. *awliyā'*): one who is close to God; hence, a protégé or friend of God, a saint

waqf: a pious endowment established in perpetuity to support a religious or charitable institution or to benefit the founder's family

waqfiyya: the legal document establishing the endowment of a *waqf* and the terms stipulated by the founder

wird: a litany

wilāya (or *walāya*): in Sufi usage, the *walī*'s intimacy or closeness to God and the spiritual authority or charisma that this bestows on him

zandaqa: a term used in medieval times primarily in reference to Manichaeism but also more loosely to refer to heretical unbelief; in sixteenth-century Ottoman usage it was employed interchangeably with *ilḥād*

zāwiya: a Sufi lodge (in our sources, used interchangeably with *tekke*); in some contexts, *zāwiya* meant a smaller urban lodge, or one on the road or in a mountain pass

Bibliography

The following abbreviations are used in the bibliography, with full titles given only in the main entry:

Cook	M. A. Cook, ed., *A History of the Ottoman Empire to 1730*
EI[2]	*The Encyclopaedia of Islam*, 2nd edition
EIr	*Encyclopaedia Iranica*
Evliya	Martin van Bruinessen and Hendrik Boeschoten, eds., *Evliya Çelebi in Diyarbekir*, the relevant section of the Seyahatname, edited with translation, commentary and introduction
İA	*İslâm Ansiklopedisi*
IJMES	*International Journal of Middle East Studies*
JMIAS	*Journal of the Muhyiddin Ibn 'Arabi Society*
Levtzion	Nehemia Levtzion and John O. Voll, eds., *Eighteenth-Century Renewal and Reform in Islam*
Lewisohn	Leonard Lewisohn, ed., *The Legacy of Medieval Persian Sufism*
Lifchez	Raymond Lifchez, ed., *The Dervish Lodge: Architecture, Art, and Sufism in Ottoman Turkey*
Naqshbandis	Marc Gaborieau, Alexandre Popovic, and Thierry Zarcone, eds., *Naqshbandis: Cheminements et situation actuelle d'un ordre mystique Musulman*
REI	*Revue des études Islamique*
SI	*Studia Islamica*
Studies	Butrus Abu-Manneh, *Studies on Islam and the Ottoman Empire in the 19th Century (1826–1876)*

PRIMARY SOURCES

Aḥmed Muhtār, Ḥāccı Beyzāde. *Brusa sergisi rehberi*. Istanbul, 1339/1920–21.

Ahmet Refik. *Onaltıncı Asırda Râfizîlik ve Bektâşîlik*. 1932. Reprint, with different pagination, Istanbul, 1994.

'Alī Emīrī. *Tezkere-i şu'arā'-i Āmid*. Incomplete, one of three planned volumes published. Istanbul, 1328/1910–11.

'Alī Mınıḳ. *Al-'Iqd al-manẓūm fī dhikr afāḍil al-Rūm*. Printed on the margin of Ibn Khallikān, *Ta'rīkh wafayāt al-a'yān*. 2 vols. Būlāq, 1299/1881–82.

Arberry, Arthur J., trans. *The Koran Interpreted*. London, 1964.

'Āşıḳ Çelebi. *Meşā'ir üş-şu'arā*. Edited in facsimile by G. M. Meredith-Owens. Gibb Memorial Series, n.s., 24. London, 1971.

Āsitāne-i 'aliye ve bilād-i selāsede kā'in al-ān mevcūd ve muḥterik olmuş tekyelerin ism ve şöhretleri ve mukābele-i şerīfe günleri beyān olunur. Istanbul, 1256/1840.

Ayvānsarāyı, Ḥāfiẓ Ḥüseyn b. Ismā'īl. *Ḥadīḳat ül-cevāmi'*. 2 vols. Istanbul, 1281/1864–5.

Baldırzāde, Meḥmed b. Muṣṭafā. *Revżat el-evliyā'*. MS Staatsbibliothek (Berlin), or. oct. 2937.

Bāqī Bi'llāh, Muḥammad. *Maktūbāt-i Khwāja Bāqī Bi'llāh*. In the *Kulliyāt*. Edited by Abū'l-Ḥasan Fārūqī and Burhān Aḥmad Fārūqī. Lahore, n.d.

Barkan, Ömer Lutfî, and Ekrem Hakkı Ayverdi, eds. *İstanbul Vakıfları Tahrîr Defteri: 953 (1546) Târîhli*. Istanbul, 1970.

Barzanjī, Muḥammad b. 'Abd al-Rasūl al-. *Qadḥ al-zand wa-qadaḥ al-rand fī radd jahālat ahl Sirhind*. MS Süleymaniye Library (Istanbul), Laleli 3744, 73a–107a.

Belīğ-i Bursevī, Ismā'īl Efendi. *Güldeste-i riyāż-i 'irfān*. Bursa, 1302/1884–5.

Bukhārī, Muḥammad b. Ismā'īl al-. *Ṣaḥīḥ al-Bukhārī*. 8 vols. in four. Cairo, 1315/1898.

Bukhārī, Ṣalāḥ b. Mubārak [=Muḥammad Pārsā?]. *Anīs al-ṭālibīn va-'uddat al-sālikīn*. Edited by Khalīl Ibrāhīm Ṣārīughlī [Sarıoğlu] Tehran, 1371 *sh.*/1992.

Būrīnī, Ḥasan b. Muḥammad al-. *Tarājim al-a'yān min abnā' al-zamān*. Edited by Ṣalāḥ al-Dīn al-Munajjid. Incomplete, only two vols. published. Damascus, 1959–63.

Bursalı, Meḥmed Ṭāhir. *'Osmānlı mü'ellifleri*. 3 vols. in two. Istanbul, 1333–42/1914–24.

[Erżurūmī], Ibrāhīm Ḥaḳḳı. *Ma'rifetnāme*. Istanbul, 1330/1911–12.

Evliyā Çelebi. *Evliya Çelebi in Bitlis*. The relevant sections of the Seyahatname, edited with translation, commentary and introduction by Robert Dankoff. Leiden, 1990.

———. *Evliya Çelebi in Diyarbekir*. The relevant section of the Seyahatname, edited with translation, commentary and introduction by Martin van Bruinessen and Hendrik Boeschoten. Leiden, 1988.

———. *Seyāḥatnāme*. 10 vols. Istanbul, 1314–57/1896–1938.

Eyyūbī, 'Abdürrezzāḳ. *Hediyet ül-aṣdiḳā'*. MS Süleymaniye Library (Istanbul), Es'ad Efendi 3622.

Faṣl fī'l-kalimāt al-qudsiyya. MS Süleymaniye Library (Istanbul), Fātiḥ 2658, 78b–80a.

[Ghujduvānī, 'Abd al-Khāliq?]. *Risāla-yi ṣāḥibiyya.* Published with an introduction and commentary by Sa'īd Nafīsī in *Farhang-i Īrān zamīn* 1 (1332 *sh.*/1953): 70–101.

Ḥamawī, Muṣṭafā Fatḥallāh al-. *Fawā'id al-irtiḥāl wa-natā'ij al-safar fī akhbār al-qarn al-ḥādī 'ashar.* (1) MS Dār al-Kutub Library (Cairo), Ta'rīkh 1093. (2) MS Dār al-Kutub Library (Cairo), Ta'rīkh Taymūr 923.

Hujwīrī, 'Alī b. 'Uthmān al-Jullābī al-. *Kashf al-maḥjūb.* Translated by Reynold A. Nicholson. E. J. W. Gibb Memorial Series. London, 1976.

Ḥusaynī, Maḥmūd b. Ashraf al-. *Tuḥfat al-sālikīn fī dhikr tāj al-'ārifīn.* MS Dār al-Kutub Library (Cairo), Muṣawwarāt Khārij al-Dār 116/13 (copy of MS in the Qāḍī Ḥasan al-Siyāghī Library in San'a, Yemen), 615-40.

Ibn al-Buṣrawī, 'Abdallāh b. Zayn al-Dīn. *Safīna farīda mushtamila 'alā tarājim wa-tawārīkh.* MS Staatsbibliothek (Berlin), We. 409.

Ibn al-Mīmī, Ḥusayn b. Muḥammad al-Baṣrī. *Naẓm al-sumūṭ al-zabrajiyya fī silsilat al-sāda al-naqshbandiyya.* MS Süleymaniye Library (Istanbul), 'Āşir Efendi 176.

Ibn Sulaymān, Muḥammad al-Ḥanafī al-Baghdādī. *Al-Ḥadīqa al-nadiyya fī ādāb al-ṭarīqa al-Naqshbandiyya wa'l-bahja al-Khālidiyya.* Printed on the margin of 'Uthmān b. Sanad al-Wā'ilī, *Aṣfā al-mawārid min silsāl aḥwāl al-imām Khālid.* Cairo, 1313/1896.

Ibn al-'Ujaymī, Muḥammad Ḥasan al-Makkī. *Khabāyā al-zawāyā.* MS Dār al-Kutub Library (Cairo), Ta'rīkh 2410.

Ilāhī, 'Abdullāh. *Ervāḥ ül-müştāḳīn.* MS Süleymaniye Library (Istanbul), Ibrāhīm Efendi 420.

———. *Meslek eṭ-ṭālibīn ve'l-'ābidīn.* MS Staatsbibliothek (Berlin), or. quart. 1471/2.

———. *Risale-i molla Ilāhī.* (1) Istanbul, 1261/1845. (2) MS Süleymaniye Library (Istanbul), Pertev Paşa 616.

Irbīlī, Muḥammad As'ad al-. *Al-Risāla al-as'adiyya fī'l-ṭarīqa al-'aliyya.* Istanbul, 1343/1924.

Jabartī, 'Abd al-Raḥmān al-. *'Ajā'ib al-āthār fī'l-tarājim wa'l-akhbār.* 4 vols. Būlāq, [1297/1879–80].

Jāmī, 'Abd al-Raḥmān. *Nafaḥāt al-uns min khażarāt al-quds.* Edited by Mehdī Tawḥīdīpūr. Tehran, 1336 *sh.*/1957.

Karbalā'ī Tabrīzī, Ḥāfiẓ Ḥusayn. *Ravżat al-jinān va jannat al-janān.* Edited by Ja'far Sulṭān al-Qurrā'ī. 2 vols. Tehran 1344 *sh.*/1965.

Kāshifī, Fakhr al-Dīn 'Alī b. Ḥusayn Vā'iẓ. *Rashaḥāt-i 'ayn al-ḥayāt.* Edited by 'Alī Aṣghar Mu'īniyān. 2 vols. with consecutive pagination. Tehran, 2536 Imperial/1977–78.

———. *Rashaḥāt-i 'ayn al-ḥayāt.* Translated into Ottoman Turkish by Meḥmed Şerīf al-'Abbāsī [Ma'rūf al-Ṭrābzūnī]. Published in lithograph. Istanbul, 1291/1874.

Kātib Çelebi. *Fezleke-i Kātib Çelebi.* 2 vols. Istanbul, 1286–87/1869–70.

———. *Mīzān ül-ḥakk fī ihtiyār il-aḥakk*. Istanbul 1286/1869–70.

Kefevī, Maḥmūd b. Süleymān. *Kitāb al-a'lām al-akhyār*. MS Topkapı Palace Library (Istanbul), AY 6504 (A. 2949).

Kermānī, 'Abd al-Razzāq. *Manāqib-i ḥażrat-i Shāh Ni'matullāh Walī*. Published by Jean Aubin in *Matériaux pour la biographie de Shah Ni'matullah Wali Kermani*, 1–131. Tehran, 1956.

Khānī, 'Abd al-Majīd al-. *Al-Ḥadā'iq al-wardiyya fī ḥaqā'iq ajillā' al-Naqshbandiyya*. Cairo, 1308/1890.

Kishmī, Khwāja Muḥammad Hāshim. *Zubdat al-maqāmāt*. Kanpur (Cawnpore), 1307/1889–90.

Kūrānī, Ibrāhīm b. Ḥasan al-. *Al-Amam li-īqāẓ al-himam*. Hyderabad, Deccan, 1328/1910–11.

———. *Itḥāf al-munīb al-awwāh bi-faḍl al-jahr bi-dhikr Allāh*. MS Princeton University Library, Garrett Collection/Yahuda Section 3869/1.

———. *Nashr al-zahr fī'l-dhikr bi'l-jahr*. MS India Office (London), Delhi 710/a.

Kürkçüoğlu, Kemâl Edîb, ed. *Süleymaniye Vakfiyesi*. Ankara, 1962.

Lāmi'ī Çelebi, Maḥmūd b. 'Osmān. *Terceme-i nefaḥāt ül-üns*. Istanbul, 1289/1872–73.

Laṭīfī. *Tezkere-i Laṭīfī*. Edited by Aḥmed Cevdet. Istanbul, 1314/1896–97.

Mecdī Efendi. *Terceme-i şaḳā'iḳ-i nu'māniye*. Istanbul, 1269/1852.

Meḥmed 'Aṭā'ullāh. *Silsile-i şerīfe-i hōcagān-i 'ālīşa'n* (*Risāla fī rijāl ṭarīqat al-Naqshbandiyya*). MS Dār al-Kutub Library (Cairo), Majāmī' 334, 20a–23b.

Meḥmed Es'ad Efendi, Ṣaḥḥāflar Şeyhīzāde [Esad Efendi]. *Üss-i ẓafer*. 1243/1828. Reprint, Istanbul, 1293/ 1876–77.

Meḥmed Şemseddīn. *Bursa Dergâhları: Yâdigâr-i Şemsî*. Edited by Mustafa Kara and Kadir Atlansoy. 2 vols in one, with consecutive pagination. Bursa, 1997.

Meḥmed Tevfīḳ. *Mecmū'at üt-terācim*. MS Istanbul University Library, TY 192.

Muḥibbī, Muḥammad Amīn b. Faḍlallāh al-. *Khulāṣat al-athar fī a'yān al-qarn al-ḥādī 'ashar*. 4 vols. Cairo, 1284/1867–68. Reprint, Beirut, n.d.

Murādī, Muḥammad Khalīl al-. *Maṭmaḥ al-wājid fī tarjamat al-wālid al-mājid*. MS British Library (London), or. 4050.

———. *Silk al-durar fī a'yān al-qarn al-thānī 'ashar*. 4 vols. in two. Būlāq, 1291–1301/ 1874–83.

Muṣṭafā b. Hayreddīn. *Silsile-i hōcagān-i Naḳşbendiye*. MS Süleymaniye Library (Istanbul), Hüsrev Paşa 408.

Nābulusī, 'Abd al-Ghanī al-. *Al-Ḥaqīqa wa'l-majāz fī riḥlat bilād al-Shām wa-Miṣr wa'l-Ḥijāz*. Edited by Riyāḍ 'Abd al-Ḥamīd Murād. Damascus, 1989.

———. *Iḍāḥ al-dalālāt fī samā' al-ālāt*. MS Princeton University Library, Garrett Collection 3232.

———. *Miftāḥ al-ma'iyya fī ṭarīq al-Naqshbandiyya*. MS Princeton University Library, Garrett Collection 929.

Na'īmā, Muṣṭafā. *Ta'rīh-i Na'īmā*. 3rd ed. 6 vols. in three. [Istanbul, 1281–83/ 1864–66].

Nakhlī, Aḥmad al-Makkī al-. *Bughyat al-ṭālibīn li-bayān al-mashā'ikh al-muḥaqqaqīn al-mu'tamadīn.* Hyderabad, Deccan, 1328/1910–11.

Nev'īzāde 'Aṭā'ī, 'Aṭā'ullāh. *Ḥadā'iḳ ül-ḥaḳā'iḳ fī tekmilet iş-şaḳā'iḳ.* 2 vols. with consecutive pagination. Istanbul, 1268/1852.

Niyāzī, Muṣṭafā Müstaḳīm. *Sülūk-i ḳavīm ve ṣirāṭ-ı müstaḳīm.* MS Süleymaniye Library (Istanbul), Çelebi 'Abdullāh Efendi 173.

Niẓāmī-i Bākharzī, 'Abd al-Vāsī'. *Maqāmāt-i Jāmī.* Edited by Najīb Mā'il Haravī. Tehran, 1371 *sh.*/1992.

Pārsā, Khwājā Muḥammad b. Muḥammad. *Qudsiyya: Kalimāt-i Bahā' al-Dīn Naqshband.* Edited by Aḥmad Ṭāherī 'Irāqī. Tehran, 1354 *sh.*/1975.

——— *Faṣl al-khiṭāb.* Translated as *Tevhide Giriş* by Ali Hüsrevoğlu. Istanbul, 1989.

Peçevī, Ibrāhīm. *Ta'rīh-i Peçevī.* 2 vols. Istanbul, 1283/1866.

Qazvīnī, Nūr al-Dīn Muḥammad. *Silsilanāma-yi khwājagān-i Naqshband.* MS Bibliothèque Nationale (Paris), Suppl. Persan 1418.

Qushāshī, Ṣafī al-Dīn Aḥmad al-. *Al-Simṭ al-majīd fī sha'n al-bay'a wa'l-dhikr wa-talqīnihi wa-salāsil ahl al-tawḥīd.* Hyderabad, Deccan, 1327/1909–10.

Risāle-i şerīfe-i mağrūbe fī uṣūl-i ṭā'ife-i 'aliye-i naḳşbendiye. MS Süleymaniye Library (Istanbul), Es'ad Efendi 3702, 159b–79a (and note on fol. 159a).

Ṣādiqī, Muṣṭafā b. Ḥusayn al-. *Al-Manhaj al-muwaṣṣil ilā al-ṭarīq al-abhaj.* MS Princeton University Library, Arabic Collection/New Series 974.

[———]. *Risāla fī bayān ṭarīq al-Naqshband.* MS Süleymaniye Library (Istanbul), Es'ad Efendi 3772, 159a–161b.

Sālim Efendi, Meḥmed Emīn. *Tezkere-i Sālim.* Istanbul, 1315/1897–98.

Ṣarı 'Abdullāh Efendi [pseud. 'Abdī]. *Cevheret el-bidāye ve dürret en-nihāye.* MS Staatsbibliothek (Berlin), or. oct. 2667.

Selānīkī, Muṣṭafā. *Ta'rīh-i Selānīkī.* (1) [To 1000/1592]. Istanbul, 1281/1864. Reprint, Freiburg, 1970. (2) Edited by Mehmet İpşirli. 2 vols. with consecutive pagination. Istanbul, 1989.

Şerā'iṭ ve naṣā'iḥ-i meşā'ih. MS Süleymaniye Library (Istanbul), Fātiḥ 2658, 71a–76a.

Şeyhī, Meḥmed b. Ḥasan. *Zeyl-i zeyl-i 'Aṭā'ī.* MS Staatsbibliothek (Berlin), or. quart. 1372.

Shirvānī, Shaykhim b. Mavlānā Bābā. *Silsilanāma.* MS in private collection of Necdet Tosun (Istanbul).

Shushtarī, Nūrallāh. *Majālis al-mu'minīn.* 2 vols. Tehran, 1365 *sh.*/1986.

Sīdī ['Alī] Re'īs. *Mir'āt ül-memālik.* Edited by Aḥmed Cevdet. Istanbul, 1313/1895–96.

Silsile-i hōcagān-i naḳşbendiye nisbet-i kulliye-i bekriye. MS Süleymaniye Library (Istanbul), Fātiḥ 2658, 76b–78a.

Silsilenāme-i ṭurūḳ i 'aliye. MS Istanbul University Library, TY 95.

Silsilet eṭ-ṭurūḳ fī't-taṣavvuf. MS Süleymaniye Library (Istanbul), Es'ad Efendi 3680.

Süleymān Fā'iḳ. *Mecmū'a.* MS Istanbul University Library, TY 9577.

Süreyya, Meḥmed. *Sicill-i 'osmānī.* 4 vols. Istanbul, 1308–15/1890–97.

Ṭabbākh, Muḥammad Rāghib al-Ḥalabī al-. *A'lām al-nubalā' bi-ta'rīkh Ḥalab al-shahbā'*. 7 vols. Aleppo 1342–45/1923–26.

Ṭaşköprüzāde, Aḥmed b. Muṣṭafā. *Al-Shaqā'iq al-nu'māniyya fī 'ulamā' al-dawla al-'uthmāniyya*. Printed on the margin of Ibn Khallikān, *Ta'rīkh wafayāt al-a'yān*. 2 vols. Būlāq, 1299/1881–82.

Tüḥfet eṭ-ṭālibīn ve 'ümdet el-vāṣilīn. MS Süleymaniye Library (Istanbul), Fātiḥ 5385, 68b–91b.

Urmavī, Maḥmūd b. Seyyid Meḥmed en-Naḳşbendī el-. *Tecvīd-i güzide*. MS Staatsbibliothek (Berlin), or. 4685.

'Uşāḳīzāde, [Ibrāhīm Ḥasīb Efendi]. *Zeyl-i şaḳā'iḳ*. Edited in facsimile by Hans Joachim Kissling. Wiesbaden, 1965.

[Üsküdarī], Seyyid Ḥasīb. *Menāḳib-i Aḥmed Yekdest ve Meḥmed Emīn Tōkādı*. MS Istanbul University Library, TY 6480.

'Uthmānī, Tāj al-Dīn al-. *Jāmi' al-fu'ād*. MS Istanbul University Library, AY 5490.

———. *Risāla fī ādāb al-mashyakha wa'l-murīdīn al-ṭālibīn wa-sharā'iṭihima*. (1) MS India Office Library (London), Bījāpūr 459b, 125a–143a. (2) MS Süleymaniye Library (Istanbul), Serez 1530. (3) MS Staatsbibliothek (Berlin), We 1760.

———. *Risāla [fī bayān sulūk al-] Naqshbandiyya*. MS Al-Azhar Mosque Library (Cairo), Ḥalīm 33602 [968], 162a–173a.

Walīullāh Dihlawī, Shāh. *Anfās al-'ārifīn*. Delhi, 1315/1897.

Wāsiṭī, Taqī al-Dīn 'Abd al-Raḥmān al-. *Tiryāq al-muḥibbīn fī ṭabaqāt khirqat al-mashā'ikh al-'ārifīn*. Cairo, 1305/1887.

Zâkir Şükrî Efendi. *Die Istanbuler Derwisch-Konvente und ihre Scheiche (Mecmu'a-ı tekaya)*. Edited by Klaus Kreiser from a typescript of Mehmet Serhan Tayşı. Freiburg, 1980.

SECONDARY SOURCES

'Abdīzāde, Ḥüseyn Ḥüsāmeddīn. *Amasya ta'rīhi*. Vol. 1. Istanbul, 1328–30/1910–12.

Abou-El-Haj, Rifa'at 'Ali. *Formation of the Modern State: The Ottoman Empire, Sixteenth to Eighteenth Centuries*. Albany, NY, 1991.

Abu-Manneh, Butrus. "*Khalwa* and *Rābiṭa* in the Khālidī Suborder." In *Naqshbandis*, 289–302. Istanbul, 1990.

———. "The Naqshbandi-Mujaddidi and the Bektashi Orders in 1826." In *Studies*, 59–71. Istanbul, 2001.

———. "The Naqshbandiyya-Mujaddidiyya and the Khālidiyya in Istanbul in the Early Nineteenth Century." In *Studies*, 41–57. Istanbul, 2001.

———. "The Naqshbandiyya-Mujaddidiyya in Istanbul in the Early Tanzimat Period." In *Studies*, 99–114. Istanbul, 2001.

———. "The Naqshbandiyya-Mujaddidiyya in the Ottoman Lands in the Early 19th Century." *Die Welt des Islams*, n.s., 22 (1982, published 1984): 1–36.

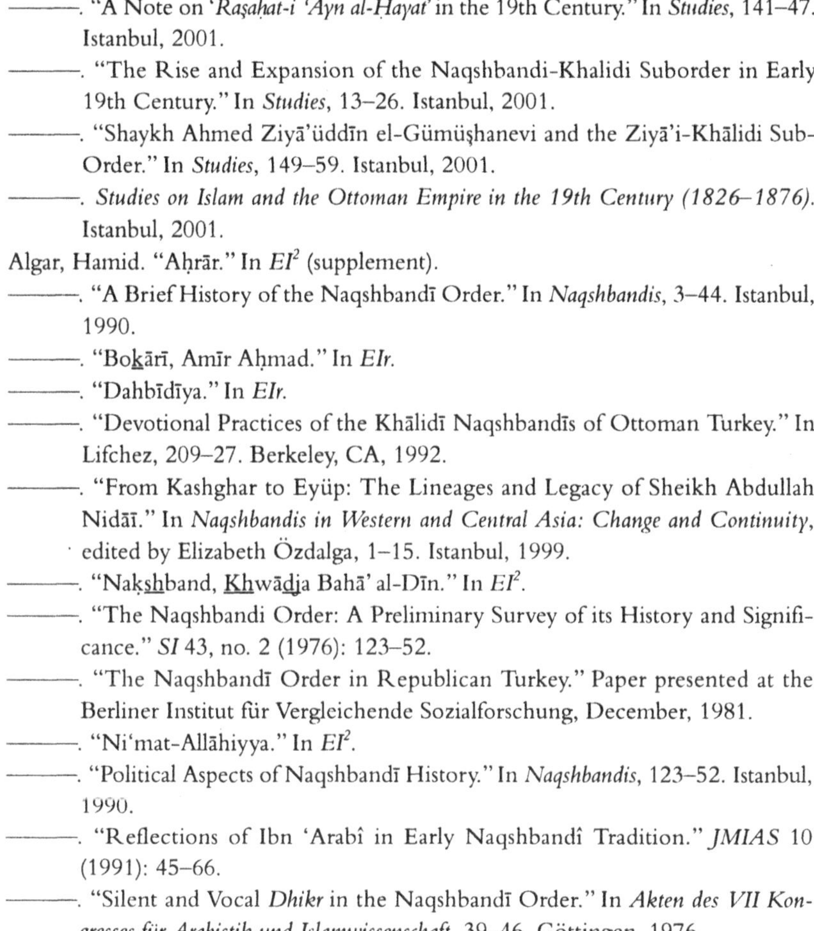

———. "A Note on '*Raşahat-i 'Ayn al-Ḥayat*' in the 19th Century." In *Studies*, 141–47. Istanbul, 2001.

———. "The Rise and Expansion of the Naqshbandi-Khalidi Suborder in Early 19th Century." In *Studies*, 13–26. Istanbul, 2001.

———. "Shaykh Ahmed Ziyā'üddīn el-Gümüşhanevi and the Ziyā'i-Khālidi Sub-Order." In *Studies*, 149–59. Istanbul, 2001.

———. *Studies on Islam and the Ottoman Empire in the 19th Century (1826–1876)*. Istanbul, 2001.

Algar, Hamid. "Aḥrār." In *EI*[2] (supplement).

———. "A Brief History of the Naqshbandī Order." In *Naqshbandis*, 3–44. Istanbul, 1990.

———. "Bok̲ārī, Amīr Aḥmad." In *EIr*.

———. "Dahbīdīya." In *EIr*.

———. "Devotional Practices of the Khālidī Naqshbandīs of Ottoman Turkey." In Lifchez, 209–27. Berkeley, CA, 1992.

———. "From Kashghar to Eyüp: The Lineages and Legacy of Sheikh Abdullah Nidāī." In *Naqshbandis in Western and Central Asia: Change and Continuity*, edited by Elizabeth Özdalga, 1–15. Istanbul, 1999.

———. "Nak̲s̲h̲band, K̲h̲wād̲j̲a Bahā' al-Dīn." In *EI*[2].

———. "The Naqshbandi Order: A Preliminary Survey of its History and Significance." *SI* 43, no. 2 (1976): 123–52.

———. "The Naqshbandī Order in Republican Turkey." Paper presented at the Berliner Institut für Vergleichende Sozialforschung, December, 1981.

———. "Ni'mat-Allāhiyya." In *EI*[2].

———. "Political Aspects of Naqshbandī History." In *Naqshbandis*, 123–52. Istanbul, 1990.

———. "Reflections of Ibn 'Arabî in Early Naqshbandî Tradition." *JMIAS* 10 (1991): 45–66.

———. "Silent and Vocal *Dhikr* in the Naqshbandī Order." In *Akten des VII Kongresses für Arabistik und Islamwissenschaft*, 39–46. Göttingen, 1976.

Altundağ, Ş., and Ş. Turan. "Rüstem Paşa." In *İA*.

'Ammār, 'Alī Sālim. *Abū'l-Ḥasan al-Shādhilī*. 2 vols. Cairo, 1951.

Amoretti, B. S. "Religion in the Timurid and Safavid Periods." In *The Timurid and Safavid Periods*, edited by Peter Jackson and Laurence Lockhart, 610–55. Vol. 6 of *The Cambridge History of Iran*. Cambridge, 1986.

Arjomand, Said Amir. *The Shadow of God and the Hidden Imam: Religion, Political Order, and Societal Change in Shi'ite Iran from the Beginning to 1890*. Chicago, 1984.

Ateş, A. "Ibn al-'Arabī." In *EI*[2].

Aubin, Jean. *Matériaux pour la biographie de Shah Ni'matullah Wali Kermani*. Persian texts with an introduction. Tehran, 1956.

Babad anov, Baxtiyor. "On the History of the Naqšbandīya Muǧaddidīya in Central Māwarā'annahr in the Late 18th and Early 19th Centuries." In *Muslim Cul-*

ture in Russia and Central Asia from the 18th to the Early 20th Centuries, edited by Michael Kemper, Anke von Kügelgen, and Dmitriy Yermakov, 385–414. Berlin, 1996.

Babajanov, Bakhtiyar [Babad anov, Baxtiyor]. "La Naqshbandiyya sous les premiers Sheybanides." *Cahiers d'Asie Centrale* 3–4 (1997): 69–90.

Bacqué-Grammont, Jean-Louis. "Études turco-safavides, I: Notes sur le blocus du commerce iranien par Selîm 1er." *Turcica* 6 (1975): 68–88.

———. "Notes sur une saisie de soies d'Iran en 1518." *Turcica* 8, no. 2 (1976): 236–53.

Baer, Gabriel. "Women and Waqf: An Analysis of the Istanbul *Tahrîr* of 1546." In *Studies in Islamic Society: Contributions in Memory of Gabriel Baer*, edited by Gabriel Warburg and Gad G. Gilbar, 9–27. Haifa, Israel, 1984.

Baldick, J. "Uways al-Ḳaranī." In *EI*[2].

———. "Uwaysiyya." In *EI*[2].

Banani, Amin, Richard Hovannisian, and Georges Sabagh, eds. *Poetry and Mysticism in Islam: The Heritage of Rumi*. Cambridge, 1994.

Barkan, Ömer Lütfî. "Osmanlı İmparatorluğunda bir İskan ve Kolonizasyon Metodu olarak Vakıflar ve Temlikler I. İstilâ Devrilerinin Kolonizatör Türk Dervişleri ve Zâviyeler." *Vakıflar Dergisi* 2 (1942): 279–353.

Barthold, V. V. *Four Studies on the History of Central Asia*. Translated by V. Minorsky and T. Minorsky. 3 vols. Leiden, 1956–62.

———. "Mīr 'Alī-Shīr." In vol. 3 of *Four Studies on the History of Central Asia*, translated by V. Minorsky and T. Minorsky, 1–72. Leiden, 1962.

Barthold, W. "S̲h̲īrwān." Revised by C. E. Bosworth. In *EI*[2].

———. "S̲h̲īrwān S̲h̲āh." In *EI*[2].

Baysun, M. Cavid. "Ebüssu'ûd Efendi." In *İA*.

Behrens-Abouseif, Doris, and Leonor Fernandes. "Sufi Architecture in Early Ottoman Cairo." *Annales Islamologiques* 20 (1984): 103–14.

Beldiceanu-Steinherr, Irène. "À propos d'un ouvrage sur la polémique ottomane contre les Safawides." *REI* 39, no. 2 (1971): 395–400.

———. "Le règne de Selim 1er: Tournant dans la vie politique et religieuse de l'empire ottoman." *Turcica* 6 (1975): 34–48.

Bennigsen, Alexandre, and Chantal Lemercier-Quelquejay. "La grande horde Nogay et le problème des communications entre l'empire ottoman et l'Asie Centrale en 1552–1556." *Turcica* 8, no. 2 (1976): 203–36.

Bois, Th. "Kurds, Kurdistān." With V. Minorsky and D. N. MacKenzie. In *EI*[2].

Brockelmann, Carl. *Geschichte der arabischen Litteratur.* 2 vols. and 3 supplements. Leiden, 1937–49.

Bruinessen, Martin van. "Agah, Shaikh and State: On the Social and Political Organization of Kurdistan." Ph. D. dissertation, Utrecht University, 1978.

———. "Economic Life in Diyarbekir in the 17th Century." In *Evliya*, 36–44. Leiden, 1988.

———. "Evliya Çelebi and His Seyahatname." In *Evliya*, 3–12. Leiden, 1988.

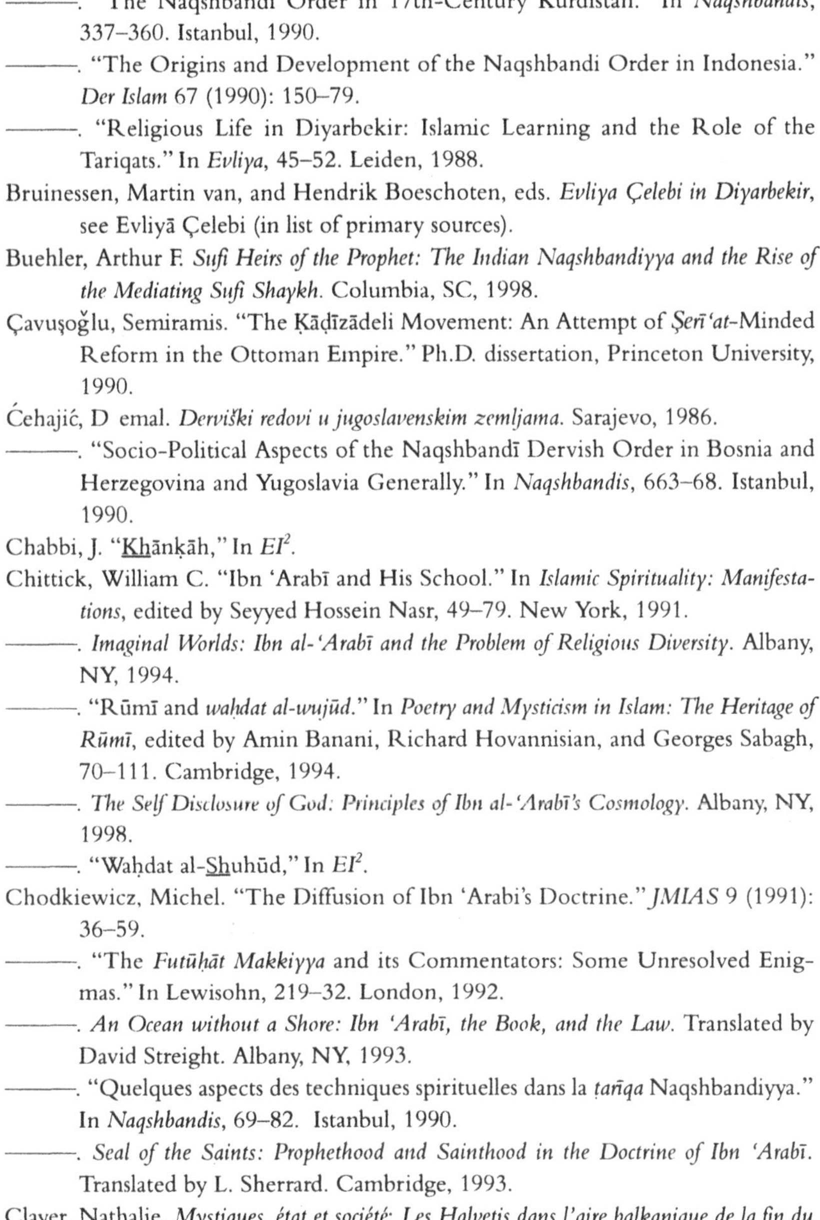

———. "The Naqshbandī Order in 17th-Century Kurdistan." In *Naqshbandis*, 337–360. Istanbul, 1990.

———. "The Origins and Development of the Naqshbandi Order in Indonesia." *Der Islam* 67 (1990): 150–79.

———. "Religious Life in Diyarbekir: Islamic Learning and the Role of the Tariqats." In *Evliya*, 45–52. Leiden, 1988.

Bruinessen, Martin van, and Hendrik Boeschoten, eds. *Evliya Çelebi in Diyarbekir*, see Evliyā Çelebi (in list of primary sources).

Buehler, Arthur F. *Sufi Heirs of the Prophet: The Indian Naqshbandiyya and the Rise of the Mediating Sufi Shaykh*. Columbia, SC, 1998.

Çavuşoğlu, Semiramis. "The Ḳāḍīzādeli Movement: An Attempt of *Şerī'at*-Minded Reform in the Ottoman Empire." Ph.D. dissertation, Princeton University, 1990.

Ćehajić, D emal. *Derviški redovi u jugoslavenskim zemljama*. Sarajevo, 1986.

———. "Socio-Political Aspects of the Naqshbandī Dervish Order in Bosnia and Herzegovina and Yugoslavia Generally." In *Naqshbandis*, 663–68. Istanbul, 1990.

Chabbi, J. "Khānḳāh," In *EI*[2].

Chittick, William C. "Ibn 'Arabī and His School." In *Islamic Spirituality: Manifestations*, edited by Seyyed Hossein Nasr, 49–79. New York, 1991.

———. *Imaginal Worlds: Ibn al-'Arabī and the Problem of Religious Diversity*. Albany, NY, 1994.

———. "Rūmī and *waḥdat al-wujūd*." In *Poetry and Mysticism in Islam: The Heritage of Rūmī*, edited by Amin Banani, Richard Hovannisian, and Georges Sabagh, 70–111. Cambridge, 1994.

———. *The Self Disclosure of God: Principles of Ibn al-'Arabī's Cosmology*. Albany, NY, 1998.

———. "Waḥdat al-Shuhūd," In *EI*[2].

Chodkiewicz, Michel. "The Diffusion of Ibn 'Arabi's Doctrine." *JMIAS* 9 (1991): 36–59.

———. "The *Futūḥāt Makkiyya* and its Commentators: Some Unresolved Enigmas." In Lewisohn, 219–32. London, 1992.

———. *An Ocean without a Shore: Ibn 'Arabī, the Book, and the Law*. Translated by David Streight. Albany, NY, 1993.

———. "Quelques aspects des techniques spirituelles dans la *ṭarīqa* Naqshbandiyya." In *Naqshbandis*, 69–82. Istanbul, 1990.

———. *Seal of the Saints: Prophethood and Sainthood in the Doctrine of Ibn 'Arabī*. Translated by L. Sherrard. Cambridge, 1993.

Clayer, Nathalie. *Mystiques, état et société: Les Halvetis dans l'aire balkanique de la fin du XVe siècle à nos jours*. Leiden, 1994.

Clayer, Nathalie, Alexandre Popovic, and Thierry Zarcone, eds. *Melâmis-Bayrâmis: Ètudes sur trois movements mystiques musulmans*. Istanbul, 1998.

Cook, Michael. *Commanding Right and Forbidding Wrong in Islamic Thought.* Cambridge, 2000.

———, ed. *A History of the Ottoman Empire to 1730.* Cambridge, 1976.

———, ed. *Studies in the Economic History of the Middle East from the Rise of Islam to the Present Day.* Oxford, 1970.

Cornell, Vincent J. *Realm of the Saint: Power and Authority in Moroccan Sufism.* Austin, TX, 1998.

DeWeese, Devin. "Khojagānī Origins and the Critique of Sufism: The Rhetoric of Communal Uniqueness in the *Manāqib* of Khoja 'Alī 'Azīzān Rāmītanī." In *Islamic Mysticism Contested: Thirteen Centuries of Controversies and Polemics,* edited by Frederick de Jong and Bernd Radtke, 492–519. Leiden, 1999.

———. "The Mashā'ikh-i Turk and the Khojagān: Rethinking the Links between the Yasavī and Naqshbandī Sufi Traditions." *Journal of Islamic Studies* 7, no. 2 (1996): 180–207.

———. "A Neglected Source on Central Asian History: The Seventeenth-Century Yasavī Hagiography *Manāqib al-Akhyār.*" In *Essays on Uzbek History, Culture, and Language,* edited by Bakhtiyar A. Nazarov and Denis Sinor, with Devin DeWeese, 38–50. Bloomington, IN, 1993.

———. *An "Uvaysī" Sufi in Timurid Mawarannahr: Notes on Hagiography and the Taxonomy of Sanctity in the Religious History of Central Asia.* Papers on Inner Asia, no. 22. Bloomington, IN, 1993.

———. "Yasavī Šayḫs in the Timurid Era: Notes on the Social and Political Role of Communal Sufi Affiliations in the 14th and 15th Centuries." *Oriente Moderno,* n.s., 15 (76), no. 2 (1996), 173–88.

Dickson, Martin B. "Shāh Ṭahmāsb and the Ūzbeks: The Duel for Khurāsān with 'Ubayd Khān, 930–946/1524–1540." Ph.D. dissertation, Princeton University, 1958.

Digbi, Simon. "The Naqshbandîs in the Deccan in the Late Seventeenth and Early Eighteenth Century A.D.: Bâbâ Palangposh, Bâbâ Musâfir and Their adherents." In *Naqshbandis,* 167–207. Istanbul, 1990.

During, J. "Samā' (in music and mysticism)." In *EI*[2].

Eaton, Richard M. *Sufis of Bijapur (1300–1700): Social Roles of Sufis in Medieval India.* Princeton, NJ, 1978.

Eberhard, Elke. *Osmanische Polemik gegen die Safawiden im 16. Jahrhundert nach arabischen Handschriften.* Freiburg, 1970.

Elias, Jamal. *The Throne Carrier of God: The Life and Thought of 'Alā' ad-Dawla as-Simnānī.* Albany, NY, 1995.

Encyclopaedia Iranica. Edited by Ehsan Yarshater. London, 1982–.

Encyclopaedia of Islam. 2nd ed. Leiden 1960–2002.

Ende, W. "Mudjāwir." In *EI*[2].

Ernst, Carl W. *Eternal Garden: Mysticism, History, and Politics at a South Asian Sufi Center.* Albany, NY, 1992.

Fahd, T. "Sakīna." In *EI*[2].

Farooqi, Naim R. "Moguls, Ottomans, and Pilgrims: Protecting the Routes to Mecca in the Sixteenth and Seventeenth Centuries." *International History Review* 10, no. 2 (1988): 198–220.

Faroqhi, Suraiya. *Der Bektaschi-Orden in Anatolien (vom späten fünfzehnten Jahrhundert bis 1826)*. Vienna, 1981.

———. "Crisis and Change, 1590–1699." Pt. 2 of *An Economic and Social History of the Ottoman Empire*, edited by Halil İnalcık, with Donald Quataert, 413–636. 2 vols. with consecutive pagination. Cambridge, 1994.

———. "Seyyid Gazi Revisited: The Foundation as Seen through Sixteenth and Seventeenth-Century Documents." *Turcica* 13 (1981): 90–122.

———. "The Tekke of Haci Bektaş: Social Position and Economic Activities." *IJMES* 7 (1976): 183–208.

Fay, Mary Ann. "Women and *Waqf*: Property, Power, and the Domain of Gender in Eighteenth-Century Egypt." In *Women in the Ottoman Empire: Middle Eastern Women in the Early Modern Era*, edited by Madeline C. Zilfi, 28–47. Leiden, 1997.

Fernandes, Leonor. *The Evolution of the Sufi Institution in Mamluk Egypt: The Khanqah*. Berlin, 1988.

Fleischer, Cornell H. *Bureaucrat and Intellectual in the Ottoman Empire: The Historian Mustafa Âli (1541–1600)*. Princeton, NJ, 1986.

Flemming, Barbara. "Lāmiʿī." In *EI*[2].

Fletcher, Joseph. "The Naqshbandiyya in Northwest China." Edited posthumously by Jonathan N. Lipman. In *Studies on Chinese and Islamic Inner Asia*, edited by Bratrice Forbes Manz, Variorum reprint, with various paginations, Aldershot, U.K., 1995.

———. *Studies on Chinese and Islamic Inner Asia*. Edited by Bratrice Forbes Manz. Variorum reprint, Aldershot, U.K., 1995.

———. "Les 'voies' (*turuq*) soufies en Chine." In *Les orders mystiques dans l'Islam: Cheminements et situation actuelle*, edited by A. Popovic and G. Veinstein, 13–26. Paris, 1985.

Friedmann, Yohanan. *Shaykh Aḥmad Sirhindī: An Outline of His Thought and a Study of His Image in the Eyes of Posterity*. Montreal, 1971.

Frye, R. N. "Harāt." In *EI*[2].

Gaborieau, Marc, Alexandre Popovic, and Thierry Zarcone, eds. *Naqshbandis: Cheminements et situation actuelle d'un ordre mystique musulman*. Istanbul, 1990.

Gandjeï, T. "Ḥusayn (Mīrzā B. Manṣūr B. Bayḳara)." In *EI*[2].

Gardet, L. "D̲h̲ikr." In *EI*[2].

Geoffroy, Éric. *Le soufisme en Égypte et en Syrie sous les derniers mamelouks et les premiers Ottomans: Orientations spirituelles et enjeux culturels*. Damascus, 1995.

Goldziher, I. "ʿAzīma." In *EI*[2].

Gölpınarlı, Abdülbaki. *100 Soruda Türkiye' de Mezhepler ve Tarikatlar*. Istanbul, 1969.

Graham, Terry. "Shāh Ni'matullāh Walī: Founder of the Ni'matullāhī Sufi Order." In Lewisohn, 173–90. London, 1992.

Gross, Jo-Ann. "Khoja Ahrar: A Study of the Perceptions of Religious Power and Prestige in the Late Timurid Period." Ph.D. dissertation, New York University, 1982.

Gündüz, İrfan, *Gümüşhânevî Ahmed Ziyâüddîn (KS): Hayatı-Eserleri-Tarîkat Anlayışı ve Hâlidiyye Tarîkatı*. Ankara, 1984.

———. *Osmanlılarda Devlet-Tekke Münasabetleri*. Istanbul, 1984.

Haar, J. G. J. ter. *Follower and Heir of the Prophet: Shaykh Aḥmad Sirhindī (1564–1624) as Mystic*. Leiden, 1992.

———. "The Importance of the Spiritual Guide in the Naqshbandī Order." In Lewisohn, 311–21. London, 1992.

Harrison, Christopher. *France and Islam in West Africa*. Cambridge, 1988.

Headley, R. L. "Bayt al-Faḳīh." In EI^2.

Ḥikmat, 'Alī Aṣghar. *Jāmī*. Tehran, 1363 *sh.*/1984.

Holt, P. M., Ann K. S. Lambton, and Bernard Lewis, eds. *The Cambridge History of Islam*. 2 vols. Cambridge, 1970.

Huart, Cl. "Djāmī." Revised by H. Massé. In EI^2.

Imber, C. H. "The Persecution of the Ottoman Shī'ites according to the Mühimme Defterleri, 1565–1585." *Der Islam* 56 (1979): 245–73.

İnalcık, Halil, ed. *An Economic and Social History of the Ottoman Empire*. With Donald Quataert, 2 vols. with consecutive pagination. Cambridge, 1994.

———. "Istanbul." In EI^2.

———. "The Ottoman Economic Mind and Aspects of the Ottoman Economy." In *Studies in the Economic History of the Middle East from the Rise of Islam to the Present Day*, edited by M. A. Cook, 207–18. Oxford, 1970.

———. *The Ottoman Empire: The Classical Age, 1300–1600*. Translated by Norman Itzkowitz and Colin Imber. New York, 1973.

———. "The Rise of the Ottoman Empire." In *The Cambridge History of Islam*, edited by P. M. Holt, Ann K. S. Lambton, and Bernard Lewis, 1:295–323. Cambridge, 1970.

'Irāqī, Aḥmad Ṭāherī. Introduction to *Qudsiyya: Kalimāt-i Bahā' al-Dīn Naqshband* by Khwaja Muḥammad b. Muḥammad Pārsā. Tehran, 1975.

İslâm Ansiklopedisi. Istanbul, 1976–86.

Issawi, Charles. "The Decline of Middle Eastern Trade, 1100–1850." In *Islam and the Trade of Asia*, edited by D. S. Richards, 245–66. Oxford, 1970.

Jackson, Peter, and Laurence Lockhart, eds. *The Timurid and Safavid Periods*. Vol. 6 of *The Cambridge History of Iran*. Cambridge, 1986.

Johns, A. H. "Friends in Grace: Ibrahim al-Kurani and 'Abd al-Ra'uf al-Singkeli." In *Spectrum: Essays Presented to Sutan Takdir Alisjahbana on His Seventieth Birthday*, edited by S. Udin, 469–85. Jakarta, 1978.

———. "Kūrānī." In EI^2.

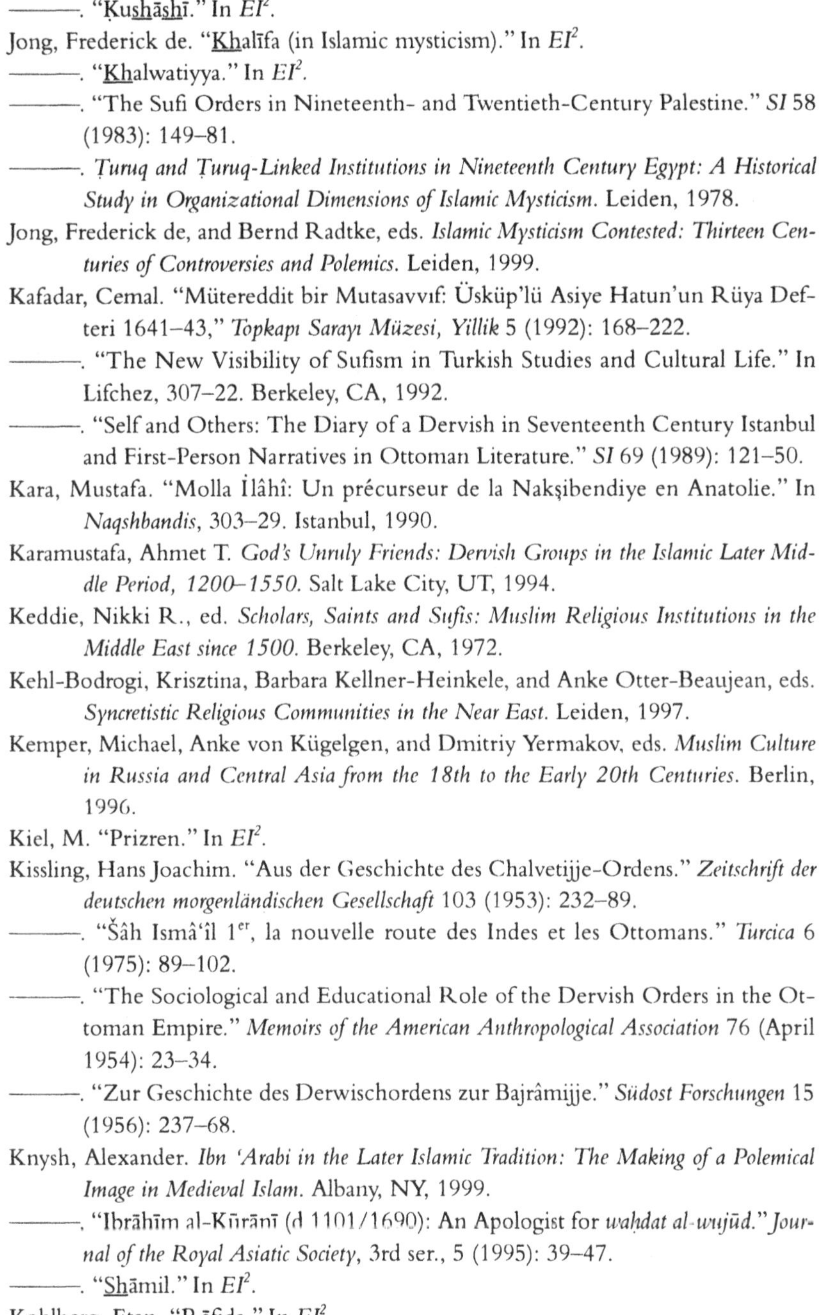

———. "Ḳushāshī." In *EI*^{2}.

Jong, Frederick de. "Khalīfa (in Islamic mysticism)." In *EI*^{2}.

———. "Khalwatiyya." In *EI*^{2}.

———. "The Sufi Orders in Nineteenth- and Twentieth-Century Palestine." *SI* 58 (1983): 149–81.

———. *Ṭuruq and Ṭuruq-Linked Institutions in Nineteenth Century Egypt: A Historical Study in Organizational Dimensions of Islamic Mysticism*. Leiden, 1978.

Jong, Frederick de, and Bernd Radtke, eds. *Islamic Mysticism Contested: Thirteen Centuries of Controversies and Polemics*. Leiden, 1999.

Kafadar, Cemal. "Mütereddit bir Mutasavvıf: Üsküp'lü Asiye Hatun'un Rüya Defteri 1641–43," *Topkapı Sarayı Müzesi, Yillik* 5 (1992): 168–222.

———. "The New Visibility of Sufism in Turkish Studies and Cultural Life." In Lifchez, 307–22. Berkeley, CA, 1992.

———. "Self and Others: The Diary of a Dervish in Seventeenth Century Istanbul and First-Person Narratives in Ottoman Literature." *SI* 69 (1989): 121–50.

Kara, Mustafa. "Molla İlâhî: Un précurseur de la Nakşibendiye en Anatolie." In *Naqshbandis*, 303–29. Istanbul, 1990.

Karamustafa, Ahmet T. *God's Unruly Friends: Dervish Groups in the Islamic Later Middle Period, 1200–1550*. Salt Lake City, UT, 1994.

Keddie, Nikki R., ed. *Scholars, Saints and Sufis: Muslim Religious Institutions in the Middle East since 1500*. Berkeley, CA, 1972.

Kehl-Bodrogi, Krisztina, Barbara Kellner-Heinkele, and Anke Otter-Beaujean, eds. *Syncretistic Religious Communities in the Near East*. Leiden, 1997.

Kemper, Michael, Anke von Kügelgen, and Dmitriy Yermakov, eds. *Muslim Culture in Russia and Central Asia from the 18th to the Early 20th Centuries*. Berlin, 1996.

Kiel, M. "Prizren." In *EI*^{2}.

Kissling, Hans Joachim. "Aus der Geschichte des Chalvetijje-Ordens." *Zeitschrift der deutschen morgenländischen Gesellschaft* 103 (1953): 232–89.

———. "Šâh Ismâ'îl 1er, la nouvelle route des Indes et les Ottomans." *Turcica* 6 (1975): 89–102.

———. "The Sociological and Educational Role of the Dervish Orders in the Ottoman Empire." *Memoirs of the American Anthropological Association* 76 (April 1954): 23–34.

———. "Zur Geschichte des Derwischordens zur Bajrâmijje." *Südost Forschungen* 15 (1956): 237–68.

Knysh, Alexander. *Ibn 'Arabi in the Later Islamic Tradition: The Making of a Polemical Image in Medieval Islam*. Albany, NY, 1999.

———. "Ibrāhīm al-Kūrānī (d 1101/1690): An Apologist for *waḥdat al-wujūd*." *Journal of the Royal Asiatic Society*, 3rd ser., 5 (1995): 39–47.

———. "Shāmil." In *EI*^{2}.

Kohlberg, Etan. "Rāfiḍa," In *EI*^{2}.

———. "The Term 'Rāfiḍa' in Imāmī Shī'ī Usage." *Journal of the American Oriental Society* 99 (1979): 677–79.

Konyalı, İbrahim Hakkı. *Abideleri ve Kitabeleriyle Üsküdar Tarihi*. 2 vols. Istanbul, 1976–77.

Köprülü, Mehmed Fuad. "Abdal." *Türk Halkedebiyatı Ansiklopedisi*. Fasc. 1, nothing further published. Istanbul, 1935.

———. *Islam in Anatolia after the Turkish Invasion (Prolegomena)*. Translated and edited by Gary Leiser. Salt Lake City, UT, 1993.

Köprülü, Orhan F. "Feyzullah Efendi." In *İA*.

Kraus, Werner. "Some Notes on the Introduction of the Naqshbandiyya-Khalidiyya into Indonesia." In *Naqshbandis*, 691–706. Istanbul, 1990.

Kufralı, Kasım. "Molla İlâhî ve Kendisinden Sonraki Nakşbendîye Muhiti." *Türk Dili ve Edebiyatı Dergisi* 3 (1949): 129–51.

———. "Nakşbendiliğin Kuruluş ve Yayılışı." Ph. D. dissertation, Istanbul University, 1949 (MS Istanbul University, Türkiyat Enstitüsü, TY 337).

Kufrevî [Kufralı], Kasım. "Birgewī." In *EI*[2].

Kütükoğlu, Bekir. *Osmanlı-İran Siyasi Münasabetleri, 1578–1590*. Istanbul, 1962.

Lambton, A. K. S. "Ḳazwīn." In *EI*[2].

Lane, Edward William. *An Arabic-English Lexicon*. 8 vols. London, 1863–93. Reprint, Beirut, 1968.

Levtzion, Nehemia. "Eighteenth Century Sufi Brotherhoods: Structural, Organizational and Ritual Change." In *Islam: Essays on Scripture, Thought and Society: A Festschrift in Honour of Anthony H. Johns*, edited by Peter G. Riddell and Tony Street, 147–60. Leiden, 1997.

Levtzion, Nehemia, and John O. Voll, eds. *Eighteenth-Century Renewal and Reform in Islam*. Syracuse, NY, 1987.

———. Introduction to *Eighteenth-Century Renewal and Reform in Islam*. Syracuse, NY, 1987.

Lewis, Bernard. "*Watan*." *Journal of Contemporary History* 26 (1991): 523–33.

Lewisohn, Leonard, ed. *The Legacy of Mediaeval Persian Sufism*. London, 1992.

Lifchez, Raymond, ed. *The Dervish Lodge: Architecture, Art, and Sufism in Ottoman Turkey*. Berkeley, CA, 1992.

Lipman, Jonathan N. *Familiar Strangers: A History of Muslims in Northwest China*. Seattle, 1997.

Madelung, Wilfred. "Yūsuf al-Hamadānī and the Naqšbandiyya." *Quaderni di Studi Arabi* 5–6 (1987–88): 499–509.

Mardin, Şerif. "The Nakshibendi Order of Turkey." In *Fundamentalisms and the State: Remaking Polities, Economies, and Militance*, edited by Martin E. Marty and R. Scott Appleby, 204–32. The Fundamentalism Project, vol. 3. Chicago, 1993.

Martin, B. G. "A Short History of the Khalwati Order of Dervishes." In *Scholars, Saints and Sufis: Muslim Religious Institutions in the Middle East since 1500*, edited by Nikki R. Keddie, 275–305. Berkeley, CA, 1972.

Marty, Martin E., and R. Scott Appleby, eds. *Fundamentalisms and the State: Remaking Polities, Economies, and Militance.* The Fundamentalism Project, vol. 3. Chicago, 1993.

McChesney, Robert D. "'Barrier of Heterodoxy'? Rethinking the Ties between Iran and Central Asia in the 17th Century." In *Safavid Persia: The History and Politics of an Islamic Society*, edited by Charles Melville, 231–67. London, 1996.

———. *Waqf in Central Asia: Four Hundred Years in the History of a Muslim Shrine, 1480–1889.* Princeton, NJ, 1991.

Meier, Fritz. *Meister und Schüler im Orden der Naqšbandiyya.* Heidelberg, 1995.

———. *Zwei Abhandlungen über die Naqšbandiyya.* Istanbul, 1994.

Mélikoff, Irène. *Hadji Bektach: Un mythe et ses avatars.* Leiden, 1998.

———. "Le problème Ḳızılbaş." *Turcica* 6 (1975): 49–67.

Melville, Charles, ed. *Safavid Persia: The History and Politics of an Islamic Society.* London, 1996.

Memon, M. U. *Ibn Taymīya's Struggle against Popular Religion.* The Hague, 1976.

Merad, A. "Iṣlāḥ (i.—the Arab World)." In *EI²*.

Meriwether, Margaret L. "Women and *Waqf* Revisited: The Case of Aleppo, 1770–1840." In *Women in the Ottoman Empire: Middle Eastern Women in the Early Modern Era*, edited by Madeline C. Zilfi, 128–52. Leiden, 1997.

Molé, M. "Autour du Daré Mansour: L'apprentissage mystique de Bahā' al-Dīn Naqshband." *REI* 27 (1959): 35–66.

Mottahedeh, Roy P. *Loyalty and Leadership in an Early Islamic Society.* Princeton, NJ, 1980.

Nasr, Seyyed Hussein, ed. *Islamic Spirituality: Manifestations.* New York, 1991.

Nazarov, Bakhtiyar A., and Denis Sinor, eds. *Essays on Uzbek History, Culture, and Language.* With Devin DeWeese. Bloomington, IN, 1993.

Nizami, K. A. "The Naqshbandiyyah Order." In *Islamic Spirituality: Manifestations*, edited by Seyyed Hossein Nasr, 162–93. New York, 1991.

Ocak, Ahmet Yaşar. "Un aperçu général sur l'hétérodoxie musulmane en Turquie: Réflexions sur les origines et les caractéristiques du Kızılbachisme (Alévisme) dans la perspective de l'histoire." In *Syncretistic Religious Communities in the Near East*, edited by Krisztina Kehl-Bodrogi, Barbara Kellner-Heinkele, and Anke Otter-Beaujean, 195–204. Leiden, 1997.

———. *Veysel Karanî ve Üveysîlik.* Istanbul, 1982.

Ocak, A. Y., and S. Farûkî [Faroqhi]. "Zâviye." In *İA*.

O'Fahey, R. S. *Enigmatic Saint: Ahmad Ibn Idris and the Idrisi Tradition.* London, 1990.

O'Fahey, R. S., and Bernd Radtke. "Neo-Sufism Reconsidered." *Der Islam* 70 (1993): 52–87.

Özdalga, Elizabeth, ed. *Naqshbandis in Western and Central Asia: Change and Continuity.* Istanbul, 1999.

Öztürk, N. "Islamic Orthodoxy among the Ottomans in the Seventeenth Century with Special Reference to the Qāḍī-Zāde Movement." Ph.D. dissertation, Edinburgh University, 1987.

Parry, V. J. "The Period of Murād IV, 1617–48." In Cook, 133–56. Cambridge, 1976.

———. "The Reign of Sulaimān the Magnificent, 1520–1566." In Cook, 79–102. Cambridge, 1976.

———. "The Successors of Sulaimān, 1566–1617." In Cook, 103–32. Cambridge, 1976.

Paul, Jürgen. *Doctrine and Organization: The Khwājagān/Naqshbandīya in the First Generation after Bahā'uddīn.* ANOR series, no. 1. Berlin, 1998.

———."Forming a Faction: The *Ḥimāyāt* System of Khwaja Ahrar." *IJMES* 23 (1991): 533–48.

———. *Die politische und soziale Bedeutung der Naqšbandiyya in Mittelasien im 15. Jahrhundert.* Berlin, 1991.

Peirce, Leslie. *The Imperial Harem: Women and Sovereignty in the Ottoman Empire.* New York, 1993.

Peters, R. "The Battered Dervishes of Bab Zuwayla: A Religious Riot in Eighteenth-Century Cairo." In Levtzion, 93–115. Syracuse, NY, 1987.

Peters, R. and J. G. J. ter Haar. "Ru<u>kh</u>ṣa." In *EI*[2].

Popovic, Alexandre, and Gilles Veinstein, eds. *Bektachiyya: Études sur l'ordre mystique des Bektachis et les groupes relevant de Hadji Bektach.* Istanbul, 1995.

———. *Les ordres mystiques dans l'Islam: Cheminements et situation actuelle.* Paris, 1985.

Repp, R. C. *The Müfti of Istanbul: A Study in the Development of the Ottoman Learned Hierarchy.* London, 1986.

Richards, D. S., ed. *Islam and the Trade of Asia.* Oxford, 1970.

Riddell, Peter G., and Tony Street, eds. *Islam: Essays on Scripture, Thought and Society; A Festschrift in Honour of Anthony H. Johns.* Leiden, 1997.

Rizvi, Saiyid Athar Abbas. *A History of Sufism in India.* 2 vols. New Delhi, 1978–83.

———. "Sixteenth Century Naqshbandiyya Leadership in India." In *Naqshbandis,* 289–302. Istanbul, 1990.

Robinson, Francis. "Ottomans-Safawids-Mughals: Shared Knowledge and Connective Systems." In *The 'Ulama of Farangi Mahall and Islamic Culture in South Asia,* 211–39. London, 2001.

———."Perso-Islamic Culture in India from the Seventeenth to the Early Twentieth Century." In *The 'Ulama of Farangi Mahall and Islamic Culture in South Asia,* 9–40. London, 2001.

———. *The 'Ulama of Farangi Mahall and Islamic Culture in South Asia.* London, 2001.

Roemer, H. R. "The Safavid Period." In *The Timurid and Safavid Periods,* edited by Peter Jackson and Laurence Lockhart, 189–350. Vol. 6 of *The Cambridge History of Iran.* Cambridge, 1986.

Rogers, J. M. "Aḥrār." In *EIr.*

Sāmarrā'ī, Yūnus al-Shaykh Ibrāhīm. *Ta'rīkh 'ulamā' Sāmarrā'.* Baghdād, 1386/1966.

Şapolyo, E. Behnan. *Mezhepler ve Tarikatlar Tarihi.* Istanbul, 1964.

Savory, Roger. *Iran under the Safavids.* Cambridge, 1980.

———. "Ṣafawids." In *EI*².

Schimmel, Annemarie. *Mystical Dimensions of Islam.* Chapel Hill, NC, 1975.

Schlegell, Barbara Rosenow von. "Sufism in the Ottoman Arab World: Shaykh ʿAbd al-Ghanī al-Nābulusī (d. 1143/1731)." Ph.D. dissertation, University of California, Berkeley, 1997.

Schwarz, Florian. *Unser Weg schliesst tausend Wege ein: Derwische und Gesellschaft im islamischen Mittelasien im 16. Jahrhundert.* Berlin, 2000.

Smith, Grace Martin. "The Özbek Tekkes of Istanbul." *Der Islam* 57 (1980): 130–39.

Sohrweide, Hanna. "Der Sieg der Ṣafaviden in Persien und Seine Rückwirkungen auf die Schiiten Anatoliens im 16 Jahrhundert." *Der Islam* 41 (1965): 95–223.

Soucek, S. "Sīdī ʿAlī Reʾīs." In *EI*².

Subtelny, Maria Eva. "Arts and Politics in Early 16th Century Central Asia." *Central Asiatic Journal* 27, no. 1–2 (1983): 121–48.

———. "Mīr ʿAlī S̲h̲īr Nawāʾī." In *EI*².

———. "Scenes from the Literary Life of Timurid Herat." In *Logos Islamikos: Studia Islamica in Honorem Georgii Michaelis Wickens*, edited by Roger M. Savory and Dionisius A. Agius, 137–55. Toronto, 1984.

———. "Socioeconomic Bases of Cultural Patronage under the Late Timurids." *IJMES* 20 (1988): 475–505.

Tansel, Selahattin. *Yavuz Sultan Selim.* Istanbul, 1969.

Taylor, Christopher. *In the Vicinity of the Righteous: Ziyāra and the Veneration of Muslim Saints in Late Medieval Egypt.* Leiden, 1999.

Togan, A. Zeki Velidi. "Ali Şîr Nevai." In *İA*.

Triaud, Jean-Louis. "Le thème confrérique en Afrique de l'ouest: Essai historique et bibliographique." In *Les ordres mystiques dans l'Islam: Ceminements et situation actuelle*, edited by Alexandre Popovic and Gilles Veinstein, 271–82. Paris, 1985.

Trimingham, J. Spencer. *The Sufi Orders in Islam.* Oxford, 1971. Reprint, with a foreword by John O. Voll, New York, 1998.

Tschudi, R. "Bektās̲h̲iyya." In *EI*².

Udin, S., ed., *Spectrum: Essays Presented to Sutan Takdir Alisjahbana on His Seventieth Birthday.* Jakarta, 1978.

Voll, John O. Foreword to *The Sufi Orders in Islam*, by Spencer J. Trimingham. New York, 1998.

———. *Islam: Continuity and Change in the Modern World.* Boulder, CO, 1982.

———. "Linking Groups in the Networks of Eighteenth-Century Revivalist Scholars: The Mizjaji Family in Yemen." In Levtzion, 69–92. Syracuse, NY, 1987.

———. "Muḥammad Ḥayyā al-Sindī and Muḥammad ibn ʿAbd al Wahhāb: An Analysis of an Intellectual Group in Eighteenth-Century Medīna." *Bulletin of the School of Oriental and African Studies* 38, no. 1 (1975): 32–39.

Voorhoeve, P. "ʿAbd al-Raʾūf al-Sinkilī." In *EI*².

Warburg, Gabriel, and Gad G. Gilbar, eds. *Studies in Islamic Society: Contributions in Memory of Gabriel Baer*. Haifa, Israel, 1984.

Winter, Michael. *Egyptian Society under Ottoman Rule, 1517–1798*. London, 1992.

———. "Sheikh 'Alī Ibn Maymūn and Syrian Sufism in the Sixteenth Century." *Israel Oriental Studies* 7 (1977): 281–308.

———. *Society and Religion in Early Ottoman Egypt: Studies in the Writings of 'Abd al-Wahhāb al- Sha'rānī*. New Brunswick, NJ, 1982.

Woodhead, Christine. "Rüstem Pasha." In *EI*[2].

Woods, John L. *The Aqquyunlu: Clan, Confederation, Empire; A Study in 15th/9th Century Turko-Iranian Politics*. Minneapolis, 1976.

Yazıcı, Tahsin. "Safî (Ṣafi Fahr al-Dīn 'Alī B. al-Ḥusayn al-Vā'iẓ al-Kāşifī)." In *İA*.

Yousofi, Gholam Hosein. "Kāshifī." In *EI*[2].

Zarcone, Thierry. "Histoire et croyances des derviches turkestanais et indiens à Istanbul." In *Derviches et cimetières ottomans*, edited by Thierry Zarcone, Edhem Eldem, et al., under the direction of Jean-Louis Bacqué-Grammont, 137–200. Vol. 2 of *Anatolia Moderna/Yeni Anadolu*. Paris, 1991.

Zilfi, Madeline C. "The Kadizadelis: Discordant Revivalism in Seventeenth-Century Istanbul." *Journal of Near Eastern Studies* 45, no. 4 (1986): 251–69.

———. *The Politics of Piety: The Ottoman Ulema in the Postclassical Age (1600–1800)*. Minneapolis, 1988.

———, ed. *Women in the Ottoman Empire: Middle Eastern Women in the Early Modern Era*. Leiden, 1997.

Index